WASHINGTON SUMMIT PUBLISHERS
2015

Also by Richard Lynn

Dysgenics: Genetic Deterioration in Modern Populations (1996)
Eugenics: A Reassessment (2001)
The Global Bell Curve (2008)
The Chosen People: A Study of Jewish Intelligence and Achievement (2011)

With Tatu Vanhannen
IQ and the Wealth of Nations (2002)
IQ and Global Inequality (2006)
Intelligence: A Unifying Construct for the Social Sciences (2012)

RACE DIFFERENCES IN INTELLIGENCE

An Evolutionary Analysis

Second, Revised Edition

BY RICHARD LYNN

Washington Summit Publishers
P.O. Box 100563
Arlington VA 22210

email : Info@WashSummit.com
web: www.WashSummit.com

Cataloging-in-Publication Data is on file with the Library of Congress

  ISBN: 978-1-59368-019-0
eISBN: 978-1-59368-022-0

Printed in the United States of America
10 9 8 7 6 5 4 3 2
Second Edition

CONTENTS

ix

FIGURES AND TABLES

PREFACE
To the Second Edition

THE FIRST EDITION OF THIS BOOK summarized studies on race differences in intelligence published up to 2006. The present second edition adds a large number of subsequent studies published up through the first half of 2014. There are some minor differences in the conclusions; for instance, the average IQ of sub-Saharan Africans has changed from 67 to 71. But the general pattern of results has not shown any significant changes.

The major new feature concerns European peoples. In the first edition, the IQs of these were treated as minor departures from the British IQ of 100, the standard against which all other IQs are calibrated. It has now become evident that IQs are consistently several points lower throughout the far south of Europe, i.e., in the Balkans, Italy, and southern Spain. The explanation for this is that the populations of these regions are a genetic mix of European peoples with those from the Near East and North Africa, with the result that their IQs are intermediate between the parent populations.

The IQs given in the present book are the basis from which the IQs of all nations in the world are calculated and given in my work *The Global Bell Curve*, as well as books I co-authored with Tatu Vanhanen, *IQ and Global Inequality* and, most recently, *Intelligence: A Unifying Construct for the Social Sciences*. We show in these that national IQs explain substantial proportions of the variance across nations in educational attainment, cognitive achievements, per capita income, economic growth, political institutions, health, fertility, and a number of other demographic and sociological variables. These results have been obtained not only by ourselves but by numerous scholars. I cannot list here all the many people who have contributed to these results, but I should like to acknowledge my debt to the important works of Gerhard Meisenberg, Heiner Rindermann, and especially my co-author Tatu Vanhanen.

RACE
DIFFERENCES
IN
INTELLIGENCE

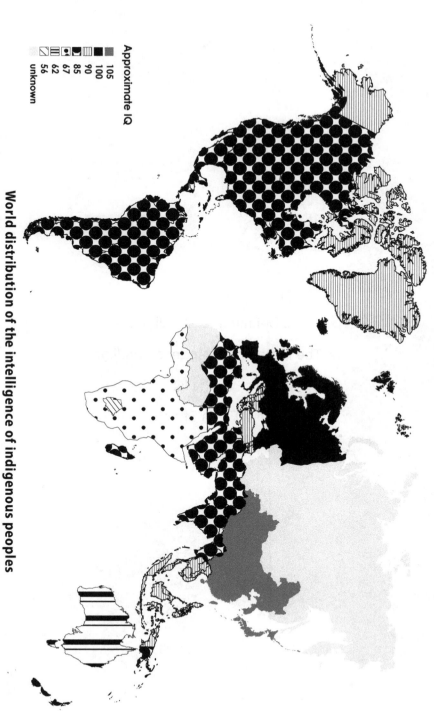

Figure 1. World distribution of the intelligence of indigenous peoples

Approximate IQ

105
100
90
85
67
62
56
unknown

World distribution of the intelligence of indigenous peoples

For a full-color version of this map, see: washsummit.com/world-iq-map

3

CHAPTER 1

THE MEANING AND MEASUREMENT OF INTELLIGENCE

RACE DIFFERENCES IN INTELLIGENCE began to be analyzed scientifically in the middle years of the 19th century. In the 1830s, Samuel George Morton (1799-1851) of the United States assembled a collection of skulls, measured their volume, and calculated that Europeans had the largest brains, followed by Chinese, Malays, and Native American Indians, while Africans and finally Australian Aborigines had the smallest brains. He concluded that these differences in brain size accounted for the race differences in intelligence (Morton, 1849). A similar view was advanced a few years later in France by Paul Broca: "in general, the brain is larger in eminent men than in men of mediocre talent, in superior than in inferior races" (Broca, 1861, p. 304). About the same time Francis Galton (1822-1911) in England arrived at the same conclusion by a different route. He assessed the intelligence of the races by the numbers of geniuses they produced in relation to the size of their populations. He concluded that the Greeks of classical Athens were the most intelligent people, followed in descending order by the lowland Scots, the English, the Africans, and the Australian Aborigines.

In the 20th century, this question continued to be debated. The intelligence test was constructed by Alfred Binet (1857-1911) in France in 1905. In 1916, it was translated into English by Lewis

5

Terman (1877-1956) at Stanford University, and later in the century a number of other intelligence tests were constructed. This made it possible to measure and compare the intelligence of the various races, and by the end of the 20th century, many hundreds of studies had been published on this issue. Most of these have been concerned with the difference between Blacks and Whites in the United States, but studies have also been made of the intelligence of peoples in virtually every part of the world. For the difference between Blacks and Whites in the United States, the most authoritative studies are by Shuey (1966), who summarized all the studies from World War I up to 1965, Osborne and McGurk (1982), who updated this summary to 1980, Loehlin, Lindzey, and Spuhler's *Race Differences in Intelligence* (1975), Richard Herrnstein and Charles Murray's *The Bell Curve* (1994), and a series of publications by Arthur Jensen, culminating in *The g Factor* (1998). There has been some interest in the intelligence of the Chinese and Japanese, which was reviewed by Vernon in *The Abilities and Achievements of Orientals in North America* (1982). A number of studies of the intelligence of Africans, Caucasians, and East Asians have been summarized by J.P. Rushton in *Race, Evolution and Behavior* (2000).

All of these studies have been concerned with two problems. These are the evidence on race differences in intelligence and the degree to which these differences are determined by genetic and environmental factors. It is widely accepted that race differences in intelligence exist, but no consensus has emerged on whether these have any genetic basis. All those named above have argued that there is some genetic basis for race differences. However, a number of authorities have concluded that there is no compelling evidence for genetic factors. This position has been adopted by James Flynn in his *Race, IQ and Jensen* (1980), Nathan Brody in *Intelligence* (1992), and Nicholas Mackintosh in *IQ and Human Intelligence* (1998).

The present book differs from previous studies in four respects. It is the first fully comprehensive review that has ever been made of the evidence on race differences in intelligence worldwide. Second, it reviews these for 10 races rather than the three major races (sub-Saharan Africans, Caucasians, and Northeast Asians) analyzed by Rushton (2000). The races analyzed here are the Europeans, sub-Saharan Africans, Bushmen, South Asians and North Africans, Southeast Asians, Australian Aborigines, Pacific Islanders, Northeast Asians, Arctic Peoples, and Native American Indians. Studies of these are presented in Chapters 3 through 12; Chapter 13 summarizes these studies and gives evidence on the reliability and validity of the IQs of the races. Third, Chapter 14 discusses the extent to which race differences in intelligence are determined by environmental and genetic factors. Fourth, Chapters 15, 16, and 17 discuss how race differences in intelligence have evolved over the course of approximately the last 100,000 years. These discussions are preceded by accounts of the nature of intelligence and the measurement of race differences given in this chapter, and of the concept of race in Chapter 2.

1. DEFINITION OF INTELLIGENCE

There is a widespread consensus that intelligence is a unitary construct that determines the efficiency of problem solving, learning, and remembering. A useful definition of intelligence was provided by a committee established by the American Psychological Association in 1995 under the chairmanship of Ulrich Neisser and consisting of 11 American psychologists whose mandate was to produce a report on what is generally known and accepted about intelligence. The definition of intelligence proposed by the Task Force was that intelligence is the ability "to understand complex ideas, to adapt effectively to the environment, to learn from experience, to engage in various forms of reasoning, to overcome obstacles by taking thought" (Neisser,1996, p.1). This definition is generally acceptable, except for the component of effective adaptation to the environment. All living species are adapted effectively to their environment or they would not have survived, but many living species, such as snakes and other reptiles, cannot be regarded as intelligent. In economically developed nations, the underclass, with its culture of long-term unemployment, crime, drug dependency, and welfare-dependent single mothers, is well adapted to its environment in so far as it is able to live on welfare and reproduce, but it has a low average IQ, as shown in detail by Herrnstein and Murray (1994), and is not intelligent in any reasonable sense of the word or as measured by intelligence tests.

A definition which avoids this misconception was proposed by Gottfredson and endorsed by 52 leading experts and published in the *Wall Street Journal* in 1994:

> Intelligence is a very general mental capacity which, among other things, involves the ability to reason, plan, solve problems, think abstractly, comprehend complex ideas, learn quickly and learn from experience. It is not merely book learning, a narrow academic skill, or test taking smarts. Rather, it reflects a broader and deeper capability for comprehending our surroundings—"catching on," "making sense" of things, or "figuring out" what to do (Gottfredson, 1997, p. 13).

Intelligence conceptualized as a single entity can be measured by intelligence tests and quantified by the IQ (intelligence quotient). The theory of intelligence as largely a single entity was formulated in the first decade of the 20th century by Charles Spearman (1863-1945), who showed that all cognitive abilities are positively intercorrelated, such that people who do well on some tasks tend to do well on all the others. Spearman devised the statistical method of factor analysis to show that the performance of all cognitive tasks is partly determined by a common factor. He designated this common factor *g* for "general intelligence" (1904). To explain the existence of the common factor, Spearman proposed that there must be some general mental power determining performance on all cognitive tasks and responsible for their positive intercorrelation.

2. THE HIERARCHICAL MODEL OF INTELLIGENCE

Spearman also proposed that, in addition to *g*, there are a number of specific abilities that determine performance on particular tasks over and above the effect of g. In the 1930s, an alternative theory was advanced by Louis Leon Thurstone (1887-1935) that there are seven "primary abilities," which he designated reasoning, verbal comprehension, numerical ability, spatial ability, word fluency (the ability to produce a number of words as exemplars of a concept in a short period of time), memory, and perceptual speed (1938). In the second half of the 20th century, a general consensus emerged that both the Spearman and the Thurstone models were partially correct and that intelligence is best conceptualized as a hierarchical structure that can be envisioned as a pyramid in which there are some 70 narrow abilities at the base (Spearman's specific abilities), eight to 10 second-order or group factors at the next level (Thurstone's primary abilities), and a single general factor (Spearman's g) at the apex.

The leading contemporary formulations of this model have been set out by John L. Horn (1991), John Carroll (1993), and Kevin McGrew and Dawn Flanagan (1998). Their models are closely similar and propose that the eight to 10 second-order factors consist of "fluid ability" (reasoning), "crystallized ability" (verbal comprehension), long-term memory, short-term memory, visualization (visual and spatial ability), numerical ability (arithmetic), mathematical ability, cultural knowledge, processing speed, and reaction time. This hierarchical model of intelligence is widely accepted among contemporary authorities such as the American Task Force on Intelligence (Neisser, 1996), Jensen (1998), Deary (2000), Mackintosh (2011), Earl Hunt (2011), and many others.

An extensive exposition of g and its structure, heritability, biology, and correlates has been presented by Jensen (1998) in his book *The g Factor*. He conceptualizes g as a construct or factor that he defines as "a hypothetical variable that *underlies* an observed or measured variable" (p. 88). It is not possible to measure g directly, but the nonverbal reasoning IQs and scores obtained from intelligence tests and expressed as IQs (intelligence quotients) are approximate measures of g. However, the IQs presented in this book are not intended as measures of g but of the IQ defined as the sum of cognitive abilities.

3. THE IQ

The metric employed for the measurement of the intelligence of the races has been to adopt an IQ of 100 (with a standard deviation of 15) for Britain as what has become known as the "Greenwich standard" (analogous to lines of latitude that are set in relation to zero through Greenwich). The IQs of other peoples are calculated in relation to this standard. British IQs are derived almost entirely from Whites (or were until recent years). The IQs of Europeans in the United States, Australia, New Zealand, and in northern and central Europe are virtually identical to those in Britain as shown in Chapter 3 (Table 3.1), so tests constructed and standardized on Europeans in these countries provide equivalent instruments for racial comparisons.

In the United States, in the first half of the 20th century, intelligence tests were normally standardized on Europeans, but in the second half of the century, tests were normally standardized on the total population, which included significant numbers of Blacks and Hispanics. In these standardization samples, the mean IQ of the total population is set at 100; the mean IQ of Europeans is approximately 102, while that of Blacks is 87, and of Hispanics about 92 (Jensen and Reynolds, 1982; Herrnstein & Murray, 1994). This means that when the IQs of other races are assessed with an American test standardized with an IQ of 100 for the total American population, two IQ points have to be deducted to obtain an IQ in relation to 100 for American Europeans. This problem does not arise with the only British test used in cross-cultural studies of intelligence. This is the Progressive Matrices, which has been standardized on British Caucasians. The tests used in the studies of racial intelligence are identified by acronyms in the tables in which the results are presented. The full names of the tests and description of the abilities they measure are given in the Appendix.

Following the calculations of national IQs given in the first edition of this book, Gerhard Meisenberg and I have calculated IQs for a number of nations based on international studies of the educational attainment of school students in mathematics, science, and reading (Meisenberg & Lynn (2011). This is a legitimate procedure because, (1) there is no clear distinction on theoretical grounds between intelligence measured by IQ tests and by tests of educational attainment, i.e., they are all measures of cognitive ability; and (2) scores on these educational tests are very highly correlated with national IQs; Heiner Rindermann (2007) has calculated the correlation at 0.87, and Lynn and Jaan Mikk (2007) at 0.92. IQs derived from studies of educational attainment are identified as EDUC in the tables that follow.

4. FLYNN EFFECTS

A problem with the quantification of race differences in intelligence is that IQs have been increasing since the 1920s in many parts of the world. These secular increases were shown by Smith (1942) in Hawaii and have been confirmed in several subsequent studies, such as that of Raymond Cattell (1951) in Britain. They have become known as the "Flynn effect," following their documentation by James Flynn (1984, 1987). When results are reported for the IQs of populations, an adjustment needs to be made for Flynn effects, as otherwise populations obtain spuriously high means when they are scored on norms obtained from Europeans a number of years previously. The magnitude of the Flynn effect varies with different tests. Mean IQs on the Wechsler tests increased in several countries by approximately 3 IQ points per decade from the mid-1930s to the 1990s, but the Verbal IQ increased by approximately 2 IQ points per decade, and the Performance IQ by approximately 4 IQ points per decade (Flynn, 1984, 1998; Lynn and Pagliari, 1994). For the Standard Progressive Matrices, the British mean IQ increased at a rate of approximately 2 IQ points per decade from 1938, when the test was constructed, up to 1979, when a further British standardization on children was carried out (Raven, 1981; Lynn and Hampson, 1986), and continued to increase at this rate among young children, but not among those aged 14 and older, up to 2008 (Lynn, 2009). For the Goodenough (1926) Draw-a-Man IQ Test, the scores increased in the United States by 3 IQ points a decade between 1955 and 1968, calculated from the Harris (1963) and the United States Department of Health, Education and Welfare (1970, p.20) standardizations. The same rate of increase on this test has been found for Blacks in South Africa from 1950 to 1988 (Richter, Griesel, and Wortley, 1989). Adjustments for Flynn effects have been made in all the figures for IQs presented for the populations in subsequent chapters. Where tests have been used for which the magnitude of the secular increase is not known, an increase of 3 IQ points per decade has been assumed.

CHAPTER 2

THE MEANING
AND
FORMATION
OF RACES

A BOOK CONCERNED WITH RACE differences in intelligence needs to define both intelligence and race. In the last chapter, intelligence was defined, and in this chapter, a definition is offered of race. A simple and straightforward definition of race is that it consists of a group that is recognizably different in a number of inherited characteristics from other groups. A fuller definition is that a race is a breeding population that is to some degree genetically different from neighboring populations as a result of geographical isolation, cultural factors, and endogamy, and which shows observable patterns of genotypic frequency differences for a number of intercorrelated, genetically determined characteristics, compared with other breeding populations. Geographical contact zones between races generally contain racial hybrids who show intermediate values of gene frequencies from the more central distributions of the breeding groups. These hybrid and mixed race populations are known as *clines*.

1. THE FORMATION OF RACES, VARIETIES, AND BREEDS

It is a general principle of evolutionary biology that when populations of species become isolated from one another, they evolve into two or more sub-species. These are generally termed varieties, strains, or breeds. In the case of humans these different varieties are called races. These different varieties evolve as a result of the four processes of founder effects, genetic drift, mutation, and adaptation. The founder effect is that when a population splits and one group migrates to a new territory to form a new population, the group that migrates will not be genetically identical to the one left behind. Hence the two populations differ genetically. The genetic drift effect is that gene frequencies change over time to some extent as a matter of chance, and this leads to differences between populations. Drift continues with time, increasing differences between races. The mutation effect is that new alleles (alleles are alternative forms of genes) appear through chance in some populations and, if they are advantageous for survival and reproduction, will gradually spread through the population. An advantageous new allele may appear as a mutation in one race, but not in others. The adaptation effect is that, when a population migrates to a new territory, some alleles will be advantageous that were not advantageous in the old location. Individuals possessing advantageous alleles in the new territory have more surviving offspring, so their alleles will be selected for and will gradually spread though the population. New varieties of several species have evolved as adaptations when populations have migrated into arctic environments. Some of these, such as foxes, bears, and hares, have evolved white fur to give them camouflage so they are not so easily seen by predators or prey. In all these cases, mutations for white fur have appeared and spread through the population because they have given the animals possessing them a selective advantage. Eventually the new advantageous alleles entirely replace the less advantageous alleles and are then said to have become "fixed."

In many cases, it is uncertain why different strains have evolved different characteristics. For instance, the fur of the European squirrel is red, while that of the North American squirrel is grey. Possibly one of these colors confers a selective advantage and appeared by chance in one of these populations through a genetic mutation.

2. VARIETIES IN NON-HUMAN SPECIES

It has long been recognized that most species have several varieties or what in humans are called *races*. Early in his career, Charles Darwin (1809-1882) noted the different varieties of turtles on the Galapagos Islands, and it was this that set him thinking how these had evolved. Later in his book *The Variation of Animals and Plants under Domestication* (1868), he described the different varieties of a number of species such as pigeons, each of which have their own distinctive manner of flight, movement, and cooing.

There are a number of different varieties or races among the apes. There are four races of common chimpanzee. These are the western chimpanzee (*Pan troglodytes versus*), indigenous to West Africa between Guinea and Nigeria, the central chimpanzee (*Pan troglodytes troglodytes*) of Cameroon and Gabon, the Nigeria-Cameroon chimpanzee (*Pan troglodytes ellioti*) of Nigeria and Cameroon, and the eastern chimpanzee (*Pan troglodytes schweinfurthii*) of central Africa. These races differ in physical appearance, genotypes, distribution of blood groups, and the cries they utter. Different races have evolved among animal species in accordance with the same principles as among humans. For instance, there are two races of gorilla. These are the eastern gorilla (*Gorilla beringei*), native to the mountains around lakes Edward and Kivu in eastern Democratic Republic of Congo, Rwanda, and western Uganda, and the western gorilla (*Gorilla gorilla*) of the forests of Cameroon, Gabon and the Republic of Congo. The two races are geographically isolated from one another by about a thousand miles and have evolved differences in physical appearance and blood group. The eastern mountain gorilla has a narrower skull, shorter arms, longer legs, thicker hair, and blood group A, while the western gorilla has a broader skull, longer arms, shorter legs, thinner hair, and blood group B (Baker, 1974). Some of the differences between the two races have evolved as adaptations to their different environments. The eastern gorilla inhabits a colder and open environment, while the western gorilla inhabits a warmer and densely forested environment. The eastern mountain gorilla has developed thicker hair than the western gorilla as a protection against the cold. The western gorilla has developed longer arms to swing from tree to tree. There is no obvious explanation for why the eastern mountain gorilla has a narrower skull, longer legs, and blood group A. These differences may have arisen through founder effects, genetic drift, or chance mutations, or they may confer some unknown advantage.

There are also a number of varieties among domestic animals. These are normally called *breeds* and have been generated by humans to serve a variety of useful purposes. Frequently, they have been bred for greater size or, in the case of cattle, milk yields. In some cases, they have been bred to adapt better to certain environments. For instance, varieties of hardy sheep have been bred that flourish on mountains and differ from lowland sheep. Humans have bred as many as 79 different breeds of dogs for a variety of abilities, such as retrievers for retrieving game, sheep dogs for rounding up sheep, rottweilers for guarding premises, cocker spaniels for house pets, and so on. These breeds differ in their general intelligence, their specific abilities, and the ease with which they can be socialized and made obedient (Coren, 1994).

3. TAXONOMIES OF RACES

Biologists and anthropologists began to analyze and classify races in the middle years of the 18th century. The first taxonomy of races was advanced by the Swedish biologist Carl Linnaeus (1708-1778) in 1758. In his *System Naturae*, he proposed that there are four races, which he designated *Europaeus* (Europeans), *Afer* (Black Africans), *Asiaticus* (Asians), and *Americanus* (Native Americans). In 1776, the German physician Johann Friedrich Blumenbach (1752-1840) added a fifth race and proposed a classification based principally on skin color. He designated these five races the Caucasian (white), Mongolian (yellow), Ethiopian (black), American (red), and Malayan (brown). These taxonomies were based on the clustering of morphological features and coloration in different races, such as the Europeans' white skin, straight hair, and narrow nose, the sub-Saharan Africans' black skin, frizzy hair, and wide nose, the Mongolians' (East Asians) black hair, yellowish skin, and flattened nose, the Native Americans' reddish skin and beaky nose, and the Malaysians' brown skin. Morton (1849) used Blumenbach's five-race classification when he made the first analysis of brain size in relation to race.

In the early 20th century, data were collected on differences in the frequencies of blood groups in various populations throughout the world. Ludwik Hirszfeld (1884-1954) showed (in a paper co-authored with his wife, Hanna) that the frequencies of a number of blood groups are consistent with race differences in coloration and morphology. For instance, blood group A is present in 41 to 48 percent in Europeans but in only about 28 percent of sub-Saharan Africans, while blood group B is present in between 10 and 20 percent of Europeans and about 34 percent of sub-Saharan Africans. Native Americans have virtually no A or B blood groups and almost all of them have the O blood group (Hirszfeld & Hirszfeld, 1919).

The accumulation of data on the distribution of the Rhesus (Rh) blood groups was used by William Boyd (1950) to advance a five-race taxonomy consisting of (1) Europeans with high frequencies of blood groups Rh cde and cde; (2) Africans with very high frequencies of Rh cde; (3) East Asians with high frequency of B and virtually no cde; (4) American Indians with very high frequency of O, absence of B, and few cde; and (5) Australids with high A, negligible B, and cde. This analysis showed that blood-group distributions were consistent with the morphological and coloration racial taxonomies of classical anthropology.

A more detailed taxonomy of races was advanced by Carleton S. Coon, Stanley M. Garn, and Joseph Benjamin Birdsell (1950), who proposed seven major races, each of which was subdivided into two or more subraces. These were (1) Caucasoids, subdivided into Nordics of Northwest Europe, Slavs of Northeast Europe, Alpines of Central Europe, Mediterraneans of South Europe, North Africa, and the Near East, and Hindi of India and Pakistan; (2) East Asians, subdivided into Tibetans, North Chinese, Classic East Asians (Koreans, Japanese,

Mongolians), and Eskimos; (3) Southeast Asians, subdivided into South Chinese, Thais, Burmese, Malays, and Indonesians; (4) American Indians, subdivided into north, central, south, and Fuegians; (5) Africans, subdivided into East Africans, Sudanese, West Africans, Bantu, Bushmen, and Pygmies; (6) Pacific Islanders, subdivided into Melanesians, Micronesians, Polynesians, and Negritos; and (7) Australian Aborigines, subdivided into the Murrayian peoples of southeastern Australia and the Carpentarian people of northern and central Australia. A closely similar seven-race taxonomy was proposed by John Baker (1974) comprising the five major races of Blumenbach and the Khoi Bushmen, consisting of the Hottentots and Bushmen of southwest Africa and the Kalahari desert, and the Australids, consisting of the Australian Aborigines and Melanesians.

In the 1980s and 1990s, Masatoshi Nei and A.K. Roychoudhury (1993) and Luigi Cavalli-Sforza, Paolo Menozzi and Alberto Piazza (1994) developed a new method of classifying humans into races on the basis of a number of genetic polymorphisms (meaning that a gene has more than one allele or alternative form). The technique is to take a number of polymorphic genes for blood groups, blood proteins, lymphocyte antigens, and immunoglobins, and tabulate the different allele frequencies in populations throughout the world. These tabulations are then factor analyzed to find the degree to which the allele frequencies are associated to form clusters of populations that are genetically similar to one another. The Nei and Roychoudhury data for 26 populations have been factor analyzed by Jensen (1998) to show the existence of six major groups of humans that correspond closely to the races proposed by classical anthropologists. Using the traditional terminology, these are (1) Africans of sub-Saharan Africa (Pygmies, Nigerians, Bantu, Bushmen); (2) Caucasoids (Lapps, Finns, Germans, English, Italians, Iranians, North Indians); (3) East Asians (Japanese, Chinese, Koreans, Tibetans, Mongolians); (4) Southeast Asians (Southern Chinese, Thais, Filipinos, Indonesians, Polynesians, Micronesians); (5) Amerindians (North and South Native American Indians and Inuit); and (6) Australian Aborigines (Australian Aborigines and New Guineans).

The same technique has been used by Cavalli-Sforza, Menozzi, and Piazza (1994) to analyze a larger data set of 120 alleles for 42 populations. These data were used to calculate the genetic differences between each population and every other population. From these, they calculated a genetic linkage tree that groups the populations into what they called "clusters." They have found 10 major clusters. These are (1) Bushmen and Pygmies; (2) sub-Saharan Africans; (3) South Asians and North Africans; (4) Europeans; (5) East Asians; (6) Arctic Peoples; (7) Native American Indians; (8) Southeast Asians; (9) Pacific Islanders; and (10) the Australian Aborigines and the Aboriginal New Guineans. It is clear that this classification corresponds closely to the racial taxonomies of classical anthropology based on visible characteristics of color of skin, hair, eyes, body shape, limb length, and the like, but for some reason Cavalli-Sforza, Menozzi, and Piazza (1994) prefer the term "clusters."

4. RACE DIFFERENCES IN DISEASES

There are race differences in a number of diseases that have a genetic basis including cystic fibrosis, PKU (phenylketonuria), hypertension, stroke, diabetes, prostate cancer, breast cancer, obesity, myopia, and schizophrenia. These differences have arisen through the processes of founder effects, genetic drift, mutation, and adaptation. There is such an extensive body of research on these that it would take a book to summarize it. The differences are illustrated here by the gene frequencies of cystic fibrosis and PKU in Europeans, sub-Saharan Africans, and East Asians (Orientals) given by W.F. Bodmer and Cavalli-Sforza (1976). These are shown in Table 2.1.

Table 2.1. Gene frequencies (percentages) of cystic fibrosis and PKU in Europeans, sub-Saharan Africans, and East Asians

RACE	CYSTIC FIBROSIS	PKU
Africans	0.4	0.3
East Asians	0.3	0.5
Europeans	2.0	1.1
Austria		1.2

Australia	2.2	1.1
Canada		0.9
England	1.9	1.5
United States	1.9	0.9

The figures represent the gene frequencies (percentage prevalence rates) in the population. Gene frequencies of cystic fibrosis in Europeans are four or five times higher than in sub-Saharan Africans and East Asians, while gene frequencies of PKU are slightly more than twice as high in Europeans than in the other two races. The lower half of the table shows that the gene frequencies of the two diseases are quite similar in different European populations as widely dispersed as Austria, Australia, Canada, England, and the United States.

5. DO RACES EXIST?

From the 18th century until the middle years of the 20th, all anthropologists, biologists and social scientists accepted that the human species contains a number of biologically distinct races. Thus, in the 1920s the British anthropologist Sir Arthur Keith (1866-1955) wrote:

> So clearly differentiated are the types of mankind that, were an anthropologist presented with a crowd of men drawn from the Australoid, the Negroid, East Asian or Caucasoid types, he could separate the one human element from the other without hesitation or mistake (Keith, 1922, p. xviii).

Curiously, this seemingly indisputable observation began to be disputed from the middle decades of the 20th century, when a number of anthropologists began to assert that races do not exist. One of the first to adopt this position was the anthropologist Ashley Montagu (1905-1999) in his book *Man's Most Dangerous Myth: The Fallacy of Race* (1945). The title suggests that the concept of race is a myth and therefore that there is no such thing as race. However, in the book, Montagu made it clear that he believed that races do exist. He wrote:

> [I]n biological usage a race is conceived to be a subdivision of a species which inherits the physical characteristics serving to distinguish it from other populations of the species. In the genetic sense a race may be defined as a population which differs in the incidence of certain genes from other populations, with one or more of which it is capable of exchanging genes across whatever boundaries (usually geographic) may separate them. If we are asked whether in this sense there exist a fair number of races in the human species, the answer is that there do (p. 6).

It is clear from this that race is neither a "myth" nor a "fallacy." Considering that Montagu evidently accepted that races exist, it seems strange that he should have given his book such a misleading title.

Later in the second half of the 20th century, a number of anthropologists and geneticists came to assert that there is no such thing as race. In 1962, the anthropologist F. B. Livingstone (1962) published a paper "On the non-existence of the human races," in which he declared, "There are no races, there are only clines" (p. 279), that is, hybrids between races. Clines invariably appear at the junction between races who interbreed and produce mixed-racial hybrids. In Latin America, for instance, there is a large population of Mestizos who have European and Amerindian ancestry and can be considered a cline. Similarly, the Pacific Islanders are a mixed race cline derived from the interbreeding of Southeast Asians and Northeast Asians. It has often been asserted that the existence of intermediate forms, clines, or hybrids invalidates the concept of races. But this is illogical. Among dogs, clines and hybrids are called mongrels, but the existence of mongrels does not mean that there are no pure breeds.

However, in the next decade, the geneticists Walter Bodmer and Luigi Cavalli-Sforza (1976, p. 698) were to write of "the existence of many different racial groups in man" and that the "races could be called sub-species, if we adopted for man a criterion. . .[from]

systematic zoology. The criterion is that two or more groups become sub-species when 75 percent or more of all individuals constituting the groups can be unequivocally classified as belonging to a particular group." They go on to say that when human races are defined broadly, it is possible to identify the race of many more than 75 percent of the population. Hence, races certainly exist among humans. Some 20 years later, this same Luigi Cavalli-Sforza opted to go with the flow, and we find him writing of the "scientific failure of the concept of human races" and that "the concept of race has failed to gain any acceptance" (Cavalli-Sforza, Menozzi, and Piazza, 1994, p. 19). However, they write "we can identify 'clusters' of populations." These "clusters" turn out to be the same as the races of classical anthropology, and later in their book, we find the authors using the classical racial terminology. For instance, they write that Africa "is inhabited by two aboriginal groups, Caucasoids in the north almost down to the southern borders of the Sahara, and Negroids in sub-Saharan Africa" (p. 167). Evidently they had forgotten their previous assertion that the "scientific failure of the concept of human races." "Clusters" is a transparent euphemism for races. Only six years later, this same Luigi Cavalli-Sforza apparently changed his mind again, because he pronounced that races do exist and that a race can be defined as "a group of individuals that we can recognize as biologically different from others" (Cavalli-Sforza, 2000, p. 25). It appears that he has made a resolution to deny the existence of race, but every now and then he forgets and the r-word slips out.

In 1985, a survey of the views of American anthropologists found that the existence of races was accepted by 59 percent of biological and physical anthropologists and about one third of cultural anthropologists (Lieberman and Reynolds, 1996). But by the beginning of the 21st century, the denial of the existence of races became increasingly frequent. "There are no biological races," asserts Jefferson Fish (2002, p. xii), a professor of psychology at St. John's University in New York. (He does not explain the grounds on which he makes this assertion.) Joseph Graves, a biologist at the University of Arizona, also asserts that "biological races do not exist"; he writes that "the term race implies the existence of some nontrivial underlying hereditary features shared by a group of people and not present in other groups" and that this is not true for humans. Contrary to this assertion, there are a number of "hereditary features" that are present in some races and absent in others. For instance, the genes for black skin are present in Africans and absent in Europeans, East Asians, and American Indians, while the genes for the epicanthic eyefold are present only in East Asians, Arctic peoples, and in some American Indians. Furthermore, the concept of race need not imply that there are some alleles that are only present in some races but are absent in others. It is sufficient that there are differences in allele frequencies between different races. There are a number of alleles for which this is the case. For example, the allele for sickle cell anemia is much more frequent in Africans than in other races, while the allele for cystic fibrosis is much more common in Europeans (Table 2.1, p. 12).

Graves (2002, p. 5) writes "The majority of geneticists, evolutionary biologists and anthropologists agree that there are no biological races in the human species." Mark Cohen (2002, p. 211) likewise asserts, "Almost all anthropologists agree that races in the popular sense do not exist and never have existed." In 2004, the American Anthropological Association announced on its website that "race is not a scientifically valid biological category." More recently, Heather J.H. Edgar and Keith Huntley (2009, p.1) write that "we have been teaching for years that race does not exist . . . race is not an accurate or productive way to describe human variation."

Despite the denials of the existence of race by a number of American anthropologists, the reality of race is widely accepted throughout the rest of society. Medical journals contain numerous papers on race differences in a variety of diseases and disabilities, including the prevalence of HIV infection. There is a journal, *Ethnicity and Health*, devoted to racial differences in the prevalence of diseases. In the social sciences, there are two journals devoted to race differences (*Race and Class* and *Ethnic and Racial Studies*), and other journals contain numerous papers on race differences in intelligence, educational attainment, earnings, socioeconomic status, unemployment, prejudice, discrimination, alcohol consumption, tobacco use, drug addiction, sexual experience, longevity, crime, and mental retardation. Corporations promote equal opportunities for the races in their employment and often grant preferences for non-

Whites in hiring. Employees sue corporations for racial discrimination and frequently obtain substantial compensation awarded by juries who have no problem in understanding the meaning of race. Many universities discrimination in favor of Black and Hispanic applicants. Judges pronounce that racially segregated schools are unconstitutional. Citizens in many countries state their race in census returns, and these are analyzed by sociologists and demographers. In Britain, there is a Race Relations Commission whose task is to promote racial equality and prosecute employers for racial discrimination. Neither the people responsible for this work nor the general public has any difficulty in understanding what race means and no doubt would be amazed to learn that many American anthropologists assert that race does not exist.

It may be wondered why a number of American anthropologists reject the concept of race. The answer has been given by two Polish anthropologists, Katarzyna Kaszycka and Goran Štrkalj (2002, p. 334). They write:

> Americans have become very sensitive to race, and the term has acquired strongly sensitive connotations. Many American scientists have opted for the non-existence of human races. Furthermore, the growing demands of "political correctness" militate against the use of the term in and outside science. . . . Few scientists dare to study racial origins, lest they be branded racists simply for being interested in the problem.

The reason for the rejection of the concept of race by a number of American anthropologists is apparent from the title of Montagu's book, *Man's Most Dangerous Myth*. Montagu evidently believed that people's consciousness of race is dangerous because it tends to foster racial antagonisms that can escalate into conflict. To prevent this, it would be better for the concept of race to be suppressed. In Europe, most anthropologists accept the validity of the concept of race. Thus, a survey of Polish anthropologists carried out in 2001 found that 75 percent agreed with the proposition, "There are biological races within the species *Homo sapiens*" (Kaszycka and Strzalko, 2003). It is mainly in the United States that the existence of race has come to be denied by a number of anthropologists and a few biologists and social scientists who have sacrificed their scientific integrity to political correctness.

1. Intelligence of Indigenous Europeans

2. Lower average IQs in Southern Europe

3. Europeans outside Europe

4. European University Students

5. Brain Size

6. The Heritability of Intelligence in Europeans

CHAPTER 3

EUROPEANS

THE EUROPEANS HAVE BEEN RECOGNIZED by all the classical anthropologists as one of the major races. Linnaeus (1758) described them as Europaeus. They have frequently been designated Caucasians or Caucasoids because of the belief that they originated in the Caucasus. A number of anthropologists have categorized them together with the South Asians and North Africans in a single Caucasoid group. However, the Europeans are distinguishable from the South Asians and North Africans by their lighter skin color and, in the northern Europeans, blonde hair and blue eyes. The distinction between the Europeans and the South Asians and North Africans has been confirmed by Cavalli-Sforza, Menozzi, and Piazza (1994) in their classification of the human races on the basis of a number of genetic markers. This has shown that Europeans represented by Italians, Danes, English, and Basques comprise a homogeneous "cluster" differentiating them from other races. Coon, Garn, and Birdsell (1950), Cole (1965), and a number of other anthropologists have sub-divided the Europeans into seven sub-races:

- Mediterranean peoples of Spain, Italy, and southeast Europe;

- Alpine peoples of France and central and southern Germany;

- Nordic peoples of England, the east of Ireland, and Scotland, the Netherlands, Belgium and Northern Germany, Denmark, Norway, Sweden, and Western Finland;

- Celtic peoples of Wales, the west of Ireland, and the western highlands of Scotland;

- Dinaric peoples of east-central Europe;

- Slavic peoples of northern Poland, the Baltic states, and Russia west of the Urals;

- Basque peoples of northern Spain and southwest France.

The Nordic peoples generally have lighter skin color, blond hair, and blue eyes, while the central and south Europeans more typically have darker skins, darker or black hair, and dark eyes.

Europe is defined as ending at the Dardanelles, the Ural mountains, and the Caucasus mountains, and therefore excludes Georgia, Armenia, Kazakstan, and Azerbaijan, which are included in South Asia.

1. INTELLIGENCE OF INDIGENOUS EUROPEANS

Studies of the IQs of Europeans in Europe are summarized in Table 3.1.

These IQs are calculated in relation to a British mean of 100 and standard deviation of 15. Twenty-one of the studies were carried out by Vinko Buj (1981) on samples of adults from major European cities. The Buj results are sometimes regarded as suspect (Rindermann, 2007) because some of them are inconsistent with other studies (for example, those carried out in Germany, Poland, and Portugal), and because the standard deviations differ remarkably in the different samples. However, Buj's data have been defended by Martin Voracek (2007) and are included here. Most of the others are derived from one of the three versions of the Progressive Matrices (CPM, SPM, and APM), and from the international studies of math, reading, and science integrated in a recent study by Meisenberg and Lynn (2011).

Table 3.1. IQs of indigenous Europeans

	COUNTRY	AGE	N	TEST	IQ	REFERENCE
1	Albania	8/15	-	EDUC	84.2	Meisenberg & Lynn, 2011
2	Austria	14	67	SPM	98	Moyles & Wolins, 1973
3	Austria	Adults	187	CF	101	Buj, 1981

	COUNTRY	AGE	N	TEST	IQ	REFERENCE
4	Austria	8/15	-	EDUC	99.8	Meisenberg & Lynn, 2011
5	Belgium	7/13	944	CPM	99	Goosens, 1952a
6	Belgium	10/16	920	CF	103	Goosens, 1952b
7	Belgium	Adults	247	CF	99	Buj, 1981
8	Belgium	8/15	-	EDUC	101.6	Meisenberg & Lynn, 2011
9	Bosnia-Herz	12/16	605	SPM	94	Djapo & Lynn, 2010
10	Bosnia-Herz	8/15	-	EDUC	93.1	Meisenberg & Lynn, 2011
11	Britain	Adults	1405	CF	100	Buj, 1981
12	Britain	6/15	3250	SPM	100	Raven et al., 1998
13	Britain	8/15	-	EDUC	99.8	Meisenberg & Lynn, 2011
14	Bulgaria	3/18	1153	Binet-S	94	Piryov, 1974
15	Bulgaria	3/18	1153	Binet-S	93	Piryov, 1974
16	Bulgaria	Adults	215	CF	94	Buj, 1981
17	Bulgaria	11/17	1456	CF	91	Lynn et al., 1998
18	Bulgaria	8/15	-	EDUC	95	Meisenberg & Lynn, 2011
19	Croatia	13/16	299	SPM	90	Sorokin, 1954
20	Croatia	Adults	525	CF	104	Buj, 1981
21	Croatia	7/14	999	SPM	99	Lugomer & Zarevski, 1985
22	Croatia	8/15	-	EDUC	96.1	Meisenberg & Lynn, 2011
23	Czech Rep.	Adults	363	CF	98	Buj, 1981
24	Czech Rep.	5/11	832	CPM	96	Raven et al., 1995
25	Czech Rep.	11	64	SPM	100	Persaud, 1972

	COUNTRY	AGE	N	TEST	IQ	REFERENCE
26	Czech Rep.	8/15	-	EDUC	100.5	Meisenberg & Lynn, 2011
27	Denmark	5/11	628	SPM	96	Vejleskov, 1968
28	Denmark	Adults	122	CF	99	Buj, 1981
29	Denmark	8/15	-	EDUC	98.3	Meisenberg & Lynn, 2011
30	England	8/15	-	EDUC	100.2	Meisenberg & Lynn, 2011
31	Estonia	12/18	2689	SPM	100	Lynn et al., 2002
32	Estonia	7/11	1835	SPM	98	Lynn et al., 2003
33	Estonia	8/15	-	EDUC	102.0	Meisenberg & Lynn, 2011
34	Finland	7	755	CPM	98	Kyostio, 1972
35	Finland	Adults	122	CF	99	Buj, 1981
36	Finland	8/15	-	EDUC	104.0	Meisenberg & Lynn, 2011
37	France	6/9	618	CPM	97	Bourdier, 1964
38	France	6/11	328	CMM	102	Dague et al., 1964
39	France	Adults	1320	CF	94	Buj, 1981
40	France	6/12	670	SPM	102	Raven et al., 2000
41	France	6/16	1120	WISC-3	98	Georgas et al., 2003
42	France	9/10	785	CPM	97	Pry & Manderscheid, 1993
43	France	8/15	-	EDUC	99.3	Meisenberg & Lynn, 2011
44	Germany	7/11	454	SPM	90	Kurth, 1969
45	Germany	5/7	563	SPM	99	Winkelman, 1972
46	Germany	11/15	2068	SPM	105	Raven, 1981

	COUNTRY	AGE	N	TEST	IQ	REFERENCE
47	Germany	11/15	1000	SPM	99	Raven, 1981
48	Germany	Adults	1320	CF	107	Buj, 1981
49	Germany	7	200	CPM	97	Guthke & Al-Zoubi, 1987
50	Germany	6/10	3607	CPM	101	Raven et al., 1995
51	Germany	5/10	980	CPM	97	Raven et al., 1995
52	Germany	14/25	880	SPM	96	Raven et al., 2000
53	Germany	6/16	990	WISC-3	99	Georgas et al., 2003
54	Germany	8/15	-	EDUC	99.3	Meisenberg & Lynn, 2011
55	Germany	7/10	205	SPM	100	Jaarsveld et al., 2012
56	Greece	6/11	290	DAM	95	Papavassiliou, 1953
57	Greece	5	30	DAM	93	Georgas & Papadopoulou, 1968
58	Greece	9/14	400	WISC	88	Fatouros, 1972
59	Greece	6/12	227	DAM	97	Georgas & Georgas, 1972
60	Greece	Adults	220	CF	95	Buj, 1981
61	Greece	6/17	731	MAT	89	Petrogiannis et al., 1999
62	Greece	6/16	990	WISC-3	92	Georgas et al., 2003
63	Greece	8/15	-	EDUC	92.0	Meisenberg & Lynn, 2011
64	Hungary	Adults	260	CF	98	Buj, 1981
65	Hungary	8/15	-	EDUC	99.0	Meisenberg & Lynn, 2011
66	Hungary	18	7588	SPM+	95	Dobrean et al., 2008

	COUNTRY	AGE	N	TEST	IQ	REFERENCE
67	Hungary	15	-	EDUC	100.3	Meisenberg & Lynn, 2011
68	Iceland	6/16	550	SPM	101	Pind et al., 2003
69	Iceland	8/15	-	EDUC	98.7	Meisenberg & Lynn, 2011
70	Ireland	10/13	96	MHE	90	Macnamara, 1964
71	Ireland	6/13	3088	SPM	87	Gill & Byrt, 1973
72	Ireland	Adults	75	CF	97	Buj, 1981
73	Ireland	6/12	1361	SPM	97	O'Connor et al., 1988
74	Ireland	9	191	SPM	87	Lynn & Wilson, 1990
75	Ireland	9/12	2029	SPM	96	Jeffers & Fitzgerald, 1991
76	Ireland	6/12	1361	SPM	93	Carr, 1993
77	Ireland	9/12	2029	SPM	91	Carr, 1993
78	Ireland	23/49	10000	SPM	95	Raven et al., 2000
79	Ireland	8/15	-	EDUC	100.1	Meisenberg & Lynn, 2011
80	Ireland	6	200	WPPSI	92	Lynn, 2012b
81	Italy	11/16	2432	SPM	103	Tesi & Young, 1962
82	Italy	6/11	700	CPM	95	Galeazzi et al., 1979
83	Italy	Adults	1380	CF	102	Buj, 1981
84	Italy	6/11	476	CPM	103	Prunetti et al., 1985
85	Italy	6/11	459	CPM	99	Prunetti et al., 1985
86	Italy	18	5370	CF	90	Pace & Sprini, 1998

	COUNTRY	AGE	N	TEST	IQ	REFERENCE
87	Italy	6/11	1384	CPM	95	Belacchi et al., 2008
88	Italy	8/15	-	EDUC	96.4	Meisenberg & Lynn, 2011
89	Latvia	8/15	-	EDUC	97.4	Meisenberg & Lynn, 2011
90	Liechtenstein	8/15	-	EDUC	101.7	Meisenberg & Lynn, 2011
91	Lithuania	6/16	381	WISC-3	92	Georgas et al., 2003
92	Lithuania	8/12	1067	CPM	96	Gintilienë & Butkienë, 2005
93	Lithuania	8/15	-	EDUC	97.0	Meisenberg & Lynn, 2011
94	Luxembourg	8/15	-	EDUC	96.7	Meisenberg & Lynn, 2011
95	Macedonia	8/15	-	EDUC	91.8	Meisenberg & Lynn, 2011
96	Malta	5	134	CPM	97	Martinelli & Lynn, 2005
97	Malta	8/15		EDUC	94.7	Meisenberg & Lynn, 2011
98	Moldova	8/15	-	EDUC	93.8	Meisenberg & Lynn, 2011
99	Montenegro	15	-	EDUC	87.1	Meisenberg & Lynn, 2011
100	Netherlands	Adults	333	CF	107	Buj, 1981
101	Netherlands	5/10	1920	CPM	99	Raven et al., 1995
102	Netherlands	6/12	4032	SPM	101	Raven et al., 1996
103	Netherlands	6/16	1100	WISC-3	99	Georgas et al., 2003
104	Netherlands	8/15	-	EDUC	102.0	Meisenberg & Lynn, 2011
105	N. Ireland	7/10	2000	MH	97	Wilson, 1973

	COUNTRY	AGE	N	TEST	IQ	REFERENCE
106	Norway	Adults	333	CF	100	Buj, 1981
107	Norway	8/15	-	EDUC	97.9	Meisenberg & Lynn, 2011
108	Poland	Adults	15643	SPM	98	Wysocki & Cankardas, 1957
109	Poland	Adults	835	CF	106	Buj, 1981
110	Poland	6/15	4006	SPM	92	Jaworowska & Szustrowa, 1991
111	Poland	15/79	660	SPM	92	Raven et al., 2000
112	Poland	5/10	756	CPM	102	Raven, 2008
113	Poland	18	395	SPM+	90	Dobrean et al., 2008
114	Poland	8/15	-	EDUC	99.1	Meisenberg & Lynn, 2011
115	Portugal	Adults	242	CF	101	Buj, 1981
116	Portugal	6/12	807	CPM	88	Simoes, 1989
117	Portugal	8/15	-	EDUC	95.8	Meisenberg & Lynn, 2011
118	Romania	6/10	300	CPM	94	Zahirnic et al., 1974
119	Romania	8/15	-	EDUC	90.7	Meisenberg & Lynn, 2011
120	Romania	7/18	1310	SPM+	88	Dobrean et al., 2008
121	Romania	8/15	-	EDUC	92.0	Meisenberg & Lynn, 2011
122	Russia	14/15	432	SPM	97	Lynn, 2001
123	Russia	27/55	745	CF	96	Grigorenko & Sternberg, 2001
124	Russia	8/15	-	EDUC	97.8	Meisenberg & Lynn, 2011
125	Russia	2/10	293	Vocab	97.6	Grigoriev et al., 2102

	COUNTRY	AGE	N	TEST	IQ	REFERENCE
126	Scotland	Adults	90000	SPM	97	Vernon, 1947
127	Scotland	Adults	9000	SPM	97	Vernon, 1947
128	Scotland	8/15	5000	NFER	98	Lynn, 1979
129	Scotland	8/15	-	EDUC	97.4	Meisenberg & Lynn, 2011
130	Serbia	15	76	SPM	89	Moyles & Wolins, 1973
131	Serbia	3/18	447	Binet-S	96	Piryov, 1974
132	Serbia	30	608	SPM	88	Rushton & Čvorović, 2009
133	Serbia	4-11	2334	CPM	98	Fajgelj et al., 2010
134	Serbia	8/15	-	EDUC	92.1	Meisenberg & Lynn, 2011
135	Serbia	6	214	CPM	90	Bala et al. 2013
136	Slovakia	9/17	3070	SPM	97	Bazany, 1963
137	Slovakia	5/11	823	CPM	96	Raven et al., 1995
138	Slovakia	11/18	1291	SPM	100	Raven et al., 2000
139	Slovakia	2/7	252	SON-R	98	Dockal, 2009
140	Slovakia	8/15	-	EDUC	99.1	Meisenberg & Lynn, 2011
141	Slovenia	6/11	1730	CPM	103	Boben, 2003
142	Slovenia	6/16	1080	WISC-3	95	Georgas et al., 2003
143	Slovenia	8/15	1556	SPM	95	Boben, 2003
144	Slovenia	11/17	610	SPM+	96	Boben, 2008
145	Slovenia	13/19	1363	APM	99	Boben, 2008
146	Slovenia	8/15	-	EDUC	101.2	Meisenberg & Lynn, 2011
147	Spain	Adults	848	CF	98	Buj, 1981
148	Spain	6/9	854	CPM	97	Raven et al., 1995

	COUNTRY	AGE	N	TEST	IQ	REFERENCE
149	Spain	11/18	3271	APM	102	Albalde Paz & Muñoz, 1993
150	Spain	Adults	202	SPM	97	Diaz et al., 2010
151	Spain	16/69	1369	WAIS-3-P	94	Roivainen, 2010
152	Spain	8/15	-	EDUC	97.3	Meisenberg & Lynn, 2011
153	Sweden	6/14	1106	WISC-P	97	Skandinaviska, 1970
154	Sweden	Adults	205	CF	104	Buj, 1981
155	Sweden	6/16	2231	WISC-3	99	Georgas et al., 2003
156	Sweden	8/15	-	EDUC	99.7	Meisenberg & Lynn, 2011
157	Switzerland	Adults	163	CF	101	Buj, 1981
158	Switzerland	6/10	200	CPM	101	Raven et al., 1995
159	Switzerland	9/15	246	SPM	104	Spicher, 1993
160	Switzerland	8/15	-	EDUC	99.2	Meisenberg & Lynn, 2011
161	Ukraine	14/17	132	SPM	96	Prozorovskaya et al., 2010
162	Ukraine	8/15	-	EDUC	94.9	Meisenberg & Lynn, 2011

The most striking features of the results are that IQs in central and western Europe are generally close to 100. The only exception is Ireland where the median of the 11 studies is an IQ of 93. There are two probable explanations for this. First, there has been a long history of emigration in which there has been some tendency for the more intelligent to migrate, leaving the less intelligent behind. Secondly, there is a dysgenic effect of Roman Catholicism, in which clerical celibacy has reduced the fertility of some of the most intelligent, who have become priests and nuns. The adverse effect of selective emigration has also been present, but to a lesser extent, in Scotland, where the average IQ in the 1940s was calculated at 97, in relation to an English IQ of 100 (Lynn, 1979). There is also strong evidence for the higher IQ of Scottish emigrants (Lynn, 1977c). Approximately the same lower IQ in Scotland was still present in the 2009 PISA study (given in row 129), in which the IQ in Scotland is computed at 97.4, compared with 100.2 in England.

IQs in Eastern Europe are a little lower than in Western and Central Europe: 98 in Poland, 97 in Russia and Latvia, 96 in Lithuania, and 95 in Ukraine, and Moldova 94, although Estonia is an exception with an IQ of 100. These six results have a median 96.5. These slightly lower IQs are probably attributable to the much lower living standards that have been present for several centuries. In the case of Russia, further adverse factors may have been the numerous Bolshevik executions and the large numbers of deaths in the Second World War, both of which probably affected predominantly the more intelligent. Considering all these adverse conditions, it may be surprising that the intelligence of the populations has been so little impaired.

2. LOWER AVERAGE IQS IN SOUTHERN EUROPE

IQs throughout southern Europe are consistently lower than in Central and Western Europe. Median IQs are 84 for Albania, 93.5 for Bosnia, 94 for Bulgaria, 97.5 for Croatia, 92.5 for Greece, 97.5 for Italy, 92 for Macedonia, 96 for Malta, 87 for Montenegro, 96 for Portugal, 91.5 for Romania, 92 for Serbia, and 97 for Spain. The median of these results is an IQ of 94. These IQs in Southern Europe decline with latitude in the Balkans, Italy, and Spain. In the Balkans, the IQ declines from 97.5 in Croatia to 92.5 in Greece and 84 in Albania. In Italy, the IQ is highest at 103 in the north (Pace & Sprini, 1998) and declines steadily to 90 in Sicily (Prunetti et al. 1985). In a more detailed analysis, it has been shown that in 16 regions of Italy, IQ is correlated with latitude at 0.963 (Lynn, 2010; 2012). These regional differences in IQs in Italy are also present in brain size, given for females as 1,401 cc. in the north (Trentino), 1,294 cc. in the center (Naples), and 1,256 cc. in the south (Sicily), and similar differences for males (Martin & Saller, 1959, vol.2, p.1,217).

Similar north-south differences are present in Spain. This was first reported by Roberto Colom (2002) for the Spanish standardization sample of the WAIS-R, in which the average IQ in the south was 4.45 IQ points lower than that in the central and northern regions. This difference has been confirmed in a more detailed analysis of 15 Spanish regions, in which it has been shown that IQ is correlated with latitude at 0.834 (Lynn, 2012a).

The probable explanation for the lower IQs in the Balkans, southern Italy, and southern Spain is that all these peoples have some genetic admixture with Near Eastern and North African populations. This has brought about hybrid or mixed-race peoples of partly European and partly Near Eastern and North African origin. Hybrid populations (or clines) invariably arise in the borderlands between two races as a result of interbreeding. In Southern Europe, they have come about through immigration from the Near East and North Africa over the course of millennia and the interbreeding of these with indigenous populations. The explanation proposed for the lower IQ in the Balkans is that the populations of this region are a cline of partly European and partly Near Eastern origin. Average IQs in the Near East (Lebanon, Syria, Jordan, Iraq, and Iran) are approximately 84, while in Turkey the IQ is 87.5, and in the Balkans IQs are in the high 80s and low 90s. These IQs in the Balkans and Turkey are, therefore, intermediate between those of approximately 100 in northern and central Europe, and 84 in the Near East, as would be expected in a cline of the two ancestral populations.

The reason that the populations of the Balkans are a mixed European-Near Eastern cline is that the Balkans are separated from southwest Asia by only about a mile of water (the Dardanelles), which has been easily and frequently crossed for millennia. It appears from archaeological evidence that Near Eastern peoples migrated into the Balkans several thousand years ago and interbred with indigenous peoples (Menozzi, Piazza, & Cavalli-Sforza, 1978).

In historical times, the exchange of populations across the Dardanelles was facilitated during the many centuries in which the Balkans and the Near East were unified in single states. Between the 9th and 4th centuries BC, the Greeks established colonies in Anatolia (present day Turkey). The Romans and later the Byzantines ruled the Balkans and Southeast Asia from around 100 BC to around AD 1300. In 1354, the Ottoman Empire based in present day Turkey began to colonize the south of the Balkans. By 1430, the Ottomans had conquered most of this region; and they continued to expand their control until 1683, when they reached the outskirts of Vienna but were defeated. The Ottomans retained, however, most of the Balkans until 1821, when they were pushed back into the south, and then to 1918, when they retreated further into the region around Istanbul. For several centuries during the last millennium, the Turks also occupied Malta where the IQ is 96. During these millennia, peoples moved freely between the Balkans and the Near East. The mix of European and Near Eastern genes in the Balkans has been illustrated by studies of Cavalli-Sforza, Menozzi, and Piazza (1994); in their genetic linkage tree, Greeks are shown to be more closely related to Iranians and other southwest Asian peoples than to Italians, Danes, and the English.

The lower IQs in the south of Spain and Italy are also attributable to the immigration of North African and Near Eastern peoples and interbreeding with indigenous populations. The immigration of North African and Near Eastern peoples into southern Spain has been easy since only about two miles separate southern Spain and North Africa. North African and Near Eastern migrants have made this crossing over the course of millennia and have settled mainly where they landed, in southern Spain. In more recent times, Arabs invaded and conquered southern Spain in AD 711 and ruled it for 781 years, until they were expelled in AD 1492. During some of this period, from approximately 814 to 1100, they conquered central Spain, but they never conquered the whole of the north, and from 1100 on, they were pushed back into the south. The longer they occupied the different Spanish regions, the greater the interbreeding with indigenous peoples and the lower the IQ, producing a correlation of 0.928 between the number of years of North African occupation and regional IQ (Lynn, 2012a). All these immigrants and invaders have left their genetic footprints, mainly in the south. The Portuguese geneticists Luísa Pereira, Maria João Prata and Antonio Amorim (2000) write:

[M]ost historical sources document a deeper influence of Berber (as well as Arab) people in Central and particularly South Iberia (as judged from toponyms and general cultural aænities), compared to North Iberia where the Muslim presence is recorded to have been more ephemeral and consequently to have made less cultural and demographic impact.

The Spanish geneticists Ana Gonzalez, Antonio Brehm, Jose Perez (2003) have analyzed the genetics of the populations of Spain and North Africa and conclude:

[O]ur results are in agreement with the gene flow (19.5%) from northwest Africa to the Iberian Peninsula estimated in a recent study of variation in the autosomic CD4 locus, and with the evidence of northwest African male input in Iberia calculated at around 20%, using the relative frequency of northwest African Y-chromosome-specific markers in Iberian samples.

They report that north African genes are more common in the south.

The lower IQs in southern Italy, Sicily, and Sardinia are also attributable to the immigration over the course of millennia of peoples from North Africa. By 750 BC, the Phoenicians (from present day Lebanon) and later the Carthaginians from North Africa colonized all these southern Italian regions. Later, in the seventh through 9th centuries, Sicily, Sardinia and Southern Italy were occupied by Arabs (Cavalli-Sforza, Menozzi, and Piazza, 1994, p. 261). These colonizations have had a genetic impact:

[N]orthern Italy shows similarities with countries of central Europe, whereas central and southern Italy are more similar to Greece and other Mediterranean countries. . . . This corresponds to the well-known differences in physical type (especially pigmentation and size) between the northern and north-central Italians on the one side and southern Italians on the other" (1994, p. 277).

By "Mediterranean countries" Cavalli-Sforza, Menozzi, and Piazza mean the countries that border the Mediterranean, including those of North Africa and the Near East. They note also that the Sardinians also are genetically more closely related to the Greeks, Lebanese, and North African Berbers than to central and northern Europeans (Cavalli-Sforza, Menozzi, and Piazza, 1994, pp.78, 274). Thus, as in the Balkans and southern Spain, genetic admixture of European peoples with those from the Near East and North Africa has brought about mixed race peoples whose IQs are intermediate between those of Central and Northern Europe and those of the Near East and North Africa.

With a median of 95.8, Portugal also has a lower IQ than that in central and northern Europe (see rows 115-118), and this is likewise attributable to considerable immigration of North African, Near Eastern, and sub-Saharan peoples over the course of many centuries. The Arabs, who invaded southern Spain in AD 711, conquered southern Portugal as well and ruled it until they were expelled in about AD 1250. During some of this time, they occupied northern Portugal. The Portuguese geneticists Luísa Pereira, Maria João Prata, and Antonio Amorim write:

> In Portugal, as well as generally in Iberia, many migration waves from both North and sub-Saharan African populations are well documented. The geographical proximity of North Africa and the Iberian Peninsula certainly afforded many opportunities for mutual population contacts. Among them, we stress the movement of Berbers and Arabs that took place during the very recent Muslim rule of Iberia (from the 8th century to the end of the 15th, in some regions). In addition, many sub-Saharan individuals entered the region during the slave trade period, from its very beginning (middle 15th century) until its total ban in the late 19th century (Pereira, Prata, & Amorim, 2000).

Portugal differs from Spain in that it experienced significant immigration of sub-Saharan Africans imported as slaves from around 1500 to the late 19th century, and these have also had a genetic impact on the Portuguese population. Luisa Pereira, Maria João Prata and Antonio Amorim (2000) write:

43

There were more African slaves in Portugal than in any other European country: in 1550, Lisbon boasted 10,000 resident slaves in a population of 100,000, and Portugal as a whole probably had over 40,000. In the mid-sixteenth century the birth of slaves' children was stimulated in Portugal for internal traffic purposes. Inter-breeding between autochthonous [indigenous] individuals and African slaves certainly occurred and the predominant mating must have been between slave African females and autochthonous males, due to social pressures and also for legal reasons: offspring of slave females would be slaves, whereas offspring of slave males would not. Therefore, breeding between slave African males and white females, besides being socially repressed, would not bring any economic profit. If the pattern of genetic admixture was markedly sex influenced, the signature of this recent African influence would be expected to be very different in the maternally inherited gene pool and in the paternally inherited one. In a recent study based on Y chromosome biallelic markers we have reported the absence of typical sub-Saharan haplogroups in the Y chromosome Portuguese pool. This finding, and the detection of L sequences at 7.1% in the mitochondrial pool, both seem to support the above-mentioned pattern of admixture with African slaves....

The introduction of L sequences in Portugal was tentatively imputed mainly to the modern slave trade that occurred between the 15th and 19th centuries. Both the great number of slaves that entered Portugal and their very diverse African geographic origin are consistent with the data set now reported.

It has been estimated that the percentage of sub-Saharan African mtDNA is 11.7 percent in southern Portugal (Gonzalez, 2003). The average IQ in sub-Saharan Africa is approximately 70 (see Chapter 4), so the introduction of a significant number of sub-Saharan African genes into the Portuguese gene pool, in addition to those from North Africa, can account for the lower IQ in Portugal than in the rest of western Europe, including Spain and Italy. It appears that the total North African contribution is about the same in Spain and Portugal (Capelli et al. 2009). On the other hand, Portugal received a considerable genetic input from sub-Saharan populations thanks to the slave trade carried out by the Portuguese (mainly in the 15th and 16th centuries), with a well-documented import in Southern Portugal (which did not affect the Spanish population) (Godinho 1983; Pereira et al. 2000). Hugo Rocha et al. (1999) have demonstrated that the mtDNA T3308C mutation is found only in Western African populations (affecting some 10 to 20 percent of the population). In Europe, it has been found only in Spain and in Portugal, where it reaches its highest frequency (two to three percent), that is, about one sixth of its frequency in Western Africa, suggesting an input from North African and Sub-Saharan African populations.

Studies of gene frequencies have confirmed the genetic impact of immigration from the Near East and North Africa into the Balkans, southern Italy, and southern Spain. The results of three of these studies are summarized in Table 3.2. Column 2 gives the frequency of an allele (the Taql, p1 2f2-8-kb allele) that is common in the Near East and North Africa and is also present at a lower frequency in southern Italy and southern Spain, but which is rare in central and northern Italy, northern Spain, and in central Europe (Semino, Passarino, Brega, Fellous & Santachiara-Benerecetti, 1996). The allele has a frequency of between 28.3 and 43.7 percent in the Near East and North Africa, 27.3 in Greece, 20.8 in Albania, 26.4 in southern Italy (including Sicily), and 8.5 percent in southern Spain (Andalusia). The frequency of the allele falls to 14.1 percent in central and northern Italy, and to between 1.7 and 6.0 percent in northern and central Europe.

Column 3 gives the frequency of the pYa1 allele and shows the same gradient of a high frequency in North Africa represented by Egypt (85.0), lower frequencies in Greece (79.2) and southern Italy (including Sicily and Sardinia) (70.5), falling to 51.4 in north-central Italy, and to 33.0 in England (Mitchell, Earl, & Fricke, 1997). These results confirm the genetic penetration of genes from North Africa and the Near East into southern Italy, southern Spain, and the Balkans. Further evidence for this is given in a more extensive genetic analysis by Zoe Rosser, Tatiana Zerjal, Mathew Hurles, Maarja Adojaan et al. (2000).

Column 4 gives the frequency of the Y-chromosome haplogroup E (Hg E) in a number of populations in North Africa, the Near East, and southern and central Europe reported by Ornella Semino, Chiara Magri, Giorgia Benuzzi, Alice Lin et al. (2004). The haplogroup has a frequency of between 55.2 and 81.1 percent in the North Africa. In the south of Europe, it falls to 23.8 in Greece, 26.6 in southern Italy (including Sicily), and 10.0 percent in southern Spain (Andalusia). The frequency of the gene falls further to 10.7 percent in central and northern Italy, and to 6.1 percent in northern Spain, 9.4 percent in Hungary, and 8.8 percent in Croatia. At more northern latitudes, it appears at a frequency of 4.0 percent in Poland and 0 percent in the Netherlands. This gene is also relatively common in the Near East, appearing at a frequency of 19.0 percent in Lebanon and 13.8 in Turkey. The high frequencies of the 8-kb allele, pYα1 allele, and the Y-chromosome haplogroup Hg E in the Near East and North Africa— as well as their frequencies in the clines in the Balkans, southern Italy, southern Spain, and central, northern Europe—correspond very closely to the IQs in these countries and regions.

Table 3.2. Frequencies of the Taql, p1 2f2-8-kb allele, the pYα1 allele, and the haplogroup E (Hg E), in the Near East and North Africa, the Balkans, southern Italy, central and northern Italy, southern and northern Spain, and central Europe.

COUNTRY / REGION	8-KB ALLELE	PYA1 ALLELE	HG E ALLELE
Egypt	-	85.0	-
Morocco	81.8	-	-
Lebanon	43.7	-	19.0
Tunisia	34.1	-	55.2
Turkey	33.0	-	13.8
Algeria	28.3	-	65.6
Greece	27.3	79.2	23.8
Albania	20.8	-	-
Italy: South	26.4	70.5	23.6
Italy: North-Central	14.1	51.4	10.7
Spain: South	8.5	-	10.0

COUNTRY / REGION	8-KB ALLELE	PYA1 ALLELE	HG E ALLELE
Spain: North	1.7	-	6.1
Croatia	8.8	-	-
Czech Republic	6.0	-	-
Hungary	4.2		9.4
Poland	4.0	-	-
France	3.8	-	-
Netherlands	3.5	-	0
England	-	33.0	-

These results showing lower IQs in southern Europe are further confirmed by the lower IQ of 96 in Malta and of approximately 94 in Corsica (Lynn, 1980).

The lower IQ in southern Europe than in central and northern Europe is corroborated by the work of Charles Murray (2003), who has assembled the numbers of what he calls "significant figures" (i.e. those who have made important contributions to literature, art, science, and music) from around 500 BC to the present. For the years 1400-1600, he lists 62 European "significant figures" in science, of which only one (unidentified) came from southern Europe (i.e. southern Italy, southern Spain, southern Portugal, and the Balkans). For the years 1600-1800, he lists 80 European "significant figures" in science, of which, again, only one (unidentified) came from southern Europe. For the years 1800-1950, he lists many hundreds of European "significant figures" in science, of which five (unidentified) came from southern Europe (two from southern Italy, one from southern Spain, and two from Lisbon in southern Portugal). Southern Europe is similarly under-represented in "significant figures" in literature, art, and music (Murray, 2003, pp. 301-3).

Because the peoples of southeast Europe are a European-Middle Eastern-North African cline, it is considered appropriate to exclude these in estimating the European IQ. The median IQ of the remaining countries is 99 and is considered the best estimate of the IQ of pure Europeans.

3. EUROPEANS OUTSIDE EUROPE

Europeans have migrated to many parts of the world. Studies of the intelligence of these populations are summarized in Table 3.3.

Table 3.3. IQs of Europeans Outside Europe

	COUNTRY	AGE	N	TEST	IQ	REFERENCE
1	Argentina	9/15	1680	SPM	93	Rimoldi, 1948
2	Argentina	5/11	690	SPM	99	Leibovich de Figueroa, 1992
3	Argentina	5/11	420	CPM	98	Raven et al., 1998
4	Argentina	10	4000	V-R	93	UNESCO, 1998
5	Argentina	14	1740	SPM	102	Raven, 2008
6	Argentina	13/30	1695	SPM	97	Flynn &Rossi-Casé, 2011
7	Argentina	8/15		EDUC	85.4	Meisenberg & Lynn, 2011
8	Australia	9/13	35000	Otis	97	McIntyre, 1938
9	Australia	18	6700	SPM	100	Craig, 1974
10	Australia	5/11	693	CPM	98	Reddington & Jackson, 1981
11	Australia	8/17	4000	SPM	100	Raven et al., 2000
12	Australia	6/11	618	CPM	93	Cotton et al., 2005
13	Australia	8/15	-	EDUC	101.2	Meisenberg & Lynn, 2011
14	Brazil	9/10	735	SPM	95	Fernandez, 2001
15	Canada	6/10	629	MAT	100	Tamaoka et al., 1993
16	Canada	7/12	313	SPM	97	Raven et al., 1996

	COUNTRY	AGE	N	TEST	IQ	REFERENCE
17	Canada	6/16	2200	WISC-3	100	Prifitera et al., 1998
18	Canada	5/17	407	MAT	100	Naglieri & Bardos, 1988
19	Canada	8/15	-	EDUC	101.9	Meisenberg & Lynn, 2011
20	Chile	8/15	-	EDUC	89.5	Meisenberg & Lynn, 2011
21	Colombia	13/16	50	WISC-R	95	Ardila et al., 2000
22	Costa Rica	5/16	199	SPM	87	Rindermann et al., 2013
23	Mexico	7/10	155	SPM	98	Lynn et al., 2005
24	N. Zealand	9/15	26000	OTIS	99	Redmond & Davies, 1940
25	N. Zealand	9/17	3108	SPM	101	Reid & Gilmore, 1989
26	N. Zealand	8/9	1692	WISC-R	102	Fergusson & Horwood, 1997
27	N. Zealand	8/15	-	EDUC	100.7	Meisenberg & Lynn, 2011
28	S. Africa	15	1056	SPM	94	Owen, 1992
29	USA	11	1000	SB	100	Scottish Council, 1933
30	USA	11	1215	TM	99	Scottish Council, 1949
31	USA	14/18	10000	DAT	101	Lynn et al., 1987b
32	USA	18/70	625	SPM	100	Raven et al., 1996
33	USA	4/14	2097	PPVT	103	Michael, 2003
34	USA	16/80	340	WAIS-3	96	Roivainen, 2010
35	USA	8/15	-	EDUC	98.8	Meisenberg & Lynn, 2011
36	Uruguay	12/25	1634	SPM	96	Risso, 1961

	COUNTRY	AGE	N	TEST	IQ	REFERENCE
37	Uruguay	8/15	-	EDUC	90.4	Meisenberg & Lynn, 2011
38	Zimbabwe	7	265	SB	100	Weyl, 1967a & b

Whites in Argentina have an average IQ of 91 (Rows 1 through 7). The explanation for this being lower than the European IQ of 99 may lie in genetic admixture with Native Americans and Africans. It has been shown that the population has 82 percent European genes and 18 percent Native Americans and African genes (Micheo et al. 1988). A more recent study has demonstrated that the Argentine population has 79 percent European genes, 18.8 percent Native American genes, and 4.3 percent African genes (Avena et al., 2006). In addition, many of the European immigrants to Argentina came from southern Italy where the average IQ is 90.

Rows 8 through 13 give six IQs for Australia, for which the median is 99. The IQ of European children in Brazil from Sao Paulo has been measured at 95 (Row 14). The median IQ for Canadian Whites is the "Greenwich Standard" of 100 (Rows 15-19). European children in Colombia have an average IQ of 95 (Row 21), and White children living in Baja California in Mexico have an average of 98 (Row 23). The intelligence of European children in Costa Rica has been measured at 87 (Row 22), which is an exceptionally low; the explanation is that the population is only 87 percent European (and this may be an overestimation (Phillip's, 1996)). In New Zealand, Whites obtained an IQ of 99 from a standardization of the Otis test in the 1930s (Row 24), a score of 101 from the standardization of the Progressive Matrices yielded (Row 25), and 102 (Row 26) from the the Christchurch Child Development Study. New Zealand Whites educational IQ is scored at 100.7 (Row 27).

European 16-year-olds in Natal in South Africa have an average IQ of 94 (Row 28). Rows 28 through 34 give seven IQs in the range between 96 and 103 for Europeans in the United States compared with those in Britain. The IQ of 101 given in row 30 is derived from the standardization of the WAIS-3 in Britain.

In Uruguay, Whites have an average IQ of 96, from a standardization of the Progressive Matrices (Row 35). Row 36 gives a lower IQ of 90.4 based on educational tests. The studies on which this score was based appear to include the racial minorities, consisting of eight percent Mestizo and six percent Black. The remaining 86 percent of the population is European. European seven-year-olds in Zimbabwe scored at Greenwich mean of 100 (Row 37).

The median of these IQs is 99, the same as that of Europeans in Europe. The results show that even in the quite poor countries of Latin America (Argentina, Brazil, Colombia, Mexico, and Uruguay), which have per capita incomes about one third of those in North America and Western Europe, the IQs of Europeans are only fractionally below those in affluent nations. This confirms the results in Europe, in which the poorer former Communist countries have only marginally lower IQs than their cousins in the West.

4. EUROPEAN UNIVERSITY STUDENTS

Studies of the intelligence of European university students are summarized in Table 3.4.

Table 3.4. Intelligence of European university students

	COUNTRY	UNIVERSITY	N	TEST	IQ	REFERENCE
1	Australia	-	745	APM	106	Yates & Forbes, 1967
2	Britain	-	-	APM	109	Raven et al., 1994
3	Canada	West Ontario	211	MAB	119	Rushton, 1992b
4	Chile	Cath Valp	177	-	105	Broer, 1996
5	Netherlands	Tilberg	30	SPM	105	Sonke, 2001
6	New Zealand	-	381	APM	106	Yates & Forbes, 1967
7	Poland	-	2072	APM	103	Raven et al., 1994

	COUNTRY	UNIVERSITY	N	TEST	IQ	REFERENCE
8	Romania	Cluj-Napoca	962	APM	100	Pitariu, 1986
9	Romania	-	1316	APM	101	Raven et al., 1994
10	S. Africa	-	40	APM	103	Poortinga,1971
11	S. Africa	-	50	Blox	100	Poortinga & Foden,1975
12	S. Africa	-	197	Blox	100	Taylor & Radford,1986
13	S. Africa	Wits	398	SPM	110	Rushton, 2008
14	USA	Wyoming	-	Stanford	106	Maity, 1926
15	USA	Stanford	-	Stanford	113	Maity, 1926
16	USA	Berkeley	300	APM	108	Paul, 1985
17	USA	Wisconsin	40	-	103	Osmon and Jackson, 2002
18	USA	-	139	Wonderlic	107	Pesta & Poznanski, 2008

All the samples have IQs of 100 or above, as would be expected, and the median IQ is 105. The IQs of students in Romania (100 and 101) are a little lower than those of other European students, consistent with the lower IQ of the population. The principal interest of the results is for comparison with university students in Africa and South Asia, where IQs are typically about 6 to 20 points lower. In the last study in which European students obtained an IQ of 107, Afro-American students (n=40) at the same university obtained an IQ of 101.7.

European students at the Universidad Católica de Valparaíso in Chile have an average IQ of 105 (Row 4), based on a study finding that had the same IQ as Austrian students (n=320) (Broer, 1996).

5. BRAIN SIZE

In Section 1, we noted that IQs are lower in southeast Europe, southern Italy, and southern Spain than in the remainder of Europe. We would thus expect that these differences would also be present in brain size, due to the correlation between brain size and intelligence of 0.40 (Vernon, Wickett, Bazana, and Stelmack, 2000). Differences in IQ between subpopulations of Europeans demonstrate that this is very much the case.

The data on the brain sizes of a large number of populations, collected by Hans Jurgens, Ivar Aune, and Ursula Pieper (1990), are shown in Table 3.5 together with IQs. Europeans in North America have the largest brain size and IQs (Row 1). They are followed by Europeans in North, Central, and Eastern Europe (Row 2). Slightly smaller brain sizes (and IQs) have been measured in Spain and Portugal (Row 3). Rows 4 and 5 shows a continuation of the downward trend, with progressively smaller brain size and IQ measurement in southeast Europe in the Near East (the latter obtained from samples of South Asians from Turkey and Iraq.) The lowest brain-size and IQ measurements are found in South Asians in India (Row 6). (Details of the IQs of the South Asians in Turkey, Iraq, and India are given in Chapter 6.)

Table 3.5. Brain size (cc) and intelligence in Europeans and South Asians

	COUNTRY	N. STUDIES	BRAIN SIZE	IQ
1	North America	34	1322	100
2	N. C. & E. Europe	104	1320	99
3	Spain & Portugal	6	1315	97
4	Southeast Europe	40	1312	92
5	Near East	5	1249	89
6	India	26	1185	82

6. THE HERITABILITY OF INTELLIGENCE IN EUROPEANS

The heritability of intelligence is the extent to which differences in intelligence are determined by genetic factors. Here, we are interested in the question of the heritability of race differences in intelligence, but before discussing this, we need to consider the heritability of individual differences in intelligence within countries. There are three sources of evidence on this problem. These consist of studies of identical twins reared apart, a comparison of identical and non-identical twins reared in the same families, and a comparison of unrelated adopted children reared in the same families. All three kinds of evidence show that the heritability of intelligence for adults is approximately 0.80 (or 80 percent.) This means that if all individuals were reared in identical environments, the differences between individuals would be reduced to 80 percent of the actual differences.

Studies on the heritability of intelligence for adults and children have been summarized by Thomas Bouchard (1993, p. 58). For adults, the evidence from identical twins reared apart is based on five studies for which the average correlation weighted by sample size is 0.75. This figure needs to be corrected for test reliability (that is, correction for attenuation), for which a reasonable figure is about 0.9 (Bouchard, 1993, p. 49; Mackintosh, 1998). This correction increases the correlation to 0.83. This is a sound measure of heritability.

The significance of heritability of intelligence is further corroborated by studies that compare the degree of similarity between identical twins and same-sex, non-identical twins brought up in the same families. There is a correlation of 0.88 for identical twins and 0.51 for same-sex non-identical twins. Correcting the correlations for the reliability of the tests and adopting a reliability coefficient of 0.9, the corrected correlations become 0.98 for identicals and 0.56 for same-sex non-identicals. The heritability can be calculated by Falconer's formula (1960), which consists of doubling the difference between the correlations of identicals and same-sex non-identicals. The difference between the two correlations is 0.42; doubling this gives a heritability of 0.84.

A third method of estimating the heritability of intelligence is to examine the correlation between the IQs of unrelated children adopted and reared in the same families. The magnitude of the adopted family environmental effect (the "between family effect") is expressed by the correlation between the twin pairs. In his summary of the research literature, Bouchard (1998) concludes that among adults the correlation is 0.04, indicating an environmental effect of 0.04—and therefore a heritability of 0.96. However, this method underestimates the environmental effect, because it does not take into account effects operating on one child but not on the other, such as prenatal and perinatal effects. The two twin methods yielding heritabilities of intelligence of 0.83 and 0.84 are more accurate. These figures are very close to Arthur Jensen heritability estimate of 0.85 (1998, p. 179).

The heritability of intelligence among children is considerably lower, at approximately 0.42 among 4- to 6-year-olds and 0.55 for the age group 6 to 20 (Bouchard, 1993, p. 58; Jensen, 1998, p. 179). The reason for this is probably that parents exert environmental effects on children that progressively wear off during adolescence. It is by including the lower heritability figures derived from children with the higher figures for adults that some scholars put the heritability of intelligence at between around 0.40 to 0.80. For instance, the statement drawn up by Gottfredson (1997, p. 14), and endorsed by 52 experts, states, "Heritability estimates range from 0.4 to 0.8 (on a scale from 0 to 1), most thereby indicating that genetics plays a bigger role than does environment in creating IQ differences among individuals." Most of the studies from which these high heritability figures are obtained come from Europeans in affluent Western nations. However, a study of 144 identical and non-identical twin pairs in Russia yielded a heritability of 0.78, which corrected for test unreliability increase to 0.87 (Lipovechaja, Kantonistowa, & Chamaganova, 1978).

CHAPTER 4

SUB-SAHARAN AFRICANS

THE TERM SUB-SAHARAN AFRICANS is used here for the principal indigenous peoples of sub-Saharan Africa. They should be distinguished from the North Africans, indigenous to Africa north of the Sahara; from the pygmies; and from the Bushmen or Khoisans, which consists of two races in sub-Saharan Africa, of whom only a few tens of thousands now survive, principally in the Kalahari Desert and as Hottentots in South Africa.

A variety of terms have been used for the Sub-Saharan African peoples, including *Afer* (Linnaeus, 1758), *Ethiopians* (Blumenbach, 1776), and *Negroids* (Cole, 1965). Whatever the might be named, the Sub-Saharan Africans have always been regarded as one of the major races in the taxonomies of classical anthropology, including those of Linnaeus (1758), Blumenbach (1776), and Coon, Garn, and Birdsell (1950). Cavalli-Sforza, Menozzi, and Piazza (1994) have confirmed the distinctive genetic characteristics of the Africans in their classification of humans into genetic "clusters," in which these peoples are represented by West Africans of the region west of Nigeria, Nilotics of the upper Nile in South Sudan, Ethiopians, and Bantus, a large group present in most of sub-Saharan Africa from Nigeria in the west to Kenya. The most distinctive features of Africans are their very dark skin, dark eyes, broad nose, thick everted lips, and woolly hair. Their blood groups differ from Europeans in having a lower frequency of group A, which is present in about 27 percent of Africans (compared to around 46 percent in Europeans), and a higher frequency of group B, which is present in about 34 percent of the population (as compared to around 14 percent in Europeans).

1. INTELLIGENCE OF SUB-SAHARAN AFRICANS IN AFRICA

The first attempt to estimate the intelligence of Sub-Saharan Africans was made by Sir Francis Galton on the basis of his own experience of them during his travels in southwest Africa and the accounts of other travelers (Galton 1869). He constructed a scale of grades of intelligence in which one grade was equivalent to 10.425 IQ points on the IQ scale. He estimated that Africans were about two grades below the English, giving them an IQ of 79. Subsequent studies of the IQs of general population samples of Sub-Saharan Africans in Africa have shown that this estimate was in the right ballpark, although it appears to have been a slight overestimate.

Shortly after the construction of the intelligence test, studies began to be made of the IQs of Africans in sub-Saharan Africa. The first of these was carried out in the mid-1920s by M. Laurence Fick (1929) using the nonverbal American Army Beta. He found that a sample of Black 10- to 12-year-olds at school obtained an average IQ of 65 in relation to an IQ of 100 of South African European children. Remarkably, "Coloreds," a largely mixed race African-European in South Africa, obtained an IQ of 83, exactly half way between that of Europeans and the Blacks.

During the subsequent 90 or so years, this early result has been broadly confirmed by numerous studies throughout sub-Saharan Africa. A problem with many of these studies is that most of them are based on samples that are not strictly representative of the populations. The studies that are considered to be broadly representative are summarized in Table 4.1. It may be that some of the samples have IQs below the Sub-Saharan African average, but these are likely counterbalanced by others that are above the average.

Table 4.1. IQs of Sub-Saharan Africans in Africa

	COUNTRY	AGE	N	TEST	IQ	REFERENCE
1	Benin	15	-	EDUC	69	Meisenberg & Lynn, 2011
2	Botswana	17/20	140	SPM	72	Lynn, 2010a
3	Botswana	15	-	EDUC	81.7	Meisenberg & Lynn, 2011
4	Burkina Faso	15	-	EDUC	72.3	Meisenberg & Lynn, 2011
5	Burundi	15	-	EDUC	76.4	Meisenberg & Lynn, 2011
6	Cameroon	Adults	80	CPM	64	Berlioz, 1955
7	Cameroon	15	-	EDUC	78	Meisenberg & Lynn, 2011
8	Cent. African Rep.	Adults	1,144	SPM	64	Latouche & Dormeau,1956
9	Chad	15	-	EDUC	68.4	Meisenberg & Lynn, 2011
10	Comoros	15	-	EDUC	71.9	Meisenberg & Lynn, 2011
11	Congo–Brazz.	13	88	SPM	73	Nkaya et al., 1994
12	Congo–Brazz.	Adults	580	SPM	75	Latouche & Dormeau,1956
13	Congo–Brazz.	Adults	1,596	SPM	74	Latouche & Dormeau,1956
14	Congo–Brazz.	15	-	EDUC	71.8	Meisenberg & Lynn, 2011
15	Congo–Zaire	6/10	693	CPM	73	Ombredane et al., 1956
16	Congo–Zaire	Adults	67	SPM	64	Verhagen, 1956
17	Congo–Zaire	17/29	320	SPM	69	Ombredane et al., 1957
18	Congo–Zaire	8	50	KAB	67	Boivin & Giordani, 1993
19	Congo–Zaire	7/12	95	KAB	68	Boivin et al., 1995

	COUNTRY	AGE	N	TEST	IQ	REFERENCE
20	Congo–Zaire	7/9	130	KAB	65	Giordani et al., 1996
21	Congo–Zaire	7/9	139	KAB	61	Conant et al., 1999
22	Congo–Zaire	7/9	183	CPM	74	Kashala et al., 2005
23	Eritrea	4/7	148	CPM	85	Wolff et al., 1995
24	Eritrea	11	152	SPM	66	Wolff & Fessada, 1999
25	Ethiopia	5/14	162	CPM	64	Aboud et al., 1991
26	Ethiopia	15	250	SPM	68	Kaniel & Fisherman, 1991
27	Ethiopia	14/16	46	SPM	69	Kozulin, 1998
28	Ethiopia	6/7	29	CPM	86	Tzuriel & Kaufman, 1999
29	Ethiopia	7/11	108	CPM	70	Ayalew, 2005
30	Gabon	15	-	EDUC	77.9	Meisenberg & Lynn, 2011
31	Gambia	17	579	CPM	64	Jukes et al., 2006
32	Gambia-Mandinka	17	418	CPM	60	Jukes & Grigorenko, 2010
33	Gambia-Wolof	17	114	CPM	60	Jukes & Grigorenko, 2010
34	Ghana	8/15	2,894	SPM	70	Bulley, 1973
35	Ghana	18/30	2,16	SPM	77	Bulley, 1973
36	Ghana	Adults	225	CF	76	Buj, 1981
37	Ghana	15	1,693	CPM	62	Glewwe & Jacoby, 1992
38	Ghana	9/18	1,563	CPM	67	Heady, 2003
39	Ghana	15	-	EDUC	72.4	Meisenberg & Lynn, 2011
40	Guinea	5/14	50	AAB	63	Nissen et al., 1935
41	Guinea	Adults	1,144	SPM	70	Faverge & Falmagne, 1962

	COUNTRY	AGE	N	TEST	IQ	REFERENCE
42	Ivory Coast	7/14	67	Piagetian	71	Dasen & Ngini, 1979
43	Ivory Coast	15	-	EDUC	65	Meisenberg & Lynn, 2011
44	Kenya	Adults	205	CPM	69	Boissiere et al., 1985
45	Kenya	6/10	1,222	CPM	78	Costenbader & Ngari, 2000
46	Kenya	12/15	85	CPM/ MH	67	Sternberg et al., 2001
47	Kenya	7	118	CPM	76	Daley et al., 2003
48	Kenya	7	537	CPM	87	Daley et al., 2003
49	Kenya	6	184	KAB	63	Holding et al., 2004
50	Kenya	6/14	528	CPM	74	Neumann et al., 2007
51	Kenya	15	-	EDUC	81.9	Meisenberg & Lynn, 2011
52	Kenya	14	851	Various	76	Rindermann, 2012
53	Lesotho	15	-	EDUC	70	Meisenberg & Lynn, 2011
54	Madagascar	Adults	147	CPM	82	Raveau et al., 1976
55	Madagascar	15	-	EDUC	76	Meisenberg & Lynn, 2011
56	Malawi	7/14	268	CPM	71	Van der Vijver, 2009
57	Malawi	15	-	EDUC	65.1	Meisenberg & Lynn, 2011
58	Mali	9/12	746	CPM	74	Fontaine, 1963
59	Mali	adults	790	SPM	68	Fontaine, 1963
60	Mali	adults	270	SPM	71	Fontaine, 1963
61	Mali	8/85	413	CPM	64	Bellis et al., 1988
62	Mali	15	-	EDUC	69.8	Meisenberg & Lynn, 2011
63	Mozambique	20	149	CPM	64	Kendall, 1976

	COUNTRY	AGE	N	TEST	IQ	REFERENCE
64	Mozambique	15	-	EDUC	76	Meisenberg & Lynn, 2011
65	Namibia	7/12	116	CPM	72	Veii & Everatt, 2005
66	Namibia	15	-	EDUC	70	Meisenberg & Lynn, 2011
67	Niger	15	-	EDUC	62.4	Meisenberg & Lynn, 2011
68	Nigeria	26	30	DAM	67	Haward & Roland, 1954
69	Nigeria	6/14	480	Leone	70	Ferron, 1966
70	Nigeria	Adults	86	SPM	64	Wober, 1969
71	Nigeria	6/13	375	CPM/ PMA	69	Fahrmeier, 1975
72	Nigeria	5/7	150	SPM	87	Okunrotifa, 1976
73	Nigeria	9/10	88	SPM	83	Nguga, 1977
74	Nigeria	9/10	165	SPM	80	Nwuga, 1977
75	Nigeria	11/12	120	SPM	72	Maqsud, 1980a
76	Nigeria	11/17	98	WISC-R	73	Ani et al., 1998
77	Nigeria	11	402	SPM	69	Ijarotimi & Ijadunola, 2007
78	Nigeria	15	-	EDUC	79.1	Meisenberg & Lynn, 2011
79	Nigeria	14	413	SPM	70	Hur & Lynn, 2013
80	Nigeria	16	140	SPM	70	Hur & Lynn, 2013
81	Rwanda	5/17	148	Piagetian	76	Laurendeau-Bendavid, 1977
82	Senegal	7/14	559	DAM	67	Bardet, 1960
83	Senegal	5/12	58	KABC	74	Boivin, 2002
84	Senegal	15	-	EDUC	72	Meisenberg & Lynn, 2011
85	Sierra Leone	Adults	122	CPM	64	Berry, 1966
86	Sierra Leone	Adults	33	CPM	64	Binnie-Dawson, 1984

	COUNTRY	AGE	N	TEST	IQ	REFERENCE
87	South Africa	10/14	293	AAB	65	Fick, 1929
88	South Africa	12/14	80	KB	68	Dent, 1937
89	South Africa	10/16	532	Non-verbal	72	Fick, 1939
90	South Africa	6/10	1,076	DAM	75	Hunkin, 1950
91	South Africa	8/16	1,008	SPM	75	Notcutt, 1950
92	South Africa	Adults	703	SPM	70	Notcutt, 1950
93	South Africa	10/12	278	NVR	74	Lloyd & Pidgeon, 1961
94	South Africa	25	140	WAIS-R	69	Avenant, 1988
95	South Africa	5/13	415	DAM	75	Richter et al., 1989
96	South Africa	9	350	SPM	67	Lynn & Holmshaw, 1990
97	South Africa	16	1,096	SPM	68	Owen, 1992
98	South Africa	19	711	CPM	71	Vass,1992
99	South Africa	15/16	1,093	JAT	68	Lynn & Owen, 1994
100	South Africa	13	49	WISC-R	70	Murdoch, 1994
101	South Africa	17/20	140	SPM	77	Maqsud, 1997
102	South Africa	43	157	WAIS-R	69	Nell, 2000
103	South Africa	16	17	SPM	68	Sonke, 2000
104	South Africa	8	63	WPPSI/ WCST	71	Akande, 2000
105	South Africa	14	152	WCST/ WISC-R	65	Skuy et al., 2001
106	South Africa	17	100	WCST/ WISC-R/ DAM	65	Skuy et al., 2001
107	South Africa	30	196	WAIS-3	82	Claassen et al., 2001
108	South Africa	8/10	806	CPM	68	Jinabhai et al., 2004
109	South Africa	11	379	CPM	71	Knoetze et al., 2005
110	South Africa	6/12	1,333	CPM	71	Linstrom, 2008

	COUNTRY	AGE	N	TEST	IQ	REFERENCE
111	South Africa	9	340	SPM	69	Malda et al., 2010
112	South Africa	15	-	EDUC	72	Meisenberg & Lynn, 2011
113	South Africa	11	379	CPM	67.5	Bakheit & Lunn, 2014a
114	South Sudan	7/16	291	Various	69	Fahmy, 1964
115	Sudan	9/18	1,006	SPM	67	Khaleefa & Lynn, 2010
116	Swaziland	15	-	EDUC	81.8	Meisenberg & Lynn, 2011
117	Tanzania	Adults	179	CPM	60	Boissiere et al., 1985
118	Tanzania	11/13	458	WCST	72	Sternberg et al., 2002
119	Tanzania	15	-	EDUC	80.3	Meisenberg & Lynn, 2011
120	Tanzania	16	171	APM	75	Rindermann, 2012
121	Tanzania	14	891	Various	64	Rindermann, 2012
122	Uganda	11	514	DAM	82	Minde & Kantor, 1976
123	Uganda	14	-	SPM	66	Heyneman, 1977
124	Uganda	11	2,019	CPM	73	Heyneman & Jamison, 1980
125	Uganda	15	-	EDUC	74	Meisenberg & Lynn, 2011
126	Uganda	14	872	Various	76	Rindermann, 2012
127	Zaire	6/30	693	CPM	73	Ombredane et al, 1956
128	Zaire	Adults	67	SPM	82	Verhagen, 1956
129	Zaire	17/29	320	SPM	69	Ombredane et al., 1957
130	Zaire	10/15	222	SPM	68	Laroche, 1959

	COUNTRY	AGE	N	TEST	IQ	REFERENCE
131	Zaire	8	47	KABC	62	Boivin & Giordani,1993
132	Zaire	7/12	95	KABC	68	Boivin et al.,1995
133	Zaire	7/9	130	KABC	65	Giordani et al.,1996
134	Zaire	8	183	CPM	74	Kashala et al.,2005
135	Zambia	15	759	SPM	75	MacArthur et al., 1964
136	Zambia	16	292	SPM	75	MacArthur et al., 1964
137	Zambia	Adults	152	SPM	64	Pons, 1974
138	Zambia	Adults	1,011	SPM	80	Pons, 1974
139	Zambia	15	-	EDUC	66.2	Meisenberg & Lynn, 2011
140	Zanzibar	15	-	EDUC	74.3	Meisenberg & Lynn, 2011
141	Zimbabwe	15	200	SPM	72	Irvine, 1969
142	Zimbabwe	12/14	204	WISC-R	71	Zindi, 1994
143	Zimbabwe	15	-	EDUC	76.2	Meisenberg & Lynn, 2011

Explanations of the results of the studies summarized in Table 4.1 are given where appropriate.

Row 18: This study from Congo-Zaire also gives an IQ of 62 for a sample with malarial infection, indicating that infection likely impairs the IQ by 5 points. However, Anna Helena Muntendam et al. (1996) have reported a study finding that cerebral malaria had no adverse effect on intelligence.

Rows 23 and 24 present discrepant results for Eritrea. Row 23 gives an IQ of 87 for 5-to 6-year-olds, while row 24 gives an IQ of 66 for 11-year-olds. The explanation of this difference is that five- and six-year-olds in Africa and other economically developing countries perform better than older children on the Progressive Matrices. This has been found in Syria, the United Arab Emirates, and Libya (Khaleefa & Lynn, 2008a and 2008b; Lynn, Abdalla & Al- Shahomee, 2008; Al- Shahomee & Lynn, 2008). As has been demonstrated (Lynn, Allik & Irwing, 2004), the reason for this age difference appears to be that the initial items in the CPM and the SPM tests are measures of visualization ability, while the later items are measures of abstract reasoning ability. The five- and six-year-olds are scored mainly on the initial visualization items because the abstract reasoning ability items are too difficult for them. Older children aged 10 and 11 are scored mainly on the abstract reasoning ability items, because the visualization are so easy that they mostly get them all right; the visualization items are largely a constant that is added to their scores on the abstract reasoning ability items. The best way of dealing with these two discrepant IQs for Eritrea is to average them to give an IQ of 75.5. This is a little above the average for sub-Saharan Africa. The explanation for this may be that there is a significant Arab component in the population of Eritrea, arising from migration of Arab peoples from Sudan and across the Red Sea from present day Yemen and Saudi Arabia. The average Arab IQ is about 84 (see Chapter 6), so this admixture may explain the higher IQ in Eritrea.

Rows 32 and 33 give IQs of 60 for Gambia. These low IQs are based on studies of two tribes, the Mandinka and the Wolof, living in rural areas and are likely underestimates.

Row 48 gives an IQ of 87 for Kenya. This is based on a sample of seven-year-olds tested in 1998 and is much higher than the other IQs for Kenya and any other studies of IQs in sub-Saharan African populations. The validity of the IQ of 87 is questionable because the same investigators reported an IQ of 76 in their previous 1984 study (Row 47). A gain of 11 IQ points from an IQ of 76 to 87 over the 14 year period is uniquely high in studies of the secular rise of IQs and cannot be accepted as credible. Furthermore, the IQ of 78 given in row 45 is obtained from a standardization of the same test for the whole of Kenya carried out in the same year, and the other IQs for Kenya are all in the normal range for sub-Saharan Africa. In addition, it is difficult to believe that children in Kenya can have a higher IQ than African-Americans in the United States, where the IQ has remained constant at approximately 85 since the 1920s, but where the living standards and nutrition of Africans are much higher than in Kenya. For these reasons, we should consider the reported IQ of 87 for Kenya to be unreliable.

Row 54 and 55 give IQs of 82 and 76 for Madagascar, a little higher than the average in sub-Saharan Africa. Although usually counted as part of sub-Saharan Africa, the population consists not only of Africans but also a significant number with South East Asian ancestry, originating from peoples in modern-day Indonesia who migrated to the island about the first century AD (Cole, 1965), and of hybrids of the two races on the island. South East Asians have an average IQ of around 87 (see Chapter 7). This element in the population may explain the higher IQ than is typically present in sub-Saharan Africa.

Row 56: This study in Malawi administered the Ab scales of the CPM. The score is scaled up to the equivalent on the complete test using the table given in the CPM manual.

Row 81 gives an IQ of 76 for Rwanda calculated from a study comparing 148 children at school in Rwanda with 139 European children in Montreal on five Piagetian tests. Results are given for the ages at which 50 percent of the two groups of children attained the last Piagetian stage on the tasks. The average of these ages for the five tasks was 9.7 for the European children and 12.8 for the Rwandan children. Thus, Rwandan children aged 12.8 are at the same level of mental development as European children aged 9.7. Using the original method for calculating the IQ as mental age divided by chronological age multiplied by 100, the IQ of the Rwandan children can be estimated at 76.

Row 89 gives an IQ of 72 obtained in the mid-1930s in South Africa for Black school children "who had already spent a considerable time under the alleged equalizing environmental influence of the schoolroom" (Fick, 1939, p.11). The same study gave IQs for European school children. The average IQ difference between Blacks and Whites was 28 IQ points, giving Blacks an IQ of 72. Row 102 gives an IQ of 69 for a sample of South African adults described as "competent men, all in long standing employment in a sophisticated environment...." (Nell, 2000, p. 27). Row 111 gives an IQ of 69 for South Africa derived from a study of the SPM administered to 161 White Afrikaans nine-year-olds, 181 urban Blacks, and 151 rural Blacks. In relation to an IQ of 100 for the White Afrikaans children, the urban Blacks obtained an IQ of 70.5, and the rural Blacks obtained an IQ of 66.75. The two Black IQs are averaged to 69.

Row 114 gives an IQ of 69 for the new state of South Sudan that came into existence in 2011. The population is Negroid, and the sample consisted of Shilluk children and adolescents described as one of the primitive Nilotic Negro tribes (Fahmy, 1964, p.164). Nilotics are one of the four subraces of Negroids given by Baker (1974, p. 329). The study administered four tests to a sample of 291 7- to 16-year-old school children inhabiting the west bank of the White Nile. The four tests and the mean American IQs obtained by the sample were the Goddard Formboard (73.5), the Porteus mazes (76.5), the Alexander Passalong (94.4), and the Goodenough Draw-a-Man (DAM) (53.4). The average American IQ on the four tests is 74.5. It is not known whether the American tests were standardized on Whites, or on the whole population including Blacks. Many of these early tests were standardized on Whites, and we assume that this was the case for these. These IQs do not take account of the increases in intelligence of approximately 3 IQ points a decade that have taken place over time in the United States (Flynn, 1984). The norms for the American tests were collected in the 1920s and 1930s, and an adjustment for a 6 IQ point increase in these in the United Sates reduces the IQ of the Sudanese sample to 68.5. Row 114 gives an IQ of 67 for a sample of Negroids in the Darfur region of southwest Sudan. Row 141 gives an IQ of 71 for school children in Zimbabwe obtained by Zindi (1994), an African psychologist at the University of Zimbabwe.

The most striking feature of the IQs of sub-Saharan Africans in sub-Saharan Africa is that they are consistently so much lower than those of Europeans set out in Table 3.1 of Chapter 3. It is also remarkable that the average IQ of sub-Saharan Africans has shown little change since the first studies published by Laurence Fick (1929, 1939) and Dent (1937) obtained IQs of 65, 72, and 68 for Africans in South Africa. The three most recent studies of Africans in South Africa published between 2005 and 2010 found virtually the same IQs of 71 (Knoetze et al., 2005; Linstrom, 2008) and 69 (Malda et al., 2010).

The median IQ of the 143 studies summarized in Table 4.1 is 71. This is a little higher than the IQ of 67 given in the first edition based on 57 studies and is proposed as the best estimate currently available of the sub-Saharan African IQ.

A higher figure for the IQ in sub-Saharan Africa has been proposed by Wicherts and his colleagues who have argued that the average IQ in sub-Saharan Africa assessed by the Progressive Matrices is 76 in relation to a British norm (Wicherts, Dolan, Carlson & Van der Maas, 2010) and assessed by tests other than the Progressive Matrices is 82 in relation to British norms (Wicherts, Dolan & Van der Maas, 2010). These estimates were obtained by including a number studies of unrepresentative elite samples and by excluding many studies of low scoring samples (Lynn, 2010b; Lynn & Meisenberg, 2010). The excluded studies of unrepresentative elite samples are listed in Table 4.2.

Table 4.2. Excluded studies of IQs of Sub-Saharan Africans

	COUNTRY	AGE	N	TEST	IQ	REFERENCES
1	Nigeria	6/11	393	DAM	83	Bakare, 1972
2	Nigeria	2/6	118	McCarth	89	Ashern & Janes, 1978
3	Nigeria	13	803	CCF	95	Nenty & Dinero, 1981
4	Nigeria	adults	28	SPM	89	Morakinyo, 1985
5	Sierra Leone	8	202	DAM	91	Ohuche & Ohuche, 1973
6	South Africa	19	228	SPM	87	Crawford-Nutt, 1976
7	South Africa	24	40	WAIS-3	84	Shuttleworth, Edwards et al., 2004
8	Zimbabwe	8	52	PMA	84	Wilson et al., 1991
9	Zimbabwe	12/14	204	SPM	70	Zindi, 1994

Row 1: This study (Bakare, 1972) gives DAM data for upper-class and lower-class Nigerian children. The fathers of the upper-class children were senior civil servants or university administrators, lecturers, and professors. All the fathers had university educations,

and the mothers had at least a secondary school education. The fathers of the lower-class children were farmers, petty traders, taxi drivers, or office messengers. The average IQ of the upper-class children was approximately 100.5, whereas the average of the lower class was 65. Jelte Wicherts averages these to give an IQ of 83. The sampling is unsatisfactory because the upper-class children were selected from a small elite group and cannot be weighted equally with the lower-class children to yield a representative sample of the population.

The results from Row 2 (Nenty & Dinero, 1981) are excluded because the sample was given additional time. The results in Row 3 (Ashem & Janes, 1978) are rejected because the study contained samples of well nourished "higher socioeconomic children" (IQ=109), adequately nourished, mainly middle-class children (IQ=91.4), and poorly nourished rural children (IQ=79.6). Wicherts averages the three IQs to 92.6 and deducts four for the Flynn effect and the British IQ adjustments to give 89. The combined sample cannot be accepted as representative. This small sample from Row 4 (Morakinyo, 1985) consisted of 28 psychiatric patients. These cannot be regarded as representative; they have to pay medical fees and are therefore likely more affluent than the general population.

The results from Row 5 (Ohuche & Ohuche, 1973) were excluded because, as the study states, the sample students attended an "experimental school of Njala University College. . . . All pupils who were repeating the year were excluded [i.e. those with low IQs who were performing poorly] . . . as were all those children who were obviously outside the age range." The ages of the children were unknown but guessed from their grades. Scores and American IQs are reported for 7 grades from "approximately 5 years to about 12 years." American IQs are given as 73 for grade one, 97.5 for grade two, and about the same figure for successive grades up to 95.5 for grade seven. This is rejected because of too many inconsistencies, problems, and unknowns.

Row 6 is excluded (Crawford-Nutt, 1976) because the sample of secondary-school students were given extensive training on the SPM, at the end of which this students obtained an average score of 45. This is the 16th percentile of the 1993 American standardization norms, which equals an IQ of 85. Two points should be deducted to equate to the British IQ and four added for the Flynn effect, which yeilds an IQ of 87. Numerous studies have shown that IQs can be increased considerably by training on the test, so this study is excluded.

Row 7 (Shuttlewoth Edwards et al., 2004) features a study that gives an IQ of 84 for a small sample of South African educated Blacks compared with White adults on the South African WAIS-3. The high IQ of this sample is attributable to its being an unrepresentative elite group and thus the study is excluded.

This study of 52 Black primary-school girls, found in Row 8 (Wilson et al., 1991), obtained an IQ of 84. The Blacks attended a primary school with Whites in a middle-class neighborhood, so the sample cannot be accepted as representative. In the study from Row 9 (Zindi, 1994), students were give only 36 out of the 60 items in the test; the IQ of 70 given by Zindi cannot be accurately calculated.

2. HIGH-SCHOOL AND UNIVERSITY STUDENTS

In addition to the studies listed in Table 4.1, there are a number of further studies based on secondary-school students. These have almost invariably been selected for ability by entrance examinations; admissions are competitive, and those with higher IQs gain entrance (Klingelhofer, 1967, p. 207). For instance, in Uganda in the mid-1960s, Philip Vernon (1969, p. 182) reported an IQ of approximately 80 for secondary school students and commented that these were "much superior to the East African population in general"; in 1970, only two percent of children in Uganda attended secondary school (Silvey, 1972, p.42), and these were admitted on the basis of their academic ability determined by examinations. As recently as 1999, it was noted that "in most developing countries, the demand for secondary school places is greater than the supply of these places. Consequently, governments in these countries resort to selecting students on merit who are then offered the few available places. The students who find themselves in government or government-assisted secondary schools are not ordinary students; they are a highly selected group" (Dzama & Osborne, 1999, p. 388).

Consequently, these secondary school samples can be assumed to have had average IQs higher than those of the general population. The exception is South Africa, where most Africans have attended secondary school in the second half of the 20th century.

Studies of the IQs these secondary school samples are, therefore, given separately in Table 4.3.

Table 4.3. IQs of Sub-Saharan secondary school students in Africa

	COUNTRY	AGE	N	TEST	IQ	REFERENCES
1	Botswana	17/20	140	SPM	75	Maqsud, 1997
2	Congo-Brazz	13	88	SPM	72	Nkaya et al, 1994
3	Congo–Zaire	10/15	222	SPM	79	Laroche, 1959
4	Nigeria	-	179	Leone	81	Ferrron, 1965
5	Nigeria	15	516	LT	86	Yoloye, 1971
6	Nigeria	13/15	136	SPM	85	Maqsud, 1980b
7	Nigeria	13	755	SPM	75	Jedege & Bamgboye, 1981
8	Nigeria	8/11	73	CPM	89	Okonji, 1974
9	Sierra Leone	13	400	MH	78	Dunstan, 1961
10	Sierra Leone	-	100	Leone	93	Ferrron, 1965
11	South Africa	17/20	140	SPM	77	Maqsud, 1997
12	Tanzania	13/17	2,959	SPM	78	Klingelhofer, 1967
13	Uganda	12	50	Various	80	Vernon, 1969
14	Uganda	13	211	SPM	77	Silvey, 1972
15	Zambia	13	649	SPM	83	MacArthur et al., 1964
16	Zambia	18/27	195	SPM	79	MacArthur et al., 1964
17	Zimbabwe	14/18	200	SPM	73	Irvine, 1969b

Worthy of attention is Row 4, which gives an IQ of 81 for a sample of boys at a selective secondary school in Nigeria. Unselected children attending schools in the same town of Zaria obtained an IQ of 70. The test was the Leone Test, which is described by the author as "devised by an African for African children" (Ferron, 1965, p. 53). The result belies the assertion often made that Africans are handicapped on tests constructed by Europeans. Row 6 gives an IQ of 85 for a sample of girls at a selective secondary school in Kano (Nigeria). Row 8 gives an IQ of 89 for a sample at a private school "considered one of the best in Lagos; the fathers of all the children with the exception of eight were higher professionals and top civil servants" (Okonji, 1974, p.18).

A 2010 study (Row 9), conducted by Jelte Wicherts, Conor Dolan and Han van der Maas, reported an IQ of 78 for a sample at a selective secondary school in Sierra Leone. A sample of secondary school students in Tanzania achieved an IQ score of 78 (Row 12). The test was given with a time limit, which may have reduced the scores. Selective-school students in Uganda had a score of 80 (Row 13), derived as the average of reasoning (81), verbal (80), and visual-spatial (78) abilities. The school students were described as "much superior to the East African population in general" (Vernon, 1969, p. 182).

The median IQ of the studies summarized in Table 4.3 is 79. This is predictably higher than the median of 71 of general-population studies summarized in Table 4.1; this fact is informative in so far as it shows that selected samples of sub-Saharan with secondary-school education obtain IQs well below Europeans

Studies of the intelligence of Sub-Saharan African university students are summarized in Table 4.4. Some of these studies also give IQs of European students tested at the same time.

Row 1 gives an IQ of 75 for Sub-Saharan African students at Legon University in Ghana tested with the Block Design (Kohs Blocks) test from the Wechsler Test. All the remaining rows present the results for South Africa.

Row 2 gives an IQ of 84 for Sub-Saharan African and 103 for European university students, calculated in relation to American adult norms (Raven, Court, and Raven, 1994). Rows 3 and 4 present results for students taking the Blox test, giving the IQs of Africans in relation to South African European student norms of 100. Row 5 shows results for the WAIS-R for students (average age of 25) at the African universities of Fort Hare, Zululand, the North, and the Medical University of South Africa. The average Verbal IQ was 78 and the Performance IQ, 73, demonstrating, once again, that the Sub-Saharan Africans have low IQs in all major cognitive abilities and disconfirming the claim sometimes made that Sub-Saharan Africans are handicapped in language tasks. Science students at the University of the North achieved an IQ of 100 (Row 6), while students at a less prestigious African university scored 77 (Row 7). Row 8 gives an IQ of 84 for students at the University of the Witwatersrand and the Rand Afrikaans University in Johannesburg. Row 9 gives an IQ of 82 for Sub-Saharan African students at the Venda University in the Northern Transvaal. The comparison European group was at the University of Tilberg in the Netherlands. Psychology students at the University of the Witwatersrand were measured at 81 (Row 10), while first-year engineering students at the University of the Witwatersrand scored 93. Row 12 gives an IQ of 99 for a slightly reduced number of the same students who took the Advanced Progressive Matrices 16 months later. Both Sub-Saharan Africans and Europeans obtained IQs approximately six points higher on the second testing, probably a result of what is known as the "practice effect." Row 13 gives an IQ of 101 for a further sample of Sub-Saharan African engineering students at the University of the Witwatersrand and shows that the Sub-Saharan African students scored 15 IQ points lower than the European Whites. A further sample of Sub-Saharan African students at the University of the Witwatersrand achieved an average of of 95 (Row 14), 15 IQ points lower than the Europeans. Row 15 gives IQs of sample of Black and White students at an American university; there, Black students scored 6.4 IQ points lower than their European peers.

The mean IQs of general student samples shown in rows 1 to 5 and 7 to 9 all fall in the narrow range of 72 to 84 with a median of 81. The IQs of 100 in Row 6, 93 in Row 11, and 99 in Row 12 are higher than the others because they are for science and engineering students, who were admitted to the universities on the basis of their performance in entrance tests of mathematics and physics; such students normally have higher reasoning ability than students in most other academic disciplines. For instance, in Iran, 18-year-olds studying math scored 10 IQ points higher than those studying literature (Mehryar, Shapurian, and Bassiri, 1972). In Britain, education students with degrees in science scored 9 IQ points higher than those with degrees in arts (Heim, 1968). The IQs of European students in South Africa are in the range between 100 and 105 and are about the same as those of European students in other countries (see Chapter 3, Table 3.3).

The interest of these results is that they show that typical African students who have had some 12 years of school and have gained entry to university obtain IQs in the range of 72–84. Since these students are part of an African cognitive elite, these results suggest that the IQ of the general population is approximately 70. The results also show that IQs of Sub-Saharan African students in South Africa are on average about 20 IQ points lower than those of European students, and that a considerable gap between the IQs of Sub-Saharan Africans and Europeans remains when they are matched for years of education. Sub-Saharan African university students have had 10 to 12 years of formal education, but apart from those studying math and physics, they obtain IQs in the range of 72–84.

Table 4.4. IQs of Sub-Saharan African and European university students

			AFRICANS		EUROPEANS			
	COUNTRY	TEST	N	IQ	N	IQ	IQ DIFF	REFERENCE
1	Ghana	BD	66	79	-	-		Jahoda, 1970
2	S. Africa	APM	40	84	40	103	19	Poortinga, 1971
3	S. Africa	Blox	47	72	50	100	28	Poortinga & Foden, 1975
4	S. Africa	Blox	403	79	197	100	21	Taylor & Radford, 1986

	COUNTRY	TEST	AFRICANS		EUROPEANS		IQ DIFF	REFERENCE
			N	IQ	N	IQ		
5	S. Africa	WISC-R	63	75	-	-	-	Avenant, 1988
6	S. Africa	SPM	147	100	-	-	-	Zaaiman, 1998
7	S. Africa	SPM	30	77	-	-	-	Grieve & Viljoen, 2000
8	S. Africa	SPM	173	84	136	103	19	Rushton & Skuy, 2000
9	S. Africa	SPM	30	82	30	105	23	Sonke, 2000
10	S. Africa	SPM	70	81	-	-	-	Skuy et al., 2002
11	S. Africa	SPM	198	93	86	106	13	Rushton et al., 2002
12	S. Africa	APM	187	99	67	113	14	Rushton et al., 2003
13	S. Africa	APM	306	103	72	116	15	Rushton et al., 2004
14	S. Africa	SPM	887	95	398	110	15	Rushton, 2008
15	USA	Wonderlic	40	101.7	139	107.3	6.4	Pesta & Poznanski, 2008

3. SUB-SAHARAN AFRICANS IN THE CARIBBEAN AND LATIN AMERICA

Studies of the IQs of Africans in the Caribbean and Latin America are summarized in Table 4.5. The average IQ of African children in Barbados is estimated to be 80 (Row 1); this figure is calculated from the IQ of 83 of well-nourished children and 68 of malnourished children, reported in a study led by Janina Galler, and weighted by the results of a 1968 survey finding a prevalence of moderate and severe malnutrition in preschool children in Barbados of 16.5 percent (Galler, Ramsay, Solimano et al., 1983). Africans in Brazil attending school in a *favela* (shanty town) in Brasilia were found to have an average IQ of 70. Row 3 gives an IQ of 64 for the mothers of these children; and Row 4 shows an IQ of 71 for Africans in Sao Paulo in Brazil.

Table 4.5. IQs of Africans in the Caribbean and Latin America

	COUNTRY	AGE	N	TEST	IQ	REFERENCE
1	Barbados	9–15	207	WISC-R	80	Galler et al., 1986
2	Brazil	9	100	DAM	70	Paine et al., 1992
3	Brazil	Adult	88	SPM	64	Paine et al., 1992
4	Brazil	9–10	223	SPM	71	Fernandez, 2001
5	Dominica	3	64	PPVT	67	Wein & Stevenson, 1972
6	Dominica	20-70	67	CPM	67	Meisenberg et al., 2006
7	Dominican Rep	15	-	EDUC	75.1	Meisenberg & Lynn, 2011
8	Jamaica	11	1730	MH	72	Manley, 1963
9	Jamaica	11	50	Matrices	75	Vernon, 1969
10	Jamaica	5–12	71	WISC	60	Hertzig et al., 1972
11	Jamaica	10	128	CEFT	75	Bagley et al., 1983
12	Jamaica	15	31	WISC-R	67	Grantham-McGregor et al., 1994
13	Jamaica	25	54	PPVT	60	Grantham-McGregor et al., 1994
14	Jamaica	9–10	30	PPVT	71	Simeon & Grantham-McGregor, 1989
15	Antillies	9-11	97	CPM	87	Van de Vijfeijken et al., 1997
16	St. Lucia	4	60	PPVT	62	Murray, 1983
17	St.Vincent	8–11	174	CPM	71	Durbrow et al., 2002
18	Trinidad	15	-	EDUC	88	Meisenberg & Lynn, 2011

Two samples in Dominica achieved scores of 67 (Rows 5 and 6). The low IQ of three-year-old African infants suggests that poor education is not a factor responsible for the low IQs of Africans in the Caribbean. The higher score found in the Dominican Republic (75.1) can be attributed to its nation's racial composition: the population is 73 percent Mulatto, 11 percent Black, and 16 percent White (Phillips, 1996). Rows 8 through 14 give IQs from seven studies of the IQ in Jamaica in the range of 60–75 with a median of 67. Row 15 gives an IQ of 87 for 9- to 11-year-olds in Netherlands Antillies, where the population is 85 percent of African descent. Row 15 gives an IQ of 60 for four-year-olds in St. Lucia and row 16 an IQ of 70 for children in St. Vincent. Trinidad's score (88) reflects its population make-up, which is 40 percent Indian, 40 percent Black, 18 percent mixed, and 1 percent White (Phillips, 1996).

The median of the 18 studies of intelligence of sub-Saharan Africans in the Caribbean and Latin America is an IQ of 71. This is the same as the median IQ of Africans in sub-Saharan Africa. Unlike most of their brethren on the African continent, Africans in the Caribbean and Latin America have some admixture of genes from Europeans. It has been estimated that the proportion of European genes in the population of Jamaica is 6.8 percent (Parra, Marcini, and Akey, 1998), but this does not seem to have had any significant effect in increasing the intelligence of the people.

4. SUB-SAHARAN AFRICAN-AMERICANS IN THE UNITED STATES

There have been many hundreds of studies of the intelligence of African-Americans in the United States. The most important of these are summarized in Table 4.6.

Row 1 gives results of the first major study based on military conscripts in World War I, who were tested with the combined Army Alpha and Beta tests that measured nonverbal and verbal IQs; on these exams, African-Americans obtained an IQ of 83. An African-American sample in West Virginia confirmed this result (Row 2). An African-American group on the island of St. Helena, studied in 1935, had an exceptionally low average IQ of 67 (Row 3). These were "of practically pure Negro blood" (Nissen, 1935) and their IQ is approximately the same as that in sub-Saharan Africa. This is an early study showing that African-Americans with little White ancestry have lower IQs than those with greater White ancestry. This has been confirmed in later studies showing that light skin color is associated with higher intelligence in African-Americans (Lynn, 2002a).

Row 4 gives an IQ of 77 for military conscripts in World War II, and Row 5, the same IQ for military conscripts in the Vietnam War. It is noteworthy that the mean IQ of 77 of Africans was lower in World War II and the Vietnam War than in World War I, and was also lower than the average IQ of 85 that is generally given for the mean IQ of African-Americans in the United States. Rows 6 through 9 give the results of Audrey Shuey's compilation of all American studies for the period 1916–65. Her results include: an IQ of 87, derived from 17 studies of pre-school children; an IQ of 85, calculated from 26 studies of primary-school children using individual tests such as the Stanford-Binet; an IQ of 85 for primary-school children, derived from 103 studies for group tests of verbal ability and 41 studies of group tests of nonverbal ability; and finally an IQ of 85 for high school students. Rows 10, 11, and 12 give the results of Robert Osborne and Frank McGurk's (1982) updated summary of American studies, published from 1976 through 1980. They report an IQ of 80, derived from 66 studies of preschool three- to five-year-olds (Row 10); an IQ of 87 (Row 11), calculated from 126 studies of primary school children; and an IQ of 87 (Row 12), derived from 17 studies of high school students.

Rows 13, 14, and 15 (Broman et al., 1975) give results for large samples not included in the Osborne and McGurk review. Row 13 gives an IQ of 85 for African mothers tested in the National Collaborative Perinatal Project and rows 14 and 15 give IQs of 87 for their children at the age of four years and seven years.

Table 4.6. IQs of African Americans in the United States

	YEAR	AGE	AFRICAN N	EURO. N	TEST	IQ	REFERENCE
1	1918	Adults	23,596	93,973	AA&B	83	Yerkes, 1921
2	1927	7/15	129	-	PPT	83	Nissen et al., 1935
3	1928	12	84	-	PPT	67	Nissen et al., 1935
4	1944	Adults	-	-	AGCT	77	Davenport, 1946
5	1964	Adults	-	-	AFQT	77	Karpinos, 1966

	YEAR	AGE	AFRICAN N	EURO. N	TEST	IQ	REFERENCE
6	1916-65	3/6	1,700	-	Various	87	Shuey, 1966
7	1916-65	6/11	7,000	-	Various	85	Shuey, 1966
8	1916-65	6/11	75,050	-	Various	85	Shuey, 1966
9	1916-65	12/18	23,000	-	Various	85	Shuey, 1966
10	1966-80	3/6	-	-	Various	80	Osborne & McGurk, 1982
11	1966-80	6/11	100,000	-	Various	87	Osborne & McGurk, 1982
12	1966-80	12–18	16,000	-	Various	82	Osborne & McGurk, 1982
13	1966	24	7,300	5,733	SRAT	85	Broman et al., 1975
14	1970	4	12,029	9,730	SB	87	Broman et al., 1975
15	1974	7	19,968	18,474	WISC	87	Broman et al., 1975
16	1972	6/16	305	1,870	WISC-R	84	Kaufman & Doppelt, 1976
17	1977	16/74	7,270	16,134	GATB	81	Avolio & Waldman, 1994
18	1977	5/11	456	604	WISC-R	85	Mercer & Lewis, 1984
19	1978	16/74	192	1,664	WAIS-R	85	Reynolds et al., 1987
20	1980	14/22	3,022	6,502	AFQT	82	Herrnstein & Murray, 1994
21	1981	2/12	311	1,450	KABC	93	Kaufman & Kaufman, 1983
22	1982	3/18	932	4,519	PPVT	84	Dunn, 1988
23	1984	12/23	210	1,303	SB-4	83	Thorndike et al., 1986
24	1984	3	86	86	SB-LM	86	Montie & Fagan, 1988
25	1985	37	502	3,535	Various	83	Nyborg & Jensen, 2000
26	1989	6/16	338	1,620	WISC-3	85	Prifitera et al., 1998

	YEAR	AGE	AFRICAN N	EURO. N	TEST	IQ	REFERENCE
27	1990	3/4	1134	2071	PPVT	82	Jencks & Phillips, 1998
28	1991	11/93	241	1,547	KAIT	88	Kaufman et al., 1994
29	1991	16/74	7,214	14,503	GATB	81	Avolio & Waldman, 1994
30	1991	6/16	711	776	WISC-R	85	Kramer et al., 1995
31	1993	3	33	33	SB-4	85	Peoples et al., 1995
32	1993	70+	833	5,122	MMSE	85	Zsembik & Peek, 2001
33	1993	Adults	806	5,300	Vocabulary	90	Lynn, 2004
34	1996	76	317	147	WAIS-Sim	87	Manley et al.,1998
35	1998	Adults	2,113	8,751	Literacy	86	Raudenbush & Kasim, 1998
36	1998	5/17	77	77	UNIT	86	Kane, 2007
37	2002	Adults	-	-	SB	88	Dickens & Flynn, 2006
38	2002	6/16s	-	-	WISC	88	Dickens & Flynn, 2006
39	2002	24	-	-	-	92	Flynn, 2007
40	2008	17	-	-	NAEP	81	Rushton & Jensen, 2010

Row 16 gives a g IQ of 84 for Africans from the standardization sample of the WISC-R. In Row 17, we find an IQ of 81 for g in a study that gave IQs of 86 for verbal and 84 for visualization abilities for employed individuals collected by the United States Employment Service. A sample of African-Americans in California achieved an IQ of 85 for g (Row 18). Row 19 shows IQs of 85 for g, in a study that measured IQs of 87 for verbal ability and 86 for visualization ability, obtained from the standardization sample of the WAIS-R. Row 20 gives an IQ of 82 from the AFQT. Row 21 gives an IQ of 93 from the standardization sample of the K-ABC. Row 22 gives a vocabulary IQ of 84 from the standardization sample of the Peabody Picture Vocabulary Test. Row 23 gives an IQ of 83 from the standardization sample of the Stanford-Binet-4; in this sample African Americans obtained a short-term memory IQ of 89, consistent with a number of other studies finding they do relatively well on tests of short-term memory.

Three-year-olds from the standardization sample of the Stanford-Binet-LM (Row 24) achieved an average IQ of 86; pre-school children obtain the same IQ as school age and adults. Such data undermine the notion that poor schools are responsible for the low IQ of African-Americans. Row 25 gives an IQ of 83, calculated from the first principal component as a measure of g obtained from military personnel. Row 26 gives an IQ of 85 from the standardization sample of the WISC-3. Row 27 gives an IQ of 82 for three- to four-year-olds from the National Longitudinal Survey of Youth. Row 28 gives an IQ of 88 from the standardization sample of the Kaufman Adolescent and Adult Intelligence Test. Row 29 gives an IQ of 81 for a sample of employed individuals collected by the United States Employment Service. Row 30 gives a visualization IQ of 85 derived from the block design subtest of the WISC-R obtained from the national NHANES III sample.

Row 31 gives an IQ of 85 for infants aged 3.0 to 3.4 years from the standardization sample of the Stanford-Binet-4 and confirms the result in rows 24 and 27, showing that the low Black IQ is present in pre-school children. A representative sample aged 70 and older from the continental United States (i.e. excluding Alaska and Hawaii) had an average IQ of 86 (Row 32). Row 33 gives an IQ of 90 for vocabulary for African adults obtained in the NORC surveys for 1990–96 from a representative sample from the continental United States. This unusually high figure is attributable to the shortness of the test, consisting of defining the meaning of 10 words. Row 34 gives an IQ of 87 for the WAIS similarities verbal reasoning test; this study also gives means for Blacks and Whites for a number of other tests, on all of which Blacks score lower than Whites by about the same amount. In the 1992 National Adult Literacy Survey (Row 35), a test consisting of verbal comprehension and arithmetic administered to a representative sample from the continental United States, African-Africans achieved a score of 86. Row 36 presents the same result, from the standardization sample of the UNIT test.

There are five conclusions to be drawn from the studies of the intelligence of African-Americans. First, the median IQ is 85 and is widely accepted as the best estimate of the African-American IQ. This estimate is close to the 83.5 obtained by Philip Roth, Craig Bevier, Philip Bobko, Fred Switzer, and Peggy Tyler (2001) from a meta-analysis of 105 studies based on 6,246,729 individuals. The variations in the means obtained in different studies are probably due to sampling, measurement errors, and differences in the abilities measured in different tests. It has been shown in many studies that sub-Saharan Africans do relatively well in tests of memory, so the size of the African-European difference reflects to some degree the extent to which memory is examined in the tests of IQ. For instance, one of the higher IQs in the table is the 88 obtained in Kaufman's KAIT. This test contains seven subtests, of which one is a memory for faces test that requires the identification of the faces of famous people. On this subtest Africans obtained a mean IQ of 92.5.

Second, the African-American IQ of approximately 85 appears in children aged 3, as can be seen in rows 22, 24, and 31. These results belie the theory, often advanced by environmentalists, that poor education and racism are responsible for (or at least contribute to) the low IQ of Africans. Even among two-year-olds, Africans have an IQ of 92 (row 21). This is not as low as in the other studies because African infants mature earlier than Europeans up to the age of two years (Lynn, 1998d; Rushton, 2000). It is not until their third or fourth years that their IQ declines to reach approximately 85, as shown in Rows 22 and 27.

Third, the IQ of approximately 85 of African Americans is substantially higher than the average IQ of 71 of Africans in sub-Saharan Africa. Two factors can explain this difference. The first is that American-Africans enjoy a better environment than Africans in Africa in a number of respects, including much higher living standards and better nutrition and health. The second is that African-Americans have, on average, about 25 percent European ancestry, resulting from their inter-breeding with White Americans over the centuries; these genes have generally increased the intelligence of African-Americans. (Reed, 1969; Chakraborty, Kamboh, Nwanko, and Ferrell, 1992).

Fourth, in the five studies giving verbal and visualization IQs, American-Africans score one or two points higher on the verbal IQs. The verbal IQs appear to be more culturally biased, so this, again, contradicts the environmentalist theory that Africans perform poorly because the tests are "biased" against them. Moreover, this result confirms the conclusions reached by McGurk (1953a, 1953b) and Jensen (1980): African-Americans are not more impaired on what can be considered "culturally biased" general-information problems, nor are IQ tests as a whole biased against African Americans.

Fifth, there appears to have been no improvement in the IQs of African Americans over the course of the 20th century. The median IQ of the 14 studies carried out from 1980 to 1998 is 85, the same as that of the earlier studies. This conclusion is confirmed by the absence of any tendency for the Black-White difference to be smaller in younger age groups. African-European IQ differences at different ages have been reported by Cecil Reynolds, Robert Chastain, Alan Kaufman, and James McLean (1987) for the WAIS-R standardization sample collected in 1978. The African IQs are 86 in 16- to 19-year-olds, 85 for 20- to 34- and 35- to 54-year-olds, and 86 for 55- to 74-year-olds. It has also been shown in bi-yearly data that there has been no difference in Black-White intelligence over the period 1974–1996 (Lynn, 1998e). Finally, in the standardization sample of the KAIT (Kaufman Adolescent and Adult Intelligence Test, Kaufman et al., 1994), there was no significant difference between the youngest and oldest age groups. In fact, the youngest age group, born between 1980 and 1991, had a slightly lower IQ of 83 compared with an IQ of 88 of the oldest age group, born on average in 1921.

5. SUB-SAHARAN AFRICANS IN BRITAIN

Africans began to migrate to Britain in substantial numbers shortly after the end of World War II. The first immigrants came mainly from the Caribbean, and in the last quarter of the 20th century, a number came from Africa. From the 1960s on, studies were published of the IQs of African immigrants. The results of these are given in Table 4.7.

The first published intelligence study (Row 1) of the children of West Indian Africans determined their IQ 88; the population sample was of Caribbean children in London, where the majority of these immigrants settled. Philip Vernon (1969) calculated an IQ of 82 for another sample in London in the 1960s (Row 2). Row 3 gives a reasoning IQ of 88 and a vocabulary IQ of 82 for West Indian children compared with European English children attending the same secondary school in the district of Haringey in London; the district is poor and the European children will have scored below the national average, thereby inflating the IQs of the West Indians. To adjust for this, the IQ of the Europeans is assumed to be 95. In Row 4, we find an IQ of 89 for a sample of children in London. Row 5 gives an IQ of 86 for samples of children in Birmingham and in Deptford, London.

Row 6 gives an IQ of 104 for nine African children taken into institutions as infants because their mothers were unable to look after them. In the same study the IQs of mixed-race children and White children also taken into institutions were measured; the mixed race had an average IQ of 110 (n=15) and the Whites, 104 (n=36). The results are out of line with the other studies in the table, all of which show that African children in Britain have IQs well below Whites. Moreover, it would normally be expected that the IQs of the children would be below average intelligence because the mothers who institutionalized them were predominantly unskilled and likely of low intelligence themselves. The results, in which these children had IQs above average, are remarkable and need replication. If they can be confirmed as valid, they suggest that in general Black mothers do not provide such a good environment as the White foster parents who reared these children, but there is little evidence to support this inference. The number of children (9) was very small and possibly this is simply a fluke result.

A national sample of Afro-Caribbean children in Britain scored an IQ of 86 (Row 7). In Rows 8 and 9, we see than in another study, African children in Britain who were born in the Caribbean had IQs of 73, whereas those born in Britain scored 82. The IQ of 73 for those born in the Caribbean is closely similar to that of 71 of indigenous Caribbean children given in Table 4.2.

Row 10 gives a verbal IQ of 86 for West Indian children tested with the English Picture Vocabulary Test. West Indian children at a comprehensive school in the town of Ilford in Essex achieved an IQ of 85 (Row 11); the 85 score is lower than that of children from the Indian subcontinent in the same school, who obtained an IQ of 91; this is the first of a number of studies in Britain finding that Caribbean immigrants have lower IQs than Indian immigrants from the sub-continent. Row 12 gives a vocabulary IQ of 78 for all West Indian children at maintained (public) schools in an education authority in the Midlands.

In Row 13, we find an IQ of 86 derived from a reading test on a very large national sample of 12,530 15-year-olds. Row 14 gives an IQ of 85 obtained on a vocabulary test by West Indian children in the north of England compared with 851 Europeans attending the same schools. West Indian children at school in a town in the Midlands scored an IQ of 87 (Row 15); Indians from the Indian sub-continent attending the same schools obtained an IQ of 96, showing, once again, that South Asians in the same environment as Africans obtain higher IQs. Row 16 and 17 show studies in which a sample of West Indian children in London achieved an IQ of 90 and West Indian four-year-olds scored an average of 87.

Row 18 gives an IQ of 89 for a national sample from the whole of Britain of Caribbean children born in 1958 and who had been in Britain for more than four years; a further group of 39, who had been in Britain for fewer than four years, obtained an IQ of 83, suggesting that residence in Britain raises the IQs of Caribbean children by around six IQ points. It has sometimes been suggested that many of the recent immigrant children from the Caribbean spoke a form of Creole West Indian English that made it difficult for them to understand the teachers, but the fact that immigrant West Indians performed about the same on nonverbal reasoning tests as on verbal comprehension makes this unlikely.

Table 4.7. IQs of Africans in Britain

	AGE	N	TEST	IQ	REFERENCE
1	10	71	SB	88	Houghton, 1966
2	11	476	VR	82	ILEA, 1967
3	12/15	174	SPM/MH	80	Bhatnagar, 1970
4	5/15	61	WISC	89	McFie & Thompson, 1970
5	11	394	EPVT	86	Halsey, 1972
6	4/5	9	WPPSI	104	Tizard, 1972
7	5/10	548	EPVT	86	Payne, 1974
8	10	143	NV5	73	Yule et al., 1975
9	10	201	NV5	82	Yule et al., 1975
10	5/10	548	EPVT	86	Little, 1975
11	10	66	VR	85	Black Peoples, 1978
12	7	139	EPVT	78	Phillips, 1979
13	15	12,530	Reading	86	Mabey, 1981
14	12	149	Vocabulary	85	Pumfrey, 1983
15	11/12	205	NFER	87	Scarr et al., 1983
16	10	88	CEFT	90	Bagley et al., 1983
17	4	106	WPPSI	87	Blatchford et al., 1985
18	11	74	NFER	89	Mackintosh & Mascie-Taylor, 1985
19	10	125	BAS	94	Mackintosh & Mascie-Taylor, 1985
20	14	250	NFER	88	Maugham & Rutter, 1986
21	65/75	248	MMSE	89	Stewart et al., 2002
22	5	340	BAS	91	Lynn & Cheng, 2013

Row 19 gives an IQ of 94 for a national British sample born in 1970; the high IQ of this sample may indicate that the IQ of Caribbean children has increased slightly, but the subsequent studies in the table show no improvement in the IQs of African children from the 1960s through the 1980s, so this may be a chance result. Row 20 gives an IQ of 88 for a sample of African schoolchildren in schools in London, the majority of whom had been born in Britain. In Row 21, we find an IQ of 89 for a sample of 65- to 75-year-old Africans in London obtained in 1996–98 compared with a national sample of 5,379 indigenous British. In 2006, a sample of 5-year-old Africans in Britain scored an an average IQ of 91 (Row 22).

The results of the studies of the intelligence of Africans in Britain raise three points of interest.

1. The median IQ of the studies is 86 and is almost exactly the same as the average of 85 of Africans in the United States. These figures are substantially higher than the median IQ of 71 of Africans in sub-Saharan Africa and in the Caribbean, from where most Africans in Britain have come in the post-World War II decades.

2. The higher IQ of Africans in Britain is attributable to the better environment and to the selective migration of those with higher IQs. The effect of the better environment is shown in the study by William Yule, Michael Berger, Michael Rutter, and Bridget Yule (1975) given in rows 8 and 9, which shows IQs of 73 for those born in the West Indies and 82 for those born in Britain, suggesting that residence in Britain raises the IQs of Caribbean children by around 9 points. This result is confirmed by a study conducted by Nicholas Mackintosh and Nicholas Mascie-Taylor (1985) shown in Row 18; the West Indian children from the Caribbean who had been in Britain for more than four years had an IQ of 89, while the IQ of a further group of 39 who had been in Britain for fewer than four years obtained an IQ of 83, suggesting that residence in Britain raises the IQs of Caribbean children by around six IQ points. The two results suggest that environmental factors of being reared in a First World country can raise a child's IQ by some eight IQ points. This increase is probably largely a result of better nutrition and healthcare and perhaps education, although there seems to be no evidence that education in the West Indies is poorer than in Britain (it is sometimes asserted to be better). The effect of improved nutrition for West Indian immigrants was shown by the Yule et al. (1975), who found that West Indian Africans born in Britain are taller than those born in the Caribbean who had come to Britain some time during childhood, a difference of $0.67d$ (standard deviation units).

3. The IQ of 87 for a sample of West Indian four-year-olds given in Row 17 is virtually the same as that obtained by older West Indian children at school and shows that the low IQs of West Indian children cannot be blamed on schools, the prejudices of teachers, difficulties understanding the teachers' spoken English, and so on. This result confirms those found in the United States, where the relatively lower IQ of Africans is present in pre-school children.

The higher IQ of Blacks in Britain compared with those in Africa and the Caribbean is also partly attributable to selective migration. Typically, when people emigrate from poor regions to more affluent regions, these migrants tend to have higher-than-average IQs. The reason for this is that a higher IQ is needed to envision the advantages of the First World and find the resources to migrate. Numerous studies summarized by Suzanne Model (2008) have found that migrants from the Caribbean and Africa to the United States have greater educational attainment (a proxy for intelligence) than non-migrants; this conclusion has been confirmed by a study by Prachi Mishra (2007). Jacob Vigdor (2002) and Model (2008) have also summarized studies finding that in the United States Blacks who migrated from the southern states to the northern states have had greater educational attainment than non-migrants. The result of this has been that Blacks in the northern states have an IQ about 10 points higher than those in the south. Kaufman & Doppelt (1976) report an average IQ of 90.5 for Blacks in the northern states compared with approximately 85 for all American Blacks and around 80 for those in the southern states. Further evidence that migration is typically selective for intelligence, and that selective migration has been for Scotland, was found by Maxwell (1967) in a follow-up study of 1,000 11-year-olds whose IQs were tested in 1947. He found that by the age of 30, 17.2 percent had emigrated and that the IQ of these was 108.1.

6. SUB-SAHARAN AFRICANS IN CANADA

There have been only three studies of the intelligence of Blacks in Canada. They are summarized in Table 4.8. All were carried out on samples of Blacks living in Ontario and compared with Whites attending the same schools (n=211 in the first study). The Blacks had been settled in the region for several generations. In the first study, Blacks obtained a mean IQ of 81. The second study found an IQ of 78 for "full-blooded" Blacks, and 93 for mixed-race mulattos. This confirms a number of studies finding that mixed-race Blacks obtain higher IQs than pure Africans. The author of these studies describes the Blacks as not overtly discriminated against. In addition to attending the same schools as Whites, they attended the same churches, and were allowed sit together with Whites in buses, restaurants, and other public places. The results of the three studies are averaged to give an IQ of 84 for Blacks in Canada.

Table 4.8. IQs of Africans in Canada

	AGE	N	TEST	IQ	REFERENCE
1	5/15	162	Pinter Pat	81	Tanser, 1939
2	7/12	46	Pinter Pat	78	Tanser, 1941
3	7/12	46	Pinter Pat	93	Tanser, 1941

7. SUB-SAHARAN AFRICANS IN THE NETHERLANDS, FRANCE, AND BELGIUM

During the second half of the 20th century, a number of Africans migrated to the Netherlands from the former Dutch colony of Surinam in the northeast of South America and from the Netherlands Antilles, the former Dutch colony in the Caribbean. Studies of their intelligence are summarized in Table 4.9. Row 1 gives an IQ of 86 for the children of immigrants from Surinam. The test used and the age of the sample are not given. The population of Surinam consists of 35 percent Creoles of mixed African-European ancestry, 10 percent Africans, 33 percent Asian Indian, 16 percent Indonesian, and 3 percent American Indian. The IQ of 86 is about what would be predicted from this racially mixed population, because the largest group, the Creoles, would be expected to have an IQ about midway between Africans in Africa (71) and Northwest Europeans (100), and the second largest group, the Asian Indians, should have an IQ of approximately 82 (see Chapter 6).

As seen in Table 4.9, the IQ of a sample of the children of first-generation immigrants from Surinam and the Netherlands Antilles was measured at 84 (Row 2). A sample of the children of second-generation immigrants from Surinam and the Netherlands Antilles achieved a higher score of 88. This increase of four points confirms the studies in Britain showing that second-generation immigrants obtain higher IQs than first-generation immigrants of the same race.

In Row 4, we find an IQ of 85 for a further sample of the children of immigrants from Surinam. (The test used and the age of the sample are not given.) Another sample of immigrants from Surinam and the Netherlands Antilles achieve a score of 83 (Row 5); adult immigrants from Surinam . Row 7 gives an IQ of 85 for immigrants from the Dutch Antilles, whose population is 85 percent African and mixed African-European. Row 8 gives an IQ of 82 for immigrants from sub-Saharan Africa in France. Finally, a study of sub-Saharan African immigrants in Belgium yielded a score of 70 (Row 9). The median IQ of these studies is 85, the same as that of Africans in the United States.

Table 4.9. IQs of Africans in the Netherlands, France, and Belgium

	AGE	N	TEST	IQ	REFERENCE
1	Children	110	GALO	86	De Jong & van Batenburg, 1984
2	Children	123	RAKIT	84	Resing et al., 1986
3	Children	77	RAKIT	88	Resing et al., 1986
4	Children	138	-	85	De Jong, 1988

	AGE	N	TEST	IQ	REFERENCE
5	11	404	CITO	83	Pieke, 1988
6	Adults	535	GATB	85	Te Nijenhuis, 1997
7	Adults	129	GATB	85	Te Nijenhuis, 1997
8	Adults	588	PM	82	Raveau et al.,1976
9	Adults	28	CCF	70	Klein et al., 2007

8. SUB-SAHARAN AFRICANS IN ISRAEL

A number of Ethiopians who adhered to the Jewish religion were recognized as Jews by the Israeli government in the 1970s and were permitted to migrate to Israel. By 1998, virtually all of them had done so. In the year 2000, the number of Ethiopian Jews in Israel was approximately 80,000, representing approximately 1.4 percent of the population. There have been three studies of their intelligence, and these are summarized in Table 4.10. Row 1 gives the results of a study of the intelligence of a sample of 15-year-olds assessed using the Standard Progressive Matrices. The researchers write:

> The Ethiopian Jews were tested one year after they arrived in Israel. All the subjects were tested in groups in their schools, using standard procedure. Each group was shown the first practice item of the test and solved it together. Special care was taken to make sure the Ethiopian Jews understood how the test was organized, to ensure their ability to fill out the answer sheet. There was no time limit (Kaniel & Fisherman, 1991, p. 28).

The leaders of the study made errors in the calculation of the IQ of the Ethiopians. I corrected their figures in study published in the *International Journal of Psychology* (1994b). The mean score on the test was 27, equivalent to the first percentile on the British 1979 standardization norms and to an IQ of 65. It is assumed that the Israeli data were collected in 1989 and that the British IQ increased by two IQ points between 1979 and 1989. To adjust for this increase, the IQ of the Ethiopian Jews needs to be reduced to 63.

Row 2 presents the results of the second study of the IQ of Ethiopian Jews. These were 14- to 16-year-olds who had been in Israel for four or more years, were attending Israeli boarding schools, and were tested with the Progressive Matrices. Their mean IQ was 66. These results suggest that education in Western schools does not benefit the African intelligence.

In Row 2, we find the results of the third study of the IQ of Ethiopian Jews, which consists of a small sample of 29 six-to seven-year-olds tested with the Colored Progressive Matrices. These obtained a higher IQ of 87. The explanation for this is that the Colored Progressive Matrices gives higher IQs for younger children than for older ones, because it is a measure of visualization rather than problem-solving ability (Lynn, Allik and Irwing, 2004). The weighted average of the three studies is an IQ of 70, virtually identical to the average IQ throughout sub-Saharan Africa.

Table 4.10. IQs of Africans in Israel

	AGE	N	TEST	IQ	REFERENCE
1	15	250	SPM	68	Kaniel & Fisherman, 1991
2	1416	46	SPM	66	Kozulin, 1998
3	6-7	29	CPM	87	Tuzuriel & Kaufman, 1999

9. SHORT-TERM MEMORY AND PERCEPTUAL SPEED ABILITIES OF SUB-SAHARAN AFRICANS

Hitherto African intelligence has been considered in terms of *g* (general intelligence). We now consider studies on the short-term memory and perceptual-speed ability of Africans. Short-term memory is typically measured by the Digit Span test, consisting of the ability to recall a series of numbers either in the order in which they are presented (forward Digit Span) or in reverse order (backward Digit

Span). Perceptual Speed is typically measured by the Coding and Digit Symbol subtests in the Wechsler tests that require accurate and rapid scanning of visual information. These studies have shown that Africans have relatively strong short-term memory and perceptual speed abilities. The results are summarized in Table 4.11.

In Row 1, African 10- to 12-year-olds (n=1,123) scored IQ IQs of 75 and 76, compared with Europeans (n=1,489); these were obtained for nonverbal reasoning and for verbal ability measured by the Lorge-Thorndike test. The African subjects achieved a much higher IQ of 90 for short-term memory, measured by Digit Span, and a remarkable IQ of 102 for Perceptual Speed. The authors comment: "given a test that involves only speed but no appreciable cognitive factor, the Negro children perform as well as or better than the European children" (Jensen & Rohwer, 1970, p. 60). Row 2 gives a typical IQ of 85 for the verbal and performance scales of the WISC-R obtained for 622 African 5- to 11-year-olds, compared with 669 Europeans and a short-term memory IQ of 94 as the average of forward (IQ 96) and backward (IQ 92) digit span. IQs for African 12- to 18-year-olds obtained from the Project Talent data set and shows a relatively high IQ of 94 for immediate memory as compared with 89 for abstract reasoning (Row 3). Five-to nine-year-old African Surinamese immigrants in the Netherlands (n=183) achieved an IQ of 94 for short-term memory, compared with European children. The test consisted of the presentation of ten drawings, each of which was given an arbitrary name; the task was to remember as many of the names as possible. Row 5 gives IQs for African 6- to 16-year-olds (n=711) compared with Europeans (n=776) of 85 for verbal reasoning, 83 for verbal ability, and 85 for visualization ability.

Row 6 gives an IQ of 90 for short-term memory for African Americans, compared with IQs of 82 for verbal comprehension, and 78 for visualization. In Row 7, we find an IQ of 94 for short-term memory for Africans, obtained from a meta-analysis of 31 studies of children and adults. Row 8 gives IQs for a number of primary abilities from South Africa from the study of 1,093 African and 1,056 European 16-year-olds tested with the Junior Aptitude Test, a test constructed in South Africa that provides measures of Abstract Reasoning (AR),

Verbal Reasoning (VR), Verbal Comprehension (Verb), Visualization (Vis), Short-Term Memory (STM), and Perceptual Speed (PS); the sample also obtained a Mechanical Ability IQ of 68.

African short-term memory IQ (79) and the perceptual-speed IQ (69) are both higher than their Abstract Reasoning Ability (58) and their Verbal Reasoning Ability (63), confirming the American studies. In this sample, the visualization and mechanical abilities are also all stronger than abstract and verbal reasoning ability. Row 9 gives a short-term memory IQ of 74 for a sample of 196 ten-year-olds in Jamaica, compared with 67 entered as the median of the seven studies given in Table 4.3.

The most striking feature of these results is that Africans perform better on short-term memory than on other abilities. Arthur Jensen (1998) interpreted these and other results as showing that the African-European differences in intelligence are largely differences in complex problem-solving ability and Spearman's g. According to this theory, short-term memory, and also perceptual speed, are weak measures of g, so Africans do relatively well on them. The theory has received considerable support (summarized by J.P. Rushton (2003)), but has also attracted some criticism from Conor Dolan and Ellen Hamaker (2001).

Table 4.11. Primary abilities of sub-Saharan Africans

	COUNTRY	AR	VR	VERB	VIS	STM	PS	REFERENCE
1	USA	75	-	76	-	90	102	Jensen & Rohwer, 1970
2	USA	-	-	85	85	94	-	Jensen & Figueroa, 1975
3	USA	89	-	86	90	94	-	Humphreys, 1988
4	Netherlands	-	-	-	-	94	-	Sijtsma & Resing, 1991
5	Netherlands	-	85	83	85			Te Nijenhuis, 1997
6	USA	-	-	82	78	90	-	Kramer et al., 1995
7	USA	-	-	-	-	94	-	Verive & McDaniel, 1996
8	South Africa	58	63	58	69	79	69	Lynn & Owen, 1994
9	Jamaica	67	-	-	-	74	-	Sternberg et al., 1997

Table 4.12. Performance of sub-Saharan Africans on digit span

	COUNTRY	AGE	N	DS	REFERENCES
1	Congo, DR	8.4	183	82.5	Kashala et al., 2005
2	Zimbabwe	14.8	35	79	Van der Vijver, 2008

In Table 4.12, Row 1 results give a Digit Span (DS) IQ of 82.5 in the Democratic Republic of the Congo and Row 2, a DS IQ of 79, obtained in a study in which the digit-span test was administered to 35 children in Zimbabwe (age 14.8) and 35 children in the Netherlands (aged 12.6). The Dutch children performed better by 21 IQ points, giving the Zimbabwe sample an IQ of 79. However, the Zimbabwean children were 2 years older, and this would give them an advantage. The results suggest that sub-Saharan Africans perform better on digit span than on general intelligence.

10. MUSICAL ABILITIES OF SUB-SAHARAN AFRICANS

Africans, it has often been asserted, have good musical abilities and a particularly strong sense of rhythm. As far back as the 14th century, the Arab writer Ibn Butlan wrote, "if a Zanji [i.e. an African] were to fall from heaven to earth he would beat time as he goes down" (Lewis, 1990, p. 94). Regarding African-Americans, William Bevis (1921, p.71) wrote, "their natural musical ability and their sense of rhythm are too well known to make any necessary comment"; Kenneth Bean (1936) added, "they sing while at work or play, swaying in rhythm with their songs. . . ."

Musical abilities are associated with intelligence, so it is interesting to consider whether Africans actually have the superior musical abilities often attributed to them, or rather the poor musical abilities consistent with the low IQs they obtain on intelligence tests.

Musical abilities have most frequently been measured by the Seashore Test, which consists of some simple tasks:

- Pitch identification: The subject is asked to identify whether the pitch of one tone is higher or lower than that of another; in the initial items, the difference between the tones is great, but as the test progresses, the tones become closer until it is extremely difficult to distinguish which is higher).

- Memory: A tune is played twice, and on the second playing, one note is altered; the task is to identify the altered note). C

- Chord analysis: The subject is asked to identify the number of notes in a chord).

- Rhythm: Two pieces of music are played, and the problem is to identify whether the rhythms are the same or different.

The association between intelligence and musical ability was shown in an early study by C.T. Gray and C.W. Bingham (1929), who reported correlations between 0.52 and 0.70 between the two. This has also been shown in two studies carried out by Richard Lynn, Graham Wilson, and Adrienne Gault (1986). In the first, a sample of 217 10-year-olds were given a number of tests of reasoning, vocabulary, visualization, and perceptual speed abilities, together with four musical-ability tests (pitch, memory, chords, and rhythm). All the tests were positively intercorrelated and loaded on the first principal component as a measure of general intelligence (g). The loadings of the four musical tests lay between 0.45 (chords) and 0.59 (rhythm). This shows that the musical tests are measures of g. In the second study, 93 9- to 11-year-olds were given three tests of musical ability (pitch change, chord analysis, and memory), together with the Standard Progressive Matrices (again, a measure of g). The three musical tests were significantly correlated with the Progressive Matrices at 0.27, 0.40, and 0.37. Further evidence for this correlation has been provided by John Carroll (1993).

Research has been conducted on the musical ability of African Americans, but it is little known because it has not been summarized in general textbooks on intelligence, such as those of Nathan Brody (1992), Nicholas Mackintosh (1998) and Earl Hunt

(2011), or in specialist textbooks on race differences in intelligence such as those by John Loehlin, Gardner Lindzey, and James Spuhler (1975) and Arthur Jensen (1980, 1998). The general outcome of these studies is that African Americans perform less well than Europeans on tests of musical abilities of pitch discrimination, tone discrimination, and memory, but they perform slightly better than Europeans on tests of rhythm. To demonstrate this pattern of musical abilities, the results of these studies have been aggregated to give a Rhythm Quotient (RQ) and a Musical Quotient (MQ), derived from tests of musical ability other than rhythm. The results of these studies are summarized in Table 4.13. These show a median Musical Quotient of 90 and a median Rhythm Quotient of 102. The studies consistently find that African-Americans have Rhythm IQs substantially greater than general Musical IQs by about 12 IQ points. There appears to be no change in the musical abilities of Africans over the period of approximately half a century from the 1920s to the early 1980s over which the studies have been conducted. The relatively high rhythm ability of Africans is expressed in their music, in which a strong rhythmic element is frequently present. This is notably the case in the hymns sung by congregations in African and African-American churches. It also appears in jazz, which was first developed by African Americans in New Orleans in the early years of the 20th century, and in its subsequent development in "swing" with its strong syncopated rhythms. In more recent musical styles like Rap and Hip-Hop, rhythmic talking or chanting more or less replaces melodies.

Several twin studies have shown that there is a genetic basis for musical abilities. For instance, a study by Steven G. Vandenberg (1962) of the heritability of rhythm ability obtained from the correlations of 33 pairs of identical twins and 43 pairs of same-sex fraternal twins calculated a heritability of 0.52, not corrected for measurement error. Heritabilities of this magnitude make it likely that the low general musical abilities and the high rhythm ability of Africans have some genetic basis.

Table 4.13. Musical (MQ) and Rhythm (RQ) Quotients of African Americans

SAMPLE	AGE	N	TEST	MQ	RQ	REFERENCE
1 Carolinas	11/20	3,300	Seashore	90	106	Johnson, 1928
2 Tennessee	18/20	288	Seashore	88	102	Peterson & Lanier, 1929
3 Texas	13/14	258	Seashore	95	-	Gray & Bingham, 1929
4 New York	9/12	678	Seashore	-	102	Streep, 1931
5 Carolinas	11	187	Seashore	101	102	Johnson, 1931
6 Carolinas	14	271	Seashore	95	103	Johnson, 1931
7 Carolinas	Adults	219	Seashore	94	100	Johnson, 1931
8 Washington	13/14	85	Seashore	83	96	Dawkins & Snyder, 1977
9 NY State	5/8	167	PMMA	89	104	Gordon, 1980
10 Texas	18	272	Seashore	86	100	Sung & Dawis, 1981

The low musical abilities of Africans, except for their strong sense of rhythm, are consistent with their generally poor achievements in classical music. There are no African composers, conductors, or instrumentalists of the first rank, and it is rare to see African players in the leading symphony orchestras.

11. REACTION TIMES OF SUB-SAHARAN AFRICANS

Reaction-times tests measure the speed of a subject's reaction to a simple stimulus, such as the onset of a light. The task is to press a button when this occurs, and the reaction time is the time taken to respond, which typically takes about a third of a second. Numerous studies reviewed by Jensen (1998) and Ian Deary (2000) have shown that reaction times are positively related to intelligence at a magnitude of around 0.2 to 0.3. It has been persuasively argued by Jensen (1998) that reaction times are a measure of the neurological efficiency of the brain in processing information. It is thus an interesting question whether the differences between Europeans and Africans in intelligence are also present in reaction times. If they are, it means that there are race differences in the efficiency of the brain.

If they are not, it means that there are no race differences in the efficiency of the brain, and the differences in intelligence must be due to some other factors, such as opportunities for learning the problems in the tests, educational experiences, or test bias.

The most complete studies of African-European differences in reaction times have been carried out by Jensen (1993) in the United States and Lynn and Manda Holmshaw (1990) and Jacoba Sonke (2000) in South Africa. Jensen's study compared 585 European and 235 African 10-year-olds, whose IQs, as assessed by the Progressive Matrices, differed by 11 IQ points. The Lynn and Holmshaw study compared 350 African and 239 British nine-year-olds, whose IQs differed by 37 IQ points. Both studies used the same computer-controlled apparatus, so that no human error can affect the times registered. Both studies measured the 12 components of reaction times. And in both studies, three different kinds of reaction-times were measured. These were simple reaction time (SRT), consisting of reactions to a single light; choice reaction time (CRT), involving responses to one of eight lights; and odd-man reaction time (OMRT), which measure the reaction to the one of three lights that was farthest from the other two. Each of these three reaction times was measured for four components consisting of the reaction time proper (RT, the decision time), the movement time (MT, time taken to move the finger to the button), and the standard deviations of the reaction times and movement times.

The results are shown in Table 4.14. Column 1 gives the different measures of reaction time. Columns 2 and 3 give the Jensen data for the correlation with the Progressive Matrices IQ and the d (i.e., difference) between Africans and Europeans with negative signs denoting faster times by Europeans. Columns 4 and 5 give the same data for the Lynn and Holmshaw data. Correlations between reaction times and IQs are consistently positive in all the data, and 16 of the 24 correlations are statistically significant (designated by the asterisks); still, the correlations are very low. Reaction times shown in rows 1, 5, and 9 are faster in Europeans than Africans, except for CMT in the Jensen data. Simple movement times show no difference, but Africans are significantly faster than Europeans in both CRT and OMMT in the Lynn and Holmshaw data. The faster movement times of Africans may be related to their widely noted physical abilities in sprinting and jumping and their success in sports that require such skills (Entine, 2001). The standard deviations are consistently greater in Africans in the Lynn and Holmshaw data and in four of the six differences in the Jensen data. In general the African-European differences are much greater and more consistent in the Lynn and Holmshaw data than in the Jensen data. This would be expected because the intelligence difference is some four times greater in the Lynn and Holmshaw data. However, in the Lynn and Holmshaw data, the mean of differences of the six reaction times and standard deviations between the Africans and Europeans amounts to only $0.67d$, as compared with a $2.5\ d$ difference in IQ. The best interpretation of the results is that approximately a quarter of the African-European difference in intelligence may be explicable by the speed of neurological processing, while the remainder must be attributed to other processes.

The two right-hand columns give results of a study of 40 Black and 139 White American college students by Bryan Pesta and Peter Poznanski (2008). The Blacks scored 6.75 IQ points lower than the Whites. IQ was significantly correlated with simple reaction time (SRT) and the simple-reaction-time variability (SRT:SD). IQ was also significantly correlated with inspection time (IT) and the inspection time variability (IT:SD). Blacks scored significantly lower than Whites on all four measures of reaction time and inspection time.

A study comparing the reaction times of children aged 6-12 years in the Ivory Coast and Switzerland has been carried out by Rafael Nunez, Diego Corti, and Jean Retschitzki (1998). They reported that the Ivory Coast children had reaction times of approximately 4000 ms and were considerably slower than those of approximately 2500 ms of the Swiss children.

A review of 14 studies of Black-White differences in reaction times has been published by Leah Sheppard and Philip Vernon (2008). The average of the studies was a White advantage of $.14\ d$, equivalent to an IQ advantage of 2.1 IQ points and therefore suggesting that the White advantage in reaction times makes only a small contribution to their advantage in intelligence.

Reaction times have a significant heritability of around 50 percent (Deary, 2000), but they are also affected by nutrition. An Italian study found that children aged 6–10 in iodine deficient villages had slower reaction times as well as lower IQs (Vitti et al., 1992). (Similar results have also been reported by Bleichrodt et al. (1987).)

Table 4.14. Correlations between reaction times and IQ and differences between Africans and Europeans

VARIABLE	JENSEN		LYNN & HOLM-SHAW		PESTA & POZNANSKI	
	R	D	R	D	R	D
SRT	0.053	-0.003	0.11*	- 0.40*	-0.24*	0.40*
SMT	0.042	0.114	0.15*	0.01		
SRT: SD	0.174*	-0.167*	0.09	-1.17*		
	-0.29*	0.55*				
SMT: SD	0.114*	-0.097	0.10*	-0.60*		
CRT	0.116*	0.053	0.14*	-0.12		
CMT	0.072	0.063	0.20*	0.47*		
CRT: SD	0.132*	-0.086	0.02	-1.50*		
CMT: SD	0.072	0.063	0.16*	-0.62*		
OMRT	0.203*	-0.189*	0.09	-0.38*		
OMMT	0.09	-0.057	0.21*	0.49*		
OMRT: SD	0.203*	-0.258*	0.07	-0.49		
OMMT: SD	0.187*	0.009	0.15*	-0.18*		
IT					-0.39*	0.79*
IT:SD					-0.30*	0.57

* = statistically significant

Cornelia Sonke (2000) has reported another study of much slower reaction times of Africans than of Europeans. This study compared three groups consisting of 26 illiterate Africans in South Africa aged 16, with "only a few years of schooling"; 29 African university students at Venda University in the Northern Transvaal; and 30 European Dutch university students at Tilberg University. The three groups were given an intelligence test (Raven's Progressive Matrices) and simple and complex reaction-time tasks, and an EEG measure was taken of the latency of the evoked potential (P3) to the presentation of the reaction-time stimuli, a measure of the speed with which the stimulus is registered in the brain. There were equal numbers of males and females in all three groups.

The results are shown in Table 4.15. In Row 1, we find the IQs of the three groups. Row 2 gives the mean simple reaction times, showing slowest reaction times in the African illiterates and fastest in the European students. Row 3 present complex reaction times, with the same group differences. Row 4 gives the evoked potential latencies for task B1, showing longest latencies in the African illiterates, and the shortest latencies in the European university students. All the group differences are statistically significant.

Table 4.15. Reaction times and EEGs of Africans and Europeans

	TEST	AFRICAN ILLITERATES	AFRICAN STUDENTS	EUROPEANS
1	IQ	68	82	105
2	RT-S	420	400	350
3	RT-C	1,950	1,650	1,220
4	EEG	534	526	506

There are six points of interest in this study. First, the South African illiterate sample's Progressive Matrices IQ of 68 is closely similar to that of a large number of samples of Africans in South Africa and in other countries of sub-Saharan Africa. Second, the African university students have a somewhat higher IQ of 82, again similar to that of other African South African university student samples. Third, there are significant differences between the three groups in reaction times, confirming other studies summarized in this chapter. Fourth, there are significant African-European differences in the EEG evoked potential, demonstrating that in European students, the brain reacts more rapidly to a stimulus than in African students. Fifth, there is a statistically significant correlation of 0.213 between the complex reaction times and the Progressive Matrices, confirming many other studies of this association. Sixth, the correlation between the Progressive Matrices and the EEG evoked potential is not statistically significant. The differences between the African illiterates and the African students on reaction times and evoked potentials are probably attributable to the students having higher IQs.

A further study of reaction times in African children has been by published by Fons van der Vijver (2008), who reported on the reaction times of 35 children in Zimbabwe (age 14.8) and 35 children in the Netherlands (aged 12.6). The Dutch children performed better by 1.4 d (equivalent to 21 IQ points). As the Zimbabwe children were two years older, this would give them an advantage, and the true difference would be greater. Another report of much slower reaction times of African children (in the Ivory Coast compared with Swiss children) has been published by Rafael Nunez, Diego Corti, and Jean Retschitzki (1998).

12. BRAIN SIZE OF SUB-SAHARAN AFRICANS AND EUROPEANS

Studies showing that Africans have a smaller average brain size than Europeans are summarized in Table 4.16. The figures given in the table are in cubic centimeters (the data have been converted from cubic inches given by Morton and Gould, and from grams given by Khang-Cheng Ho et al., 1980). It should be noted that estimates of cranial capacities are to some degree affected by the method of measurement. The cranial volume of skulls is measured by filling them with lead shot or mustard seed and measuring the volume of the shot or seed. Lead shot gives slightly larger volumes than mustard seed, because it cannot be compressed so tightly. For living humans, brain size is calculated from the length, breadth, and height of the head, or from the circumference. These different methods of measurement explain some of the differences obtained in the studies. Though despite inconsistencies of measures, there is considerable consistency in the relative brain sizes.

In Table 4.16, the results are given of eight studies of the brain size of samples of Europeans and Africans and the differences between the means. All the studies show that Europeans have a larger average brain size than Africans. In the 19th century, the American physician Samuel

Morton (1849) assembled a collection of skulls, categorized them by race, and calculated their average cranial capacities; Morton found significant differences in European-African brain sizes. These results, summarized in Row 1, were criticized by Stephen Jay Gould (1996), who accused Morton of massaging the figures to reach his desired conclusion. Gould actually recalculated Morton's skull sizes, and his results were closely similar. It is Gould's figures that are given in the table. He dismissed the 41cubic centimeter (cc) difference as of no consequence. Gould characteristically failed to mention any of the other studies that all confirmed Morton's conclusions and found larger differences.

The numbers of skulls in Morton's collection are quite low, consisting of 52 Europeans and 29 Africans. In Row 2, an analysis of a much larger collection of skulls held at Western Reserve University in Ohio shows a 50cc African-European differences in brain size. Row 3 gives results presented by Phillip Tobias, a committed equalitarian, who asserted that there is no race difference in brain size; his results, however, reveal a rather larger African-European brain size difference than those of Morton. Results from autopsies in the United States (Row 4) present a larger African-European difference, of 103cc, than in the other studies. Row 5 gives results from the largest collection of approximately 20,000 skulls from all over the world analyzed by the American anthropologist Kenneth Beals. Colin Groves (1991) calculated his results (Row 6) by combining estimates of cranial capacities of 36 samples of males from figures given by Coon, Molnar, and Martin and Saller; here again, Europeans have larger average brain size than Africans. Row 7 gives results for the United States for military personnel. These figures are adjusted for height and weight. The brain sizes of the Europeans are virtually identical to those found by Khang-Cheng Ho et al. given in row 4, but the brain size of the Africans is much greater, at 1,359 as compared with 1,267. The explanation for this is that the U.S. military screens applicants for intelligence and rejects those with IQs below 81 (Nyborg and Jensen, 2000). James Flynn (1980) has estimated that military rejection rates for low IQ are 3.4 percent for Europeans and 30 percent for Africans, and that the result of this is that Africans in the military have an average IQ of 91.5. The effect of not accepting Africans with low IQs is to screen out many of those with low intelligence and thus smaller brains, making the African-European brain size difference much smaller than in other samples. Row 8 gives average brain size of six samples of male Europeans from North America and Europe and two samples from sub-Saharan Africa from data compiled by Hans Jurgens, Ivar Aune, and Ursula Pieper (1990) and analyzed by J.P. Rushton (2000, p.124); here the European advantage is calculated at 109cc. The results in the eight data sets all show that Europeans have larger average brain sizes than Africans; they are also reasonably consistent, considering that they were compiled using different methods and different kinds of samples, including autopsies (Ho et al., 1980), skull volumes (Beals et al., 1984), and external head measurements of living individuals.

These results are corroborated by a further large-scale study of children carried out by Broman, Nichols, Shaughnessy, and Kennedy (1987). They examined and followed up approximately 17,000 European and 19,000 African children in the United States from conception to the age of 7 years. At the age of 7 there was the typical gap of approximately 15 IQ points between the two groups. The head circumferences of the two groups calculated from the published data are 50.9cm (sd 1.6) for Africans and 51.7cm (sd 1.6) for Europeans. This difference is statistically highly significant and provides an approximate measure of differences in brain size, since head circumference and brain size are correlated at about 0.8 (Brandt, 1978). The brain volumes have been estimated by Rushton (1997) at 1,134 for Africans and 1,150 for Europeans. The difference is much smaller than in the other samples, possibly because Europeans mature later than Africans. In this study the African children were slightly taller than the Europeans, suggesting that possible differences in nutrition are not likely to be responsible for the differences in head size.

Table 4.16. Brain size (cc) of Europeans and Africans

		EUROPEANS		AFRICANS			
LOCATION	SEX	N	MEAN	N	MEAN	DIFF.	REFERENCE
1 World	mf	52	1,401	29	1,360	41	Morton, 1849
2 World	mf	1,840	1,364	880	1,314	50	Simmons, 1942
3 World	mf	-	1,427	-	1,363	64	Tobias, 1970
4 USA	mf	811	1,370	450	1,267	103	Ho et al., 1980
5 World	mf	-	1,369	-	1,283	86	Smith & Beals, 1990

6	World	m	-	1,476	-	1,416	60	Groves, 1991
7	USA	mf	2,871	1,380	2,676	1,359	21	Rushton, 1992
8	World	mf	-	1,320	-	1,211	109	Rushton, 2000

13. SUB-SAHARAN AFRICAN-EUROPEAN HYBRIDS

We now consider studies of the IQs of African-European hybrids. The prediction from the genetic theory of race differences is that the IQs of racial hybrids should fall approximately midway between those of Europeans and Africans. To examine this prediction, studies of African-European racial hybrids are summarized in Table 4.17. Results for Brazil (Row 1) show that hybrids (there, known as "browns") score intermediate between Europeans and Africans. Rows 2-3 give similar results from Canada and Germany; the latter, from Eyferth (1961) study, shows the IQ of African-European hybrid children was 94 (in relation to 100 for European children. The mean IQ of the African-European hybrids was 96.5, but this is reduced in the table to 94, allowing for the secular increase of the IQ from the date of the standardization. Row 4 gives results from South Africa for Europeans, Africans, and "Coloreds," who are largely African-European. The IQ of 83 of the Coloreds falls exactly half way between that of Europeans (100) and that of Africans (65). In Row 5, a more recent study in South Africa collected approximately 60 years later shows a sample of Coloreds with an IQ of 86 compared with an IQ of 100 for Europeans. Africans were not included in this study, but the IQ of 86 is much higher than that of pure Africans in South Africa. Row 6 gives results from a further South African study showing an IQ of 80 for Coloreds.

Table 4.17 IQs of Europeans, African-European Hybrids, and Africans

		EUROPEANS				
COUNTRY	AGE	TEST	N	IQ	REFERENCE	
1 Brazil	10	SPM	735	95	Fernandez, 2001	

2	Canada	7/12	PP	100		Tanser, 1941
3	Germany	5/13	WISC	1,099	100	Eyferth, 1961
4	South Africa	10/12	AAB	10,000	100	Fick, 1929
5	South Africa	13	GSAT	746	100	Claassen, 1990
6	South Africa	15	SPM	1,056	100	Owen, 1992
7	USA	17	WISCR	16	102	Weinberg et al.,1992
8	USA	Adult	Otis	-	100	Codwell, 1947
9	USA	Adult	Vocab	1,245	100	Lynn, 2002
10	USA	Adult	Vocab	10,315	100	Rowe, 2002

HYBRIDS

	COUNTRY	AGE	TEST	N	IQ	REFERENCE
1	Brazil	10	SPM	718	81	Fernandez, 2001
2	Canada	7/12	PP	46	93	Tanser, 1941
3	Germany	5/13	WISC	170	94	Eyferth, 1961
4	South Africa	10/12	AAB	6,196	83	Fick, 1929
5	South Africa	13	GSAT	815	86	Claassen, 1990
6	South Africa	15	SPM	778	80	Owen, 1992
7	USA	17	WISCR	55	94	Weinberg et al.,1992
8	USA	Adult	Otis	284	91	Codwell, 1947
9	USA	Adult	Vocab	304	92	Lynn, 2002
10	USA	Adult	Vocab	116	97	Rowe, 2002

AFRICANS

	COUNTRY	AGE	TEST	N	IQ	REFERENCE
1	Brazil	10	SPM	223	71	Fernandez, 2001
2	Canada	7/12	PP	46	78	Tanser, 1941
3	Germany	5/13	WISC	-	-	Eyferth, 1961
4	South Africa	10/12	AAB	293	65	Fick, 1929
5	South Africa	13	GSAT	-	-	Claassen, 1990
6	South Africa	15	SPM	1,093	74	Owen, 1992
7	USA	17	WISCR	17	85	Weinberg et al.,1992
8	USA	Adult	Otis	176	87	Codwell, 1947
9	USA	Adult	Vocab	146	85	Lynn, 2002
10	USA	Adult	Vocab	4,271	89	Rowe, 2002

Rows 7-10 give four results for hybrids in the United States. In Row 7, we find the Minnesota Transracial Adoption Study, showing that hybrids score halfway between African-Americans and Europeans. The numbers are very low, but the results are informative because all three groups were reared by European adoptive parents, and this rules out any reasonable environmental interpretation of the differences. Row 8 gives a further result from the United States showing once again that hybrids score intermediate between Europeans and African Americans (results of this study are given by Loehlin, Lindzey, and Spuhler, 1975). Row 9 gives another result from the United States that divided African Americans into dark skinned and lighter skinned and showed that the lighter skinned African Americans, taken as an index of hybridization with Europeans, have an IQ of 92, halfway between the Europeans and Africans. Row 10 gives the last result, showing that African-American–European hybrids have an IQ of 97 and again score intermediate between African Americans and Europeans.

14. HIGH INTELLIGENCE OF SUB-SAHARAN AFRICAN INFANTS

African infants are more advanced that Europeans during their first 15 months. This has become known as "Black infant precocity" and was first observed for motor development by Solange Falade (1955) using the Gesell test in a study in Senegal. This observation was confirmed by Marcelle Geber (1958) in Uganda and by Daniel Freedman in Nigeria (Freedman, 1974). It was confirmed in the United Sates for motor development by Nancy Bayley (1965), who showed Black infants aged 2-14 months were advanced compared with Whites by five DQ (Developmental Quotient) points. It has been further confirmed in South Africa, where two-to 15-month-old Blacks out-performed American Whites by 11 points in motor development and by 15 DQ points in mental development (Lynn, 1998). On these tests, Blacks begin to fall behind Whites at about the age of 30 months. (Further studies of the developmental precocity of

Black infants have been reviewed by Emmy Werner (1972) and Holly Cintas (1988).)

15. HERITABILITY OF INTELLIGENCE IN SUB-SAHARAN AFRICAN-AMERICANS

There have been three studies of the heritability of African-Americans in the United States. They are all obtained from a comparison of identical (Mz) and non-identical twins (Dz). The results are given in Table 4.18. THe table presents the ages of the samples; the numbers of identical (Mz) and non-identical (Dz) twins; the correlations between the twin pairs; the heritabilities, obtained by doubling the difference between the Mz and Dz correlations, and the corrected heritability, corrected for attenuation assuming a test reliability of 0.9.

Row 1 includes data from John Loehlin, Gardner Lindzey, and James Spuhler (1975), which were obtained from a doctoral dissertation by P. L. Nichols for four-year-olds tested with the Stanford-Binet. These show a corrected heritability of 0.56, a little higher than that of Europeans of this age. Row 2 gives results of a further data set from FN. Osborne (1980, p. 72) for general intelligence calculated as the average of 12 tests; here, the corrected heritability is measured at 1.00. Row 3 shows data for the Progressive Matrices (Scarr, 1981, p. 282) giving a corrected heritability of 0.60. Taken together the three results calculate a heritability of 0.72 in African-Americans; there is higher heritability in the two studies of adolescents than in the four-year-olds. The heritabilities of the African-Americans are virtually the same as those in Europeans given in Chapter 3.

Table 4.18. Heritability of intelligence of African Americans

	AGE	MZ −N	R	DZ-N	R	H2	C-H2	REFERENCE
1	4	60	0.77	84	0.52	0.5	0.56	Loehlin et al., 1975
2	15	76	0.8	47	0.34	0.92	1	Osborne, 1980
3	10-15	65	0.63	95	0.36	0.54	0.6	Scarr, 1981

16. VALIDITY OF LOW AFRICAN IQS

It has often been asserted that IQ tests are not valid, i.e. that Africans do not have lower intelligence than Europeans, but that they just perform poorly on tests. For instance, Nell (2000, p. 27) reports of a sample of Blacks in South Africa "that these competent men, all in longstanding employment, in a sophisticated environment, score about between 1 and 2 standard deviations below the U.S. WAIS-R norms. There is no reason to believe that these individuals have a lower ability level than the age-matched U.S. and English norm groups with whom they are compared. The alternative hypothesis is that for whatever reason, the Wechsler tests lack validity for these subjects."

Contrary to this assertion, several studies have shown that IQs are valid in sub-Saharan Africa. IQ tests predict school grades in sub-Saharan Africa at about the same level as in the U.S. and Britain, e.g. at r = 0.40 in Kenya (Sternberg et al., 2001), and at r = 0.30 for university students in South Africa (Rushton, Skuy and Bons, (2004). Furthermore, sub-Saharan Africans perform about as poorly on tests of educational attainment in math and science as they do on IQ tests as shown in the Educ studies given by Meisenberg and Lynn (2001).

17. GENETIC AND ENVIRONMENTAL EXPLANATIONS OF THE LOW SUB-SAHARAN AFRICAN IQ

The problem of the genetic and environmental contributions to the low IQ of Africans has been debated since the early decades of the twentieth century, particularly in regard to the problem of the low IQs obtained by African Americans in the United States. Three positions have been taken on this question.

1. The IQ difference between Blacks and Whites is wholly environmentally determined or at least there is no compelling evidence for any genetic contribution to the

low Black IQ. This position has been taken by Flynn (1980), Mackintosh (1998), Nisbett (1998), Fish (2002), Brody (2003), and many others.

2. The IQ difference is determined by some mix of genetic and environmental factors. This position has been taken by Loehlin, Lindzey and Spuhler (1975), Vernon (1979), and Waldman, Weinberg, and Scarr (1994, p. 31), who conducted one of the most important studies of this question involving the IQs of Black children adopted by White couples.

3. The IQ difference is largely genetically determined. This position has been taken by Henry Garrett (1945, 1961); Frank McGurk (1953a, 1953b), who showed that when Blacks and Whites were matched for socioeconomic status, Blacks scored 7.5 IQ points below Whites; Kuttner (1962), who argued that Black-White differences in intelligence were reflected in the differences in the building of early civilizations; Shuey (1966), who made the first compilation of Black-White IQ differences, from 1916 up to 1965; Robert Osborne and McGurk (1982), who made an updated compilation of Shuey's work covering the years 1966–1980; and Jensen (1969, 1974, 1980, 1998), who made numerous contributions to this issue and concluded that about two thirds of the American Black-White IQ difference is attributable to genetic factors. Others who have taken the largely genetic position are Shockley (1969), Eysenck (1971), Baker (1974), Levin (1997), Rushton (2003), and the writer (Lynn, 1994c, 2001).

There are seven major arguments for the presence of some genetic determination of the intelligence difference between sub-Saharan Africans and Europeans.

First, the two races have evolved independently in different environments over a period of approximately 100,000 years (Mellars and Stringer, 1989; Cavalli-Sforza, 2000). When two populations evolve largely in isolation from each other for this period of time, genetic differences between them inevitably evolve for all characteristics for which there is genetic variability. These differences evolve as a result of genetic drift, mutations, founder effects, and most important, adaptation to different environments. The extreme environmentalist position that there is no genetic difference between the two races for intelligence defies this general principle of evolutionary biology and should be ruled out as impossible.

Second, the consistency with which Africans obtain low IQs in so many different locations can only be explained by the operation of a strong genetic factor. If only environmental factors were responsible for the different IQs of different populations, we should expect to find some countries where Africans had higher IQs than Europeans. The failure to find a single country where this is the case points to the presence of a strong genetic factor.

Third, the high heritability of intelligence found in twin studies of Blacks and Whites in the United States, in Europe, Japan, and India shows that intelligence is powerfully affected by genetic factors and makes it improbable that the differences between Africans and Europeans, or between any other pairs of races, can be solely environmentally determined.

Fourth, the brain size difference between Blacks and Whites points to a genetic difference, considering the high heritability of about 0.9 of brain size and the correlation of approximately 0.4 between brain size and intelligence.

Fifth, several egalitarians have proposed that White racism may be responsible for impairing the IQs of the Blacks. Thus, Weinberg, Scarr, and Waldman write that their result that Black children adopted by Whites have low IQs "could indicate the results of environmental influences such as the pervasive effect of racism in American life" (1992, p. 41) and "the IQ results are consistent with racially based environmental effects in the order of group means" (p. 40). Mackintosh (1998, p. 152) also falls back on White racism in a final attempt to argue that the low IQ of the Black adoptees can be explained environmentally and suggests that perhaps "it is precisely the experience of being Black in a society permeated by White racism that is responsible for lowering Black children's IQ scores." These egalitarians do not explain how hypothetical White racism could impair the IQs of Black children reared by middle class White parents. There is no known or plausible mechanism by which supposed White racism could impair the IQs of Blacks. Nor do they attempt to explain how it is that Africans throughout sub-Saharan Africa, who are not exposed to White racism, except in South Africa, have IQs of approximately 71.

Furthermore, if racism lowers intelligence, it is remarkable that Jews in the United States and Britain should have IQs of around 110 (Lynn, 2011b), since Jews have been exposed to racism for many centuries. The high IQ of American Jews has been well known since the 1930s and has been extensively documented by Storfer (1990), MacDonald (1994), and Herrnstein and Murray (1994), yet it goes curiously unmentioned by environmentalists like Flynn (1980), Brody (1992, 2003), Neisser (1996), Mackintosh (1998), Jencks and Phillips (1998), Nisbett (1998), Montagu (1999), and Fish (2002).

Sixth, Black infant precocity is impossible to explain in environmental terms and can only be attributed to a genetically based maturation difference.

Seventh, the Minnesota Transracial Adoption Study carried out by Waldman, Scarr, and Weinberg (1994) was designed to show that when Black infants are adopted by White parents they would have the same IQs as Whites. The authors of this study examined groups of Black, White, and interracial babies all adopted by White middle-class couples. It turned out that at the age of 17, the IQs were 89 for the Blacks, 98 for the interracial individuals, and 106 for the Whites. Thus, a 17 IQ point difference between Blacks and Whites remains even when they are reared in the same conditions. Being raised by White adoptive parents had no beneficial effects on the intelligence of the Black children because their IQ of 89 is the same as that of Blacks in the north-central states from which the infants came. The interracial group with its IQ of 98 falls midway between the Black and the White, as would be predicted from the genetic cause of the difference. A full analysis and discussion of this study has been given by Levin (1994) and Lynn (1994c), together with an unconvincing reply by Waldman, Weinberg, and Scarr (1994, p. 43), in which they assert "we feel that the balance of the evidence, although not conclusive, favors a predominantly environmental etiology underlying racial differences in intelligence and that the burden of proof is on researchers who argue for the predominance of genetic racial differences." Notice that their use of the phrase "predominantly environmental etiology" concedes that they accept that genetic factors are also present.

While the results of this study show that differences in family environment cannot explain the low Black IQ, it remains possible that Blacks provide an inferior prenatal environment as a result of poorer nutrition of pregnant Black women or possibly of the greater use of cigarettes that might impair the growth of the fetal brain. These possibilities are rendered improbable by studies showing that the nutrition of American Blacks throughout the twentieth century was not inferior to that of Whites (see Chapter 13, Section 7). Another possibility is that Black babies might suffer greater impairment of the brain because pregnant Black women might smoke cigarettes more, since there is some evidence that smoking retards fetal growth, but this is rendered improbable by numerous studies showing that Blacks smoke cigarettes less than Whites.

Despite their commitment to the egalitarian position, it is interesting to note that Waldman, Scarr, and Weinberg (1994) concluded that their evidence shows that both genetic and environmental differences contribute to the Black-White IQ difference: "We think it is exceedingly implausible that these differences are either entirely genetically based or entirely environmentally based" (p. 31). Thus, while there is nothing in their data that can justify this conclusion, because they provide no evidence for any environmental contribution to the low Black IQ, their final position is not greatly different from that advanced by Jensen (1969), that both genetic and environmental factors are responsible for the low Black IQ; but where Jensen proposed that the relative contributions are about two thirds genetic and one third environmental, Waldman, Scarr, and Weinberg have concluded that both factors are involved, although they do not suggest a quantification of the magnitude of the respective contributions.

In fact, the results of the Minnesota Interracial Adoption Study show that both conclusions are incorrect. The conclusion to be drawn from this study is that rearing Black children in a White middle-class environment has no effect at all on their IQs at age 17.

17. ESTIMATION OF THE GENOTYPIC SUB-SAHARAN AFRICAN IQ

The average IQ of 71 of sub-Saharan Africans shown in Table 4.1 is a function of both genetic and environmental factors. We now undertake the task of estimating the genotypic African IQ. This is the IQ that Africans would have if they were raised in the same environment as Europeans. The starting point of this analysis is the Minnesota Transracial Adoption Study, the results of which showed that a 17 IQ point difference between African Americans and Europeans is still present when they are reared in the same family environments. The conclusion to be drawn from this is that the African-American–European IQ difference in the United States is wholly genetically determined. Although this study showed a 17 IQ point African-European IQ difference, it is reasonable to assume that the true African-American–European difference is 15 IQ points, as shown by the numerous studies summarized in Table 4.5, and that the 17 IQ point difference obtained in this study is a sampling error. We conclude therefore that the genotypic IQ of African Americans is 15 IQ points below that of American Europeans. A further argument for believing that the IQ of African Americans is wholly genetically determined is that it has remained constant over a period of approximately 80 years despite the great improvements in the environment of African Americans relative to that of Europeans.

The conclusion that African Americans have a genotypic IQ of 85 does not mean that Africans in sub-Saharan Africa also have a genotypic IQ of 85. African Americans are not pure Africans but are a hybrid population with a significant amount of European ancestry. This has been estimated at 25 percent by Reed (1971) and by Chakraborty, Kamboh, Nwankwo, and Ferrell (1992). We can estimate that pure Africans in Africa and in the United States have a genotypic IQ of 80 and that this IQ increases by 0.2 IQ points for every one percent of Caucasoid genes. Thus, the average African American will have an IQ of 85 (80 + [25 x 0.2] = 85), a figure confirmed by numerous studies summarized in Table 4.4. In the Southeastern states the percentage of European genes among African Americans is quite low. For instance, in South Carolina it has been estimated at six percent (Workman, 1968), and in Georgia at 11 percent (Reed, 1969). These admixtures of European genes should raise their IQ by 1.2 and 2.2 IQ points, respectively, giving them an IQ of 81.2 and 82.2. This prediction has been confirmed by the study of 1,800 African Americans in five Southeastern states by Wallace Kennedy, Van der Reit, and White (1963), which found their IQ on the 1960 Stanford-Binet was 80.7.

African Americans with 50 percent European genes will have an average IQ of 90 (80 + [50 x 0.2] = 90). This is about the mean IQ of African Americans in the northern states, where the proportion of European ancestry approaches 50 percent. African Americans with 75 percent European genes will have an IQ 15 points higher at 95 (80 + [75 x 0.2] = 95), which is very close to the IQ of 94 of the interracial children in the Minnesota Transracial Adoption Study. Europeans with 100 percent European genes will have an average IQ at 100.

This estimate of the genotypic African IQ as 80 means that the average IQ that Africans would obtain if the environments in which they were raised were the same as those of Europeans would be 80. Throughout sub-Saharan Africa the mean IQ of Africans is approximately 71, so it can be inferred that adverse environmental conditions in sub-Saharan Africa impair the sub-Saharan African IQ by around nine IQ points.

CHAPTER 5

BUSHMEN

AND

PYGMIES

THE BUSHMEN (also called Khoisans, Sanids or Capoids) and the Pygmies are two of the minor races of sub-Saharan Africa in the taxonomies of classical anthropology such as those of Coon, Garn and Birdsell (1950). In their genetic analysis of human populations, Cavalli-Sforza, Menozzi, and Piazza (1994) confirmed that these two peoples have distinctive but closely related genetic characteristics and form two related "clusters." The Bushmen together with the Pygmies and Africans evolved from the original *Homo sapiens* peoples of equatorial East Africa. The ancestors of the Bushmen migrated south and, by about 100,000 years ago, occupied most of southern Africa. Extensive human bones and artifacts have been found in the Border Cave in present day Swaziland and have been dated to be about 100,000 years old. The morphology of the bones indicates that these peoples were a mix of Africans and Bushmen (Beaumont, de Villiers and Vogel, 1978).

Until around 1,500 years ago, the Bushmen occupied most of Southern Africa, and the Pygmies occupied the rain forests of West and Central Africa. From about AD 500, Africans (i.e. Negroids) from the north encroached on their lands, killed large numbers of them, and drove most of the surviving Bushmen into the Kalahari Desert and the Pygmies into the dense rain forests of Central Africa. Related to the Bushmen are the Hottentots, small groups of whom survive in a few locations in Southern Africa. Although the two groups are genetically closely similar, there are some genetic differences, such as the low incidence of the B blood group in the Bushmen and the high incidence in the Hottentots.

Many of the Hottentots are racial hybrids with Bushmen and European ancestry, which has given them lighter skin color and taller stature than the Bushmen (Cole, 1965). The Bushmen survive principally in the Kalahari Desert, where they number about 50,000 (roughly the same population size of the Hottentots). The largest surviving Bushmen group is the Nama in Southwest Africa, where they are around 24,000 (Cole, 1965), and there are a few other smaller groups north of the Orange River.

The Bushmen have a number of physical characteristics that distinguish them from Negroid Africans. They have peppercorn hair that grows in spirals with open spaces between tufts, whereas most Africans have helical woolly hair that forms a tight mat. Scientists believe that the peppercorn hair of the Bushmen evolved as an adaptation in hot and damp forests in which they lived for many millennia, as it affords protection from strong sunlight but at the same time the open spaces between the tufts allow sweat to evaporate. Pygmies who have remained in tropical rain forests have the same peppercorn hair. The mat woolly hair of Negroid Africans is a more advantageous adaptation in dry hot environments because it gives greater protection from strong sunlight and reduces sweating. The skin color of the Bushmen is yellowish brown, whereas that of Negroid Africans is black or dark. Some of the Bushmen have an epicanthic fold on the upper eyelid, similar to (but less pronounced than) that of East Asians and Arctic Peoples. The advantage of the epicanthic fold for Bushmen is probably that it reduces the dazzling effect of glare from strong sunlight reflected from the desert, much like epicanthic fold attenuates glare from snow for the East Asians and Arctic Peoples. This characteristic must have arisen independently through convergent evolution.

A distinctive characteristic of Bushmen is the very large buttocks of the women, known as steatopygia. The adaptive advantage of these may have been to store food and water in times of famine and shortage. The genitalia of the Bushmen are unique among the human races. Bushmen have penises that stick out horizontally, while Bushwomen have prominent minor labia that descend about three inches below the vagina. The adaptive advantages of these characteristics are unknown.

1. INTELLIGENCE OF BUSHMEN

There have been only three studies of the intelligence of the Bushmen. In the 1930s, Stanley Porteus (1937) tested a sample of 25 of them with his maze test, which involves tracing the correct route with a pencil through a series of mazes of increasing difficulty. The test has norms for European children for each age, in relation to which the Bushmen obtained a mental age of seven and a half years, representing an IQ of approximately 48. In the second study, Porteus gave the Leiter International Performance Scale to 197 adult Bushmen and concluded that their mental age was approximately 10 years, giving them an IQ of 62. In the third study, Helmut Reuning (1972), a South African psychologist, tested 108 Bushmen and 159 African Negroids with a pattern completion test involving the selection of an item to complete a pattern. In the light of his experience of the test, Reuning concluded that it "can be used as a reliable instrument for the assessment of intelligence at the lower levels of cognitive development and among preliterate peoples" (1988, p. 469). On this test, the Bushmen scored approximately 15 IQ points below the sub-Saharan Africans; since African Negroids have a mean IQ of 71 (see Chapter 4), this would give the Bushmen an IQ of 56.

Reuning also presented Bushmen and the African Negroids with a figure-drawing test (involving the drawing of a man). (This test is the same as the Goodenough Draw-a-Man test (DAM), which is a reasonably good measure of intelligence. The drawings produced in the Goodenough Test are scored for detail and sophistication, which improve as children grow older. Young children typically draw stick men with little detail, while older children draw full-bodied men with many details such as eyebrows, thumbs, and so on.) Reuning (1988, p. 476) recorded that the Bushmen's drawings were significantly less advanced than those of Negroid mineworkers whom he also tested (76 percent of whom were illiterate). He described the Bushmen's drawings as characterized by "extreme simplicity," the majority were stick figures having "no details (fingers, toes, hair, eyes, etc.)." The simplicity of the Bushmen's drawings "contrasts again with the tendency of the Blacks to include much small detail in their drawings (buttons, hair, fingers, toes, a pipe, etc.). . . ." The difference between Bushmen and African Negroids in the sophistication of drawings provides further corroboration of the lower intelligence of Bushmen.

Reuning noted that there was considerable variability in intelligence between individuals among the Bushmen, just as there is among other peoples, and that they themselves recognize that some individuals are intelligent while others are dull. Their languages have the word "clever" to describe this attribute. Reuning records, "When the tester at the end of a test had praised a good performance, they let us know, through the interpreter: 'We could have told you so, he (or she) is clever'" (1988, p. 479). There is, furthermore, a general factor (g) among the Kalahari Bushmen shown by the positive intercorrelation of a number of tests and the correlation between test performance and the general consensus of who is intelligent.

In addition to administering a test of intelligence, Reuning tested Bushmen and comparison groups of African Negroids and Whites for size constancy. This is the ability to estimate the size of an object at a distance. He found that Bushmen had more accurate size constancy than Africans and Europeans and attributed this to the great advantage this trait carries for Bushmen, who often hunt animals at a distance with a bow and arrow. Reuning also found that Bushwomen have good size constancy, although they do not hunt. If this is correct, it implies that this visual ability may have deteriorated in Europeans, North Africans, and South and East Asians, as the size-constancy trait ceased to confer advantages to peoples who gave up hunting several thousand years ago and adopted agriculture.

The three studies of Bushmen by Porteus and Reuning give IQs of 48, 62, and 56, which average to 55. This is substantially lower than the average IQ of 71 of African Negroids. This is consistent with two facts. First, the Bushmen are still hunter-gatherers, while many

African Negroids have made the transition to settled agriculture and urban living. Agriculture requires a higher IQ than hunter-gathering because of the need to clear ground, store seed, and sow crops for harvesting some months later, rear animals and so on. Urban living also requires a higher IQ than hunter-gathering due to a variety of cognitive demands. Second, the African Negroids have defeated the Bushmen in warfare and driven them from more friendly environments into the Kalahari Desert. Normally when there is warfare between two races, the race with the higher intelligence wins.

It may be questioned whether a people with an average IQ of 55 could survive as hunter-gatherers in the Kalahari Desert, and therefore whether this can be a valid estimate of their intelligence. An IQ of 55 is at the low end of the range of mild mental retardation in economically developed nations. But this is less of a problem than might be thought. The great majority of the mildly mentally retarded in economically developed societies do not reside in hospitals or institutions but live normal lives in the community. Many of them have children and work either in the home or doing cognitively undemanding jobs. An IQ of 55 represents the mental age of the average European eight year-old child, and the average European eight-year-old can read, write, and do arithmetic and would have no difficulty in learning and performing the activities of gathering foods and hunting carried out by the San Bushmen. An average European 8-year-old can easily be taught to pick berries, put them in a container and carry them home, collect ostrich eggs and use the shells for storing water, and learn to use a bow and arrow and hit a target at some distance. Before the introduction of universal education for children throughout North America and Europe in the second half of the 19th century, the great majority of eight-year-old children worked productively on farms and sometimes as chimney sweeps and in factories and mines. Today, many children of this age in Africa, India, Pakistan, Bangladesh, throughout much of Latin America, and in other economically developing countries work on farms, and some of them do semi-skilled work such as carpet weaving and operating sewing machines. There is a range of intelligence among the Bushmen, and most of them will have IQs in the range of 35 to 75. An IQ of 35 represents approximately the mental age of the average European five-and-a-half-year-old, and an IQ of 75 represents approximately the mental age of the average European 11-and-a-half–year-old. The average five-and-a-half-year-old European child is verbally fluent and is capable of doing unskilled jobs, and the same should be true for even the least intelligent Bushmen.

Furthermore, apes with mental abilities about the same as those of human four-year-olds survive quite well as gatherers and occasional hunters, as did early hominids with IQs of around 40 and brain sizes much smaller than those of modern Bushmen. For these reasons there is nothing puzzling about contemporary Bushmen with average IQs of about 54 and a range of IQs mainly between 35 and 75 being able to survive as hunter-gatherers and doing the unskilled and semi-skilled farm work that a number of them took up in the closing decades of the 20th century.

2. BRAIN SIZE

The brain size of the Bushmen was estimated at 1,250cc by Mathew Drennan (1937) and a little higher at 1,270cc by Courtland Smith and Kenneth Beals (1990). The Smith and Beals data set also includes Negroid Africans, whose brain size is 1,282cc and therefore a little larger than that of Bushmen. This is consistent with the higher average IQ of Africans at 67, as compared with the 54 of Bushmen, although the brain size difference of this magnitude can only explain a small fraction of the intelligence difference. The smaller brain size and lower intelligence of the Bushmen compared with the Africans implies that the brain size of the Africans increased over the last 100,000 years or so, since contemporary Africans and Bushmen came from the same ancestral stock. The two peoples' brain sizes must have originally been the same, and the Africans' must have increased either as a result of stronger selection pressure or advantageous mutations.

3. INTELLIGENCE OF PYGMIES

The Pygmies inhabit the equatorial rain forests of Zaire, now called the Democratic Republic of the Congo and the Central African Republic. At the close of the 20th century, they were thought to number around 100,000 to 200,000. The purest Pygmies are the Mbuti, who live in the Ituri forest of northeastern Congo and are thought to number somewhere between 30,000 and 60,000. The other Pygmies are more interbred with Africans. Mbuti Pygmies average around 4'7" (ca. 140 cm) in height. Pygmy children up to the age of puberty have normal height, but when they become adolescents, they do not have the growth spurt of other peoples, due to their low output of the insulin-like growth factor 1 (somatomedin C).

Most of the Pygmies have remained hunter-gatherers. Typically they live in small groups of around 30 and move from place to place. They have made no progress in the domestication of either animals or plants. In the early 21st century, the Pygmies in the Congo were described by Priscilla Cheung (2003) as living "deep in the northeastern forests, eking out an existence by hunting and gathering food." Judging from their lifestyle, their intelligence appears to be lower than that of Negroid Africans (as mentioned above, many Negroid Africans have become farmers during the last few hundred years). In the 20th century, a number of Pygmies worked for Negroid African farmers; according to Cavalli-Sforza, Menozzi, and Piazza (1994, p. 178), these Pygmies "are always the lower caste, being the farmers' hereditary servants." The term "hereditary servants" appears to be a euphemism for slaves. The enslavement of Pygmies by Negroid Africans is consistent with the general principle that the more intelligent races typically defeat and enslave the less intelligent, just as Europeans and South Asians have frequently enslaved Africans (but not vice versa).

Robert Woodworth (1910) carried out a study of the intelligence of Pygmies using the Sequin Form Board test, which consists of a set of blocks of various shapes that have to be fitted into the appropriate holes. He found that Pygmies performed much worse than other peoples (including Eskimos, Native Americans, and Filipinos), but he did not quantify their abilities. A further study has been reported in Lynn (2011a), in which tests were given to 402 Biaka and Babinga Pygmies and Negroids living in the same region of the Central African Republic. Some of the Pygmies were hunter-gatherers, while others were settled in villages and worked as laborers for Negroid farmers. The Pygmies and Negroids were given four cognitive tests that can be regarded as tests of intelligence. These included (1) Verbal Fluency: naming the largest number of plants, parts of the body, and people known; (2) Block Design: assembling a number of colored blocks (cubes), a well-known measure of intelligence and one of the subtests in the Wechsler tests; (3) Draw-a-Person test: a variation of Goodenough's (1926) Draw-a-Man test, in this case, the task was to draw a person in sand with a stick; and (4) African Embedded Figures Test (AEFT), consisting of identifying simple figures embedded in more complex figures. The Pygmies scored 14 IQ points lower than the Negroids. The average IQ of African Negroids is 71, so it can be concluded that the average IQ of the Pygmies is 57.

1. Intelligence of Indigenous South Asians

2. Intelligence of Indigenous North Africans

3. South Asians and North Africans in Britain and Australia

4. South Asians and North Africans in Continental Europe

5. Indians in Africa, Fiji, and Malaysia

6. South Asian and North African High School and University Students

7. Brain Size of South Asians

8. The Heritability of Intelligence in South Asians

9. Genetic and Environmental Determinants of the Intelligence of South Asians and North Africans

10. Intelligence in Israel

CHAPTER 6

SOUTH ASIANS
AND
NORTH AFRICANS

THE SOUTH ASIANS AND NORTH AFRICANS are the indigenous peoples of southern Asia (from Bangladesh in the east through India, Pakistan, Iraq, Iran, the Gulf states, the Near East, and Turkey) as well as of North Africa, north of the Sahara desert. They are closely related to the Europeans and in some of the taxonomies of classical anthropology, such as that of Coon, Garn, and Birdsell (1950), the two peoples have been regarded as a single race—the Caucasoids. But Cavalli-Sforza, Menozzi, and Piazza (1994) have shown, in their genetic analysis of human differences, that the South Asians and North Africans form a distinctive genetic "cluster" that differentiates them from the Europeans. They are therefore treated here as a separate race.

1. INTELLIGENCE OF INDIGENOUS SOUTH ASIANS

Studies of the intelligence of indigenous South Asians are summarized in Table 6.1. The 77 IQs of the South Asians show reasonable consistency. All the IQs lie in the range between 66 (for one of the studies from Yemen) and 96 (for one of the studies from Turkey). The median IQ of the entire set of results is 84 and is presented as the best estimate for the IQ of South Asians.

Row 1 gives a DAM IQ of 92 for a sample of Armenian children attending schools in Lebanon. This IQ was calculated from the 1920s norms given by Florence Goodenough (1926). The DAM IQ increased by 0.8 IQ points a decade over the years 1924-1964 (U.S. Dept of Health, 1970, p.20), and this IQ for Armenia has been adjusted for this rise. In Row 2, we find an IQ of 95.8 for Armenia. These two IQs are significantly higher than the median of 84 for South Asia. The most likely explanation for this is that Armenia is close to Europe, and the population has acquired some European genes to produce a European-South Asian genetically mixed population with an IQ intermediate between Europe and South Asia. The same explanation is likely for the IQ of 92.8 in Cyprus (Row 6), which has another European-South Asian population arising partly from many years of colonization by Venice. Eighty-one percent of the population are Greek, according to Phillip's *World Atlas* (1996), so the IQ is closely similar to that of Greece. However, the IQ of 86.1 in Azerbaijan (Row 3) and the IQ of 87.8 in Georgia (Row 7) are only marginally higher than the average in South Asia.

Sixteen IQs for various locations in India, ranging between 78 and 89.5, with a median of 82.5, are given in Rows 8 through 24. Five IQs for Iran ranging between 83 and 89.3, with a median of 84, are listed in Rows 25 through 29. Row 32 gives an IQ of 86 for Arabs in Israel, obtained in the standardization sample of the WISC-R. This is closely similar to the IQ of 84.7 for Palestine given in Row 51.

The IQ of the people of Kazakstan was measured at 86 (Row 37), while that of Kyrgyzstan, 75.7 (Row 40). The higher IQ in Kazakstan is attributable to the immigration of large numbers of Russians when Kazakstan was part of the Soviet Union. In 1990, Russians were about half the population (Kazakhs comprising the remainder). As the Russian IQ is 97 (see Table 3.1), it can be inferred that the IQ of the Kazakhs is about the same as that of 75.7 in Kyrgyzstan. These possibly surprisingly low IQs confirm the work carried out in 1931 by Aleksandr Luria (1976), who reported the inability of the Uzbek peoples in this part of the former Soviet Union to think logically. He gave them syllogisms, which they were unable to solve. For instance, he asked "There are no camels in Germany; the city of B is in Germany; are their camels there?" He gave as a typical answer "I don't know, I have never seen German cities. If B is a large city, there should be camels there." The ability to solve syllogisms is correlated with conventional intelligence tests at 0.44 (Shikishima, Hiraishi, Yamagata et al., 2009).

Luria distinguished two modes of thought that he designated *graphic recall* (memories of how objects in the individual's personal experience are related) and *categorical relationships* (categorization by abstract concepts). He found that the thought processes of Uzbek peasants were confined to *graphic recall* and that they were not able to form abstract concepts. For example, they were shown a hammer, an axe, a log, and a saw, and asked which of these did not belong. The typical Uzbek answer was that they all belonged together because they are all needed to make firewood. People who are able to think in terms of *categorical relationships* identify the log as the answer because the other three are tools (an abstract concept), but Uzbeks peasants were unable to form concepts of this kind. Other early studies reporting low intelligence of peoples in these republics of the former Soviet Union have been summarized in Andrei Grigoriev and Lynn (2009).

An IQ of 83.9 for Mauritius is listed in Row 43. This is predictable because the 68 percent of the population are Indian, and the Indian IQ is 82.5. A further 27 percent of the population are Creole (of European and sub-Saharan African descent), who can be expected to have an IQ of about the same figure.

Rows 48 through 51 give four IQs for Pakistan, ranging between 82 and 86 with a median of 84, the same as that in Iran and closely similar to the IQ of 82.5 for India. Five IQs for Saudi Arabia ranging between 78 and 81.4 with a median of 80 (Rows 58-61). An IQ of 83.5 for Seychelles is found in Row 63. The population is a mix of European, South Asian, and sub-Saharan African descent, so this result is predictable.

Rows 68 through 73 present six IQs for Turkey, for which the median is 87.5. This is a little higher than the median of 84 for South Asia. The most likely explanation for this is that Turkey is close to Europe, and the population has acquired some European genes to produce a European-South Asian genetically mixed population. This is confirmed by Cavalli-Sforza, Menozzi, and Piazza (1994), who show that contemporary Turks and Greeks are genetically quite similar and belong to the same genetic cluster. This is further confirmed by the Greek IQ of 92.5, given in Table 3.1, which a little higher than that in Turkey but considerably lower than the 100 in Central and Northern Europe.

In Rows 74 through 76, we find three studies for Yemen, yielding IQs of 81, 85, and 66. These inconsistent results are probably due to sampling inadequacies. The IQ in Yemen would be expected to be a little lower than in the rest of South Asia because of some admixture of sub-Saharan Africans in the population, shown by Viktor Cerný, Connie Mulligan, Jakub Rídl et al. (2008). According to Jon Entine (2007, p. 332), "more than a third of female DNA of Yemite Arabs traces back to Black Africa."

Table 6.1. IQs of Indigenous South Asians

	LOCATION	AGE	N	TEST	IQ	REFERENCE
1	Armenia	5/10	311	DAM	92	Dennis, 1957
2	Armenia	8/15	-	EDUC	95.8	Meisenberg & Lynn, 2011
3	Azerbaijan	8/15	-	EDUC	86.1	Meisenberg & Lynn, 2011
4	Bahrain	8/15	-	EDUC	89.1	Meisenberg & Lynn, 2011
5	Bangladesh	67	672	MMSE	81	Lynn, 2007a
6	Cyprus	8/15	-	EDUC	92.8	Meisenberg & Lynn, 2011
7	Georgia	8/15	-	EDUC	87.8	Meisenberg & Lynn, 2011
8	India	8/16	1,695	CF	84	Rao, 1965
9	India	5/11	1,339	CPM	88	Gupta & Gupta, 1966
10	India	14/17	1,359	SPM	87	Chopra, 1966
11	India	12/14	5,607	CPM	81	Sinha, 1968
12	India	5/10	1,050	CPM	82	Rao & Reddy, 1968
13	India	15	3,536	SPM	84	Majumdar & Nundi, 1971
14	India	10/16	180	SPM	79	Mohanty & Babu, 1983
15	India	13	100	SPM	78	Agrawa et al., 1984
16	India	9/12	748	WISC-R	79	Afzal, 1988
17	India	7/9	90	TONI	80	Parmar, 1989
18	India	5/12	500	CPM	86	Bhogle & Prakash, 1992
19	India	6-/12	29	CPM	82	Jyothi et al., 1993
20	India	11/15	569	SPM	82	Raven et al., 1996

	LOCATION	AGE	N	TEST	IQ	REFERENCE
21	India	7/11	828	CPM	80	Barnabus et al., 1995
22	India	7/15	8,040	SPM	88	Raven et al., 2000
23	India	11/15	569	SPM	81	Raven et al., 2000
24	India	8/15	-	EDUC	89.4	Meisenberg & Lynn, 2011
25	Iran	15	627	SPM	84	Valentine, 1959
26	Iran	14	250	AH4	83	Mehryar et al., 1972
27	Iran	6/11	1,600	BG	89	Yousefi et al., 1992
28	Iran	6/10	1,195	DAM	84	Mehryer et al., 1987
29	Iran	8/15	-	EDUC	89.3	Meisenberg & Lynn, 2011
30	Iraq	14/17	204	SPM	87	Abul-Hubb, 1972
31	Iraq	18/35	1,185	SPM	87	Abul-Hubb, 1972
32	Israel-Arabs	6/16	639	WISC-R	86	Lieblich & Kugelmas, 1981
33	Jordan	6/12	210	KABC	84	El-Mneizel, 1987
34	Jordan	8/13	151	Piagetian	82	Za'rour & Khuri, 1977
35	Jordan	11/40	1,542	APM	86	Lynn & Abdel-Khalek, 2009
36	Jordan	8/15	-	EDUC	89.9	Meisenberg & Lynn, 2011
37	Kazakstan	8/15	-	EDUC	86	Meisenberg & Lynn, 2011
38	Kuwait	6/15	6,529	SPM	86	Abdel-Khalek & Lynn, 2006
39	Kuwait	7/17	8,418	SPM	87	Abdel-Khalek & Raven, 2008
40	Kyrgyzstan	8/15	-	EDUC	75.7	Meisenberg & Lynn, 2011
41	Lebanon	5/10	191	DAM	86	Dennis, 1957
42	Lebanon	8/15	-	EDUC	88.4	Meisenberg & Lynn, 2011
43	Mauritius	8/15	-	EDUC	83.9	Meisenberg & Lynn, 2011
44	Nepal	4/16	807	DAM	78	Sundberg & Ballinger, 1968
45	Oman	9/18	5,139	SPM	82	Abdel-Khalek & Lynn, 2008
46	Oman	5/11	1,042	CPM	85	Khaleefa et al., 2012a
47	Oman	8/15	-	EDUC	85.5	Meisenberg & Lynn, 2011
48	Pakistan	15	349	GEFT	84	Alvi et al., 1986
49	Pakistan	6/8	140	SPM	84	Rahman et al., 2002
50	Pakistan	12/18	1,662	SPM	82	Ahmad et al., 2009
51	Pakistan	18/45	2,016	SPM	86	Ahmad et al., 2009
52	Palestine	8/15	-	EDUC	84.7	Meisenberg & Lynn, 2011
53	Palestine	6-11	257	CPM		
53	Qatar	10/13	273	SPM	78	Bart et al., 1987

	LOCATION	AGE	N	TEST	IQ	REFERENCE
54	Qatar	6/11	1,135	SPM	88	Khaleefa & Lynn, 2008d
55	Qatar	8/15	-	EDUC	78.4	Meisenberg & Lynn, 2011
56	Qatar	6/11	1,003	SPM	90	Khaleefa et al., 2012
57	Saudi Arabia	8/14	3,967	SPM	80	Abu-Hatab et al., 1977
58	Saudi Arabia	8/24	4,659	SPM	78	Abdel-Khalek & Lynn , 2009
59	Saudi Arabia	8/15	-	EDUC	81.4	Meisenberg & Lynn, 2011
60	Saudi Arabia	8/18	3,209	SPM	80	Batterjee, 2011
61	Saudi Arabia	6/15	1,634	SPM	76	Batterjee et al., 2012
62	Seychelles	8/15	-	EDUC	83.5	Meisenberg & Lynn, 2011
63	Sri Lanka	8	46	CTMM	79	Strauss, 1954
64	Syria	7	241	CPM	83	Guthke & Al-Zoubi, 1987
65	Syria	7/18	3,489	CPM	83	Khaleefa & Lynn, 2008a
66	Syria	8/15	-	EDUC	86.6	Meisenberg & Lynn, 2011
67	Turkey	11/12	92	D 48	84	Kagitcibasi, 1972
68	Turkey	7/9	180	DAM	96	Ucman, 1972
69	Turkey	11	218	DAM	88	Kagitcibasi, 1979
70	Turkey	6/15	2,397	SPM	87	Duzen et al, 2008
71	Turkey	11	258	DAM	83	Kagitcibasi & Biricik, 2011
72	Turkey	8/15	-	EDUC	90.8	Meisenberg & Lynn, 2011
73	Yemen	6/11	1,000	CPM	85	Al-Heeti et al., 1997
74	Yemen	6/11	986	CPM	81	Khaleefa & Lynn, 2008c
75	Yemen	8/15	-	EDUC	66	Meisenberg & Lynn, 2011
76	U Arab Em	6/11	4,496	CPM	83	Khaleefa & Lynn, 2008b
77	U Arab Em	8/15	-	EDUC	94	Meisenberg & Lynn, 2011

2. INTELLIGENCE OF INDIGENOUS NORTH AFRICAN

Studies of the intelligence of indigenous North Africans are summarized in Table 6.2. The IQs lie in the range between 64 for one of the studies from Sudan and 87 for one of the studies from Libya. An IQ of 84 obtained from a mixed sample of North Africans from Algeria, Morocco, and Tunisia is found in Row 1. Rows 3 through 6 give four studies for Egypt, with a median of 82, and Rows 7 through 12 give six IQs for Libya, with a median of 82.

Two samples in Sudan found low IQs of 64 and 76 (Rows 16 and 17). These should be regarded as underestimates of Sudanese intelligence, because the children are described as living in remote rural villages and with little or no experience of the drawing skills required by the test. The racial identity of the sample is not described, and it may be that the sample was Negroid. The median of 80 for the other eight studies should be regarded as the best estimate for the IQ in Sudan. These studies come from the northern and central two thirds of the country that from 2011 became independent from South Sudan. The population of the northern and central two thirds of the country are a mixed-race people of predominantly North African Caucasoid stock but with some admixture of Negroids from the south and west, as well as some mixed-race Arabic and Negroid peoples from Eritrea and Ethiopia to the east (Cavalli-Sforza, Menozzi, and Piazza, 1994). The population of the new state of South Sudan is Negroid, and IQs for it are given in Chapter 4.

Table 6.2. IQs of Indigenous North Africans

	COUNTRY	AGE	N	TEST	IQ	REFERENCE
1	N. Africa	Adults	90	SPM	84	Raveau et al., 1976
2	Algeria	8/15	-	EDUC	84.1	Meisenberg & Lynn, 2011
3	Egypt	6/10	206	DAM	84	Dennis, 1957
4	Egypt	12/15	111	CCF	81	Sadek, 1972
5	Egypt	6/12	129	SPM	83	Abdel-Khalek, 1988
6	Egypt	8/15	-	EDUC	76	Meisenberg & Lynn, 2011
7	Libya	6/11	600	CPM	86	Lynn et al., 2008a
8	Libya	8/17	1600	SPM	78	Al-Shahomee & Lynn, 2010
9	Libya	6/16	870	WISC-R	85	Lynn et al., 2009
10	Libya	Adults	600	SPM	78	Al-Shahomee, 2012
11	Libya	Adults	520	SPM	79	Al-Shahomee & Lynn, 2012a
12	Libya	16	592	SPM	87	Al-Shahomee & Lynn, 2012b
13	Morocco	6/11	85	SPM	84	Aboussaleh et al., 2006
14	Morocco	adults	202	SPM	84	Sellami et al., 2010
15	Morocco	8/15	-	EDUC	81.4	Meisenberg & Lynn, 2011

	COUNTRY	AGE	N	TEST	IQ	REFERENCE
16	Sudan	6	80	DAM	64	Badri, 1965a
17	Sudan	9	293	DAM	76	Badri, 1965b
18	Sudan	8/12	148	SPM	75	Ahmed, 1989
19	Sudan	adults	77	ETMT	76	Stanczak et al., 2001
20	Sudan	6/9	1683	CPM	81	Khatib et al., 2006
21	Sudan	4/10	1345	DAM	83	Khaleefa et al., 2008a
22	Sudan	9/25	6202	SPM	79	Khaleefa et al., 2008b
23	Sudan	7/11	3185	SPM	79	Irwing et al., 2008
23	Sudan	50	801	WAIS-R	86	Khaleefa et al., 2009
24	Sudan	50	801	WAIS-R	84	Khaleefa & Lynn, 2009
25	Tunisia	20	509	SPM	84	Abdel-Khalek & Raven, 2006
26	Tunisia	8/15	-	EDUC	86.4	Meisenberg & Lynn, 2011

Rows 25 and 26 give two studies for Tunisia. In Row 25, we have the results of the SPM standardized in 2001. The sample obtained a score of 47 and can be compared with the mean of 54 for British 20-year-olds obtained in the 1992 standardization. The raw score difference of seven is approximately equivalent of 14 IQ points, giving the Tunisian sample an IQ of 86. Adjusting for a Flynn effect of two IQ points per decade reduces the Tunisian mean to 84. A closely similar IQ of 86.4 obtained by Tunisian school students in mathematics in the 2003 PISA study is listed in Row 26.

The median of the studies of the IQs of South Asians is an IQ of 83, virtually identical to the median of 84 for South Asians, as would be expected for these two genetically related races.

3. SOUTH ASIANS AND NORTH AFRICANS IN BRITAIN AND AUSTRALIA

IQs of South Asians in Europe and Australia are given in Table 6.3.

Table 6.3. IQs of South Asians in Britain and Australia

	COUNTRY	ASIANS	AGE	N	TEST	IQ	REFERENCE
1	Britain	Indian	11	43	VR	87	ILEA, 1967
2	Britain	Pakistani	9/10	173	CPM	93	Dickenson et al., 1975
3	Britain	Indian	10	149	VR	91	Black Peoples, 1978
4	Britain	Indian	11	173	NFER	94	Scarr et al., 1983
5	Britain	Pakistani	11	32	NFER	89	Scarr et al., 1983
6	Britain	Indian	11	37	NFER	83	Mackintosh et al., 1985
7	Britain	Indian	11	25	NFER	97	Mackintosh et al., 1985
8	Britain	Pakistani	10	91	BAS	93	Mackintosh et al, 1985
9	Britain	Pakistani	10	170	BAS	96	Mackintosh et al., 1985
10	Britain	Indian	76	149	MMSE	86	Lindesay, et al.,
11	Australia	Mixed	Adults	111	SPM	89	De Lemos, 1989

An IQ of 87 is given in Row 1 for Indian children in London collected in the mid-1960s by the Inner London Education Authority (ILEA) and calculated by Philip Vernon (1969, p. 169). Row 2 lists an IQ of 93 for a sample of Pakistani children in London. Row 3 gives an IQ of 91 for Indian children at a comprehensive school in Essex, in a study in which Afro-Caribbean children at the same school obtained an IQ of 85. IQs of 94 and 89 for Indian and Pakistani children in a town in the British Midlands are given in Rows 4 and 5. Afro-Caribbean children at the same schools obtained an IQ of 86, confirming the result in Row 3 finding higher IQs of South Asians than of Africans. Rows 6 and 7 give IQs of 83 and 97 for Indians nationwide, and the following Rows 8 and 9 give IQs of 93 and 96 of Pakistani children nationwide. A sample of Indian immigrants is found in Row 10, and Row 11 gives an IQ of 89 for South Asian immigrants in Australia.

The range of IQs of South Asians in Britain and Australia is quite large, from 83 to 97. One reason for this is that the IQs increase with length of residence in Britain. This is shown in two of the studies. First, Rows 6 and 7 give nonverbal reasoning IQs of 83 for Indian children resident for fewer than four years in Britain and 97 for those living in Britain for four or more years, indicating a gain of 14 IQ points arising from residence in Britain. It is interesting to note that the IQ of 83 of Indian children resident for fewer than four years in Britain is almost the same as the IQ of 82 for Indians in India given in Table 6.1. Second, Rows 8 and 9 give nonverbal reasoning IQs of 93 for Pakistani children resident for fewer than four years in Britain and 96 for Pakistani children resident for four or more years in Britain, indicating a gain of 3 IQ points with longer residence in Britain.

The median IQ of the studies of South Asians in Britain is 89, and the IQ of South Asian immigrants in Australia given in the last row is the same. This is a little higher than the IQ of 84 of indigenous South Asians, consistent with the results showing that IQs improve with length of residence in Britain and Australia. These IQ gains may be due to a variety of factors. Recent immigrants will have had difficulty in speaking and understanding English, and this will have impaired their performance, even on nonverbal tests, because of difficulty in understanding the instructions given in English. In addition, those who had been born in Britain may have benefited from better nutrition and education than comparable children received in their own countries.

4. SOUTH ASIANS AND NORTH AFRICANS IN CONTINENTAL EUROPE

IQs of South Asians and North Africans in Continental Europe are given in Table 6.4.

Table 6.4. IQs of South Asians and North Africans in Continental Europe

	COUNTRY	SAMPLE	AGE	N	TEST	IQ	REFERENCE
1	Germany	Turkish	10/17	330	SPM	86	Taschinski, 1985
2	Germany	Turkish	15	-	Math	86	Weiss, 2007
3	Netherlands	Turkish	-	177	RAKIT	78	Resing et al., 1986
4	Netherlands	Turkish	-	104	RAKIT	79	Resing et al., 1986

	COUNTRY	SAMPLE	AGE	N	TEST	IQ	REFERENCE
5	Netherlands	Moroccan	-	177	RAKIT	75	Resing et al., 1986
6	Netherlands	Moroccan	-	76	RAKIT	79	Resing et al., 1986
7	Netherlands	Mixed		106	GALO	83	De Jong, 1984
8	Netherlands	Turkish	11	815	CITO	85	Pieke, 1988
9	Netherlands	Moroccan	11	720	CITO	84	Pieke, 1988
10	Netherlands	Indian	11	338	CITO	88	Pieke, 1988
11	Netherlands	Mixed	10	47	Otis/ Cito	93	Van de Vijver & Willemse, 1991
12	Netherlands	Turkish & Moroccan	5–17	33	Son-R	84	Laros & Tellegren, 1991
13	Netherlands	Moroccan	5–8	194	LPTP	85	Hamers et al., 1996
14	Netherlands	Turkish	5–8	194	LPTP	84	Hamers et al., 1996
15	Netherlands	Moroccan	Adults	167	GATB	84	Te Nijenhuis, 1997
16	Netherlands	Turkish	Adults	275	GATB	88	Te Nijenhuis, 1997
17	Netherlands	Mixed	6–12	1,315	Arith	92	Driessen, 1997
18	Netherlands	Mixed	6–12	474	RAKIT	94	Helms-Lorenz et al., 2003
19	Serbia	Gypsies	Adults	323	SPM	70	Rushton et al., 2007
20	Slovakia	Gypsies	5–8	728	CPM	83	Raven et al., 1995

Rows 1 and 2 give an IQ of 86 for Turkish immigrants in Germany (second-generation in the case of the Row-2 study). The results of 16 studies of the IQs obtained by South Asians and North Africans immigrants in the Netherlands are listed in Rows 3 through 18. A useful review of a number of these studies has been given by Jan Te Nijenhuis and Henk van der Flier (2001). Row 3 gives an IQ of 78 for a sample of the children of first-generation immigrants from Turkey and Row 4 an IQ of 79 for a sample of the children of second-generation immigrants from Turkey. Both IQs are low and indicate no significant improvement in the intelligence of second-generation immigrants. An IQ of 75 for a sample of children of first-generation immigrants from Morocco is listed in Row 5, and an IQ of 79 for a sample of children of second-generation immigrants from Morocco in Row 6. Again, both IQs are low, but there appears to be some improvement in the intelligence of second-generation immigrants, as has been found in the studies of immigrants in Britain.

Row 7 gives an IQ of 83 for children of immigrants from Morocco and Turkey. The following Rows 8 and 9 list IQs of 85 and 84 for further samples of Moroccan and Turkish immigrant children. A sample of Indians achieved an average IQ of 88 (Row 10), six IQ points higher than the median IQ of 82 in India. Row 11 gives an IQ of 93 for Moroccan and Turkish children, the average of 92 obtained on the Otis and 94 on the Cito, both of which are largely verbal tests. In Row 12, an IQ of 84 for Turkish (n=24) and Moroccan (n=9) children obtained on the standardization sample of the Snijders-Oomen Nonverbal Test; IQs of those born in the Netherlands were the same as those who had only been in the country from one to six years. Rows 13 and 14 give IQs of 85 and 84 for samples of Moroccan and Turkish children, while Rows 15 and 16 list IQs of 84 and 88 for Moroccan and Turkish adults on the General Ability Test Battery (GATB); this is a Dutch test with eight subtests measuring vocabulary, arithmetical ability, perceptual speed, etc. The Turkish and Moroccan immigrants performed poorly on vocabulary because they had not learned Dutch well, and this test has therefore been omitted in the calculation of the IQs. The figures for g are the average of the remaining seven subtests. Row 17 gives an IQ of 92 for Muslims in the Netherlands from Turkey and Morocco, compared with approximately 69,000 Dutch Europeans; this figure is obtained from a test of arithmetic entered as verbal IQ. The mean vocabulary IQ of this sample was 85, but this is not entered because most of these children did not speak Dutch as their first language. An IQ of 94 for second-generation immigrant children, of whom 72 percent were from Turkey and Morocco and 10 percent from Surinam and the Netherlands Antilles, is given in Row 18. Their verbal IQ was 80, but this has been omitted on the grounds that most of them did not speak Dutch as their first language. The results of the studies from the Netherlands are closely similar to those from Britain. The median IQ of the first eight studies of first-generation immigrants is 84, the same as that of indigenous South Asians and North Africans.

IQs of 70 for Gypsies in Serbia and 83 for Gypsies in Slovakia are listed in Rows 19 and 20. The results are given here because gypsies, or Roma as they are coming to be called, are people of South Asian stock who migrated from northwest India between the ninth and 14th centuries. This has been shown by linguistic analysis of their Romani language, which has been found to have an Indian origin, and by genetic analysis (Pearson, 1985; Fraser, 1995). The IQ of 70 for gypsies in Serbia is remarkably low. Perhaps Roma with higher IQs have assimilated with the general population, leaving those with lower IQs as an underclass. Their low IQ is consistent with their high rate of infant and child mortality, which are three times higher than that of the general population (Čvorović, Rushton, & Tenjevic, 2008). The IQ of 83 for gypsies in Slovakia given in row 20 is typical of South Asians.

5. INDIANS IN AFRICA, FIJI, AND MALAYSIA

There are Indian populations in several countries in Africa. In South Africa they number about one million, of whom approximately 84 percent are in Natal and 14 percent are in the Transvaal. There are also Indians in Kenya and Tanzania, whose ancestors were brought in by the British and Germans under colonial rule to do work of various kinds, including building railways. Studies of the IQs of Indians in Africa are summarized in Table 6.5.

Row 1 gives an IQ of 77 for the first study of the IQ of Indians in South Africa, compared with 65 for Africans. An IQ of 88 for Indian computer-programming students, compared with an IQ of 100 for a sample of 243 Whites, is given in Row 2. In Row 3, an IQ of 86 is calculated from the standardization samples of the Junior South African Individual Scales. This test resembles the Wechsler. The norms for Indians have been calculated in relation to the South African White standardization sample. The test contains a scale for numerical ability, on which the Indians obtained an IQ of 86, which contributes to the overall IQ. Row 4 gives an IQ of 91 in relation to British 1979 norms. White South Africans obtained an IQ of 98; hence Indians scored seven IQ points below South African Whites. An IQ of 83 in relation to South African Whites on the South African

Junior Aptitude Test is found in row 5. This test also has two memory subtests on which the Indians obtained an IQ of 89; in the same study, Africans in South Africa obtained an IQ of 63, showing again that Indians in South Africa obtain much higher IQs than Africans.

The median IQ of Indians in South Africa derived from the five studies is 86. This is a little higher than the median IQ of 82 of Indians in India and a little lower than the IQ of approximately 89 of Indians born in Britain. Possibly, a reason for these differences is that standards of living are lowest in India, higher in South Africa, and highest in Britain, and these have had some effect on intelligence levels. There may also have been differences in the intelligence of the migrants from whom the Indians in South Africa and Britain are descended. The ancestors of the Indians in South Africa were largely recruited to work in the sugar and tobacco plantations and may not have had such high IQs as those who migrated to Britain in the second half of the twentieth century.

Table 6.5. IQs of Indians in Africa, Fiji, and Malaysia

	COUNTRY	AGE	N	TEST	IQ	REFERENCE
1	S. Africa	10/12	762	AAB	77	Fick, 1929
2	S. Africa	18	284	GFT	88	Taylor & Radford, 1986
3	S. Africa	6/8	600	JSAIS	86	Landman, 1988
4	S. Africa	15	1,063	SPM	91	Owen, 1992
5	S. Africa	15	1,063	JAT	83	Lynn & Owen, 1994
6	Tanzania	13/18	727	SPM	91	Klingelhofer, 1967
7	Fiji	8/13	140	QT	82	Chandra, 1975
8	Malaysia	7/12	555	SPM	88	Chaim, 1994

An IQ of 91 for Indians in Tanzania is listed in Row 6. The sample consisted of secondary-school students who had to pass an entrance examination, and the IQ is therefore somewhat inflated. The IQ of this sample is probably about eight IQ points higher than that of the general population of Indians in Tanzania, which can therefore be estimated at approximately 83, closely similar to the IQ of 82 of Indians in India given in Table 6.1. In the same study Africans at the same selective schools obtained an IQ of 78. This difference confirms a number of studies in South Africa and Britain showing that, when Indians and Africans are in the same environment, Indians obtain substantially higher IQs than Africans.

Row 7 gives an IQ of 82 for Indians in Fiji, where there are approximately the same number of Indians and indigenous Fijians. The Fijians obtained a mean IQ of 84 in the same study. An IQ of 88 for Indians in Malaysia, obtained from a standardization of Raven's Standard Progressive Matrices, is found in Row 8. The studies summarized in Table 6.4 lie in the range between 77 and 91 and have a median IQ of 88, a little higher than that in India and about the same as that of Indians in Europe. This is probably because Indians outside India generally enjoy higher living standards and possibly because those who have emigrated from India have had above-average intelligence.

6. SOUTH ASIAN AND NORTH AFRICAN HIGH SCHOOL AND UNIVERSITY STUDENTS

Studies of the intelligence of South Asian and North African students in high schools, colleges, and universities are summarized in Table 6.6. It would be expected that these would be somewhat higher than the intelligence of general population samples, and, indeed, this is the case.

Row 1 lists an early study of the 1920s in which Armenian students at the Constantinople Women's College obtained an IQ of 94; American college students obtained a median IQ of 118 on the same test. An IQ of 81, calculated from the administration of the PMA to 100 students aged 19-29 at the College of Arts and Education in Bahrain in 1997-8, is found in Row 2. The mean score was 45.4. This is at the 17.5th percentile for 20-year-olds in the 1982 American standardization sample, equivalent to an IQ of 86. Deducting two IQ points for a comparison with American Whites, and three IQ points for the Flynn effect, gives an IQ of 81.

Row 3 gives an IQ of 85 for students at the University of Alexandria. Intelligence was measured using the Standard

Progressive Matrices. The students obtained an average score of 42.5 , equivalent to the 9th percentile on a 1992 British standardization sample (Raven, Raven and Court, 1998, p.73) and a British IQ of 80. This should be raised by one IQ point because the Egyptian data were obtained six years before the British standardization data, giving the sample a British IQ of 81. This is approximately the same as the IQ of 83 on the same test of a general population sample in Egypt given in Table 6.2. Row 4 gives another IQ of 81 for university students in Egypt.

Table 6.6. IQs of South Asian and North African High School and University students

	COUNTRY	AGE	N	TEST	IQ	REFERENCE
1	Armenia	18/21	27	Otis	94	Wood, 1929
2	Bahrain	19/29	100	PMA	81	Khaleefa & Al Gharaibeh, 2002
3	Egypt	23	452	SPM	85	Abdel-Khalek, 1988
4	Egypt	21	452	SPM	81	Abdel-Khalek et al., 2014
5	India	21	32	Stanford	95	Maity, 1926
6	India	14	45	SPM	93	Mehrotra, 1968
7	India	18/25	165	SPM	90	Mohan, 1972
8	India	19/25	400	SPM	88	Mohan & Kumar, 1979
9	India	16/20	800	CCF	88	Gupta, 1991
10	India	21	250	SPM	107	Bhogle & Prakash, 1994
11	Iran	19/26	143	SPM	90	Amir, 1975
12	Iraq	16/18	103	CCF	92	Alzobaie, 1964
13	Libya	18/21	800	SPM	78	Al-Shahomee & Lynn, 2010b
14	Oman	21	92	SPM	94	Abdel-Khalek & Lynn, 2008
15	S. Africa	19	58	SPM	98	Rushton et al., 2002
16	S. Africa	20	40	APM	102	Rushton et al., 2003
17	S. Africa	17/23	57	APM	106	Rushton et al., 2004
18	S. Africa	17/23	212	A/SPM	103	Rushton, 2008
19	Sudan	16/19	1,001	SPM	81	Khaleefa et al., 2012b
20	Turkey	18/21	27	Otis	96	Wood, 1929
21	Turkey	18/26	103	CCF	101	Tan et al., 1999
22	Turkey	19	39	CCF	92	Dayi et al., 2002

A study from 1926, in which second-year students at the University of Calcutta obtained an IQ of 95, is found in Row 5. The test used was the Stanford, on which American students at the Stanford University obtained a mean IQ of 113. Row 6 gives an IQ of 93 for 14-year-old students at St. Xavier's School in Delhi, who were described as coming from upper-class families. Rows 6 and 7 give IQs of 90 and 88 for students at the Punjab University, while Row 8 lists an IQ of 88 for women students at various colleges in the Indian city of Amritsar. In Row 9, we find an IQ of 107 for post-graduate students at the University of Bangalore. This IQ is much higher than that of any of the other samples, as these post-grads were an elite group who had done well as undergraduates.

University students in engineering, economics, and the liberal arts in Tehran were found to have an IQ of 90 (Row 11). Row 12 gives an IQ of 92 for high-school students in Baghdad, who were described by the author of the study as "a highly selected group, since education is not compulsory at the high school level and students who do reach this level have to pass rigid examinations" (Alzobaie, 1966, p. 476).

Students at University of Omar Al–Mukhtar in Libya were found to have an average IQ of 78 (Row 13), while students at Sultan Qaboos University in Muscat, Oman, were found to have an IQ of 94 (Row 14). Rows 15 and 16 give IQs of 98 and 102 for Indian engineering students at the University of the Witwatersrand in South Africa. In this study, European students in the same faculty obtained IQs of 106 and 113, and Black African students IQs of 93 and 99. An IQ of 106 (Row 17) was found for a further sample of Indian engineering students at the University of the Witwatersrand in South Africa. European students in the same faculty obtained an IQ of 116, and Black African students, an IQ of 101. Thus, in these three studies of students, the IQs of the Indians fall midway between those of Whites and Blacks, as they do in general population samples. Also, in these studies, the IQs of the Indians are somewhat higher than those in South Asia and North Africa. This is probably attributable to the IQs of Indians in South Africa being higher and because the engineering department of the University of the Witwatersrand takes relatively talented students. Row 18 consolidates the three previous studies and adds more data to give an IQ of 103 for Indian university students in South Africa, compared with 110 for Europeans.

Row 19 gives an IQ of 81 for first-year students at the University of Khartoum. An early study of the 1920s in which Turkish students at the Constantinople Women's College obtained an IQ of 96 (Row 20). Row 22 gives an IQ of 101 for medical students at Attaturk University in the city of Ezurum in Turkey, while Row 21 gives an IQ of 92 for 15 women and 24 men students of dentistry at the same university.

The median of the studies is an IQ of 92, eight points higher than that of general population samples of South Asians and North Africans. The interest of these studies is that they show that South Asian and North African university students with extensive education and from upper- and middle-class families have lower IQs than average Europeans. This indicates that lack of education is unlikely to be a major factor responsible for the low IQs of general population samples. The IQs of South Asian and North African students are also lower than the median of 105 for European college students (Table 3.3). Thus, the 15 IQ point difference between Europeans and South Asians and North Africans in general population samples is closely similar to the 14 IQ point difference between college students.

7. BRAIN SIZE OF SOUTH ASIANS

Four sets of data on the brain size of South Asians compared with that of Europeans are shown in Table 6.7. Row 1 gives data assembled by Courtland Smith and Kenneth Beals (1990) from approximately 20,000 crania collected worldwide and shows a European advantage of 84 cubic centimeters (cc). In Row 2, we find data assembled from various sources by Colin Groves, who contends that there are no racial differences in brain size but whose research nevertheless shows a European advantage of 63cc. Row 3 gives average brain sizes of six samples of Europeans from North America and Europe and two samples from India from data, compiled by Hans Jurgens et al. (1990) and analyzed by J.P. Rushton (2000, p. 124) showing a European advantage of 134cc. The U.S. National

Aeronautics and Space Administration (NASA) compiled data of the average of 19 European and Iranian male military samples, showing a European advantage of 114cc (Row 4).

The figures in the four data sets all show greater brain size of Europeans and are reasonably consistent, considering that they were compiled using different methods. The Smith and Beals data are derived from measurements of the volume of skulls, the Groves data come from various sources, while the data sets in Rows 3 and 4 have been calculated from external measurements of the heads of living individuals. The average of the four data sets is a European Caucasoid advantage over South Asians of 97cc.

Table 6.7. Brain size (cc) of Europeans and South Asians

	EUROPEANS	SOUTH ASIANS	DIFFERENCE	REFERENCE
1	1,368	1,284	84	Smith & Beals, 1990
2	1,467	1,404	63	Groves, 1991
3	1,319	1,185	134	Jurgens et al., 1990
4	1,470	1,356	114	Rushton, 2000

8. THE HERITABILITY OF INTELLIGENCE IN SOUTH ASIANS

There have been two studies of the heritability of intelligence in India, both of which have used the method of comparing the IQs of identical (MZ) and non-identical (DZ) twins. Shich Pal, Radhey Shyam, and Rajbir Singh (1997) have reported a study of 30 MZ and 30 same-sex DZ adult twins and calculated the heritability at 0.81. If this is corrected for attenuation, assuming a test reliability of 0.9, the heritability becomes 0.90. In a second study, S.S. Nathawat and P. Puri (1995) obtained a heritability of 0.90; corrected for attenuation (assuming a test reliability of 0.9), this estimate becomes 1.0. Thus, the heritability of intelligence in India is marginally higher than that of 0.83 in Europeans.

9. GENETIC AND ENVIRONMENTAL DETERMINANTS OF THE INTELLIGENCE OF SOUTH ASIANS AND NORTH AFRICANS

We saw in Tables 6.1 and 6.2 that the median IQ of the studies of indigenous South Asians and North Africans is approximately 84. This IQ is depressed environmentally because of the low standard of living of these peoples. In 1996, UNICEF published a report on South Asia and North Africa that estimates that malnutrition stunts the maturation of 24 percent of children in the Middle East and North Africa and 60 percent of children in South Asia. There is little doubt that this has an adverse effect on intelligence.

Nevertheless, it seems likely that genetic factors are also involved. First, the very high heritabilities of intelligence in both South Asians and Europeans show that genetic factors are largely responsible for differences in intelligence within the two populations, and this makes it likely that these contribute to the differences between the two populations. Second, it has been shown that South Asians and North Africans living in the affluent European environments of Britain, Australia, and the Netherlands have median IQs of 89, 89, and 94. All of these are higher than the average IQ of 84 of those in their indigenous homelands and poorer environments. These figures show that when South Asians and North Africans are reared in European environments, their IQs increase, but they do not increase to the same level as those of Europeans. This suggests the presence of genetic factors. Third, the IQ of Indians in South Africa is 86. This is higher than the IQ of 82 in India and is attributable to the better living standards, but it is substantially below the IQ of Europeans. The Indians were brought to Natal in the 1850s to work on the sugar plantations (Johnston, 1930). They have had some four to six generations to adapt to life in South Africa, yet a large IQ difference remains; this suggests a genetic difference between the two populations. Fourth, the average brain size of South Asians is about eight percent smaller than that of Europeans; this may partly be due to sub-optimal nutrition, but it is likely also to have some genetic basis and contribute to the intelligence difference.

10. INTELLIGENCE IN ISRAEL

Intelligence in Israel is higher than in the other countries of South Asia and North Africa. Eight studies on Israeli intelligence are summarized in Table 6.8.

Table 6.8. Intelligence in Israel

	AGE	N	TEST	IQ	REFERENCE
1	13/14	200	WISC	95	Ortar, 1952
2	11/15	346	SPM	95	Moyles & Wolins, 1973
3	10/12	180	LT	97	Miron, 1977
4	10/12	268	SPM	95	Globerson, 1983
5	11	2,781	SPM	89	Lancer & Rim, 1984
6	5	52	CPM	96	Tzuriel & Caspi, 1992
7	9/15	1,740	SPM	90	Lynn, 1994a
8	13	-	SPM	96	Kozulin, 1998
9	8/15	-	Educ	95	Meisenberg & Lynn, 2011

The IQs lie in the range of 88–97 with a median of 95. This is substantially higher than the median of 84 for the remainder of South Asia, showing that Israelis have higher IQs than other South Asians. In Israel, approximately 20 percent of the population are Arabs, whose IQ of 86 (see Table 6.1) is virtually the same as that of other South Asians in the Near East. Some 40 percent of the population are European Jews (mainly Ashkenazim from Russia and Eastern Europe) and 40 percent are Oriental Jews (Mizrahim) from Asia and North Africa.

Three studies carried out in Israel have found that the Ashkenazim have a mean IQ approximately 12 IQ points higher than the Oriental Jews (Zeidner, 1987a; Burg and Belmont, 1990; Lieblich, Ninio, and Kugelmass, 1972). The IQ of 95 for Israel is the weighted mean of the IQs of 103 of the Ashkenazim Jews, 91 of the Oriental Jews (12 IQ points lower), and 86 of the Arabs. The lower IQ of Arabs in Israel compared with Jews is confirmed by Moshe Zeidner (1987a), who has reported that Arab applicants for admission to university obtained an IQ 15 points lower than that of Jewish applicants.

There are two questions concerning the Jewish IQ that require explanation. The first is why the Ashkenazim Jews in Israel have an IQ of 103. This result is not particularly surprising, because there is considerable evidence that Ashkenazim Jews in the United States and Britain have substantially higher IQs than Gentiles. In the United States, a study published in the 1920s reported that Jewish 10-year-olds had an IQ 13 points higher on the Stanford-Binet test than European Gentiles (Ns=110 and 689, respectively) (Bere, 1924). In the 1940s, Noah Nardi (1948) reported an IQ of 110 on the Stanford-Binet test for Jewish 12-year-olds (N=1,210), and in the 1950s FIRST NAME Levinson (1957) found an IQ of 109 for Jewish 12-year-olds (N=2,083), also on the Stanford-Binet test. Richard Herrnstein and Charles Murray (1994) reported an IQ of 112.6 for Jewish adolescents in their study of the National Longitudinal Study of Youth; the latest study has found an IQ of 107.5 in a nationally representative sample (N=150) of adults (Lynn, 2004).

High IQs for Jewish children have been reported in Britain. In the 1920s, Mary Davies and A.G. Hughes (1927) found that Jewish 8- to 14-year-olds in London had an IQ of 110 (N=1,081), compared with 100 for British children. In the 1960s, Jewish 10-year-olds in Glasgow had an IQ of 117.8 (N=907) compared with Scottish children in the same city (Vincent, 1966). However, this figure for the Jewish IQ is too high for a comparison with British children as a whole because the IQ of children in Glasgow is 93.7 in relation to 100 for the national average (Lynn, 1979). To compare the mean IQ of Jewish children in Glasgow with that of British non-Jewish Whites, we have therefore to subtract 6.3 IQ points from their score, giving them a mean IQ of 111.5. I have summarized studies of the IQs of Jews in the United States and Britain and concluded that they average 110 (Lynn, 2011) and are therefore higher than the 103 estimated for Ashkenazim Jews in Israel. Some possible explanations for this are that few American and British Jews have emigrated to Israel. Most of the Ashkenazim Jews in the United States and Britain fled persecution in Russia and Eastern Europe between 1880 and 1914 and in Germany between 1933 and 1939. It seems likely that these would have been the more intelligent who foresaw the dangers of staying and were able to organize emigration. Those who remained in Russia and Eastern Europe would likely have been a little less intelligent. These are the ones who emigrated to Israel after World War II to escape persecution and poverty and whose IQs are a little lower than those of Ashkenazim Jews in the United States and Britain. A further factor is that many of these supposedly European Jews are not Jews at all, but pretended to be Jews in order to get permission to leave the Soviet Union (Abbink, 2002).

A second problem concerning the intelligence of Jews is that all Jews were originally from the same stock. Hence, the question arises, Why is the intelligence of Ashkenazim Jews approximately 12 IQ points higher than that of Oriental Jews. There are probably two answers to this question. The first is that despite strict Jewish prohibitions on exogamy, there has always been some inter-marriage and inter-mating between Jews and non-Jews living in the same localities. Even a small amount of exogamy over many generations is sufficient to introduce significant proportions of non-Jewish genes into the Jewish gene pool. The effects of this are visible in European Jews, a number of whom have fair hair and blue eyes. The result of this will have been that Ashkenazim Jews in Europe will have absorbed a significant proportion of the genes for higher intelligence possessed by the Europeans, while the Oriental Jews in the Near East and North Africa will have absorbed a significant proportion of the genes for lower intelligence from the South Asians and North Africans.

The second factor that has probably increased the intelligence of Ashkenazi Jews in Europe and the United States as compared with Oriental Jews is that the Ashkenazim Jews have been more subject to persecution. Jews were less persecuted over the course of many centuries in Southwest Asia and North Africa. Oriental Jews experienced some persecution sufficient to raise their IQ to 91, as compared with 84 among other South Asians and North Africans, but not so much as that experienced by Ashkenazim Jews in Europe.

The 12 IQ point difference between Ashkenazim Jews and Oriental Jews in Israel is almost certainly to some degree a genetic difference. Genetic analysis by Michael Hammer, Alan Redd, and E.T. Wood et al. (2000) has shown that all Jews have some genetic affinity (except for the Ethiopian Jews), arising from their common original stock in the Near East. Nevertheless, European and Oriental Jews form two distinct families, with the European Jews having some genetic affinity with Gentile Europeans and the Oriental Jews, with Southwest Asians and North Africans.

1. Intelligence of Indigenous Southeast Asians

2. Southeast Asians in the United States and
the Netherlands

3. Brain Size of Southeast Asians

4. Genetic and Environmental Determinants of the Intelligence
of Southeast Asians

CHAPTER 7

SOUTHEAST ASIANS

THE SOUTHEAST ASIANS are the indigenous peoples of Burma, Thailand, Cambodia, Laos, Vietnam, Malaysia, Indonesia, the Philippines, and Brunei. In classical anthropology, they were designated the Malays (Morton, 1849; Coon, Garn, and Birdsell, 1950) or the Indonesian-Malays (Cole, 1965). Their distinctive racial identity has been confirmed by the genetic analysis made by Cavalli-Sforza, Menozzi, and Piazza (1994), in which these peoples constitute a genetic "cluster." They have some genetic affinity with the East Asians, with whom they are to some degree interbred, though Southeast Asians' flattened nose and epicanthic eyefold are less prominent.

1. INTELLIGENCE OF INDIGENOUS SOUTHEAST ASIANS

IQs for Southeast Asians from eight countries are given in Table 7.1. University students at the University of Cambodia achieved an IQ of 82 (Row 1). compared with students in Germany. This IQ is the lowest score, considerably lower than neighboring Vietnam (94), Thailand (88), and Laos (89). The explanation for this is the dysgenic effect of the mass killings of the middle and professional classes that took place in Cambodia during the Pol Pot regime from 1976 to 1979 (Lynn, 2013).

Rows 2 through 7 give IQs for various samples of Indonesian children. An IQ of 86 for children in the city of Bandung on Java is

155

listed in Row 2; in Row 3, an IQ of 87 for children and adolescents in two villages in central Java. Row 4 gives an IQ of 87 for children of families working on a tea plantation, and Row 5 gives an IQ of 87 for children in northern Jakarta.

In Laos, village children who are "not from families living in abject poverty" scored an IQ of 90 (Row 8). The mothers of the children had an average IQ of 88 (Row 9).

Row 10 gives an IQ of 89 for Malays in Malaysia, obtained in the standardization of the Standard Progressive Matrices. Malay college students at the International Islamic University in Kuala Lumpur scored an average IQ of 85, in relation to college students at universities in Germany, Russia, and the United States (Row 11). Row 16 gives an IQ of 93 for 13-year-old Malays at school in Singapore.

In Row 13, we have an IQ of 86 for the Philippines, coming from a sample of school children in Manila, while Row 15 gives an IQ of 94 for the Philippines, a score obtained from school children nationwide. (The IQ of the latter sample was 98.76. The data were collected in 2006, and since data for the NNAT (Naglieri Nonverbal Ability Test), the American standardization, were collected in 1996, the Philippines IQ needs to be reduced to 95.76. Additionally, this IQ needs to be expressed in relation to Whites (IQ=102) and so equals 93.76, rounded to 94.)

Table 7.1. IQs of Southeast Asians

Row	Country	Age	N	Test	IQ	Ver	Vis	Reference
1	Burma	6-13	93	DAM	107		107	Schuster, 1971
2	Cambodia	3-5	4,015	PPVT	65	65		Naudeau et al., 2011
3	Indonesia	5-12	1,149	DAM	86		86	Thomas & Shah, 1961
4	Indonesia	5-Adult	520	CPM	87			Bleichrodt et al., 1980
5	Indonesia	4	139	PPVT	87	87		Soewondo et al., 1989
6	Indonesia	6-8	483	CPM	87			Hadidjaja et al., 1998
7	Indonesia	7-Adult	50	SPM	79			Rindermann & Nijenhuis, 2012
8	Indonesia			EDUC	86			Meisenberg & Lynn, 201
9	Laos	5-12	22	K-ABC	90			Boivin et al., 1996

10	Laos	Adults	22	Matrix Analogies Test	91		Boivin et al., 1996
11	Malaysia	7-12	3,151	SPM	89		Chaim, 1994
12	Malaysia	20	175	EFT	85	85	Kuhnen et al., 2001
13	Malaysia	8-15		EDUC	97		Meisenberg & Lynn, 2011
14	Philippines	12-13	203	SPM	86		Flores & Evans, 1972
15	Philippines	8-15		EDUC	82		Meisenberg & Lynn, 2011
16	Philippines	12		NNAT	94		Vista & Care, 2011
17	Singapore	12	190	SPM	93		Lynn, 1977b
18	Thailand	7-12	1,385	CPM	82		Malakul, 1957
19	Thailand	7-12	892	DAM	98	98	Talapat & Suwannalert, 1966a
20	Thailand	7-14	1,438	CPM	82		Talapat & Suwannalert, 1966b
21	Thailand	7-11	70	WISC	88		Rajatasilpin et al., 1970
22	Thailand	Adults	1,462	CPM	72		Chou & Lau, 1987
23	Thailand	6-11	104	Piagetian	87		Opper, 1977
24	Thailand	9-11	1,358	CPM	91		Pollitt et al., 1989
25	Thailand	6-13	3,846	TONI	90		Thai Institute of Public Health, 1998
26	Thailand	Adults	400	SPM	90		Phatthrayuttawat et al., 2000
27	Thailand	10	427	TONI	75		Sungthong et al., 2002
28	Thailand	5-11	900	CPM	106		Phatthrayuttawat et al., 2003
29	Thailand	7-12	396	CPM/DAM	98	97	Sangtongluan, 2004
30	Thailand	6-12, 13-18	6,285	TONI	85		Ruangdaraganon, 2004
31	Thailand	12-18	5,702	APM	105		Sukhatunga et al., 2006a
32	Thailand	6-11	3,848	CPM	96		Sukhatunga et al., 2006b
33	Thailand	6-16	3,300	WISC-III	95		Wanitrommani et al., 2004
34	Thailand	13-15	319	TONI	88		Isaranurug et al., 2006
35	Thailand	7-9	100	CPM	87		Nimmalangkun, 2006
36	Thailand	7-11	390	CPM	94		Sroythong, 2008
37	Thailand	7-12	748	CPM	94		Thavornsuwanchi, 2008

38	Thailand	9	560	CPM/ WISC-III	81	91	87	Pongcharoen et al., 2011
39	Thailand	6-14	5,993	TONI	88			Aekplakorn, 2009
40	Thailand	6-15	72,780	SPM	97			Thai Department of Mental Health, 2011
41	Thailand			EDUC	91			Malloy, 2014d
42	Vietnam	8-12	47	DAM	99		99	Mayer, 1966
43	Vietnam	8	311	CPM	82			Watanabe et al., 2005
44	Vietnam	8	1,000	PPVT	95	95		Glewwe et al., 2012
45	Vietnam	5	1,747	PPVT	82	82		Glewwe et al., 2012
46	Vietnam	5	1,602	PPVT	85	85		Behrman et al., 2013
47	Vietnam	12	976	PPVT	102	102		Fink & Rockers, 2014
48	Vietnam	8	469	CPM/ WISC-III	83			Nga et al., 2011
49	Vietnam	11	60	CogAT	97			Rindermann et al., 2013
50	Vietnam			EDUC	94			Meisenberg & Lynn, 2011
51	Vietnam			EDUC	102			OECD, 2013

An IQ of 91 for school children in Thailand obtained from Chon Buri province, an agricultural area on the east coast, is listed in Row 17. Row 18 gives an IQ of 87 for Thailand derived from a study by Sylvia Opper (1977), which compares children at school in Thailand with 139 European children in Switzerland on seven Piagetian tests. Results are given for the ages at which the two groups of children attained the Piagetian concepts. The average of these ages for the seven tasks was 7.86 years for the European children and 9.0 for the Thai children. Thus, Thai children aged 9.0 are at the same level of mental development as European children aged 7.86. Using the original method for calculating the IQ as mental age divided by chronological age multiplied by 100, the IQ of the Thai children can be estimated at 87.

An IQ of 88 for Thailand in Row 19 is based on a representative sample cited by Rassamee Sungthong, Ladda Mo-suwan, and Virasakdi Chongsuvivatwong (2002). The IQ on this American test was 92. Two IQ points have been deducted for the Flynn effect, and an additional two IQ points have been deducted to equate to the

British IQ. Rows 20 and 21 give two further IQs of 86 and 92.4 for Thailand. Rows 22 and 23 give IQs of 94 and 99 for Vietnam.

Apart from Vietnam, the IQs in Table 7.1 lie in the range between 84 and 97.3; the median is 87. The two IQs for Vietnam are higher at 94 and 99, averaging 96.5. The reason for this is that the Vietnamese are a racially mixed people of Southeast Asians and southern Chinese (Cavalli-Sforza et al., 1994, p. 234); predictably, their IQ is about midway between these two peoples.

2. SOUTHEAST ASIANS IN THE UNITED STATES AND THE NETHERLANDS

IQs of Southeast Asians in the United States and the Netherlands are summarized in Table 7.2. An early study of a sample of Filipino children in Hawaii, tested with the Porteus Maze Test, achieved an IQ of 96 (Row 1). A sample of Filipinos in Honolulu, collected by Stevenson Smith (1942) in 1924 and 1938, scored an IQ of 89 (Row 2). The IQ of Filipino children on the Hawaiian island of Kauai was measured at 91 (Row 3). Row 4 gives an IQ of 93 for a sample of Filipinos in Hawaii obtained from the mathematics subtest of the STAS; and Row 5, an IQ of 87 for a sample of Filipinos in the United States calculated by James Flynn (1991).

In Row 6, we have an IQ of 94 for a sample of second-generation Indonesian immigrants in the Netherlands. Listed in Row 7, a sample of mainly Vietnamese high-school students in an American city scored an IQ of 94 (Flynn, 1991). (This sample obtained a verbal IQ of 87, measured by the Mill Hill Vocabulary Scale. This is probably slightly depressed in relation to their nonverbal reasoning IQ because many of them had not acquired fluency in English.)

The median of the seven studies is an IQ of 93, a little higher than the IQ of 87 of indigenous Southeast Asians. It is possible that a selective element in migration to the United States and the Netherlands may be part of the explanation for this; a further possible factor is that Southeast Asians in the United States and the

Netherlands enjoy a higher standard of living and of nutrition than indigenous Southeast Asians.

Table 7.2. IQs of Southeast Asians in the United States and the Netherlands

	ETHNICITY	AGE	N	TEST	IQ	REFERENCE
1	Filipino	6/14	140	PM	96	Porteus, 1937
2	Filipino	10/14	305	NV	89	Smith, 1942
3	Filipino	10	138	PMA	91	Werner et al., 1968
4	Filipino	16	4,147	STAS	93	Brandon et al., 1987
5	Filipino	9/25	263	Various	87	Flynn, 1991
6	Indonesian	6/10	84	NV	94	Tesser et al., 1999
7	Vietnamese	12/16	391	SPM	94	Flynn, 1991

3. BRAIN SIZE OF SOUTHEAST ASIANS

Studies of differences in brain size between Europeans and Southeast Asians are summarized in Table 7.3. Row 1 gives the results calculated by Stephen J. Gould (1981) from the collection of skulls assembled in the 19th century by the American physician Samuel Morton (1849). The number of skulls was quite low, consisting of 18 Southeast Asians and 52 Europeans, and not a great deal of weight should be attached to the results. They are given here largely for historical interest. Row 2 gives results from six populations of Southeast Asians compared with nine populations of Europeans, showing a difference of 37cc. The standard deviations are given by Courtland Smith, Kenneth Beals, and Stephen Dodd (1984). The numbers of individuals are not given, but are part of a total collection of approximately 20,000 and can be assumed to be several thousand. Despite the small size of Morton's sample, and Gould's accusation that Morton massaged his results to give a larger brain size for Europeans, the results agree closely with the later study of Beals, Smith, and Dodd. A much larger difference, based on average brain sizes for 190 samples of Europeans and 20 samples of Southeast Asians, is found in

Row 3. Thus, all three data sets show smaller brain size in Southeast Asians than in Europeans, consistent with their lower IQs.

Table 7.3. Brain size (cc) differences of Europeans and Southeast Asians

	EUROPEANS	SOUTHEAST ASIANS	DIFFERENCE	REFERENCE
	Mean (Sd)	**Mean (Sd)**		
1	1,426	1,393	33	Gould, 1981
2	1,369 (35)	1,332 (49)	37	Smith & Beals, 1990
3	1,319	1,217	102	Jurgens et al., 1990

4. GENETIC AND ENVIRONMENTAL DETERMINANTS OF THE INTELLIGENCE OF SOUTHEAST ASIANS

The average IQ of Southeast Asians in the United States is higher at 93 than that of indigenous Southeast Asians at 87. This difference is attributable to the better environment with higher living standards in the United States, with better nutrition, education, and welfare. The effect of these is that the IQ gap between Southeast Asians and Europeans is approximately halved. Nevertheless, a seven (7) IQ point difference remains when Southeast Asians and Europeans are raised and live in approximately the same environments. This suggests that genetic factors contribute to the difference in intelligence between the two races. The smaller average brain size of Southeast Asians compared with Europeans also indicates a genetic difference.

1. Intelligence of Australian Aborigines

2. Intelligence of Aboriginal-European Hybrids

3. Piagetian Intelligence of Australian Aborigines

4. Spatial Memory of Australian Aborigines

5. Brain Size of Australian Aborigines

6. Genotypic Intelligence of Australian Aborigines

7. Intelligence of New Guineans

8. Conclusions

CHAPTER 8

AUSTRALIAN ABORIGINES

THE AUSTRALIAN ABORIGINES, also known as the Australids, are the indigenous people of Australia. They have long been recognized as a race in classical anthropology and are one of the seven major races in the taxonomy proposed by Coon, Garn, and Birdsell (1950). They have a distinctive profile of blood groups, about 73 percent of them having O group, as compared with a little fewer than 50 percent among Europeans; the remaining 27 percent are A, and there are virtually none with the B group. Their distinctive racial identity has been confirmed by the genetic analysis made by Cavalli-Sforza, Menozzi, and Piazza (1994), in which the Australian Aborigines, together with the original New Guineans, constitute a genetic "cluster." The reason that the Australian Aborigines and the original New Guineans are closely related genetically is that the ancestors of the Australian Aborigines migrated from New Guinea to Australia about 60,000 years ago (Bradshaw, 1997). Those who migrated split from those who remained in New Guinea and today inhabit the interior highlands. Also, closely related to the Australian Aborigines are the now extinct Tasmanians. The last pure Tasmanian died in 1876, but there are still a few mixed-race Tasmanians.

It has been estimated that, before the Europeans arrived, there were around 300,000 Aborigines in Australia. Their numbers were considerably reduced following the colonization of Australia by Europeans, partly as a result of diseases contracted from Europeans from which they lacked immunities, and partly as a result of Europeans killing them. In the second half of the 20th century, the numbers of Aborigines in the censuses of 1961, 1971, and 1981 were recorded as approximately 106,000, 139,000, and 171,000. In 2006, their numbers had increased to 517,000, and they were 2.3 percent of the population. The rapid increase in numbers has been a result of high birthrates and a reduction of infant and child mortality.

In the second half of the 20th century, there were three groups of Australian Aborigines. The first lived on government reserves principally in the north and center of Australia. The second group lived on the outskirts of country towns and stations. The third lived in larger towns and cities. Both the second and third groups typically attended schools with Europeans. Many of the second and third groups have some European ancestry, while those on the reservations are largely pure Aborigines.

The Europeans who first encountered the Australian Aborigines considered they were a backward people. Thomas H. Huxley (1825-1895) regarded them as the "missing link" between apes and humans, and Chase and John von Sturmer (1974, p.6) asserted that they represented "one of the lowest rungs on the ladder of intellectual development."

1. INTELLIGENCE OF AUSTRALIAN ABORIGINES

The first estimate of the intelligence of the Australian Aborigines was made by Sir Francis Galton in 1869. On the basis of travelers' accounts of their accomplishments, he estimated their intelligence was approximately three "grades" below that of the English. In Galton's metric, a grade was equivalent to 10.4 IQ points. Hence, in terms of the IQ scale, he estimated the Australian Aborigine IQ at 68.8. Subsequent studies of the intelligence of Australian Aborigines assessed by intelligence tests have shown that this was a fairly accurate assessment. These studies are summarized in Table 8.1.

Row 1 shows the results of the first study, giving an IQ of 66 obtained by Stanley Porteus with his Maze Test, a series of paper and pencil mazes of increasing complexity from which mental age is measured as the success rate of the average child of the corresponding chronological age. The Maze Test was later incorporated into the

Wechsler tests and provides a measure of *g* and of visualization. The mean mental age of his sample adults was 10.5, the approximate equivalent of an IQ of 66. The results for the next study that used the Porteus Mazes on a sample of Aborigines at La Grange Bay in northwest Australia are listed in Row 2. The men obtained a mental age of 10.5 and the women, of 8.6. The average mental age of the two sexes was 9.55, equivalent to an IQ of 59. A closely similar result was obtained by Porteus for adults at the Beagle Bay Mission in the Kimberley region (Row 3); the Aborigines obtained a mental age of 9.35, equivalent to an IQ of 58.

Row 4 gives an IQ of 69 obtained from two visualization tests (Alexander Passalong and Fergusson Form Boards); Row 5, an IQ of 70 from a study of the Wailbiri Aborigines of Central Australia carried out by Porteus and Gregor in the 1960s. In Row 6, we find an IQ of 58 for a sample at a primary school in Maningrida in the Northern Territories. Row 7 gives an IQ of 74 for a sample of adults who obtained a mental age of 11.8. Rows 8 and 9 list IQs of 62 and 64 for two samples of Aboriginal children attending schools with White children in a town in New South Wales.

Table 8.1. IQs of Australian Aborigines

	AGE	N	TEST	IQ	VER	VIS	REFERENCE
1	Adults	56	PM	66	-	66	Porteus, 1931
2	Adults	24	PM	59	-	59	Piddington, 1932
3	Adults	268	Various	58	-	-	Porteus, 1933a, 1933b
4	Adults	31	AA/PF	69	-	69	Fowler, 1940
5	Adults	87	PM	70	-	70	Porteus & Gregor, 1963
6	11	101	QT	58	-	-	Hart, 1965
7	Adults	103	PM	74	-	74	Porteus et al., 1967
8	5	24	PPVT	62	62	-	De Lacey, 1971a, 1971b
9	6/12	40	PPVT	64	64	-	De Lacey, 1971a, 1971b
10	Adults	60	CPM	53	-	-	Berry, 1971
11	3/4	22	PPVT	64	64	-	Nurcombe & Moffit, 1973
12	6/14	55	PPVT	52	52	-	Dasen et al., 1973
13	9	458	QT	58	-	-	McElwain & Kearney, 1973

	AGE	N	TEST	IQ	VER	VIS	REFERENCE
14	13	42	SOT	62	-	-	Waldron & Gallimore, 1973
15	6/10	30	PPVT	59	59	-	De Lacey, 1976
16	25	22	CPM/KB	60	-	67	Binnie-Dawson, 1984
17	4	55	PPVT	61	61	-	Nurcombe et al., 1999

An IQ of 70 for a sample of Aboriginal adults tested with the Colored Progressive Matrices in found in Row 10. Row 11 gives a verbal IQ of 67 for three- and four-year-old Aboriginal children attending pre-school with Whites in Bourke. A verbal IQ of 52 was found for children attending schools at the Hermannsberg Mission in central Australia (Row 12), and an IQ of 58 for Aboriginals as calculated in relation to the norms for European children in New Zealand (Row 13). Row 14 gives an IQ of 62 on the Spiral Omnibus Reasoning Test for a sample of 13-year-old Aboriginal children attending school on an Aboriginal reserve in Queensland. A verbal IQ of 59 was obtained for a sample of 6–10-year-old Aboriginal children in Alice Springs in central Australia (Row 15). Row 16 gives a reasoning IQ of 60 for a sample of adults with an average age of 25, and Row 17 a vocabulary IQ of 61 for a sample of four-year-olds.

The IQs range between 52 and 74. The median IQ of the seventeen studies is 62 and represents the best estimate of the average intelligence of Australian Aborigines. Verbal ability is a little weaker than visualization ability, with median IQs of 62 and 68, respectively. The low intelligence of Australian Aborigines has been confirmed by studies showing that they have slow reaction times (Davidson, 1974) and are disproportionately over-represented in government special schools for backward students (Graham, 2012).

The abilities of 15-year-old European and Aboriginal school in math, reading comprehension, and science were tested in 2006, as part of an OECD survey of representative samples of school students in a number of countries. The results have been calculated as EQs (educational quotients, analogous to IQs), with the EQ of Europeans set at 100 (Sd, 15), and are shown in the Table 8.2. It will be seen that the Aboriginal performed better on these tests than they do on IQs, possibly because they are a selected sample.

Table 8.2. Math, reading and science abilities of Europeans and Australian Aborigines

CATEGORY	YEAR	EUROPEANS	ABORIGINES	REFERENCE
Math	2006	100	88	OECD, 2006
Reading	2006	100	87	OECD, 2006
Science	2006	100	86	OECD, 2006

2. INTELLIGENCE ABORIGINAL-EUROPEAN RACIAL HYBRIDS

A number of studies have been made of the intelligence of Aboriginal-European hybrids. These are summarized in Table 8.3.

Row 1 gives an IQ of 95 for the first of these, which was carried out by Porteus at the Mission Station in Port MacLeay, South Australia. Rows 2 and 3 list results of a study which compared 19 Aboriginal-European hybrids with European five-years-olds attending the same schools in New South Wales. In relation to IQs of 100 of the European children, the Aboriginal-European hybrids obtained IQs of 79 on the PPVT (Peabody Picture Vocabulary Test) and 77 on the ITPA (Illinois Test of Psycholinguistic Abilities). A verbal IQ of 69 was found for 13 part-Aborigines aged 6–12 years (Row 4), a little higher than the IQ of 64 of 40 full-Aborigines obtained in the same study. The visualization IQ of 95 shown in Row 1 is much higher than the verbal IQs of 79, 77, and 69 shown in rows 2, 3, and 4.

All the IQs of Aboriginal-European hybrids shown in Table 8.2 are higher than the median of the full-blooded Aborigines given in Table 8.1. This could be due to an admixture of genes from European raising the intelligence of Aborigines. Alternatively, Aborigine-European hybrids tend to be reared in better environments as regards standards of living and nutrition. None of these studies gives estimates of the proportion of European ancestry in these part-Aborigines.

Table 8.3. IQs of hybrid Australian Aborigines and Europeans

	AGE	N	TEST	IQ	VER	VIS	REFERENCE
1	10	28	PM	95	-	95	Porteus, 1917
2	5	19	PPVT	79	79	-	Teasdale & Katz, 1968
3	5	19	ITPA	77	77	-	Teasdale & Katz, 1968
4	6/12	13	PPVT	69	-	-	De Lacey, 1976, 1971a, 1971b

3. PIAGETIAN INTELLIGENCE OF AUSTRALIAN ABORIGINES

The intelligence of Australian Aborigines has been assessed by "Piagetian" tests in addition to conventional intelligence tests. This work has been carried out in the framework of the theory of the development of intelligence in children formulated by the Swiss psychologist Jean Piaget (1896-1980). This theory states that children progress through four stages of cognitive development. The first of these is the sensorimotor stage of infancy, in which the child learns about the properties of objects, space, time, and causality. At about the age of two, children make the transition to the preoperational stage in which they acquire language and abstract concepts but are not yet able to understand logical principles. This stage lasts until the age of about six years. In Western societies, children at around the age of seven make the transition to the stage of concrete operations, when they can grasp logical principles but only in concrete terms. At around the age of 12 years, European children progress to the fourth and final stage of formal operations, when they become able to think logically in terms of general principles divorced from concrete examples. A number of studies have found that the ability to understand the concepts measured in Piagetian tasks is highly correlated with IQs measured by standard intelligence tests (Jensen, 1980).

The method adopted by those who have examined the Piagetian intelligence of Australian Aborigine children is to ascertain whether they reach the stages of cognitive development at the same ages as European children. These studies have generally examined the ages at which Aboriginal children attain the concrete operational and formal operational stages of thinking. The concrete operational stage has most frequently been measured by tests of whether a child has acquired the concept of "conservation." This is the understanding of the principle that the volume and weight of a substance remain the same (i.e., are "conserved") when its shape changes. The standard test of the ability to understand the principle of the conservation of quantity is that the tester pours water or some other substance (such as beads) from a glass tumbler into a long thin glass. The child is asked whether the amount of water (or other substance) remains the same. Young children typically believe that there is more water in the tall, thin glass, apparently focusing on its greater height and ignoring its lesser width. When children grasp that the volume remains the same, whatever the shape of the container, they have achieved understanding of the concept of conservation.

The first studies of the ability of Australian Aboriginal adults to understand the principle of conservation were carried out by Marion De Lemos (1969, 1979). She showed 12 Aboriginal women two glasses of sugar. One was long and thin and was filled with a cup of sugar, while the other was wide and short and was filled with half a cup of sugar. The women were offered a choice between the two glasses, and eight of them chose the wide and short glass with less sugar. She concluded: "According to Piaget's theory this concept is basic to all logical thinking, and this retardation would therefore indicate a lower level of intellectual functioning than is normally achieved in European culture (1979, p.15)." The lack of understanding of the principle of conservation among two thirds of these adult women suggests they are at about the same mental level as White eight-year-olds. This indicates that they would have had an IQ of about 50. De Lemos (1969) also found that mixed-race Aboriginals (i.e. Aboriginal-White hybrids) performed better on the test of conservation than pure Aborigines, although not as well as Whites.

In the second study, De Lemos (1969) gave Piagetian conservation tasks to 38 pure Aboriginal children and to 34 who had approximately one eighth European ancestry. She described the environment in which they lived as follows: "There were no apparent differences in the present environment of part-Aboriginal and full-Aboriginal children . . . who formed a single integrated community and the children were brought up under the same mission conditions and attended the same school (p. 257)." The part-Aboriginal children scored significantly higher on the tasks than the pure Aboriginals, but it is not possible to quantify the results as IQs. De Lemos concluded that, as the two groups were living in the same environment, only a genetic hypothesis could explain the difference.

A study by Pierre Dasen (1973) produced similar results. He gave Piagetian conservation tasks to two samples of 55 and 90 Aboriginal children and adults in central Australia and to 80 White children in Canberra. All the Aboriginal children were attending schools. The White children had reached this stage at an average age of eight, while the Aboriginal children reached it at about the age of 15. Twenty-three percent of the Aboriginal adults attained the stage that is attained by European children at an average age of about seven to eight years. Dasen (1973, p. 92) concluded, "[A] large proportion of Aborigines do not develop these concrete operational concepts at all, even as adults." The results indicate that the Aborigines had an IQ of around 55. In a further component of the study, Dasen compared about 30 full-blooded and 30 part-Aboriginal children. He found the part-Aboriginal performed slightly but not significantly better than the pure Aborigines.

A further study of the attainment of the Piagetian concept of conservation by Australian Aboriginal children has been carried out by Gavin Seagrim and Robin Lendon (1980). They found that 10 percent of seven- to eight-year-olds, 35 percent of nine- to ten-year-olds, and 70 percent of 12-year-olds grasped the concept. Thus, 12-year-old Aborigines are at about the same mental level as seven- to eight-year-old White children. This would give them an IQ of approximately 60.

Piaget concluded on the basis of his work on Swiss children that everyone except the mentally retarded attains all the stages of cognitive development by the time they are adults. The studies of Australian Aborigines have shown that this is incorrect and that many of humans never reach the last stage of logical thought.

These studies showing retarded development of Piagetian intelligence provide further confirmation of the low intelligence of the Australian Aborigines.

4. SPATIAL MEMORY OF AUSTRALIAN ABORIGINES

A remarkable study by Judith Kearins (1981) found that Aboriginal children had much stronger spatial memory than Europeans. In this study, 132 Aboriginal children, aged seven to 16, and the same number of White Australian children, were given various tests of spatial memory. In these tests, 20 objects were laid out before the child, and he was asked to look at them for 30 seconds and try to remember their positions. The objects were then removed, and the child was asked to re-assemble them in the same positions. In all the tasks, Aboriginal children performed better than Whites. Their overall advantage is represented by a Spatial Memory IQ of 119. Kearins argued that the most probable explanation for this high spatial-memory ability is that it evolved in the Aborigines because the deserts of central Australia have few landmarks; the nomadic Aboriginal peoples needed to note and remember the country, by such landmarks as exist, to construct mental spatial maps of their environments to find their way home after going out on hunting expeditions. In support of this argument, she tested a sample of Aborigines living in a town whose families had been there for several generations. This group performed just as well on spatial memory as those from the desert. She argued that this indicated that the environment is not responsible for the high spatial-memory ability of the Aborigines and supported her view that it has an evolved genetic basis.

Kearins's results have, however, been challenged. Betty Drinkwater (1976) compared 22 Aboriginal and 22 White 12-year-olds on similar tasks and found the two groups performed at the same level, but his Aborigines came from a coastal area where the strong spatial memory required, according to Kearins's theory, would not have been necessary and would not have evolved. Nevertheless, considering the low general intelligence of Aboriginals, it is remarkable that they should have performed as well as Whites on spatial memory. Stephen Harris (1977), in his unpublished Ph.D. thesis, found that desert Aborigines performed worse than Whites on this task. P.A. Knapp and Gavin Seagrim (1981) also found that desert Aborigines performed worse than Whites, but unfortunately they did not present the data in such a way that the magnitude of the White advantage can be calculated.

Despite these negative results, Kearins's findings on the Aboriginal spatial memory remain impressive and deserve further research by Australian psychologists. The strong spatial memory of the Aborigines, if it can be confirmed, has a parallel in the strong visual memory of the Eskimos reported by Judith Kleinfeld (1971) and explained as an adaptation to living in the frozen tundra, which contains few landmarks and is similar in this regard to the deserts of Australia (see Chapter 11).

5. BRAIN SIZE OF AUSTRALIAN ABORIGINES

Seven studies of the brain size of Australian Aborigines compared with Europeans are summarized in Table 8.4. Row 1 gives Morton's figures, refined by Gould (1996). All the studies show smaller brain size in Australian Aborigines than in Europeans. These results are corroborated by a study of 281 Aboriginal primary school children aged 6–11 by Edwards and Craddock (1973), which found their average head circumference was at the 10th percentile of Whites in the United States and Australia. As discussed above, head circumference is an approximation for brain size. And since brain size is a significant determinant of intelligence (Vernon et al., 2000), the smaller average brain size of the Aborigines can be regarded as partly responsible for their lower IQ. Joerg Klekamp, Agnes Riedel, Clive Harper, and Hans-Joachim Kretschmann (1987) have reported that Australian Aborigines have a larger right visual cortex than Europeans. The right hemisphere deals with spatial abilities and the left hemisphere with verbal abilities, so the relatively larger right hemisphere of Aborigines is consistent with their good spatial memory found by Kearins (1981), summarized in Section 4, and for which she has proposed the theory that Aborigines have evolved a relatively larger right brain and visual cortex in order to solve the visual and spatial problems encountered by nomadic peoples in a featureless desert environment.

Table 8.4. Brain size (cc) of Australian Aborigines and Europeans (sample sizes in parentheses)

	EUROPEANS	ABORIGINES	DIFFERENCE	REFERENCE
1	1,426	1,229 (8)	197	Morton, 1849
2	-	1,217 (325)	-	Morant, 1927
3	-	1,198 (109)	-	Wagner, 1937
4	-	1,206 (29)	-	Klekamp et al.,1987
5	1,369	1,225	144	Smith & Beals,1990
6	1,319	1,240	79	Jurgens et al.,1990
7	-	1,178 (73)	-	Freedman et al.,1991

6. GENOTYPIC INTELLIGENCE OF AUSTRALIAN ABORIGINES

That there is some genetic component to the low intelligence of the Australian Aborigines is indicated by eight lines of evidence.

First, the most satisfactory method for assessing the extent to which genetic factors are involved in the low intelligence of the Aborigines would be a cross-racial adoption study in which Aboriginal infants are adopted by White families. Environmental theory predicts they will have the same average IQ as Whites, whereas genetic theory predicts their IQ will remain the same as that of other Aborigines. If their average IQ is intermediate between that of Aborigines and Whites, it can be inferred that both genetic and environmental factors are involved. The only study of this kind that has been carried out is by

173

Pierre Dasen, Philip de Lacey, and Gavin Seagrim (1973); it concerned 35 Aboriginal children adopted by White couples in and around Adelaide. Seventeen of these children were half Aborigine, and the remainder included seven full-blooded, two three-quarter, four one-quarter, one one-eighth, and four unknown. On average, they were about half Aborigine. The average age of adoption was 18 months. Between the ages of 5 and 13 years, they were given six tests, of which four were Piagetian, one was the Nixon test of "reclassification," and the other was the Peabody Picture Vocabulary Test. The results are given for the adopted Aborigines, and for comparison groups of Europeans and full-blooded Aborigines in central Australia. None of the test results can be accurately quantified because they are given in graph format. It can be discerned from these that, on two of the Piagetian tests (conservation of quantity and weight), the Aborigines performed about mid-way between Europeans and full-blooded Aborigines. As the adopted Aborigines were half-blooded, this is where genetic theory would expect them to fall, and the results suggest that the adoptive experience had no advantageous effect. On the third test (conservation of horizontality), the adopted Aborigines performed somewhat below the European comparison group but substantially better than the full-blooded Aborigines. On the fourth, fifth, and sixth tests, described as measures of "seriation of lengths," "reclassification" (neither of these terms is explained), and the PPVT, the Aborigines performed about the same as the European comparison group. Thus, though the performance of these adopted part-Aboriginal children varied on the different tests, as a whole, they scored below European children.

This is consistent with the authors' observation that "the majority of the children were reported, by their parents, to be below average in school work; most were reported to experience particular difficulty in mathematics (p. 98)." Whereas these adopted part-Aborigines performed at a lower level than Europeans, they seem to have performed somewhat better than part-Aborigines reared by their biological parents. The results therefore suggest that both genetic and environmental factors are responsible for the low intelligence of Aborigines. It should be noted that the average age of the children when they were tested was about eight years. The American study by Weinberg, Scarr, and Waldman (1992) of Black children adopted by

White parents found that at the age of seven years, the adoptees had an average IQ of 95, but by the age of 17, this had deteriorated to 89. This finding demonstrates that young Black children secure IQ gains from adoption, but these fade by late adolescence (see Chapter 4).

Second, the median IQ of Aborigines obtained from the 16 studies summarized in Table 8.1 is 62, while the median IQ of the four studies of Aboriginal-European hybrids summarized in Table 8.2 is 78. The higher IQ of the hybrids is consistent with the genetic hypothesis of the low Aboriginal IQ, which predicts that the IQ of the hybrids should be intermediate between the IQs of the two parent races. However, it may be that the hybrids enjoyed better living standards, and their higher IQ can be explained environmentally.

Third, all the Aboriginal children in the studies listed in Tables 8.1 and 8.2 attended schools, and in three of the studies (rows 6, 7, and 9 in Table 8.1), the Aboriginal children attended schools with White children, so their low IQs cannot be attributed to lack of opportunity to acquire the mental skills tested in intelligence tests or to radically different environments.

Fourth, the low IQs of Aborigines are present in children aged four (Table 8.1, rows 11 and 17), confirming that they cannot be attributed to inadequate schooling.

Fifth, the low IQs of Aborigines appear in a wide range of abilities including reasoning, verbal comprehension, vocabulary, spatial ability (measured by the Porteus Mazes), and Piagetian conservation tasks, showing that their low IQs cannot be explained by bias of any particular test.

Sixth, there is no tendency for the IQs of Aborigines to increase over the period of approximately half a century from the first two studies carried out around 1930, which produced IQs of 66 and 59, and the last two studies carried in the 1980s and 1990s, which produced IQs of 60 and 61 (see Table 8.1), despite improvements in the environmental conditions of Aborigines arising from increased welfare and medical attention.

Seventh, if the intelligence of some Aborigines is impaired by adverse environmental conditions, the most probable factor is likely to be poor nutrition. The prevalence of malnutrition among Aborigines has been investigated in two studies. In the first, a study of 82 preschool Aboriginal children in New South Wales, L.D. Edwards (1970) found that 31 percent were malnourished and, in a subsequent study of 281 Aboriginal children, that 21 percent were malnourished (Edwards and Craddock, 1973). Malnourishment in infancy has an adverse effect on intelligence, but these two studies taken together found that only approximately 25 percent of Aborigines are affected. Edwards and L.J. Craddock (1973) administered an intelligence test to 29 malnourished and 29 well-nourished Aboriginal children aged six to 10 years and found that the malnourished children had a mean IQ eight IQ points lower than the well-nourished. As approximately 25 percent of Aborigines are malnourished, the effect of malnutrition on the total Aboriginal population would be to reduce the IQ by about two points. This suggests that inadequate nutrition has only a negligible effect on the low IQ of Aborigines.

Eighth, the low brain size of Aborigines is a major neurological and genetic determinant of their low intelligence. Brain size affects intelligence and is significantly heritable. Brain size can be reduced by malnutrition, but as only about 25 percent of Aborigines are malnourished, their average brain size must be largely genetically based.

7. INTELLIGENCE OF NEW GUINEANSA

The Aborigines of New Guinea inhabit the interior highlands, into which they were pushed by Melanesian Pacific Islanders and Southeast Asians from Indonesia during the last 3,000 years or so. Today the population consists of the Aboriginals, Pacific Islanders, Southeast Asians, and hybrids. Generally, researchers do not describe to which of these groups their samples belong, and thus racial identity has to be inferred by location. There have been two studies of the intelligence of the Aborigines of New Guinea assessed by intelligence tests. The first, reported by Donald McElwain and George Kearney (1970), is of 26 men aged 20–29 tested with the nonverbal Queensland Test; it found an IQ of 65, compared with White Australians. The second, reported by John Berry (1971), was for a sample of 70 adults tested with the Colored Progressive Matrices. Their score was well below the first percentile of British adults, and their IQ can be estimated at approximately 62, the same as that of Australian Aborigines.

There have been three studies of the Piagetian intelligence of the New Guinean Aborigines. The first of these was carried out by J.R. Prince (1968) on a large sample of 2,700 school students and teacher-training college students. He concluded that the New Guineans "show the expected pattern of Piagetian stages, though conservation is not achieved until much later than in Western European culture." Even the college students showed "significantly poorer development in all test items requiring the concept of conservation (p. 64)." Whereas the principle of conservation is understood by approximately 85 percent of European eight-year-olds and by virtually all 12-year-olds, conservation of substance was understood by 22 percent of New Guinean eight-year-olds and 85 percent of 18-year-olds; conservation of area was understood by no eight-year-olds and 50 percent of 18-year-olds. These results suggest that the 18-year-old New Guinean Aborigines have a European mental age of about eight years, equivalent to an IQ of approximately 50.

A second study of 432 children and adolescents aged six to 19 and with a mean age of 11 years was carried out by Max Kelly (1977). The results were that 31 percent of them had attained the concept of the conservation of quantity; none attained the stage of formal operations. Because approximately 70 percent of European children attain the concept of conservation by the age of seven years, and all, except the mentally retarded, attain the stage of formal operations by the age of 12 years, the finding that 31 percent of the New Guinean sample achieved the stage of concrete operations at the age of seven, and that none of them attained the stage of formal operations, indicates that their average IQ was about 55. In this study, the New Guineans were divided into those at school and those not at school. Among the males, there was no difference between these two groups, suggesting that the late development of an understanding of the concept of conservation is not attributable to a lack of education.

Among the females, those at school performed better, but this was not necessarily an effect of schooling. The more intelligent were selected for schooling, and the two groups came from different tribes in different locations. The author comments: "the result for males is in keeping with Piaget's often repeated statement that the structures which he describes are not affected to any material extent by school (Kelly, 1977, p. 183)."

Kelly summarizes another study by Jones, which studied high-school students and university students, aged 16 to 19 years, who had been selected by competitive examination for secondary school and college and had had at least nine years of schooling; of these, 67 percent were able to do the conservation tasks. The remaining 33 percent were therefore below the mental age of the average European seven-year-old. The results suggest that the group as a whole had about the mental age of European 10-year-olds, and therefore an IQ of approximately 63. The five results are reasonably consistent with a median IQ of 63, almost exactly the same as the 62 of the Australian Aborigines.

8. CONCLUSIONS

The results of intelligence testing of the Australian Aborigines confirm the observations of anthropologists of the late 19th century and first half of the 20th, who described the Aborigines as having poor mental abilities and considered them to be a primitive survival of a stone-age people. Staniland Wake (1835-1910) (1872, p. 80) wrote that "the Australian aborigines are still but children in their general mental development." In the first decade of the 20th century, Klaatsch (1908, p. 164) published the first of a number of studies showing that the Aboriginal brain is smaller than that of Europeans and concluded that "the Australian Aborigines are a relic of the oldest type of mankind." Some years later the anthropologist Sir Arthur Keith (1866-1955) (1922, p. xi) wrote that the Australian Aborigines "represent the original stock from which the three great modern races—the Negroids, Europeans and the Mongoloids—have developed."

The second half of the 20th century witnessed a stark reversal in opinion. Anthropologists came to assert that the Aborigines are just as intelligent as Europeans. Thus, A.P.E. (1960, p. 714), writing in the *Encyclopaedia Britannica*, described the stone-age culture of the Aborigines, but went on to assert,

> [T]his material poverty was not the result of low intelligence but of the conditions of existence. The brain size of the Aborigines falls within the European range and there is no evidence to suggest that this is not true of their intelligence.

The use of the phrase "falls within the European range" for the brain size of Aborigines suggests that the author was well aware that their average brain size falls at the low end of the European range, but was apparently anxious to gloss this over. The assertion that the Aborigines are as intelligent as Europeans is probably attributable to sheer ignorance.

Jared Diamond goes even further in his book *Guns, Germs, and Steel*, which achieved widespread notoriety over the past 15 years. He begins by describing how when he was working in New Guinea, a tribesman named Yali asked him: "Why is it that you white people developed so much cargo and brought it to New Guinea, but we Black people have little cargo of our own?" ("Cargo," in the lingo of New Guinea, means goods.) Diamond says that he wrote his book to answer this question. He contends that the answer does not lie in differences in the intelligence of different peoples and that the "New Guineans impressed me as being on average more intelligent than the average European or American." Diamond cites not empirical evidence for this remarkable claim.

1. Intelligence of Indigenous Northeast Asians

2. Northeast Asians in the United States

3. Further Studies of Northeast Asians Outside Northeast Asia

4. Northeast Asians Adopted by Europeans

5. Northeast Asian-European Hybrids

6. Reaction Times of Northeast Asians

7. Visual Memory of Northeast Asians

8. Brain Size of Northeast Asians

9. The Heritability of Intelligence in Northeast Asians

10. Environmental and Genetic Explanations of the Intelligence of Northeast Asians

CHAPTER 10

NORTHEAST ASIANS

THE NORTHEAST ASIANS are the indigenous peoples of present day China, Japan, Korea, and Mongolia. Tibetans are a mixed-race people with South Asian and Northeast Asian ancestry. In classical anthropology, these groups were described as Mongoloids and were recognized as one of the major races from the first taxonomies of Linnaeus (1758) and Blumenbach (1776), and are one of the seven major races in the classification proposed by Coon, Garn, and Birdsell (1950). Their identity as a genetic "cluster" has been confirmed by Cavalli-Sforza, Menozzi, and Piazza (1994), based on a number of genetic markers taken from samples of Samoyeds, Mongols, Tibetans, Koreans, and Japanese. The most distinctive features of Northeast Asians are their straight black hair, flat nose, yellowish skin color, and the epicanthic eyefold that gives their eyes a narrow appearance.

1. INTELLIGENCE OF INDIGENOUS NORTHEAST ASIANS

Studies of the intelligence of indigenous Northeast Asians have been made in China, Japan, Hong Kong, South Korea, Taiwan, and also in Singapore, where ethnic Chinese make up 74.2 percent of the population. The results of these studies are summarized in Table 10.1.

Table 10.1. IQs of Indigenous Northeast Asians

	COUNTRY	AGE	N	TEST	IQ	VER	VIS	REFERENCE
1	China	6/16	660	WISC-R	107	-	-	Li et al., 1990
2	China	6/15	5,108	SPM	101	-	-	Lynn, 1991c
3	China	14/15	297	Various	103	-	-	Li et al., 1996
4	China	6/12	269	SPM	104	-	-	Geary et al., 1997
5	China	4	60	Arith	109	-	-	Ginsburg et al., 1997
6	China	6/13	463	DAM	103	-	-	Cox et al., 1998
7	China	6/8	160	SPM	107	-	-	Goa et al., 1998
8	China	17	218	SPM	103	-	-	Geary et al., 1999
9	China	19	218	SPM	113	-	-	Geary et al., 1999
10	China	6/8	300	BTBC-R	107	-	-	Zhou & Boehm, 2001
11	China	5	53	Arith	113	-	-	Siegler & Mau, 2008
12	China	8/15	-	EDUC	111	-	-	Meisenberg & Lynn, 2011
13	Hong Kong	9/11	1,007	CCT	105	-	-	Godman, 1964
14	Hong Kong	16	5,209	AH4	106	-	-	Vernon, 1982
15	Hong Kong	10	1,000	SPM	109	-	-	Chan & Vernon, 1988
16	Hong Kong	6/13	13,822	SPM	103	-	-	Lynn et al., 1988b
17	Hong Kong	6/15	4,500	SPM	110	-	-	Lynn et al., 1988b
18	Hong Kong	10	197	SPM	108	92	114	Lynn et al., 1988b
19	Hong Kong	9	376	CCF	104	-	-	Lynn et al., 1988a
20	Hong Kong	9	479	SPM	122	-	-	Chan et al., 1991
21	Hong Kong	15	341	APM	120	-	-	Lynn & Chan, 2003
22	Hong Kong	15	-	Math	105	-	-	Weiss, 2007
23	Hong Kong	8/15	-	EDUC	104.4	-	-	Meisenberg & Lynn, 2011
24	Japan	5/15	1,070	WISC	102	-	102	Lynn, 1977a
25	Japan	35	316	WAIS	102	-	-	Lynn, 1977a
26	Japan	5/10	760	MFFT	107	-	-	Salkind et al., 1978
27	Japan	10	212	Kyoto	106	-	-	Lynn & Dziobon, 1980
28	Japan	8/11	97	WRAT	108	108	-	Tarnopol, 1980
29	Japan	9	223	CEFT	112	-	112	Bagley et al., 1983

	COUNTRY	AGE	N	TEST	IQ	VER	VIS	REFERENCE
30	Japan	4/9	347	CMMS	107	-	-	Misawa et al., 1984
31	Japan	6/11	480	Various	105	99	111	Stevenson et al., 1985
32	Japan	6/16	1,100	WISC-R	103	100	104	Lynn & Hampson, 1986a
33	Japan	4/6	600	WPPSI	105	97	109	Lynn & Hampson, 1987
34	Japan	14	2,100	Kyoto	104	103	107	Lynn et al., 1987a
35	Japan	13/15	178	DAT	104	-	114	Lynn et al., 1987b
36	Japan	2/8	548	McCart	103	102	105	Ishikuma et al., 1988
37	Japan	6/12	142	K-ABC	101	99	103	Kaufman et al., 1989
38	Japan	16	175	A/MR/M	113	-	-	Mann et al., 1990
39	Japan	9	444	SPM	110	121	-	Shigehisa & Lynn, 1991
40	Japan	5/7	454	CCAT	109	121	109	Takeuchi & Scott, 1992
41	Japan	6/12	451	MAT	106	-	-	Tamoaka et al., 1993
42	Japan	14/15	239	Various	103	100	-	Li et al., 1996
43	Japan	6/17	93	Gen Info	105	-	102	Chen et al., 1996
44	Japan	19	72	GMRT	102	-	-	Flaherty, 1997
45	Japan	7/11	60	DAM	102	105	-	Cox et al., 2001
46	Japan	17	1,119	Gen Info	105	105	-	Evans et al., 2002
47	Japan	8/15	-	EDUC	104.4	-	-	Meisenberg & Lynn, 2011
48	Japan	18/22	60	MRT	-	-	110	Sakamoto & Spiers, 2014
49	Macau	8/15	-	EDUC	101.2	-	-	Meisenberg & Lynn, 2011
50	Mongolia	5/14	4,694	SPM	100	-	-	Lynn, 2007a
51	Singapore	13	147	SPM	107	-	-	Lynn, 1977b
52	Singapore	15	459	APM	114	-	-	Lim, 1994
53	Singapore	8/15	-	EDUC	107.5	-	-	Meisenberg & Lynn, 2011
54	Singapore	11	662	SPM	114	-	-	Pancheco et al., 2012
55	S Korea	2/12	440	KABC	113	106	120	Moon, 1988
56	S Korea	9	107	SPM	109	98	111	Lynn & Song, 1994
57	S Korea	4	56	Number	103	-	-	Ginsburg et al., 1997

	COUNTRY	AGE	N	TEST	IQ	VER	VIS	REFERENCE
58	S Korea	6/16	2,231	WISC-3	100	98	102	Georgas et al., 2003
59	S Korea	5/10	598	CPM	108	-	-	Raven, 2008
60	S Korea	8/15	-	EDUC	105.3	-	-	Meisenberg & Lynn, 2011
61	Taiwan	16	1,290	CF	103	-	-	Rodd, 1959
62	Taiwan	6/8	1,865	CPM	102	-	-	Hsu, 1971
63	Taiwan	9/10	1,384	SPM	110	-	-	Hsu et al., 1973
64	Taiwan	6/7	43,825	CPM	105	-	-	Hsu, 1976
65	Taiwan	8/11	193	WRAT	107	107	-	Tarnopol, 1980
66	Taiwan	611	480	Various	104	100	-	Stevenson et al., 1985
67	Taiwan	11	50	V/R/S	106	100	110	Vernon, 1987
68	Taiwan	6/8	764	CPM	105	-	-	Rabinowitz et al., 1991
69	Taiwan	6/11	169	Info	100	100	-	Chen et al., 1996
70	Taiwan	9/12	2,476	CPM	105	-	-	Lynn, 1997
71	Taiwan	6/15	118	SPM	105	-	-	Lai et al., 2001
72	Taiwan	17	1,469	Info	107	107	-	Evans et al., 2002
73	Taiwan	6/17	6,290	SPM	109	-	-	Lynn et al., 2011a
74	Taiwan	8/15	-	EDUC	105.3	-	-	Meisenberg & Lynn, 2011
75	Tibet	12/17	80	SPM	92	-	-	Lynn, 2008

Rows 1 to 10 give results for the People's Republic of China. Row 1 gives an IQ of 107 from a standardization of the WISC-R in Shanghai. This figure is probably a little high for China, because the IQ in Shanghai is likely to be higher than in China as a whole. An IQ of 101 for several reasoning tests for 14- and 15-year-olds, obtained in the mid-1990s, is found in Row 2. An IQ of 103 (Row 3) was calculated from a standardization of the Standard Progressive Matrices in China for the age range from 6 to 15. Row 4 gives an IQ of 104 for 12- and 18-year-olds in Shanghai, compared with Americans in Missouri and Georgia. On 10 arithmetic tests of computation and arithmetical reasoning, the Chinese scored higher by an average of 1.37d, the equivalent of 20 IQ points. This study also reports a comparison of the performance of elderly Chinese (N=56, age=66) and Americans (N=47, age=70), in which the Chinese obtained a lower mean IQ than the Americans by eight IQ points. No information is given on how representative the sampling was, and the result is not considered sufficiently reliable for entry in the table. Row 5 gives an IQ of 109 for a test of arithmetical reasoning for a sample of four-year-old pre-school children in Beijing, compared with a sample of 156 American children. In Row 6, an IQ of 103 for a drawing test of a person and a horse resembling the Draw-a-Man test is listed; the Chinese children were at school in Beijing and were compared with a sample of 489 British children. Row 7 gives an IQ of 107 for a combined sample of urban and rural children, while Row 8 shows an IQ of 103 for a sample of 17-year-olds at high school in Shanghai, compared with a sample of 55 American high-school students in Columbia, Missouri. An IQ of 113 (Row 9) was found for a sample of college students at the East China Normal University in Shanghai, compared with a sample of 239 American college students at the University of Missouri. Finally, in Row 10, we have an IQ of 107 for a sample of seven- to eight-year-olds at school in Beijing. Row 11 gives an IQ of 113 obtained on an unfamiliar arithmetic test by kindergarten children, compared with a carefully matched group in the United States. These results show that the higher IQs of Northeast Asians cannot be attributed to superior schooling (as it often is).

Eleven results for Hong Kong are listed in rows 13 through 23. Row 13 gives an IQ of 105 obtained from the Culture Fair Test for a representative sample of Chinese 9-to-11-year-olds attending five primary schools. An IQ of 106 obtained for a large sample of 16-year-olds on the AH4 test is listed in Row 14. There are no satisfactory British norms for this age for this test, so the comparison group is a sample of Canadian 16-year-olds (MacLean and McGhie, 1980). Rows 15 through 17 give IQs of 109, 103, and 110 obtained from the Standard Progressive Matrices. The results for 10-year-olds, in which reasoning ability was measured with the SPM, spatial ability with the space relations test from the Primary Mental Abilities Test, and verbal ability by word fluency are found in Row 18. This study shows an exaggerated version of the typical East Asian pattern of high reasoning IQ (108), higher spatial IQ (114), and weaker verbal IQ (92). Row 19 gives an IQ of 104 obtained from the Culture Fair Test. In Row 20, we find the unusually high IQ of 122 for a sample of 9-year-olds; while in Row 21, a closely similar IQ of 120 for the Advanced Progressive Matrices Hong Kong standardization sample, which appears to have been exceptionally well drawn. Row 22 gives an IQ of 105 for a math test taken as a proxy for IQ, and, finally, in Row 23, an IQ of 100.4 for EDUC.

Rows 24 through 48 list IQs for 23 studies in Japan. Row 24 gives a Japanese IQ of 102, calculated from the Japanese standardization sample of the WISC and based on five performance tests and digit span (the remaining verbal tests were altered in the Japanese version of the test and therefore not used); the visualization IQ of 102 is calculated from the block design and mazes subtests. Row 25 gives a Japanese IQ of 102, calculated from the standardization sample of the WAIS and based on digit symbol, block design, and digit span, the only tests that were unaltered in the Japanese version of the test. A Japanese IQ of 107 for 5- to 10-year-olds on the MFFT, calculated from error scores compared with an American sample numbering 2,676, is found in Row 26; Row 27 gives a Japanese IQ of 106 for 10-year-olds, obtained on the Japanese Kyoto Test compared with British children. An IQ of 108 for a sample of children in Hiroshima for the arithmetic subtest of the WRAT is found in Row 28. Row 29 gives an IQ of 112 for Japanese children in Nagoya and Hamamatsu; and in Row 30, an IQ of 107 was obtained from the Japanese standardization sample of the Columbia Mental Maturity Scale.

Row 31 gives results of the study by Harold Stevenson and his colleagues that compared 6- and 11-year-olds of samples drawn from the cities of Minneapolis in the United States, Sendai in Japan, and Taipei in Taiwan. While Sendai and Taipei may be acceptable as broadly representative of urban children in Japan and Taiwan, the same cannot be said of Minneapolis. Minneapolis is the principal city in Minnesota, and there is considerable evidence that the intelligence level is higher in Minnesota than in the United States as a whole. In the military draft in World War I, Whites from Minnesota obtained the highest score on the Army Beta Test of all American states (Montagu, 1945b). In the military draft for the Korean War, the percentage found unacceptable for military service in Minnesota on account of low intelligence was the second lowest among the American states (Jensen, 1973, p.107), indicative of a high average intelligence level.

In the NAEP (National Assessment of Educational Progress) math test of eighth grade students in 2003, Minnesota achieved the highest score of all the American states (National Center for Education Statistics, 2003). James Flynn (1980, p. 107) has calculated that the mean IQ of Whites in Minnesota is 105. This is accepted as the best estimate. Hence for a comparison with an American White IQ of 100, five IQ points need to be added to the samples from Japan and Taiwan, giving them an IQ of 105, consistent with the results of numerous other studies. In this study, note again the low verbal (99) / high visual abilities (111) typical of the Northeast Asian peoples.

Row 32 gives a general (full-scale) IQ of 103, derived from the Japanese standardization samples of the WISC-R, a verbal IQ of 100 based on the five verbal subtests, and a visualization IQ of 104 based on the block design subtest. The following row, Row 33, lists a general (full-scale) IQ of 105, derived from the Japanese standardization sample of the WPPSI, a verbal IQ of 97 based on five verbal subtests, and a visualization IQ of 109 based on four performance subtests.

IQs of 104 for reasoning, 103 for verbal, and 107 for visualization ability, obtained from the administration of the Kyoto Test to a representative sample of British children, are listed in Row 34; the three IQs have been averaged to give a general IQ of 104. IQs of 104 for reasoning and 114 for visualization ability, obtained from the administration of the DAT to a sample of Japanese 13- to 15-year-olds, are found in Row 35. Row 36 gives a general IQ of 103, as well as IQs of 102 for "sequential processing" (approximately equivalent to verbal ability) and 105 for "simultaneous processing" (approximately equivalent to visualization ability), calculated from the Japanese standardization sample of the McCarthy Test. An IQ of 101, derived from Alan Kaufman et al.'s (1989) analyses of the Japanese WISC-R standardization sample for Kaufman's sequential and simultaneous factors is found in Row 37. "Sequential processing" (verbal ability) correlated 0.44 with the Wechsler verbal IQ, and "simultaneous processing" (visualization ability) correlated 0.73 with the Wechsler performance IQ. The two IQs are averaged. In addition, the test contains a matrix-analogies test similar to the Progressive Matrices, the results of which are entered in the table under reasoning.

Row 38 gives an IQ of 113 for a sample of adolescents at school in Keio, compared with 121 American students in school in Florida; the verbal IQ of 116 is calculated from a test of arithmetic and the visualization IQ of 110 from tests of mental rotation and mazes. An IQ of 110 for a sample of 9-year-old children in Tokyo is found in Row 39. Row 40 compares Japanese children in the city of Nagoya with Canadian norms on the Canadian Cognitive Abilities Test (CCAT). The mean Japanese reasoning IQ of 109 is typical of a number of other studies, but the Japanese verbal IQ of 121 is an unusually high figure for Japanese children. This study also found a quantitative IQ of 112 for Japanese children. The children's age range was five to seven years, and the advantage of the Japanese five-year-olds was as great as that of the six- to seven-year-olds. The five-year-olds were at kindergarten. The high IQs obtained by Japanese five-year-olds makes it improbable that the Japanese advantage can be an effect of more efficient schooling, as proposed by Stevenson et al. (1985). Row 41 compares Japanese children in the medium-sized city of Matsuyama with American norms on the Matrix Analogies Test. The sample was from predominantly middle class families and obtained an American IQ of 114 and a British IQ of 112. There is typically a 10 IQ point gap between middle-class and working-class children; in order to account for this, the result has been adjusted down to 106. Row 41 gives an IQ of 106 for reasoning, while Row 42, a reasoning IQ of 103.

Row 43 presents a verbal IQ of 100, derived from a general-knowledge test given to 6- and 17-year-olds in the Japanese city of Sendai, compared with the American city of Minneapolis. Because the mean IQ of Whites in Minneapolis is estimated at 105 (as explained in the comment on Row 31), the Japanese mean IQ has been raised by five points. A visualization IQ of 102, obtained by comparing a sample of Japanese high-school and university students with a sample of 52 European students at University College Dublin, is found in Row 44. Row 45 lists an IQ of 102 obtained for Japanese seven and 11-year-olds, compared with a matched sample of 60 British children. A verbal IQ of 105 derived from a general knowledge test comparing Japanese 17-year-olds with Americans in Minneapolis is found in Row 46; the Japanese mean has been raised by five (5) IQ points for the reason given in the comment on Row 31. Finally, Row

47 gives an EDUC IQ of 104.4 and Row 48 gives a relatively high verbal IQ of 110 in a recent study from 2014.

Moving on to other regions of East Asia, Row 49 presents an EDUC IQ of 101.2 for Macau. Row 50 gives an IQ of 100 for Mongolia, obtained from two studies comparing the IQs of Mongolians living in the same communities and in closely similar environments as Han Chinese in Xinjiang and Inner Mongolia. The lower IQ of the Mongolians is expected, because Mongolians are a mixed-race people of Han Chinese and Arctic peoples. This has been shown by Cavalli-Sforza, Menozzi, and Piazza (1994, p. 78) in their genetic analysis of samples of world populations; specifically, they demonstrate that Mongolians are related to the Japanese, Koreans, and the Northern Chinese (genetic distance = .05), and, more distantly, to the Inuit (Eskimos) (genetic distance = .108). The Inuit have a mean IQ of 91 (see Chapter 11), so we should expect that the IQ of the Mongolians would be in a range between 91 and 105, i.e., intermediate between that of the East Asians and the Inuit, the two peoples to which Mongolians are most closely related. The genetic distance between the Mongolians and the Northeast Asians is approximately half that between the Mongolians and the Inuit (.05 compared with .108). Thus, we should expect that the Mongolians' average IQ would be on the higher end of that 91-105 range. Using this reasoning, the mean IQ of the Mongolians would be expected to be around 100, five IQ points lower than that of the Northeast Asians and nine IQ points higher than their more distant relatives, the Inuit. Rows 51 through 53 give four results for Singapore. An IQ of 107 for an early study of 13-year-olds obtained from the APM is found in Row 51, while Row 52 gives an IQ of 114 for 15-year-olds obtained from the SPM, Row 53, an EDUC IQ of 107.5, and Row 54, an SPM IQ of 114.

Rows 55 through 60 give six results for South Korea. Row 55 lists an IQ of 113 derived from the standardization sample of the Kaufman K-ABC test, an exceptionally well-constructed and standardized American test. This study shows the typical Northeast Asian pattern of high reasoning IQ (113—obtained from a matrix analogies test), high visual-spatial IQ (120), and weaker verbal IQ (106). An IQ of 109 and a similar pattern of lower verbal (98) than visual-spatial ability (111) is found in Row 56. In the following study (Row 57), we find an IQ of 103 for a socially representative sample of four-year-olds at pre-school in the region of Busan, compared with 156 American children. Row 58 gives an IQ of 100 based on the standardization sample of WISC-III and is one of very few studies finding that Northeast Asian IQ is the same as that of Europeans. Finally, we find an IQ of 108 based on the CPM in Row 59. Row 60 gives an EDUC IQ of 105.3.

Rows 61 through 74 give 14 results for Taiwan. An IQ of 103 obtained from an early result in the 1950s for Han Chinese (indigenous Taiwanese obtained an IQ of 101) is found in Row 61. Rows 62, 63, and 64 give IQs of 102, 110, and 105, which were achieved by primary school children. In Row 65, we find an IQ of 107 for a sample of children in Taipei for the arithmetic subtest of the WRAT. Row 66 lists an IQ of 104, obtained from a comparison of Taiwanese children with an American sample in Minneapolis, where, as explained in the comment on Row 31, the mean IQ of Whites is estimated at 105); the Taiwanese mean has thus been raised by five IQ points. An IQ of 106 for six- to eight-year-old primary school children in Taipei and country towns and villages is found in Row 67, again showing the familiar pattern of lower verbal (100) than visual-spatial ability (110). Row 68 gives a CPM IQ of 105, and Row 69, an IQ of 100 for a general information or knowledge test given to samples from the United States (N=1,052) and Taipei in Taiwan. General knowledge is a component of verbal intelligence, as shown in numerous factor analyses of the Wechsler tests (see also Carroll, 1993), explaining why the IQ is only 100 on this test. Rows 70 and 71 list IQs of 105 for nonverbal reasoning. An IQ of 107 for a general knowledge test given to samples in the United States (N=1,052) and Taipei is found in Row 72. The Taiwanese sample scored two IQ points higher than the American, but the American sample was taken from the city of Minneapolis where the mean IQ of Whites is estimated at 105 (as explained in the comment on Row 31), so the Taiwanese mean has been raised by five IQ points to 107. Row 73 gives an SPM IQ of 109. Finally, in Row 74, we find an EDUC IQ of 105.3.

Row 75 gives an IQ of 92 for Tibet. This is derived from

a study comparing the IQs of Tibetan and Han Chinese junior secondary-school students in Tibet. The Han Chinese scored 12.6 IQ points higher than the Tibetans. The IQ of the Han Chinese is 105, so this gives the Tibetans an IQ of 92.4. This IQ is substantially lower than any of the other IQs for Northeast Asians. The explanation for this is that the Tibetans are a mixed-race people of Northeast Asian Mongoloids and South Asians, as would be expected from their geographical position between the Mongoloid Chinese to the east and the South Asian peoples of Bhutan, Nepal, India, and Burma to the south. They have been described by Sonia Cole (1963) as a "mixture between the archaic white stock and fully evolved Mongoloids"; Cole notes further that "the Tibetan face is narrower than that of the Classic Mongoloid and is less padded with fat, while the nose is typically prominent, resembling that of the American Indians." More recently, the population geneticists Cavalli-Sforza, Menozzi, and Piazza (1994, pp. 206, 231) have written that "the Tibetans were originally nomadic pastoralists who came from the North..." and that subsequently they "have received contributions to their ethnic background from various neighbors to the southwest, southeast, and north." Consistent with this origin and subsequent admixture, Cavalli-Sforza, Menozzi, and Piazza found that, in their genetic analysis of samples of world populations, the Tibetans are genetically most closely related to the Bhutanese to the south, and they also have genetic affinities with Koreans and Japanese and with the Balti peoples of North Pakistan. Language similarities also indicate admixture of Tibetans with South Asians. The Tibetan language most closely resembles Burmese (Kapstein, 2006, p.19), and the Balti peoples of North Pakistan speak a Tibetan language (Cavalli-Sforza, Menozzi, and Piazza, 1994, pp.78, 225, 231). It appears from these genetic linkage analyses and language similarities that there must have been some interbreeding between Tibetans and their southern neighbors in Bhutan and North Pakistan. This has produced a racially mixed population of Mongoloid and South Asian ancestry.

From this anthropological and genetic evidence of their racially mixed heritage, Tibetans would be expected to have an intelligence level intermediate between the Mongoloids (Northeast

Asians) and the South Asians. The Mongoloids have an IQ of 105 while the Indians to the south have an IQ of 82 (see Chapter 6). Hence, we should expect the IQ of 92 obtained by Tibetans.

Two conclusions can be drawn from the studies summarized in Table 10.1. The first is that virtually all the Northeast Asian IQs are a little higher than those of Europeans. The median IQ of the studies is 105 and should be taken as the best estimate of the IQs of indigenous Northeast Asians. Second, many of the studies contain measures of verbal and visual-spatial abilities and show that Northeast Asians' verbal IQ is substantially lower than their visual-spatial IQ as compared with Europeans. This difference appears in a variety of tests and is so consistently present and is so large that it appears to be a real phenomenon.

2. NORTHEAST ASIANS IN THE UNITED STATES

Northeast Asians have settled in a number of countries around the world, including the United States, Canada, Europe, Brazil, and Malaysia. By far the greatest number of studies of the intelligence of Northeast Asians outside East Asia has been made in the United States. These have been summarized and discussed by Philip Vernon (1982) and James Flynn (1991). Vernon concluded that Americans of Northeast Asian ancestry have a verbal IQ of 97 and a nonverbal IQ of 110 (p. 28). His analysis is flawed on two accounts. First, there is no generally accepted meaning of "nonverbal" intelligence. This imprecise concept could refer to a variety of abilities, including abstract reasoning, visualization, and spatial perception. Second, Vernon took no account of the secular increase of test norms—the effect being that groups tested with a test normed at some earlier date have inflated IQs. Flynn's analysis is better in so far as he adjusts IQs for secular increases in norms, but he also analyzes intelligence in terms of verbal and "nonverbal" IQs and averages these to produce an "overall IQ." Flynn's conclusions are that ethnic Chinese and Japanese in America have a verbal IQ of 95.3 and a "nonverbal IQ" of 99.6; he averages these to give an "overall IQ" of 97.6. This is not a satisfactory analysis because, again, "nonverbal IQ" is today not accepted as a meaningful concept. Furthermore, Flynn's use of the two concepts of verbal and nonverbal intelligence gives verbal ability the same weight as all other abilities in calculating general intelligence; since Northeast Asians are relatively weak in verbal ability, this spuriously reduces their IQ. General intelligence (or *g*) is best measured either from a test of nonverbal reasoning or from the average of verbal, reasoning, and visualization abilities. Despite this conceptual weakness, Flynn has performed a useful literature review and analysis, and in general I have adopted his estimates in the summary that follows.

There is a problem with the studies of ethnic Northeast Asians in the United States and elsewhere in that many of the individuals sampled have continued to speak Japanese, Chinese, or Korean as their first language and have consequently performed poorly on verbal tests in English. In many cases it is impossible to tell the extent of this handicap.

Studies of ethnic Northeast Asians in the United States are summarized in Table 10.2.

Table 10.2. IQs of Northeast Asians in the United States

	LOCATION	ETHNICITY	AGE	N	TEST	IQ	VER	VIS	REFERENCE
1	California	Chinese	6/12	97	Binet	97	-	-	Yeung, 1922
2	Hawaii	Chinese	9/13	513	Pintner	99	95	-	Symonds, 1924
3	National	NE Asian	6/8	67	DAM	101	-	-	Goodenough, 1926b
4	Hawaii	Mixed	12	408	PM	100	-	-	Porteus & Babcock, 1926
5	Hawaii	Mixed	7/12	770	PM	103	-	-	Porteus, 1930
6	Honolulu	Chinese	10/14	2704	NV	99	-	-	Smith, 1942
7	Honolulu	Japanese	10/14	3312	NV	101	-	-	Smith, 1942
8	Honolulu	Korean	10/14	509	NV	102	-	-	Smith, 1942
9	National	Japanese	18	669	OSUT	96	96	-	Portenier, 1947
10	New York	Chinese	6	80	Hunter	103	97	106	Lesser et al., 1965
11	National	NE Asian	6/17	4994	Various	100	97	-	Coleman, 1966

	LOCATION	ETHNICITY	AGE	N	TEST	IQ	VER	VIS	REFERENCE
12	Hawaii	NE Asian	16	554	SCAT	96	96	-	Stewart et al., 1967
13	Kauai	Japanese	9/10	253	PMA	98	97	95	Werner et al., 1968
14	Los Angeles	NE Asian	17	390	Various	99	95	-	Flaughter, 1971
15	California	Chinese	11/15	90	Maps	103	-	103	Feldman, 1971
16	National	NE Asian	6/11	32	WISC	101	101	102	United States, 1971
17	National	NE Asian	18	150	Various	98	99	-	Backman, 1972
18	California	Chinese	9	53	WISC	101	91	101	Yee & La Forge, 1974
19	California	Chinese	6/11	478	Various	101	-	-	Jensen & Inouye, 1980
20	National	NE Asian	-	929	Various	99	-	-	Sowell, 1986
21	Hawaii	Japanese	16	4,024	STAS	107	-	-	Brandon et al., 1987
22	California	Chinese	6/11	254	Lorge-T	101	89	-	Flynn, 1991
23	California	NE Asian	10/12	234	Lorge-T	110	-	106	Flynn, 1991
24	California	Chinese	10	155	SPM	104	-	-	Jensen & Whang, 1994
25	National	E Asian	14/22	42	AFQT	103	-	-	Herrnstein & Murray, 1994
26	National	Asian	6/17	48	DAB	104	100	105	Lynn, 1996
27	National	E Asian	7	63	WISC	109	-	-	Rushton, 1997
28	National	Asian	5/17	77	UNIT	107	-	105	Kane, 2007
29	National	Asian	3/8	18	PTI	107	-	-	Lynn, 2006a
30	National	E Asian	5/9	40	DAM	114	-	-	Huntsinger et al., 2011

Row 1 gives an IQ of 97 for Chinese children in San Francisco. They were tested with the Binet test, which is largely verbal, and this probably handicapped the children, as a number of them likely spoke English as a second language. In Row 2, we find a nonverbal reasoning IQ of 99 and a word knowledge IQ of 95 for Chinese children in Hawaii. Row 3 lists an IQ of 101 for Chinese and Japanese obtained in the standardization sample of the Draw-a-Man test. IQs of 100 and 103 for Chinese and Japanese in Hawaii tested with the Porteus Mazes are found in Rows 4 and 5. Rows 6, 7, and 8 give IQs of 99, 101, and 102 for nonverbal reasoning for ethnic Chinese, Japanese, and Koreans in Honolulu compared with Whites in the same location. The Chinese, Japanese, and Koreans scored substantially lower than Whites on verbal tests (89, 86, and 88). It is impossible to determine how far the low verbal IQs of the Chinese, Japanese, and Koreans were due to their speaking their own languages at home and consequently being handicapped on verbal tests in English, and how far they were due to the typical East Asian pattern of weaker verbal than reasoning abilities. Probably both factors were involved. James Flynn calculated a verbal IQ of 96 for Japanese 18-year-olds interned during World War II (Row 9) (1991); 91 percent of the sample were second-generation immigrants and 8 percent third-generation immigrants. As with the Honolulu study, it is uncertain what percentage of these would have spoken Japanese in the home as their first language and hence were handicapped on verbal tests in English. Row 10 lists a verbal IQ of 97 and a visualization IQ of 106 for a sample of ethnic Chinese six-year-olds in New York. It is not certain whether some of these children spoke Chinese at home and were therefore handicapped on the verbal test. It is assumed that half of them were, and hence the verbal IQ is given only half the weight of the visualization IQ, yielding an estimate of their general intelligence to be 103.

In Row 11, we find IQs of 100 for reasoning and 97 for verbal ability for ethnic Chinese, Japanese, and Koreans from the nationwide Coleman study, calculated by Flynn. The reasoning IQ is adopted as the figure for g. Row 12 gives a verbal IQ of 96 for ethnic Chinese and Japanese in Hawaii, again calculated by Flynn. Results for Japanese children on the island Kauai in the Hawaiian archipelago are found in Row 13. The mean IQs were verbal, 107; spatial, 105; reasoning, 112; perception, 105; and number, 106. Flynn (1991) estimates that the norms of the test were obsolescent by 33 years and therefore that 10 points need to be deducted from the IQs. He arrives at a verbal IQ of 97 and a nonverbal IQ of 99, calculated as the average of the remaining four tests; this yields an overall IQ of 98. The results are unusual in showing a relatively low IQ of 95 for spatial (visualization) IQ. In Row 14, Flynn calculates an IQ of 99 and a verbal IQ of 95 for 17-year-olds in Los Angeles in 1969–1970. In Row 15, we find an IQ of 103 for ethnic Chinese in San Francisco matched for socioeconomic status to Whites tested with a map-understanding test described as a measure of spatial reasoning. (In the same study Blacks also matched with Whites for socioeconomic status obtained an IQ of 90.)

Row 16 gives IQs of 101 for vocabulary and 102 for block design tests measured by the WISC in a nationwide survey and averaged to 101 for g (this study was missed by Flynn in his survey). Flynn did calculate a nonverbal reasoning IQ of 98 and a verbal IQ of 99, derived from tests of information and English language obtained from a nationwide survey; these are found in Row 17. The higher verbal than reasoning IQ is unusual, and so contrary to the usual Northeast Asian higher reasoning than verbal pattern, that the result may be unreliable. Row 18 lists a WISC performance nonverbal IQ of 101 and a WISC verbal IQ of 91 for a small sample of nine-year-olds in San Francisco's Chinatown, calculated by Flynn (1991). The children attended Chinese private schools, and their low verbal IQ is probably attributable to many of the children speaking Chinese both at school and at home. The performance IQ is therefore adopted as the best measure of their general intelligence. Row 19 gives an IQ of 101 for a Chinese sample in California.

An IQ of 99 from various studies collected by Thomas Sowell and synthesized by Flynn is found in Row 20. The tests administered were not identified and are entered as measures of g. Row 21 gives an IQ of 107 obtained from the test of mathematical skills for a large sample of Japanese adolescents in Hawaii compared with a sample of 3,722 Europeans also living there.

Row 22 gives an IQ of 101 for Chinese children in California, collected by Jensen in 1975 and analyzed by Flynn. Half the children were foreign born, coming mainly from Hong Kong, which probably accounts for their low verbal IQ of 89. Row 23 lists results from an affluent district in Berkeley, California, again collected by Jensen and calculated by Flynn. The Chinese, Japanese and White children all scored quite high. The figures entered in the table are Flynn's estimates for the Northeast Asian children scored against national norms. In relation to White children (N=1,506) in the same district, the Northeast Asian children obtained IQs of 98 for reasoning and

95 for verbal IQ. The sample is not representative or satisfactory. In Row 24, we find results for a Californian Chinese sample, while in Row 25, an IQ of 103 for a small but nationally representative sample of adolescents. Row 26 lists an IQ of 104 for Asian-Americans from the standardization sample of the Differential Ability Scale. The 1980 American census showed that approximately half of American Asians are Northeast Asians, consisting of ethnic Chinese, Japanese, Koreans, and some Vietnamese. The remainder are mainly Filipinos, Vietnamese, Thais, Cambodians, and other Southeast Asians. Southeast Asians have IQs below Europeans, so the results shown in the table understate the intelligence of American Northeast Asians. An IQ of 109 for Northeast Asians obtained from the National Collaborative Perinatal Project collected in approximately 1966 is given in Row 27. Row 28 lists an IQ of 107 obtained by Asians on the standardization sample of the 1998 nonverbal UNIT test.

Row 29 gives an IQ of 107 for Asians, again including Southeast Asians, obtained in the standardization sample of French's (2001) Pictorial Test of Intelligence. An IQ of 114 for 40 Chinese American and 40 matched European American children aged 5.6 years—all from well-educated, two-parent middle-class families, who were recruited from pre-schools and kindergarten and tested using the Goodenough (1926) Draw-a-Man test—is found in Row 30. The Chinese American scored 12.5 IQ points higher than the European American children. The children were tested again at the age of nine years, when the Chinese American scored 14.9 IQ points higher than the European American children.

The median IQ of the nine studies in the first half of the 20th century is 101 and is thus a little lower than the median of 105.5 of the eight studies obtained from 1987 onwards (which is almost exactly the same as the 105 of indigenous Northeast Asians). There are three possible explanations for the increase in the intelligence of Northeast Asians in the United States during the 20th century. The first is that many of those in the early studies spoke Chinese or Japanese as their first language and would have been handicapped on tests in English. Second, there may have been a tendency for the Northeast Asians who migrated to the United States to have been a little below the average intelligence of those who remained in Northeast Asia. The Chinese and Japanese who emigrated to the United States in the second half of the 19th century were largely peasants who came to do unskilled work on the construction of the railways and similar projects. This would probably not seem an attractive option for the more intelligent, who would generally have been doing sufficiently well in their own countries. Once these early migrants had settled in the United States, their children would have shown some regression upwards towards the Northeast Asian mean of 105. Third, five of the studies contain measures of verbal and visualization abilities; in four of these, the visualization IQ is greater than the verbal IQ (the study in Row 13 is the exception). The mean difference between the two abilities is 4.4 IQ points and is present in studies using a variety of tests. This confirms the pattern found in the samples of indigenous Northeast Asians given in Table 10.1. This significant difference may affect the assessment of general IQ.

3. FURTHER STUDIES OF NORTHEAST ASIANS OUTSIDE NORTHEAST ASIA

Studies of the intelligence of Northeast Asians in locations outside Northeast Asia and the United States are summarized in Table 10.3.

Row 1 gives an IQ of 99 for ethnic Japanese in Brazil. An IQ of 107 for Japanese children in London is listed in Row 2; the actual IQ of this sample was 115, but as the children's parents were largely businessmen, diplomats, and professional people of various kinds, their IQs were unusually high. There are typically about 15 IQ points between the top and bottom socioeconomic classes (e.g. Nettle, 2003), so the IQ of average Japanese children should be about 107. Row 3 gives a verbal reasoning IQ of Chinese children in London. In Rows 4 and 5, we find IQs of 104 and 95 for early studies of Japanese and Chinese in Vancouver. According to Philip Vernon (1982), the Chinese immigrants were of poor peasant stock, whereas the Japanese were from the skilled working class and middle class, and this explains why the Japanese performed better. Row 7 gives an IQ of 101 for a later study of Chinese in Vancouver, while Rows 7 and 8 list results of two further studies of Chinese in Canada with IQs of 101 and 103. In Row 9, we have IQs of ethnic Chinese university students in Canada; note that their visualization IQ is eight points higher than their verbal IQ. Row 10 lists an IQ of 99 for ethnic Chinese in Malaysia and is 10 IQ points higher than that of Malays (see Table 7.1). The reason the IQ of the ethnic Chinese in Malaysia is a little lower than that of other Northeast Asians in Northeast Asia may be that they are relatively recent immigrants, recruited to do unskilled work, and these immigrants may have been a little below the Chinese average. A numerical reasoning IQ of 102 for the children of Chinese immigrants in the Netherlands is found in Row 11. On verbal comprehension their IQ was 85, but since they spoke Chinese as their first language, this cannot be regarded as valid assessment of intelligence. The median IQ of the studies is 101, exactly the same as that of Northeast Asians in the United States. Finally, Row 12 show an IQ of 103 for Northeast Asian university students in South Africa, compared with 100 for European students.

Table 10.3. Further Studies of Northeast Asians Outside Northeast Asia

	COUNTRY	ETHNICITY	AGE	N	TEST	IQ	VER	VIS	REFERENCE
1	Brazil	Japanese	10	186	SPM	99	-	-	Fernandez, 2001
2	Britain	Japanese	9	42	CEFT	107	-	107	Bagley et al.,1983
3	Britain	Chinese	11	626	VR	103	-	-	Lynn, 2008
4	Canada	Japanese	12	274	Pintner	104	-		Sandiford & Kerr, 1926
5	Canada	Chinese	12	224	Pintner	95	-	-	Sandiford & Kerr, 1926
6	Canada	Chinese	8	40	WISC	101	97	105	Peters & Ellis, 1970
7	Canada	Chinese	8	85	WISC	101	99	103	Kline & Lee, 1972
8	Canada	Chinese	15	182	Various	103	97	106	Vernon,1984
9	Canada	Chinese	20	73	MAB	118	113	121	Rushton, 1992b
10	Malaysia	Chinese	12	1,459	SPM	99	-	-	Chaim,1994
11	Netherlands	Chinese	11	150	CITO	102	85	-	Pieke,1988
12	S. Africa	Chinese	22	23	SPM	103			Rushton, 2008

Some conclusions can be drawn from the studies of Northeast Asians summarized in Table 10.3. First, their average IQs are a little higher than those of Europeans in similar environments. In Brazil, the IQ of 99 of ethnic Japanese is four IQ points higher than that of Europeans (see Table 3.2). The ancestors of these Japanese were recruited to work as agricultural laborers in the late 19th century, and these immigrants may have had IQs below the national average. In addition, their IQ and the IQ of 95 of Europeans in Brazil (see Table 3.2) are both slightly depressed, probably partly because of the low living standards in Brazil. The median IQ of the four Canadian studies is 101. The median IQ of all the studies in the United States is 101. This is slightly higher than Flynn's estimate of 97.6, because Flynn omits the studies by Symonds (1924), Goodenough (1926b), Feldman (1971), the United States (1971), and the four last studies published after his analysis. Thus, the IQ of Northeast Asians in the United States is a little lower than the 105 of Northeast Asians in their own native habitats in Northeast Asia. There are four possible reasons for this.

The first is that those who migrated to the United States could have had average IQs slightly lower than those who remained in Asia. This is possible because the Northeast Asians in the United States (and elsewhere) are the descendants of immigrants who migrated to take unskilled jobs and may well have been a little below the average intelligence of the populations from which they came.

The second is that many of the Chinese and Japanese spoke Chinese and Japanese as their first language, and this would have handicapped their performance in some of the tests.

Third, it may take two generations for immigrants from impoverished countries to overcome the effects of poor nutrition and reach their full potential. The mean IQ of the last six studies in Table 10.2, published from 1990 onwards, is 105, the same as that of Northeast Asians in Northeast Asia.

Fourth, three of the studies contain measures of verbal and visualization abilities, and in all of these, the visualization IQ is greater than the verbal IQ. The mean difference between the two abilities is seven IQ points. This confirms the low verbal–high visualization pattern of abilities found in Northeast Asia and the United States. A further study finding this ability pattern has been reported by Rushton

(1992a) in a sample of university students in Canada; East Asian students had a mean verbal IQ of 112.8 and a mean performance (mainly visualization) IQ of 120.6, while European students had a mean verbal IQ of 117.7 and a mean performance IQ of 118.8.

4. NORTHEAST ASIANS ADOPTED BY EUROPEANS

There have been six studies of the intelligence of Northeast Asian infants adopted by European families in Europe and the United States. These are summarized in Table 10.4.

Table 10.4. IQs of Northeast Asian Children Adopted by Europeans

	COUNTRY	ETHNICITY	AGE	N	TEST	IQ	VER	VIS	REFERENCE
1	USA	Korean	14-Jun	37	Various	102	-	-	Winick et al., 1975
2	USA	Korean	14-Jun	38	Various	106	-	-	Winick et al., 1975
3	USA	Korean	14-Jun	37	Various	112	-	-	Winick et al., 1975
4	USA	Various	3/4	25	PPVT	115	115	-	Clark & Hanisee, 1982
5	Belgium	Korean	10	19	WISC	110	104	111	Frydman & Lynn, 1989
6	Netherlands	Korean	7	36	RACIT	108	-	-	Stams et al., 2000

Rows 1 through 3 give IQs of Korean children reared by White American adoptive parents. The sample was divided into three groups consisting of those who had been severely undernourished as infants (Row 1), those who were poorly nourished (Row 2), and those who were well nourished (Row 3). The IQs of the three groups were related to their nutritional history. The severely undernourished group did not score significantly differently from American Whites, but the other two groups scored higher. No details are given of the intelligence tests used to measure the IQs, which were obtained from school records and probably inflated by obsolete norms. Row 4 shows a verbal IQ of 115 for 25 largely Northeast Asians, consisting of 12 from Vietnam (largely ethnic Chinese), 10 from Korea, three from

Cambodia, and two from Thailand.

In Rows 5 and 6 we find the results of similar studies in Europe. Row 5 gives an IQ of 110 for Korean children adopted as infants in Belgium and shows the profile of higher visualization than verbal ability characteristic of Northeast Asians. Row 6 gives an IQ of 108 for 36 Korean children who were adopted by Dutch families in the Netherlands.

The mean of the six studies is an IQ of 109, and if the two first studies of malnourished infants are excluded, the mean is 111. One reason for this high figure is probably that these were young children adopted by largely middle-class families. It is known from the Weinberg, Scarr, and Waldman (1992) study that middle-class adoptive parents boost the IQs of their adopted children in early and middle childhood, but the effect fades away in late adolescence and adulthood. In this study, Black infants adopted by White middle-class parents obtained a mean IQ of 95 at age seven, but this fell to 89 at age 17; this result indicates that being reared in White middle-class families boosts the childhood IQ by six IQ points (Levin, 1994; Lynn, 1994c). Applying this result to the IQ of 112 of adequately nourished adopted Northeast Asian children suggests that by adulthood their IQ would have declined by six IQ points, bringing it down to 106, virtually the same as that of Northeast Asians in Northeast Asia and of the most recent studies of Northeast Asians in the United States.

The results for the adopted children in Belgium given in Row 5 show once again the low verbal–high visualization ability pattern of Northeast Asians present in Northeast Asia, the United States, and elsewhere. This racial pattern has been found so consistently in such a variety of locations that it appears to be genetic in origin.

5. NORTHEAST ASIAN-EUROPEAN HYBRIDS

In Chapter 4, we saw considerable evidence that the intelligence of sub-Saharan African-European hybrids is intermediate between that of sub-Saharan Africans and Europeans. It would thus be expected that the intelligence of Northeast Asian-

European hybrids would likewise be intermediate between that of the two parent races. The only study on this issue was done by J.P. Rushton (1997), in an analysis of the data of the American National Collaborative Perinatal Project. This consists of a study of 53,043 infants for whom information of various kinds was collected at birth, in infancy, and at the age of seven; IQ data were collected, measured by the WISC, as well as head circumference. The IQs and brain size of Northeast Asians, Northeast Asian-European hybrids (of the 37 cases, five were Black, but these were not disaggregated), Europeans, and African-Americans at age seven are shown in Table 10.5. Row 1 gives the numbers of children. In Row 2, the mean IQs as reported are presented. Row 3 shows the IQs adjusted for the secular increase of test norms from 1949, the year of the standardization of the WISC, to 1966, the median year of the collection of the data; this requires the deduction of five points from the reported IQs. Finally, Row 4 gives the brain size in cubic centimeters estimated from head circumference. Notice that for all three measures, the Northeast Asian-European hybrids fall intermediate between the Northeast Asians and the Europeans. The fact that they fall closer to the Europeans is bot surprising since five of the cases were Northeast Asian-African hybrids.

Table 10.5. IQs and Brain Size (cc) of Northeast Asian-European Hybrids

		NORTHEAST ASIAN	HYBRID	EUROPEAN	AFRICAN
1	Number	63	37	17,432	19,419
2	IQ-Raw	114	103	102	90
3	IQ-Adjusted	109	98	97	85
4	Brain size	1,170	1,155	1,150	1,134

6. REACTION TIMES OF NORTHEAST ASIANS

Reaction times consist of the speed of reaction to a simple

stimulus, such as the onset of a light. Many studies have shown that reaction times are positively related to intelligence at a magnitude of around 0.2 to 0.3 (see Jensen, 1998, and Deary, 2000); Arthur Jensen (1998) has argued that reaction times are a measure of the neurological efficiency of the brain in processing information. We saw in Chapter 4 that Africans have slower reaction times than Europeans, which is consistent with their lower IQ. We consider now whether Northeast Asians have faster reaction times than Europeans, which would be consistent with their higher IQs.

Three studies of this issue are summarized in Table 10.6.

Table 10.6. Differences Between Northeast Asians and Europeans in Reaction Times

	SAMPLE	N	AGE	IQ	IQD	RTD	REFERENCE
1	Japanese	444	9	110	0.66	0.5	Lynn & Shigehisa, 1991
2	Chinese	479	9	122	1.33	0.96	Chan et al., 1991
3	Chinese	155	11	106	0.4	0.25	Jensen & Whang, 1993

In all three studies, the reaction times (RT) shown are the average of three reaction-time tasks, consisting of simple reaction times (the speed of reaction to the onset of a single light), choice reaction times (the response to one of eight lights), and odd-man reaction times (three lights appear in an array, and the correct response is to switch off the one furthest from the other two). Row 1 compares Japanese and British 9-year-olds. The IQ of the Japanese children was 110 or 0.66d higher than that of the British children, while their reaction times were 0.50d higher than those of British children. Row 2 gives results for a similarly designed study comparing Chinese children in Hong Kong with White British children. The IQ of the Chinese children was 122 or 1.33d higher than that of the British children, while their reaction times were 0.96d higher than those of British children. Finally, Row 3 shows the results for a further study of ethnic Chinese children in California compared with 77 European children. The Chinese scored six IQ points or 0.40d higher than the White children on intelligence and 0.25d higher on the average of the three reaction time tests. The results of all three studies show that the magnitude of the advantage of Northeast Asian children in reaction times, potentially representing the neurological efficiency of the brain in simple information processing, is about two thirds of their advantage in intelligence. These studies also reported differences in reaction-time variability and in movement times; these were of approximately the same magnitude as those of the reaction times. Jensen provides a more detailed description and discussion of these studies in his book *The g Factor*. David Geary et al. (1997) have also reported faster reaction times and higher IQs in Chinese as compared with American children, but they do not give standard deviations, so the difference cannot be expressed as a *d*.

7. VISUAL MEMORY OF NORTHEAST ASIANS

Visual memory is not normally assessed in intelligence tests. There have been four studies of the visual memory of the Japanese, the results of which are summarized in Table 10.7.

Table 10.7. Differences Between Northeast Asians and Europeans in Visual Memory

	N	AGE	TEST	IQ	REFERENCE
1	760	5–10	MFFT	107	Salkind et al., 1978
2	48	23	Vis. Mem	105	Flaherty & Connolly, 1996
3	72	19	Vis. Mem	110	Flaherty, 1997
4	316	16–74	Vis. Repr.	113	Sugishita & Omura, 2001

Row 1 gives a Japanese IQ of 107 for five- to 10-year-olds on the MFFT, calculated from error scores compared with an American sample numbering 2,676. The MFFT consists of the presentation of drawings of a series of objects, e.g., a boat, hen, etc., that have to be matched to an identical drawing among several that are closely similar. The task entails the memorization of the details of the drawings in order to find the perfect match. Performance on the task correlates 0.38 with the performance scale of the WISC (Plomin and Buss, 1973), so that it is a weak test of visualization ability and general intelligence as well as a test of visual memory. Row 2 shows a visual memory IQ of 105 for ethnic Japanese-Americans, compared with American Whites, on two tests of visual memory; they consist of the presentation of 20 objects for 25 seconds (which are then removed); the task was to remember and rearrange their positions. In Row 3, we have a visual memory IQ of 110, obtained by comparing a sample of Japanese high-school and university students with a sample of 52 European students at University College, Dublin. In Row 4, we find a visual memory IQ of 113, for the visual reproduction subtests of the Wechsler Memory Scale-Revised, obtained from the Japanese standardization of the test compared with the American standardization sample. The test involves the drawing from memory of geometric designs presented for 10 seconds. The authors suggest that the explanation for the Japanese superiority may be that Japanese children learn *kanji*, the Japanese idiographic script, and this develops visual-memory capacity. This hypothesis was apparently disproved by a study by Mary Flaherty and Martin Connolly (1996), whose results are shown in Row 2. Some of the ethnic Japanese-American participants had a knowledge of *kanji*, while others did not; there was no difference in visual memory between those who knew and those who did not know *kanji*, disproving this essentially environmentalist theory.

8. BRAIN SIZE OF NORTHEAST ASIANS

Studies of differences in brain size between Northeast Asians and Europeans are summarized in Table 10.8. The means and standard deviations are for brain volume in cubic centimeters. Row 1 gives the results calculated by Stephen Jay Gould (1981) from the collection of skulls assembled in the early 19th century by the American physician Samuel Morton (1849), who categorized them by race and calculated their average cranial capacities. Gould accused Morton of mistakes and re-measured the skulls, proving to his own satisfaction that the Northeast Asians and Europeans had the same brain size. However, the number of skulls was very low, consisting of 10 Northeast Asians and 52 Europeans, and is so few that little weight can be attached to it. They are given here only for historical interest. Row 2 shows results from the largest collection of skulls ever collected, numbering approximately 20,000, and shows that the Northeast Asians had a larger brain size than the Europeans by 1.2d (standard deviation units). In Row 3, we find a difference of 20cc from a study of American seven-year-old children carried out by Sarah Broman, Paul Nichols, Peter Shaughnessy, and Wallace Kennedy (1987). The brain sizes have been calculated from their data by Rushton (1997). Row 4 gives the results of data assembled by Hans Jurgens, Ivar Aune, and Ursula Pieper (1990) for many thousands of 25- to 45-year-olds. The figures in the table have been adjusted for body size by Rushton (2000). Row 5 gives the results of a data set assembled by Colin Groves (1991) by combining estimates of cranial capacities of 36 samples of males from figures given by Carleton Coon, Stephen Molnar, and Rudolph Martin and Karl Saller. The brain sizes are larger than in Row 2 because they are for men, but the European-Northeast Asian difference is similar, though slightly larger. Rushton's results for brain size adjusted for body size for 6,325 United States military personnel are given in Row 6. Finally, Row 7 shows Rushton's summary of a large number of data sets for brain size adjusted for body size. All the studies—except Morton's revised by Gould (Row 1)—have found that the Northeast Asians have a larger average brain size than Europeans.

Table 10.8. Brain Size (cc) Differences of Europeans and Northeast Asians

	EUROPEANS	NORTHEAST ASIANS	DIFFERENCE	REFERENCE
1	1,426	1,426	0	Gould, 1981
2	1,369	1,416	53	Smith & Beals, 1990
3	1,150	1,170	20	Broman et al. 1987
4	1,297	1,308	11	Jurgens et al., 1990
5	1,467	1,531	64	Groves, 1991
6	1,361	1,403	44	Rushton, 1992
7	1,347	1,364	17	Rushton , 2000

9. THE HERITABILITY OF INTELLIGENCE IN NORTHEAST ASIANS

There have been two studies of the heritability of intelligence in Northeast Asians. The first reports correlations of 543 identical and 134 non-identical twin pairs aged 12 years for a composite of 23 tests (Lynn and Hattori, 1990). The correlation was 0.782 for the identical twins and 0.491 for the non-identical twins. Heritability is obtained by doubling the difference between the two correlations, which is 0.582. Corrected for test reliability (assuming a reliability coefficient of 0.9 (Bouchard, 1993)), heritability becomes 0.65. This is about the same as the heritability for Europeans at this age, as shown in Chapter 3, Section 4. The second study reports a heritability of 0.83 for a sample of young adult twins (age 25, N=448 pairs) (Shikishama, Hiraishi, Yamagata, et al., 2009). It is evident that the heritability of intelligence in Europeans and Northeast Asians is approximately the same.

10. ENVIRONMENTAL AND GENETIC EXPLANATIONS OF THE INTELLIGENCE OF NORTHEAST ASIANS

The consistently high IQs obtained by Northeast Asians in their indigenous habitats in Northeast Asia and in Europe and the Americas have presented a problem for environmentalists. These researchers have found it relatively easy to explain the low IQs of sub-Saharan Africans, which they could ascribe to poverty, poor education, test bias, and racism. None of these can explain the lower IQ of Europeans compared with Northeast Asians. Environmentalists have adopted three strategies to deal with this problem. The first is to ignore the evidence. This is the solution adopted in most general textbooks and in specialist books on race and intelligence by Jefferson Fish (2002), Gould (1996), and Ashley Montagu (1999). The second strategy is to dispute or belittle the evidence. Thus, shortly after the first study of the high IQ of the Japanese on the WISC-R was published, Harold Stevenson and Hiroshi Azuma (1983) contended that the Japanese standardization sample under-represented lower IQ groups. Later, as more studies were published confirming the high IQ of the Japanese, it was no longer possible to dispute it, so environmentalists contended that the difference was only small. Thus, Nathan Brody (2000, p. 219) writes of the studies finding that intelligence in Japan is higher than in the United States, "there is little or no evidence that there are large differences in IQ between these groups." He does not specify what he means by "large." The third strategy adopted by environmentalists is to contend that, even if it is conceded that Northeast Asians have higher IQs than Europeans, "there is no evidence to decide whether such differences are environmental or genetic in origin (Mackintosh, 1998, p. 168)."

Contrary to this contention, the studies summarized in this chapter point to a strong genetic determination of the higher IQ of Northeast Asians as compared with Europeans.

First, there is the consistency of the higher IQs of the Northeast Asians than those of the Europeans in so many different locations, including China, Japan, Hong Kong, Singapore, South Korea, and Hong Kong (summarized in Table 10.1).

Second, the high IQs obtained by Northeast Asians in their native lands are in general confirmed by studies of Northeast Asians outside Northeast Asia, summarized in Table 10.2. In the United States, the median IQ of Northeast Asians derived from all the studies is 101, a little lower than the 105 of indigenous Northeast Asians in East Asia. As discussed above, there are two possible reasons for this. The first is that those who migrated to the United States could have had slightly lower than average IQs than those who remained in Asia. The second is that the first and second generations of immigrants generally continue to speak their own languages. and English as a second language. This may handicap them in language tests. The mean IQ of the last six studies in Table 10.2, published from 1990 onwards, is 105, the same as that of Northeast Asians in Northeast Asia.

In Table 10.3 we see that Northeast Asians consistently obtain slightly higher average IQs than Europeans in similar environments. In Brazil, the IQ of 99 of ethnic Japanese is four IQ points higher than that of Europeans (see Table 3.2). (These Japanese were brought into Brazil to work as agricultural laborers after the abolition of slavery in 1888 and are unlikely to have had higher IQs than the general population in Japan.) In Britain, Northeast Asians obtained an IQ of 107, and in the Netherlands, an IQ of 102. In Malaysia, they obtained an IQ of 99, 10 points higher than that of the indigenous Malays.

Third, environmentalists do not offer any explanation for the consistently high IQ of Northeast Asians, and it is doubtful whether any credible environmental explanation could be found. Intelligence is affected by living standards, but the living standards in most of East Asia have been lower than those in Europe. The Northeast Asians in Japan, Hong Kong, and Singapore enjoy comparable living standards to those of Europeans in Northern and Western Europe, the United States, Canada, Australia, and New Zealand; but the living standards of those in China, South Korea, and Taiwan have been much lower— yet their IQs are about five points higher than those of Europeans. The difference is consistently present, and there is no plausible environmental explanation for Northeast Asian superiority.

Fourth, the six studies of the intelligence of Korean infants adopted by European families in Europe and the United States (summarized in Table 10.4) all show that these children have higher IQs than those of the Europeans in whose environment they have been reared. It seems improbable that these infants, who were given up for adoption, were a selective sample with higher than average IQs. It should be noted, however, that these children were quite young and would probably have been adopted largely by middle-class families that would have given them some environmental advantage. Just how large this effect actually was is difficult to assess, but it is unlikely that it can have been as much as the 11 IQ point advantage of the four adequately nourished samples of adopted Northeast Asians. In the Weinberg, Scarr, and Waldman (1992) study (summarized in Section 13 of Chapter 4), it was shown that Black infants adopted by White middle-class families obtained an IQ of 95 at age seven and 89 at age 17, suggesting that the environmental advantage for the seven-year-olds was six IQ points. Applying the same rule of thumb to the adopted Northeast Asian children, the mean IQ of the adequately nourished samples of 111 should be reduced by six points to give a true IQ of 105, precisely the same as that of indigenous Northeast Asians.

Fifth, the faster reaction times of Northeast Asian children shown in Table 10.6 indicate that they have a more efficient neurological processing system, which likely makes a significant contribution to their measurable IQ; again, this superiority in reaction times cannot be plausibly explained environmentally.

Sixth, several studies, which are summarized in Table 10.8, have shown that Northeast Asians have a larger average brain size than Europeans. Brain size is a significant neurological determinant of intelligence, and it has a high heritability.   It is doubtful whether any environmental explanation is possible for the larger brain size of Northeast Asians. It can be estimated that their larger brains should give Northeast Asians a 10 IQ point advantage (see p. 216). This is the IQ advantage that they would be expected to have by virtue of their larger brain size, if they were reared in the same environments as Europeans. As the IQ of Europeans has been estimated as 99, and the IQ of Northeast Asians as 105, the actual IQ difference between them is six IQ points. Two explanations can be offered for the fact that the actual Northeast Asian advantage is greater than what would be predicted. First, some of the larger Northeast Asian brain may be devoted to visual memory, which is not measured in most intelligence tests. (Northeast Asians have displayed a high capacity for visual memory whenever it has been studied.) Second, many of the samples were conceived and reared in poorer environments with lower living standards than those of Europeans, and these may have had some depressing effect on their IQs. If this is so, when the living standards of Northeast Asia become equal to those of Europeans, it can be predicted that the IQ difference will become 10 points and will thus be explicable in terms of brain size.

1. Intelligence of Arctic Peoples

2. Visual Memory of Arctic Peoples

3. Brain Size of Arctic Peoples

4. Genotypic Intelligence of Arctic Peoples

CHAPTER 11

ARCTIC PEOPLES

The Arctic Peoples are the indigenous Inuit (formerly known as Eskimos) of Alaska, the north coast of Canada, and Greenland; the Aleuts of the Aleutian Islands; and the North Turkic and Chukchi peoples of the far northeast of Asia. They are identified as a distinctive genetic "cluster" by Cavalli-Sforza, Menozzi, and Piazza (1994) in their classification of peoples based on a number of genetic markers. The Arctic Peoples differ genetically from the Amerindians in having an appreciable percentage of the B blood group, which is absent in the Amerindians. They differ from the Amerindians and from the East Asians in that they are more highly cold adapted, with shorter legs and arms and a thick trunk to conserve heat, a more pronounced epicanthic eyefold, and a nose flattened into the face to reduce the risk of frostbite. The reason the Arctic Peoples have evolved into a distinctive race is that their ancestors were isolated from the Northeast Asians by the Chersky mountain range in northeast Asia. The Inuit split off from the Chukchi people of northwest Russia when they migrated across the Bering Straits into North America about 11–10,000 BC. Several of their prehistoric sites have been found in the Nenana river valley in Central Alaska, where their artifacts have been dated at between 11,300 to 10,000 years ago (Dixon, 1999). In the mid-20th century, there were approximately 50,000 Inuit and approximately 5,600 Aleutians.

1. INTELLIGENCE OF ARCTIC PEOPLES

Studies of the intelligence of Arctic Peoples are summarized in Table 11.1.

Table 11.1. IQs of Arctic Peoples

	AGE	N	TEST	IQ	VER	VIS	REFERENCE
1	6/11	105	DAM	93	-	-	Eells, 1933
2	8/18	-94	-	80	-	-	Anderson & Eells, 1935
3	6/11	469	DAM	89	-	-	Eells, 1933
4	8/18	389	S. BINET	74	-	-	Anderson & Eells, 1935
5	6/9	174	CPM	94	-	-	MacArthur, 1965
6	10/15	326	SPM	84	-	-	MacArthur, 1965
7	25	122	CPM	78	-	-	Berry, 1966
8	Adults	186	CPMT	93	-	93	Kunce et al., 1967
9	10	87	SPM	91	-	-	MacArthur, 1967
10	11	50	MVK	90	80	88	Vernon, 1969
11	6/12	380	WISC	91	-	91	Kaplan et al., 1973
12	9/12	69	CPM	96	-	-	Taylor & Skanes, 1976a
13	7	22	WPPSI	93	78	93	Taylor & Skanes, 1976b
14	7/10	63	CPM	95	-	-	Taylor & Skanes, 1977
15	7/14	366	WISC-R	91	-	91	Wilgosh et al., 1986
16	5	110	CPM	92	-	-	Wright et al., 1996
17	15	261	CCF/MH	86	77	-	Grigorenko et al., 2004
18	9	29	SPM+	80	-	-	Lynn & Shibaev, 2014

Studies of the intelligence of Arctic Peoples are summarized in Table 11.1. Row 1 gives an IQ of 92 for a sample of Aleutian children also tested with the Goodenough Draw-A-Man (DAM) Test. Row 2 gives an IQ of 80 for a sample of Aleutian tested with the Stanford Binet. These are the only studies of the intelligence of Aleutian children. All the other studies are of Inuit. Row 3 gives an IQ of 89 for the first study of a large sample of Inuit children tested with the DAM. Row 4 gives a lower IQ of 74 for a sample tested with the Stanford Binet. Rows 5 and 6 give results of a study of the IQs of representative samples of primary and secondary Inuit school children in the Yukon and Northwest Territories of Canada tested in 1962. The primary school children obtained an IQ of 94 and the secondary school children an IQ of 84. Row 7 gives a low IQ 78 for a sample of young adults. Row 8 gives Inuit adults a visualization IQ of 93. Row 9 gives an IQ of 91 for 10-year-olds. Row 10 gives an IQ of 90 obtained by Vernon from tests of matrices, vocabulary, and Koh's Blocks. The low IQ of 80 for vocabulary might be spuriously low, as the children might have spoken their native language at home. The IQ of 90 for reasoning has been entered as the most reasonable figure for general intelligence. In this study, Vernon also gave the DAM test, on which the Inuit children obtained an IQ of 95. This is broadly consistent with the results in Rows 1 and 3, in which Arctic children obtained DAM IQs of 89 and 92. Row 11 gives an IQ of 91 for a substantial sample of 6–12-year-olds obtained from the performance scale of the WISC; these children obtained much lower verbal IQs, but they did not speak English as their first language and their low verbal IQs cannot be regarded as valid. Row 12 gives a reasoning IQ of 96 for a sample of 9–12-year-olds. Row 13 gives verbal and performance IQs of 78 and 93, respectively, for a small sample of seven-year-olds tested with the WPPSI. The children spoke English as a second language, so the verbal IQ is spuriously low and the performance IQ of 93 is entered as the best measure of general intelligence. Row 14 gives a reasoning IQ of 95 for a sample of 7-to-10-year-olds. Row 15 gives an IQ of 91 for a substantial sample of 7-to-14-year-olds, obtained from the performance scale of the WISC-R. The verbal scale was not given because the children did not speak English as their first language. Row 16 gives an IQ of 92 for Inuit 5-year-olds living in Arctic Quebec. The authors claim that the Inuit children scored higher than Americans, but this is because American norms were depressed by the inclusion of ethnic minorities, they made no allowance for the secular increase of scores, and the children were given repeated testing at the ages of six and seven, in which they made gains attributable to practice effects. Row 17 gives a non-verbal reasoning IQ of 86 and a vocabulary IQ of 77 for Inuit 15-year-olds in Alaska. Row 18 gives a non-verbal reasoning IQ of 80 Tungus in the northeast or Russia.

The median IQ of the studies is 91 and is proposed as the best estimate of the intelligence of the Arctic Peoples. The visualization IQs are somewhat higher than the verbal IQs, as shown in Vernon's sample given in Row 10, where the visualization IQ is 88 and the verbal IQ 80, and again in the Taylor and Skanes study listed in Row

13, where the visualization IQ is 93 and the verbal IQ 78. Averaging the two results gives us a visualization IQ 11 points higher than the verbal IQ. This low verbal-high visualization pattern is also present in the related East Asian and Amerindian Peoples. It appears that there has been no tendency for the intelligence of Inuit to improve over the period of approximately 60 years, from the early 1930s, when the first study by Walter Eells (1933) found an IQ of 89, to the most recent study in the early 1990s, when Lorraine Wilgosh et al. (1986) found an IQ of 91.

2. VISUAL MEMORY OF ARCTIC PEOPLES

The Inuit have an unusually strong visual memory ability that is not measured in standard intelligence tests. This was shown by Judith Kleinfeld (1971) in a study of the visual memory of 125 Inuit village children in Alaska aged nine to sixteen compared with 501 White children in Anchorage and Fairbanks, the two principal towns in Alaska. The test consisted of the presentation of drawings for a brief period of time, after which the children were given the task of drawing them from memory. The Inuit children obtained a mean IQ of 106 in relation to a White mean of 100. Kleinfeld (p. 133) observes that this test result is consistent with the observations of travelers who have accompanied Inuit on long hunting expeditions. She writes,

> Caucasians who have traveled with the Eskimo frequently remark upon their extraordinary ability to travel through what seems to be a featureless terrain by closely observing the smallest landmarks and memorizing their spatial locations.

The strong visual memory of Inuit may explain why they are relatively good at spelling. In Vernon's (1969) study he found that Inuit ten-year-olds had a spelling IQ of 95, considerably higher than their verbal IQ of 80, of which spelling is generally considered a component (Carroll, 1993). Good visual memory helps spelling because it makes it possible to recall the shapes of words. This is probably why females are much better at spelling than males (Lynn, 1992): they have better visual memories (Halpern, 2000; Kimura, 2002).

It is likely that the strong visual memory of Inuit has a genetic basis. It has been found by Robert Osborne and Anthony Gregor (1966) that visual memory has a high heritability. Even nine-year-old Inuit children had significantly better visual memory than Europeans, and it seems unlikely that children of this young age would have acquired this strong ability through training, even if this is possible. The most probable explanation for the strong visual memory of Inuit children is that this ability developed genetically through natural selection because of the need for Arctic Peoples to remember fine details of the landscape in order to find their way home after going out on long hunting expeditions. The landscape of the frozen tundra provides few distinctive cues, so hunters would need to note and remember such few features as do exist. The strong visual memory of the Inuit is also present in the Northeast Asians (IQ 107) (Chapter 10, Section 7) and Native Americans, for whom Thomas Lombardi (1970) found an IQ of 104, very close to the IQ of 106 found by Kleinfeld for Inuit. Possibly, the ancestral population of Northeast Asia evolved strong visual memory before they diverged into the East Asians, Native Americans, and Arctic Peoples. The strong visual memory of the Inuit has a parallel with that in the Australian Aborigines reported by Kearins (1981) and explained as an adaptation to living in deserts with few landmarks and similar in this regard to the frozen tundra of the Arctic (see Chapter 8).

3. BRAIN SIZE OF ARCTIC PEOPLES

It has only proved possible to find one study of the brain size of Arctic Peoples. Courtland Smith and Kenneth Beals (1990) give brain sizes for 10 populations, of which the mean is 1,444cc. They give a brain size for Europeans of 1,368cc. The difference of 76cc is substantial. Brain size is associated with intelligence among individuals, and the same association would be expected to hold between groups. The larger brain size of the Arctic Peoples leads to the expectation that they would have higher IQs than Europeans, yet this is not the case.

There are two probable explanations for this anomaly. First, some of the large brain size of the Arctic Peoples is likely devoted to their strong visual memory found by Kleinfeld (1971) and summarized in Section 2. Second, brain size is not the sole determinant of intelligence. Some neurophysiological processes for higher intelligence may have evolved in the Europeans as a result of genetic mutations and failed to appear in the Arctic Peoples. The reason for this is probably that the Europeans were much more numerous so that the chances of favorable mutations for greater intelligence were greater.

4. GENOTYPIC INTELLIGENCE OF ARCTIC PEOPLES

It seems probable that both genetic and environmental factors contribute to the low IQ of the Arctic Peoples. There are two lines of evidence suggesting some genetic determination. First, as noted in Section 1, the IQ of the Arctic Peoples has not shown any increase relative to that of Europeans since the early 1930s, although their environment has improved in so far as in the second half of the 20th century, they received improved welfare payments and education. If the intelligence of the Arctic Peoples had been impaired by adverse environmental conditions in the 1930s, it should have increased by the early 1980s. Second, in all the studies summarized in Table 11.1 the Arctic children were at school and thus familiar with test-taking procedures, so there is no reason to suppose that they were handicapped in this regard.

1. Intelligence of Native Americans in North America

2. IQs of Native Americans Assessed by the Draw-a-Man Test

3. Intelligence of Native Americans in Latin America

4. Visual Memory of Native Americans

5. Native American-European Hybrids

6. Musical Ability of Native Americans

7. Brain Size of Native Americans

8. IQs of Hispanics in the United States

9. Genotypic Intelligence of Native Americans

CHAPTER 12

NATIVE AMERICANS

The Native Americans, also known as American Indians, Amerindians, and aboriginal Americans, are the original indigenous peoples of the Americas, whose ancestors migrated from the far northeast of Asia across the Bering Straits into present-day Alaska. They are one of the major races in the taxonomies of the classical anthropologists Linnaeus (1758), Blumenbach (1776), and Coon, Garn, and Birdsell (1950). Cavalli-Sforza, Menozzi, and Piazza (1994) have confirmed that the Native Americans form a genetic "cluster" that differentiates them from other peoples. The most distinctive features of Native Americans, which distinguish them from East Asians, are their darker and sometimes reddish skin, hooked or straight nose, and lack of the complete Northeast Asian epicanthic eyefold (although the inner eyefold is sometimes present). According to the 2010 census, 5.2 million Native Americans or Alaska Natives reside in the United States. Of these, some 2.2 million identify as Native American in combination with another race. One quarter of this population lives on certified reservations. In Central and South America, there are around 52 million indigenous peoples and some 162 million Mestizos, with mixed Native American and European ancestry.

1. INTELLIGENCE OF NATIVE AMERICANS IN NORTH AMERICA

The intelligence of the Native Americans in the United States began to be studied in the 1920s; from the 1960s on, similar studies began to be published for Native Americans in Canada. These are summarized in Table 12.1.

Table 12.1. IQs of Native Americans in North America

	COUNTRY	AGE	N	TEST	IQ	VERB	VIS	REFERENCE
1	USA	6/11	715	Otis	86	-	-	Hunter & Sommermier, 1922
2	USA	9/13	1102	National	69	-	-	Garth, 1925
3	USA	5/9	961	Pinter/Nat	85	-	-	Haught, 1934
4	USA	9/14	1000	Otis	70	-	-	Garth and Smith, 1937
5	USA	6/11	323	McArthur	88	-	-	Havighurst et al., 1944
6	USA	6/13	205	CPM	93	-	-	Turner & Penfold, 1952
7	USA	16	100	WAIS	86	82	91	Howell et al., 1958
8	USA	6/15	281	SPM	85	-	-	West & MacArthur, 1964
9	USA	8/17	4994	-	91	87	-	Coleman, 1966
10	Canada	6/14	124	CF	76	-	-	Gaddes et al., 1968
11	Canada	13	137	SPM	94	-	-	Bowd, 1973
12	Canada	5/11	111	CPM	92	-	-	Cropley & Cardey, 1975
13	USA	6/20	160	WISC	90	70	90	St. John et al., 1976
14	Canada	6/13	177	WISC-R	82	80	85	Seyfort et al., 1980
15	USA	6/13	177	WISC-R	87	-	87	Teeter et al., 1982
16	USA	6/12	236	WISC-R	94	88	100	McShane & Plas, 1984
17	USA	6/16	200	WISC-R	93	-	93	Browne, 1984
18	USA	14	124	SPM	87	-	-	Sidles & MacAvoy, 1987
19	Canada	11	50	R/V/S	87	79	87	Vernon, 1987
20	USA	6/16	1129	SPM	93	-	-	Raven & Court, 1989
21	USA	6/16	240	WISC-R	72	68	78	Reynolds et al., 1999

	COUNTRY	AGE	N	TEST	IQ	VERB	VIS	REFERENCE
22	USA	6/15	691	WISC-R	80	83	89	Beiser & Gotowiec, 2000
23	USA	9	99	WAIS	84	84	-	Tsethlikai, 2011

Row 1 gives an IQ of 86 from the first study of the intelligence of Native Americans in the United States, published in 1922. A nonverbal reasoning IQ of 91, obtained by eight-to17-year-olds in a study by James Coleman, the largest study ever published of the ability of Native American school students, is listed in Row 9. Their verbal IQ was a little lower at 87. The median of the 22 studies is an IQ of 86. The Native Americans obtained higher visualization than verbal abilities in all of the seven studies in which tests of the two abilities were given. The median visualization IQ in these studies is 89, and the median verbal IQ for the studies is 82. The same strong visualization/weak verbal profile of abilities is present among North East Asians (see Chapter 10, Section 1), to whom the Native Americans are genetically closely related.

2. IQS OF NATIVE AMERICANS ASSESSED BY THE DRAW-A-MAN TEST

There have been several studies of the intelligence of Native Americans tested with the Goodenough Draw-a-Man Test (DAM). Because this is a nonverbal test, and hence avoids the problem that some of the Native Americans sampled did not speak English as their first language, it is useful to consider these results separately. The DAM was originally devised by Florence Goodenough (1926a and 1926b) and involves the drawing of a man and a woman. The drawings are scored for the presence of details such as ears, eyebrows, etc. The DAM correlates with other established intelligence tests at a magnitude of around 0.40 to 0.60. For instance, Steven Abell, William Wood, and Samuel Liebman (2001) report correlations on studies of 100 children of the DAM with the WISC-R and WISC-111 of 0.46 and 0.35 for verbal IQ, 0.57 and 0.48 for performance IQ, and 0.54 and 0.45 for full-scale IQ. In a study in which the DAM was given to a sample of 217 10-year-olds, together with a number of other tests of vocabulary, reasoning, spatial, and perceptual abilities, the DAM loaded 0.48 on the first principal component, compared with loadings in the range of 0.58 to 0.70 for the other cognitive tests (Lynn, Wilson, and Gault, 1989). Thus, the DAM is an adequate, though not a strong, measure of g and appears to be more a measure of visualization than of verbal ability. The reason for this is probably that the child has to visualize the human body before drawing it. The results of the studies of the IQs of Native Americans in North America on the DAM are summarized in Table 12.2. The median IQ is 90. This is almost the same as the median visualization IQ of 89.5 for the studies summarized in Table 12.1 and is consistent with the interpretation of the DAM as predominantly a measure of visualization ability.

Table 12.2. IQs of Native Americans on the Draw-a-Man Test

	COUNTRY	AGE	N	IQ	REFERENCE
1	California	6/8	79	86	Goodenough, 1926b
2	N. Dakota	5/11	225	88	Telford, 1932
3	Alaska	6/11	58	91	Eells, 1933
4	Oklahoma	6/8	125	99	Rohrer, 1942
5	N. Mexico	6/8	96	90	Norman & Midkiff, 1955
6	Vancouver	6/14	124	88	Gaddes et al., 1968
7	Canada	11	50	88	Vernon, 1969
8	Canada	5/11	111	99	Cropley & Cardey, 1975

3. INTELLIGENCE OF NATIVE AMERICANS IN LATIN AMERICA

Studies of the intelligence of Native Americans in Latin America are summarized in Table 12.3. Row 1 gives an IQ of 84, obtained on a test of quantitative reasoning for four-year-old children in Colombia described as divided "approximately equally among SES groups" (p. 172). These were compared with 156 American children described as representative of the United

States. The population of Colombia is 75 percent Native American and Mestizo, 20 percent European, and five percent African. It is reasonable to assume that the higher IQ of the Europeans and the lower IQ of the Africans will approximately balance out and that the IQ of 84 represents the intelligence of the Native Americans. In Rows 2 through 5, four IQs for Ecuador (89, 88, 80, and 91) are listed. The IQ of 91 given in Row 5 is for eight-year-old Quechua children in two villages, some of whom were pure Native American, while others were of mixed racial identity. Row 6 gives an IQ of 79 for Guatemala. Rows 7 through 10 list four IQs for Mexico (87, 92, 83, 86), whose population is approximately 30 percent Native American Indian, 60 percent Mestizo, and 10 percent European (Phillip's, 1996). The IQ of 83 in Row 9 is for the Native Americans in Baja California. Finally, IQs of 87 and 85 for Native Americans in Peru are found in Rows 12 and 13.

Table 12.3. IQs of Native Americans in Latin America

	COUNTRY	AGE	N	TEST	IQ	REFERENCE
1	Colombia	4	120	QR	84	Ginsburg et al., 1997
2	Ecuador	6/7	48	DAM	89	Dodge, 1969
3	Ecuador	17	120	WISC-R	88	Fierro-Benitez et al., 1989
4	Ecuador	5/17	104	MAT	80	Proctor et al., 2000
5	Ecuador	8	41	CPM	91	Counter et al., 1998
6	Guatemala	6/12	256	DAM	79	Johnson et al., 1967
7	Mexico	6/13	520	DAM	87	Modiano, 1962
8	Mexico	6/12	197	DAM	92	Laosa et al., 1974
9	Mexico	7/11	194	SPM	83	Lynn et al., 2005
10	Mexico	15	-	PISA	86	Lynn & Mikk, 2006
11	Peru	8/11	4382	CPM	87	Raven et al., 1995
12	Peru	6/7	300	WISC	85	Llanos, 1974

The IQs lie in the range of 79 to 92 and are reasonably consistent, considering the range of countries from which the samples have been drawn. The median IQ of the studies is 86 and is the same as that of Native Americans in North America derived from the studies set out in Table 12.1. The best estimate of the IQ of Native

Americans in both North and South America is therefore 86.

4. VISUAL MEMORY OF NATIVE AMERICANS

Visual memory is an ability not generally assessed in intelligence tests. There is some evidence that Native Americans are strong in this area. A study by Thomas Lombardi (1970) compared 80 Native American with 80 White six-to-eight-year-olds tested with the Illinois Test of Psycholinguistic Abilities and found that the Native Americans obtained a verbal IQ of 73 and a visualization IQ of 93. The visualization IQ is constructed as the sum of six subtests of visualization abilities of which one is visual memory, and on this, the Native Americans obtained an IQ of 104. This was the only subtest on which the Native Americans scored higher than the Whites.

The strong visual memory of Native Americans may explain why they are relatively good at spelling. In a study of the academic achievement of approximately 13,000 Native American children in 11 states of the United States, they were found to do poorest on reading vocabulary, probably because many of them spoke English as a second language, and best on spelling (Coombs, 1958). Good visual memory assists spelling because it makes it possible to recall the visual shapes of words. This is consistent with the fact that generally females have better visual memories than males (Halpern, 2000) and are also better at spelling (Lynn, 1992).

5. NATIVE AMERICAN-EUROPEAN HYBRIDS

There have been a few studies that have compared the intelligence of pure-blood Native Americans with mixed-race Native American-European hybrids. These investigations show that the hybrids obtain higher average IQs than the pure Native Americans. The studies are summarized in Table 12.4.

Table 12.4. IQs of Native American-European Hybrids

LOCATION	AGE	TEST	EUROPEANS		HYBRIDS		NATIVE AMERICANS		REFERENCE
			N	IQ	N	IQ	N	IQ	
Kansas	Adult	OTIS	-	100	536	93	179	67	Hunter & Sommermeir, 1922
South Dakota	10/15	OTIS	-	100	68	89	15	86	Fitzgerald & Ludeman, 1925
Mexico	7/10	SPM	155	98	571	94	194	83	Lynn et al., 2005
Bolivia	6/16	WISC4	-	-	62	94	-	-	Virues-Ortega et al., 2011

Row 1 shows a much lower IQ of 67 in pure-blooded Native Americans than the 93 among hybrids, but the IQ of the pure-bloods must be regarded as spuriously depressed because the Otis is a verbal test, and the Native Americans spoke English as a second language (no information is provided on the first language of the hybrids). The study divided the hybrids into quarter, half, three-quarter, and full-blooded Native Americans and found a correlation of 0.41 between the amount of White ancestry and IQ. Row 2 gives IQs of 89 for hybrids and 86 for a small sample with 80–100 percent Native American ancestry. IQs of 94 for Mestizo hybrids and 83 for a pure-blood Native Americans in Mexico are listed in Row 3.

Throughout Latin America there are racial socioeconomic hierarchies in which Europeans (and a small number of Chinese and Japanese) have the highest status. *Mestizos* (mixed race peoples of European, Native American Indian, and sometimes African ancestry) occupy intermediate positions, and Native American Indians and Blacks are at the bottom. These racial differences have been reported over the decades by numerous sociologists and social anthropologists. For instance, the British social anthropologist Peter

Wade has written of Latin American society, "[W]hites were at the top, indians and Blacks at the bottom and positions in the middle were defined by various criteria of status, among which colour and descent were very important."

More recently, Amy Chua, a Yale Law Professor, concluded,

> Latin American society is fundamentally pigmentocratic, characterized by a social spectrum with taller, lighter-skinned, European-blooded elites at one end; shorter, darker, Indian-blooded masses at the other end.

This state of affairs in Mexico has been analyzed by Andres Villarreal, a sociologist at the University of Texas, in a paper in which he shows that skin color is strongly associated with educational attainment, socioeconomic status and affluence/poverty. He analyzed the results of a survey of a representative sample of 2,400 adults carried out in 2006. The interviewers recorded the respondents' skin color as white (European), light brown (Mestizo), or dark brown (Native American Indian). The percentages of respondents in these categories were 18.8 percent European, 50.5 percent Mestizo, and 30.7 percent Native American Indian. These percentages approximate those in the population as a whole.

Villarreala finds that there is "evidence of profound social stratification by skin color."

> Individuals with darker skin tone have significantly lower levels of educational attainment and occupational status, and they are more likely to live in poverty and less likely to be affluent, even after controlling for other individual characteristics (2010, pg. 652).

The results "indicate a very strong association between respondents' skin color and their educational attainment. Individuals with darker skin tones have substantially lower education levels (pg. 665)." For instance,

> the odds of having a college education or more are 29.5

percent lower for respondents who are light brown compared with those who are white. Similarly, the odds of having a college education are 57.6 percent lower for respondents who are dark brown compared with those who are white (pgs. 665-66).

Villarreala finds the same differences for socioeconomic status. Respondents in the lowest occupational categories, such as domestic workers, manual workers, drivers, and security guards, are much more likely to be in the dark-brown category and less likely to be in the white category than are respondents in the highest status occupations, such as office supervisors, professional workers, and employers. For example, only 9.4 percent of manual workers are considered White, compared with 28.4 percent of professionals. Respondents with darker skin tones work in occupations with significantly lower status, even once their education levels and other characteristics are taken into account. A light-brown individual has 25.2 percent lower odds of being a professional worker or employer than does a white-toned respondent, while a dark-brown respondent has 35.9 percent lower odds of being in the top two occupational categories.

Villarreala looks next at the race differences in poverty and affluence. He reports that the results "once again confirm that individuals with darker skin color face disadvantages (pg. 667)." Non-White individuals are significantly less likely than Whites to be affluent. This is particularly true of dark-brown individuals, who have 50.9 percent lower odds than Whites of being affluent.

How can these race differences in Mexico be explained? Villarreala suggests the following:

> Mexicans with darker skin tones may in fact face discrimination in the labor market. Alternatively, the observed differences in socioeconomic status could be at least partly the result of discrimination in the nineteenth century or as far back as the colonial era, when racial discrimination was more explicit and sanctioned by the state. In a society known for its historically low levels of social mobility, stratification by skin color may result from

class reproduction even without continued racial or color discrimination. Differences in socioeconomic status for Mexicans of different skin tones during the colonial era could be perpetuated if there is little class mobility and if individuals with high socioeconomic status tend to marry each other (pg. 671).

It is should not be surprising that Villarreala omits to mention that that Mestizos and Native American Indians have lower IQs than Whites, and that the socioeconomic differences he reports are predictable from these IQ differences. He adopts the explanation almost invariably advanced by sociologists for the disadvantaged socioeconomic position that is universally associated with dark skin color.

6. MUSICAL ABILITY OF NATIVE AMERICANS

Simple musical abilities, such as identification of pitch changes and memory of tunes, are correlated with intelligence and can be regarded as a component of intelligence (Carroll, 1993). It is therefore interesting to inquire whether Native Americans have low musical ability, which would be consistent with their low IQ. Two studies have been published of this issue. The first, by Thomas R. Garth and Sarah Rachel Isbell (1929), reported results for the Seashore Test for 360 full-blood and 409 mixed-blood Native American school students. The authors concluded that the subjects did not differ in their performance from Europeans. In the second study, T.R. Garth (1931) reported results for pitch identification and memory for tunes for a sample of 757 Native American school students. Their MQ (Musical Quotient), based on these two tests, was approximately 92, somewhat higher than their IQ of 86 estimated in section 1. However, on a test of rhythm, they performed better than White students, with a Rhythm Quotient (RQ) of approximately 104. These somewhat conflicting results indicate that Native Americans perform relatively better on musical ability than on intelligence. In this regard, Native Americans are like Africans, who score higher than

Whites on rhythm, as shown in Chapter 4. It is not known whether the ability to identify rhythm is related to intelligence, and there is no apparent explanation for this relatively strong aptitude in Native Americans and Africans.

7. BRAIN SIZE OF NATIVE AMERICANS

Studies of the brain size of Native Americans in relation to those of Europeans are found in Table 12.5. Row 1 gives the results calculated by Stephen J. Gould (1981) from the collection of skulls assembled in the early 19th century by the American physician Samuel Morton (1849). Gould accused Morton of massaging the data to give Europeans the largest brains, but it will be seen that the difference given by Morton is *smaller* than that in the two other studies. Row 2 lists the results obtained by the American anthropologists Courtland Smith and Kenneth Beals from a collection of approximately 20,000 human crania. The average of 20 populations of Native Americans from data assembled by Hans Jurgens, Ivar Aune, and Ursula Pieper (1990) for many thousands of 25- to 45-year-olds is listed in Row 3. It is evident that although the three studies all show larger brain size in Europeans than in Native Americans, the magnitude of the difference varies quite considerably. The first two studies show very small differences, but the 79cc difference in the third study is considerable.

Table 12.5. Brain sizes (cc) of Native Americans and Europeans

	EUROPEANS	NATIVE AMERICANS	DIFFERENCE	REFERENCE
1	1426	1420	6	Gould, 1981
2	1369	1366	3	Beals et al., 1984
3	1319	1240	79	Jurgens et al., 1990

8. IQS OF HISPANICS IN THE UNITED STATES

In the United States, the term "Hispanic" denotes individuals of Latin American and Caribbean Spanish-speaking origin. Hispanics can be pure White, Black, White-Black mixes, Native American, or Mestizo (with mixed White and Native American ancestry). There are five principal groups of Hispanics in the United States. These are from Mexico, the rest of Latin America, Cuba, Puerto Rico, and other Caribbean islands. The U.S. Census Bureau (1989) reported that 63 percent of Hispanics were from Mexico, 13 percent from Puerto Rico, 10 percent from Central and South America (outside Mexico), six percent from Cuba, and eight percent from elsewhere, mainly from Caribbean islands, particularly Dominica. Thus, by far the largest group comes from Mexico, where nine percent of the population are White, 60 percent are Mestizo, and 30 percent Native American (Philip's, 1996). Many of those from the rest of Latin America are also Mestizos. Hence, most Hispanics in the United States are Mestizos.

Studies of the IQs of Hispanics are summarized in Table 12.6. Rows 1 and 2 give IQs of 89 and 87 for the two early studies carried out in the 1920s. Row 3 lists a nonverbal reasoning IQ of 91, derived from the Progressive Matrices, Lorge-Thorndike, and Gesell Figure Copying test and a verbal IQ of 90 for a sample of Mexican children aged six to thirteen compared with 638 Whites. In Row 4, we find a nonverbal reasoning IQ of 90, tested with the Colored Progressive Matrices, for a sample of Mexican children aged six to 12 (compared with 638 Whites). They obtained a somewhat lower IQ of 84 on the Peabody Picture Vocabulary Test (PPVT), possibly partly or wholly attributable to some of the Mexican children's use of English as a second language. In Row 5, we see an IQ of 95 for Mexican children in California (compared with 744 White children); in Row 6, we find an IQ of 83, obtained from the Colored Progressive Matrices in 1972 for Hispanic children in California, who were described as a representative sample. Row 7 gives an IQ of 94 for Hispanic six- to eleven-year-old children in Texas, while row 8 an IQ of 84 for Hispanic nine- to twelve-year-olds in Texas.

Row 9 gives results from the standardization of the Stanford-

Binet 4, showing Hispanics with an IQ of 99 on nonverbal reasoning; this sample obtained an IQ of 93 on verbal reasoning. An IQ of 87, derived from the standardization sample of the PPVT-Revised, is listed in Row 10. Rows 11 and 12 show IQs of 84 and 83 for Puerto Rico, whose population is 80 percent White, eight percent Black, and eleven percent mixed race (Philip's 1996). Row 13 shows an IQ of 93 and a verbal IQ of 85; these were obtained from the standardization sample of the K-BIT. An IQ of 86 for Latinos on a largely verbal test of g, which was derived from the National Longitudinal Study of Youth, is listed in Row 14. Row 15 gives an IQ of 92, obtained from the standardization sample of the KAIT. IQs of 88 for general ability (g), 91 (verbal), and 94 (spatial) for employed individuals collected by the United States Employment Service are found in Row 16. Row 17 lists an IQ of 91, obtained from the standardization sample of the WISC-111, while Row 18 shows an IQ of 81 for a sample of Mexican Americans in Arizona. In row 19, an IQ of 92 obtained from the standardization sample of the WAIS-111 is listed. Row 20 gives an IQ of 89 obtained from a meta-analysis of 39 studies of employed adult Hispanics. Finally, Row 21 lists an IQ of 93, which was obtained from the standardization sample of the nonverbal UNIT tests. The median IQ of the studies is 89, the same as the result of the meta-analysis given in Row 20.

Table 12.6. IQs of Hispanics in the United States

	COUNTRY	AGE	N	TEST	IQ	VER	VIS	REFERENCE
1	N. Mexico	6/12	100	Binet	89	-	-	Sheldon, 1924
2	USA	6/12	367	DAM	87	-	-	Goodenough, 1926b
3	California	6/13	2025	SPM/LT/SA	91	90	-	Jensen, 1973
4	California	6/12	644	CPM/PPVT	90	84	-	Jensen, 1974
5	California	7/13	608	CPM/SPM	95	-	-	Jensen, 1974
6	California	6/11	597	CPM	83	-	-	Raven, 1986
7	Texas	6/11	434	CPM	94	-	-	Raven, 1986
8	Texas	9/12	404	SPM	84	-	-	Raven, 1986
9	USA	12/23	111	SB4	99	-	-	Thorndike et al., 1986
10	USA	3/18	550	PPVT-R	87	87	-	Dunn, 1988

	COUNTRY	AGE	N	TEST	IQ	VER	VIS	REFERENCE
11	Puerto Rico	8/15	2911	SPM	84	-	-	Raven & Court, 1989
12	Puerto Rico	5/11	2400	SPM	83	-	-	Raven et al., 1995
13	USA	20/90	37	K-BIT	93	85	-	Kaufman & Wang, 1992
14	USA	14/22	3120	AFQT	86	-	-	Herrnstein & Murray, 1994
15	USA	11/93	140	KAIT	92	87	-	Kaufman et al., 1994
16	USA	16/74	1736	GATB	88	91	94	Avolio & Waldman, 1994
17	USA	6/16	242	WISC-111	91	89	95	Prifitera et al., 1998
18	Arizona	6/16	223	WISC-R	81	81	83	Reynolds et al., 1999
19	USA	20/89	163	WAIS-111	92	89	96	Kaufman & Lichtenberger, 2002
20	USA	Adults	-	Meta-analysis	89	-	-	Roth et al., 2001
21	USA	5/17	77	UNIT	93	-	87	Kane, 2007

9. GENOTYPIC INTELLIGENCE OF NATIVE AMERICANS

The low intelligence of significant numbers of Native Americans in South and Central America is partly attributable to poor nutrition. It has been estimated that 21 percent of children are "stunted" (that is, have low stature as a result of nutritional deficiencies), and 30 percent of pregnant women are anemic, a result of iron deficiency (De Maeyerand Adiels-Tegman, 1985; UNICEF, 1996). Iodine deficiency is widespread and causes high prevalence rates of goiter and cretinism, which cause stunting and reduce intelligence. In the rural highland regions of Ecuador, it is estimated that there is a prevalence rate of cretinism of around seven percent (Fierro-Benitez, Cazar, and Sandoval, 1989). It is estimated that for every one percent of the population who are cretins, three percent have some brain damage resulting in lower intelligence, and 30 percent have a loss of energy resulting from hypothyroidism (Hetzel, 1994). Thus, in the highlands of Ecuador, around 21 percent of the population may have impaired intelligence as a result of sub-clinical cretinism and also some loss of energy. In view of these nutritional deficiencies, it may be surprising that Native Americans in South and Central America should have IQs as high as 86. Native Americans in North America have a better environment because the United States and Canada provide higher standards of living, nutrition, and health, so it may be surprising that their IQ of 86 is the same as that in South and Central America.

The low intelligence of Native Americans is most reasonably attributable to both genetic and environmental factors. There are five lines of evidence pointing to some genetic determination. First, only between 20 and 30 percent of Native Americans in South and Central America have nutritional deficiencies that could explain their low IQs. Second, the intelligence of Native Americans in the United States and Canada has shown no improvement relative to that of Europeans since the 1920s, despite great improvements in their living standards and environments. Third, the intelligence of Native American-European hybrids is related to the amount of European ancestry (as demonstrated in Section 5). Fourth, Hispanics are largely Native American-European hybrids, and their intelligence is intermediate between the two parent races. Fifth, a study by Bert Cundick, Douglas Gottfredson, and Linda Willson (1974) showed that 84 Native American children placed in White middle-class foster homes for a period of six years made no gains in intelligence. This strongly suggests that the various environmental advantages associated with being reared in a White middle class family have no beneficial effect on the intelligence of Native Americans and suggests that their IQ are to some degree genetically determined.

1. Summary of Race Differences in Intelligence

2. Reliability of Racial IQ Data

3. Validity of Racial IQs: Number Concepts

4. Validity of Racial IQs: Educational Attainment

CHAPTER 13

RELIABILITY AND VALIDITY OF RACE DIFFERENCES IN INTELLIGENCE

THE EVIDENCE ON THE INTELLIGENCE OF THE RACES has been presented in detail in the preceding chapters. This chapter contains an integrated summary of these differences as well as a consideration of the reliability and validity of these IQ scores.

1. SUMMARY OF RACE DIFFERENCES IN INTELLIGENCE

Table 13.1 gives a summary of the evidence on race differences in intelligence that has been set out in detail for the races individually in chapters three through twelve. The table lists the races ranked in ascending order of their intelligence levels and shows large differences ranging from an IQ of 55 for the Bushmen of the Kalahari to an IQ of 105 for indigenous Northeast Asians.

Table 13.1. Summary of race differences in intelligence

	RACE	LOCATION	IQ	RACE	LOCATION	IQ
1	Bushmen	S.W. Africa	55	Pacific Islanders	Pacific Islands	85
2	Pygmies	Africa	57	Maoris	New Zealand	90
3	Aborigines	Australia	62	Southeast Asians	Southeast Asia	87
4	Aborigines	New Guinea	63	Southeast Asians	United States/ Netherlands	93
5	Sub-Saharan Africans	Israel	70	Native Americans	North America	86
6	Sub-Saharan Africans	Africa	71	Native Americans	Latin America	86
7	Sub-Saharan Africans	Caribbean	71	Hispanics	United States	89
8	Sub-Saharan Africans	Canada	84	Arctic Peoples	North America	91
9	Sub-Saharan Africans	United States	85	South Europeans	South Europe	94
10	Sub-Saharan Africans	Netherlands/ France/Belgium	85	East Europeans	East Europe	96.5
11	Sub-Saharan Africans	Britain	86	Europeans	Outside Europe	99
12	North Africans	North Africa	83	Central/West Europeans	Europe	100
13	South Asians	South Asia	84	Europeans	Outside Europe	99
14	S. Asians & N. Africans	Europe	84	Northeast Asians	United States	101
15	S. Asians & N. Africans	Fiji, etc.	88	Northeast Asians	Elsewhere	102
16	S. Asians & N. Africans	Africa	86	Northeast Asians	Northeast Asia	105
17	South Asians	Britain/Australia	89			

2. RELIABILITY OF RACIAL IQ DATA

The IQs of many of the samples are likely to be inaccurate to some degree because of sampling and measurement errors. The accuracy of the results is known as their reliability and is assessed by examining how far two samples obtained for the same country give consistent results. The correlation between two IQs obtained for the same countries, taking the two extreme values where three or more IQs are available, is 0.94. This shows that the IQs are highly reliable.

The validity of the IQs is the question of the extent to which they provide genuine or valid measures of the cognitive abilities of samples. It has often been argued that the peoples who obtain low IQs are really just as intelligent as Europeans, but the tests are biased against them. The issue of test bias has been discussed at length by Jensen (1980) in his book *Bias in Mental Tests*, in which he demonstrates that the assumption that tests are biased towards Westerners is simply not tenable. Individuals and races that do well on intelligence tests also tend to do well in education, earnings, job performance, and socioeconomic status (Jensen, 1980, 1998; Herrnstein and Murray, 1994). An Australian psychologist, Murray Dyck, (1996, p. 67) has given this verdict on the "bias" thesis:

> The evidence indicates that cognitive tests are equally reliable across races, are of equivalent item difficulty across races, yield similar subtest correlations…and factor analyses yield similar results. The question of whether standard ability tests are culturally biased has been answered: they are not.

A further verdict comes from Robert Brown, Cecil Reynolds and Jean Whitaker (1999, p. 215): "[R]esearch to date consistently finds that standardized cognitive tests are not biased in terms of predictive or construct validity."

3. VALIDITY OF RACIAL IQ DATA: NUMBER CONCEPTS

The validity of racial IQ data is a different issue than its reliability; validity refers to the extent to which tests measure real differences in cognitive ability (beyond, of course the ability to solve the problems presented in the tests themselves).

There are several ways of establishing the validity of the race differences in intelligence. First to be considered are race differences in the development of the concepts of numbers. It has been shown by Brian Butterworth (1999) that sophisticated numerical systems—those that contain numbers for one to 10, tens, thousands, tens of thousands, and hundreds of thousands—were devised by the South Asian, North African, and Northeast Asians four or five thousand years ago, and a little later by the Europeans and the Native Americans. The Bushmen, Africans, Australian Aborigines, and New Guinean Aborigines only devised numbers for one, two, few, and many. In some of the languages spoken by the Bushmen and the Australian Aborigines, it is possible to express numbers up to six or seven by use of multiples of one and two. Thus seven is expressed as two, two, two, one. Larger numbers cannot be expressed because it becomes too difficult to remember the number of twos and ones. Construction of complex number systems must have required moderately high intelligence, and the racial differences in these suggest that race differences in intelligence were present several thousand years ago.

4. VALIDITY OF RACIAL IQ DATA: EDUCATIONAL ATTAINMENT

From the early years of the 20th century, the validity of intelligence tests has been examined by investigating the extent to which they are correlated with educational attainment. Numerous studies have found that IQs and educational achievement are correlated at around 0.6 to 0.7 (Jencks, 1972; Lynn, Hampson, and Magee, 1984). This shows that intelligence tests are valid measures of general cognitive ability and not merely the ability to solve the problems presented in the tests. The same procedure is adopted here to examine the validity of the national IQs. The validity of these has been established by showing that they are perfectly correlated with measures of educational attainment (Lynn & Meisenberg, 2010; Meisenberg & Lynn, 2011).

CHAPTER 14

ENVIRONMENTAL AND GENETIC DETERMINANTS OF RACE DIFFERENCES IN INTELLIGENCE

WE NOW CONSIDER THE QUESTION of the environmental and genetic determinants of race differences in intelligence. There are three possible positions on this issue. These are, first, the differences between all 10 races could be entirely environmentally determined. Second, the differences could be entirely genetically determined. Third, the differences could be determined by both genetic and environment factors. The third of these positions, that both genetic and environment factors contribute to race differences in intelligence, is by far the most probable.

The problem of whether there is a genetic contribution to race differences in intelligence has been debated for well over a century. Much, but by no means all, of this debate has been concerned with the difference between African-Americans and Europeans in the United States. Prominent scientists and writers who have argued that a significant genetic effect is present include, among others, Arthur de Gobineau (1816-1882) (1853), Francis Galton (1869), Henry Garrett (1945, 1961), Frank McGurk (1953a, 1953b), Audrey Shuey (1966), William Shockley (1968), Arthur Jensen (1969, 1980, 1998), Philip Vernon (1969, 1979), Hans Eysenck (1971), John Randall Baker (1974), Loehlin, Lindzey, and Spuhler (1976), J.P. Rushton (1988, 2000), Rushton and Jensen, (2005), Richard Lynn (1991, 1991b, 1997), Irwin Waldman, Richard Weinberg and Sandra Scarr (1994, p. 38), Scarr (1995), Michael Levin (1997), Linda Gottfredson (2005), and Earl Hunt (2011).

Prominent figures who have argued that there is no significant genetic determination of race differences include James Flynn (1980), Nathan Brody (1992, 2003), Ulrich Neisser (1996), Richard Nisbett (1998), Nicholas Mackintosh (1998, 2011), Christopher Jencks and Meredith Phillips (1998), and Jefferson Fish (2002).

Many books have been devoted to critical examinations of this issue. In *The g Factor*, Jensen (1998) devotes a 113-page chapter to this question (which amounts to a book in itself); Jensen deals almost exclusively with the difference between Blacks and Whites in the United States. It is not the objective of this book to address all the relevant evidence and arguments but rather to broaden the debate from the local issue in the United States to the much larger question of the determinants of the global differences between the 10 races (whose IQs are summarized in Table 13.1).

1. NUTRITION

There is no doubt that the low IQs of the peoples in impoverished Third World countries are to some degree determined by environmental factors. The most important of these is poor nutrition. Even in affluent economically developed countries, poor nutrition is present in significant proportions of the population and has an adverse effect on intelligence. There are many different sources of evidence showing this adverse effect, which I have reviewed in detail in previous studies (Lynn, 1990a, 1993, and 1998b). For instance, it sometimes happens that twins are born with different birth weights and brain sizes, because the heavier twin has received more nutrients in the womb than the lighter twin. The insufficient nutrition obtained by the lighter twins has a permanent adverse effect on their intelligence, shown by lower IQs, averaging a deficit of about five IQ points, in adolescence and adulthood. (I have summarized seven studies that have analyzed this effect (Lynn, 1990a).)

Several studies in economically developed countries have found that infants who are breast-fed have higher IQs later in life than those who were fed formula milk obtained from cows (Lucas, Morley, Cole, Lister, and Leeson-Payne, 1992; Lucas, Morley, and Cole, 1998). The explanation for this is that breast milk contains nutrients not present in formula milk and that the iron present in cow milk is not easily absorbable by infants.

It has also been shown that some adolescents are nutritionally deficient and that nutritional supplements can improves their intelligence. For instance, a study of adolescents in a socially deprived city in Britain found that 17 percent were iron deficient; daily iron supplements given to them for three months increased their IQs by 5.8 points (Lynn and Harland, 1998). Other studies showing positive effects of nutritional supplements on the intelligence of children in economically developed nations have been described by David Benton and Gwilym Roberts (1988), Benton and Richard Cook (1991), and Hans Eysenck and Stephen Schoenthaler (1997).

The secular increases in intelligence that have occurred in economically developed nations during most of the 20th century are largely due to improvements in nutrition, which have produced increases in height of the same magnitude of about half a standard deviation over 50 years. (I have reviewed the evidence for this (Lynn, 1990a).) In many impoverished countries, inadequate nutrition is widespread, and there is abundant evidence that this has had an adverse effect on the intelligence of the populations. The principal kinds of inadequate nutrition that have been studied are protein-energy malnutrition, iron deficiency, and iodine deficiency. Protein-energy malnutrition retards growth and, in extreme cases, causes kwashiorkor and marasmus. Iron deficiency can produce anemia and a lack of energy and can impair intelligence. Iodine deficiency produces goiter and in pregnant women can impair the neurological development of the brain of the fetus, resulting in cretinism and impaired intelligence. The adverse effect of iodine deficiency on intelligence has been synthesized by Bleichrodt and Born (1994) in a meta-analysis of 18 studies that compared intelligence in iodine deficient regions with that in non-deficient regions and the effects of the administration of iodine in iodine deficient populations. They conclude that the effect of severe iodine deficiency is to reduce intelligence by 13.5 IQ points.

Malnutrition impairs physical growth, including the growth of the brain, which is the reason it impairs intelligence. The presence of malnutrition is measured by "stunting," "wasting," and "underweight." Stunting means refers to reduce height and is usually caused by chronic insufficiency of protein for bone growth. Moderate to severe stunting is defined as less than two standard deviations below the median height in relation to age of the well-nourished population. Moderate to severe wasting consists of weighing less than two standard deviations below a healthy population's median. Underweight describes people weighing less than two standard deviations below the normal median weight measured by age.

Table 14.1 includes the prevalence rates of moderate to severe malnutrition in different regions of the "economically developing" world in the early 1990s, estimated by UNICEF (1996); it also includes dats for anemia among pregnant women in the years 1960–1982, estimated by the World Health Organization (De Maeyer and Adiels-Tegman, 1985). Surveys in individual countries confirm these results. For instance, a survey in India carried out in the 1980s found about 60 percent of children under three years, and 44 percent of those between three and five years, were anemic (Seshadri and Gopaldas, 1989). Inadequate nutrition in many Third World countries is exacerbated by diseases, particularly diarrhea and measles, which impair the absorption of nutrients.

Table 14.1. Prevalence of malnutrition in economically developing countries (percentages)

REGION	UNDERWEIGHT	WASTING	STUNTING	ANEMIA
Sub-Saharan Africa	31	7	41	40
Middle East & North Africa	12	5	24	-
South Asia	64	13	62	40
East Asia & Pacific	23	4	33	25
Latin America & Caribbean	11	3	21	30

The adverse effect of malnutrition on the intelligence of many of the peoples in Third World countries is shown by a number of studies that have compared the IQs of well-nourished and malnourished children. Donald Simeon and Sally Grantham-McGregor (1990) have reviewed 15 such studies and conclude that in 10 of them, malnourished children obtained lower IQs than adequately nourished ones. The adverse effect of inadequate nutrition on intelligence has also been shown by a number of studies in which nutritional supplements have been given to malnourished children, and the effect has been to increase their intelligence. Seven such studies in economically challenged countries have been summarized by Simeon and Grantham-McGregor (1990).

While inadequate nutrition undoubtedly impairs the intelligence of significant numbers in underdeveloped world, it does not provide a full explanation for race differences. The figures set out in Table 14.1 show that fewer than half the children in economically developing countries of sub-Saharan Africa, the Middle East and North Africa, East Asia, the Pacific Islands, Latin America, and the Caribbean suffer from malnutrition.

It is only in South Asia that more than half the children are malnourished, with 64 percent underweight and 62 percent stunted. While several studies have shown that malnourished children in Thrid World countries have lower IQs than well-nourished children, the well-nourished still have IQs well below those of Europeans and Northeast Asians in economically developed countries. For instance, Janina Galler and her colleagues have reported that children in

Barbados who were malnourished in their first year of life had an IQ of 68 at the ages of 9 to 15, while a group of well-nourished children obtained an IQ of 83 (Galler, Ramsey, and Ford, 1986). This study suggests that the effect of malnourishment in Barbados is the reduction of IQs by 15 points. However, only 16.5 percent of children in Barbados are malnourished, and the IQ of 83 of well-nourished African children is well below the IQ of 99 of Europeans and of 105 of Northeast Asians. In broad terms, the effect of malnourishment on Africans in sub-Saharan Africa and the Caribbean probably explains about half the low IQs, leaving the remaining half to genetic factors.

It has sometimes been asserted by environmentalists that poor nutrition contributes to the low IQ of African-Americans in the United States. For instance, Ken Richardson and David Spears (1972, p. 82) have written "we have overwhelming evidence that minority groups like the Blacks always tend to be less well fed than the majority." They offer no evidence for this assertion, and it is doubtful whether it is correct. Richard and Spears should remember that poor nutrition reduces height, making stature a rough index of nutrition in a country. But as early as 1918, the average heights of White American conscripts were measured at 170.96 centimetersl Black conscripts were fractionally taller at 171.99 cm (Nelson, 1933). A further study published later in the 20th century has confirmed that there is no difference in height between American Blacks and Whites at the ages of 4 and 7 years or among adults (Broman, Nichols, Shaughnessy, and Kennedy, 1985). Surveys of nutrition have also failed to find any differences between American Blacks and Whites. For instance, a survey of 1987–88 found that in a representative sample of 2,379 9-to-10-year-old girls, 20 percent of Blacks and 25 percent of Whites had below the RDA (recommended daily allowance) of 45 mg a day of vitamin C (Simon, Schreiber, Crawford, Frederick and Sabry, 1993). The First Health and Nutrition Examination Survey of girls up to the age of 15 found no difference between Blacks and Whites in low vitamin C intake (National Center for Health Statistics, 1979). Other dietary deficiencies are likely to be associated with vitamin C deficiency, so these results suggest that American Blacks do not experience any greater nutritional deficiency than Whites.

With regard to Northeast Asians, a study of Korean infants adopted by American parents before the age of 2 and intelligence-tested at the ages of 6 to 14, reported by Myron Winick, Katchadurian Meyer, and Ruth Harris (1975), found that those who had been severely malnourished as infants had an IQ of 102; those who had been moderately malnourished as infants had an IQ of 106; and those who had been well nourished had an IQ of 112. The results suggest that severe malnourishment in infancy impairs intelligence by 10 IQ points. Nevertheless, even Northeast Asians who had been severely malnourished as infants had an IQ of 102, slightly higher than that of well-nourished Europeans, suggesting that genetic factors are responsible for the higher Northeast Asian IQ.

2. THE DUTCH WORLD WAR II FAMINE STUDY

The principal study suggesting that prenatal and early postnatal malnutrition does not have an adverse effect on the intelligence of children is the Dutch World War II Famine Study of Zena Stein, Mervyn Susser, Gerhart Saenger, and Francis Marolla (1972). This study examined the effect of a famine in one region of the Netherlands in the winter and spring of 1944-45, in which the population, including pregnant women, experienced severe malnutrition for a period of six months. Food was reduced to around 700 calories a day, about a quarter to a fifth of that normally consumed in economically developed nations. During this trying period, babies had lower birth weights by around 300 grams, but at the age of 19 they had the same IQs as those who had lived in other regions of the Netherlands who had not experienced the famine or been exposed to prenatal starvation.

However, the authors warn that "the results should not be generalized to the effects of chronic malnutrition with a different set of dietary deficiencies such as often occurs in developing countries, nor to nutritional insult in postnatal life" (p. 712). This point has been elaborated by Reynaldo Martorell (1997), who contends that six months of poor nutrition does not have any adverse effect if the mothers are well nourished previously and the fetuses are well-nourished in the remainder of the pregnancy and as infants after birth. He suggests that the mothers probably had reserves of micronutrients that were used during the period of the famine. In economically backward countries, many people are chronically undernourished and no compensation of this kind is possible.

It is doubtful whether this is the correct explanation in view of the fact that the infants born in the famine region had substantially lower birth weights of approximately 300 grams, compared with 330 grams in the non-famine regions, as well as in light of substantial evidence that low birth weights are associated with reduced intelligence. If mothers had been able to draw on reserves of nutrients, the birth weight of their infants would likely have been normal. The fact that it was considerably reduced shows the malnutrition caused by the famine did have an adverse effect. The most probable explanation for the result is that the proportion of babies born to more affluent families increased in the famine areas relative to those in families headed by manual labors. The more affluent families, it can be presumed, were better able to get food from the non-famine areas, and this improved their nutrition and increased their fertility relative to that of manual laborers. There is a strong association between intelligence and socioeconomic status, so the effect of this would have been that the increase in the proportion of babies born in upper-class families compensated for the adverse effect of malnutrition.

3. NEUROPHYSIOLOGICAL EFFECT OF MALNUTRITION

The neurophysiological effect of malnutrition is to impair the growth of the brain so that it functions less effectively. Prenatal and early postnatal malnutrition has the most serious adverse effect on intelligence because about 70 percent of brain growth takes place in utero, and the remaining 30 percent including dendritic growth and synaptic branching is completed by the ages of 18–24 months (Dobbing and Smart, 1974). Malnutrition has various adverse effects on the brain of the fetus and young infant that impair later intelligence, of which the best established are the following:

1. Malnutrition impairs the growth of the brain and reduces the number of brain cells, and brain size is associated with intelligence with a correlation of 0.40 (Vernon, Wickett, Bazana, and Stelmack, 2000);

2. The effect of iron deficiency is to reduce the number of dopamine receptors, and this impairs dopamine neurotransmission, which, in turn, impairs learning and brain function in adulthood;

3. Fatty acids are essential for brain growth and efficient functioning; about half of these acids are acquired in utero and the other half, in the first 12 months of life from breast milk; these fatty acids are not present in cow milk or in most infant formulas, which is one reason why infants who are breast fed have higher subsequent IQs (Grantham-McGregor, Walker, and Powell, 1994).

4. EDUCATION

A second environmental factor that has sometimes been proposed as responsible for the low IQs of peoples in Third World countries is the lack of education. For instance, Jefferson Fish (2002, p. 14) writes "the lack of formal education of Africans in relation to European comparison groups provides an obvious explanation of their lower test performance." Simon Biesheuvel (1949) has advanced the same view and cites a study in South Africa showing that Africans who had never been to school had IQs about 10 points lower than those who had received education; he contends that this shows that a lack of schooling impairs intelligence. Stephen Ceci (1991) and Nicholas Mackintosh (1998, 2011) review several studies showing that schooling increases intelligence, and there can be no doubt that this lack of education contributes to the low IQs in economically underdeveloped counties.

However, in the studies of the intelligence of the races reviewed in Chapters 3 through 12, most of the studies have been carried out on children attending school, and, in a number of these studies, the children have attended the same schools as Europeans. In South Africa, the 16-year-olds in Kenneth Owen's (1992) sample had had eight to ten years of formal education, yet they obtained a typical mean IQ of 63. Twelve studies of African university students in South Africa who had had 10 to 12 years of schooling found that they have IQs around 20 points lower than those of Whites (see Chapter 4, Table 4.2). Similarly, in India three studies of the intelligence of university students found they obtained IQs of 88, 90, and 95, well below the average of Europeans.

Furthermore, several studies have shown that the race differences in intelligence are fully present in preschool children. For instance, African three-year-olds in Dominica have an average IQ of 67 (Wein & Stevenson, 1972), and four-year-olds in St. Lucia have an IQ of 62 (Murray, 1983). In the United States, three-year-old Africans have an IQ of 86 (Montie & Fagan, 1988) and 85 (Peoples et al., 1995), and four-year-olds have an IQ of 87 (Broman et al., 1975), just about the same as African-American adolescents and adults. These preschool studies suggest that lack of education is not a significant factor determining racial differences in intelligence.

5. BLACK INFANT PRECOCITY

While environmental factors undoubtedly contribute to the differences in intelligence between the races, there are a number of considerations that suggest that genetic factors are also involved. We consider here the phenomenon of Black infant precocity. While the low IQ of sub-Saharan Africans is fully present among three-year-olds, it is a remarkable fact that, in infancy, sub-Saharan Africans are advanced compared with Europeans, while Northeast Asians are retarded. These differences can be understood in terms of the well-known principle of evolutionary biology that the infants of more highly developed species have longer childhoods, during which they are dependent on their mothers. For instance, as soon as baby reptiles hatch out of their eggs, they can move around and fend for themselves, whereas monkeys and apes have some years of dependency on their mothers; humans have an even longer period of dependency. Among primates, the most primitive are the lemurs, who have about two years of infant and childhood dependency; macaque monkeys are more developed and require about four years of infant and childhood dependency; chimpanzees are still more developed and require about eight years of infant and childhood dependency; and humans are the most developed and require about fourteen years of infant and childhood dependency (Lovejoy, 1981; Rushton, 2000, p.205). It has been demonstrated by J.P. Rushton (2000, p.147ff.) that this principle extends to the three major human races: Northeast Asians have the slowest rate of infant and child development, the longest period of dependency, and the highest final intelligence; Caucasians (Europeans, South Asians, and North Africans collectively) mature more rapidly, while sub-Saharan Africans have the fastest rate of infant and child development, the shortest period of dependency, and the lowest final intelligence. Rushton has also shown that these differences are present for physical, motor, and mental development. In regard to physical development, they are present for skeletal maturity at birth, dental maturity in childhood, and sexual maturity at adolescence (measured by the appearance of breasts and menarche in girls and genital development in boys). Rushton's theory has been confirmed by the Japanese physical anthropologist Kunihiko Kimura (Eiben, 1998).

Race differences in motor and mental development deserve to be looked at in more detail. The accelerated early infant development of sub-Saharan Africans in mental and motor abilities during the first 18 months or so of life was first observed by Solange Falade (1955), a French physician, on the basis of a study in Senegal in which he tested Black infants with the Gesell test of infant development; he found they were more advanced in motor development than White American infants. This result was confirmed in studies of Ugandan infants by Marcelle Geber (1958), of Nigerian infants by Daniel Freedman (1974), and in the United States where Nancy Bayley (1965) found that Black infants were ahead of Whites between birth and15 months on both motor and mental development tested with her Scales of Infant Development. Subsequentresearch confirmed these results, and by the early 1970s, Neil Warren (1972) summarized 12 major studies of which 10 found that Black infants are developmentally advanced. Two years later, Freedman (1974, p.146) wrote that "African and Afro-American infants appear generally to retain their relative precocity throughout the second year." More recently, such studies have been confirmed through research on Black infants in Barbados (Galler, Harrison, Ramsey, et al., 2000) and in South Africa (Lynn, 1998). The latter study reports the mean scores obtained by Black South African infants in a standardization sample of the American Bayley Scales of Infant Development. This test was constructed and normed on White infants in the United States by Nancy Bayley (1969) and is scored to give Developmental Quotients (DQs) for infants, analogous to the IQs of children that are obtainable from the age of three years and upwards. The Bayley Scales provide measures of both motor and mental Development. The Motor Scale measures the ages at which infants are able to hold up their heads, sit up, stand, walk, jump, etc. The Mental Scale measures the ages at which infants pay attention, display curiosity, utter their first words, respond to requests, name objects, use pronouns, etc. The two scales are correlated at 0.44 in a sample tested by Bayley (1993).

Bayley Developmental Quotients (DQs) for Black South African infants, expressed in standard deviation units (d scores) in relation to American White means of zero, are found in Table 14.2 (Lynn, 1998). These show the South African infants are significantly advanced in comparison with American White infants at the ages of six and twelve months. By 21 months, and again at 30 months, the advantage of the South African Blacks has disappeared.

Table 14.2. Differences between the means of South African Black and American White infants on the Bayley Scales of Infant Development, expressed as ds

SCALE	6 MONTHS	12 MONTHS	21 MONTHS	30 MONTHS
Mental	0.47	0.64	0	-0.01
Motor	0.94	0.24	0.06	-0.01

Australian Aborigines also have a low IQ (62), and they also show infant precocity in so far as they are more advanced than Caucasians in control over the neck, back, and legs, in pull-to-sit-up, and in holding up body weight when standing (Freedman, 1974).

6. DELAYED MATURATION IN NORTHEAST ASIANS

While the early development of Black infants is advanced compared to that of Europeans, the early development of Northeast Asians is retarded. The delayed maturation of Northeast Asians appears to have been first reported independently in 1969 by William Caudill and Helen Weinstein (1969) and Daniel Freedman, and Nina Freedman (1969). Caudill and Weinstein (1969) compared Japanese and European-American White infants and reported that, at three to four months, the European-American infants were more advanced in activity, vocalization, and following moving objects with their eyes and turning their heads. Freedman and Freedman (1969) compared Chinese-American and European-American newborns and observed that European-American infants were more advanced in head turning and lifting.

There have been five further studies confirming these early reports of delayed development in Northeast Asians. In the first, Reiko Ueda (1978) reported a Japanese standardization of the American Denver Developmental Screening Test. This measures motor and cognitive development from birth to six years. The Japanese were significantly retarded from the age of one to two months in head lifting and turning towards a voice; at three to five months, in rolling over; at 15 to 20 months, in removing garments; and at two to four years, in copying a circle and in the size of their vocabularies.

In the second study, developmental norms for two- to eight-year-old Japanese children obtained from the Japanese standardization sample of McCarthy Scales of Children's Abilities were analyzed by Richard Lynn and Susan Hampson (1986); these are shown in Table 14.3. The McCarthy Scales are an American intelligence test for children aged two-and-a-half years to eight-and-a-half years. The results show that at age two-and-a-half, Japanese children (IQ 94.4) scored well below American White children (IQ 100). The data for each year of age are set out in Table 14.3 and show that Japanese children gradually improve until, by the age of six to eight years, they score virtually the same (IQ 99.1) as American White children. It is only from the age of around eight years that Northeast Asian children begin to show higher IQs than Europeans.

Table 14.3. Norms for Japan for the McCarthy Scales of Children's Abilities

AGE–YEARS				
2	3	4	5	6-8
94.4	96.7	97.1	97.9	99.1

The third and fourth studies have been reported by Jerome Kagan and his colleagues. In the first of these, Kagan, Richard Kearsley, and Philip Zelazzo (1978) compared Chinese-American and European-American infants aged up to two years; they found that European-Americans newborn infants were more advanced in motor development and vocalization. The second study compared four-month-old European infants in Boston and Dublin with Chinese infants in Beijing. Both groups of European infants were more advanced than the Chinese in motor development and vocalization (Kagan, Arcus, Snidman et al., 1994). Kagan and his colleagues suggest,

> [I]t is reasonable to at least entertain the hypothesis of genetically influenced behavioral differences belonging to populations that have been reproductively isolated for a long time.

The fifth study consists of developmental norms for Chinese infants in Taiwan aged six to 24 months measured by the Bayley Scales of Infant Development derived from a representative sample of 507 infants. The results are reported by Yen-Tzu Wu, Kuomintang-Inn Tsou, Chyong-Hsin Hsu et al. (2007) and are presented in Table 14.4 as *d* scores (standard deviation units) in relation to American means of zero. The minus signs indicate that Taiwanese infants scored lower than American infants. Thus, for those aged six months, Taiwanese babies scored .88 d below American infants on the mental scale and 1.06 d below American infants on the motor scale. It will be seen that the slower development of the Taiwanese infants is greatest at six months and that they catch up progressively up to 24 months, although at this age they are still retarded compared with European infants.

Table 14.4. Norms for Taiwan for the Bayley Scales of Infant Development

SCALE	6 MONTHS	12 MONTHS	18 MONTHS	24 MONTHS
Mental	-0.88	-0.82	-0.48	-0.23
Motor	-1.06	-0.97	-0.74	-0.27

7. GENETIC DETERMINANTS OF RACE DIFFERENCES IN INTELLIGENCE

We consider here 10 further lines of evidence that suggest that genetic factors contribute to the race differences in intelligence. First, it is a principle of evolutionary biology that when populations of a species become geographically isolated and occupy different environments, they become genetically differentiated and eventually diverge so much that they become different species. Thus, squirrels in North America have evolved gray fur while those in Europe have evolved red fur. From an original ancestral species, cats have evolved into lions, leopards, and cheetahs in Africa, tigers in Asia, and jaguars and pumas in the Americas. The general principle has been stated by Richard Dawkins (1988, pp. 238–9), who writes that when two populations become isolated from one another,

> they become so unlike each other that, after a while, naturalists would see them as belonging to different races; after a longer time, they will have diverged so far that we should classify

them as different species. . . [T]he theory of speciation resulting from initial geographical separation has long been a cornerstone of mainstream, orthodox neo-Darwinism.

The processes by which these genetic divergences take place have been described in Chapter 2. It is in accordance with this principle that the races have become genetically differentiated for all characteristics for which there is genetic variation, including body shape, color of skin, hair, and eyes, prevalence of genetic diseases, and blood groups. It is simply inconceivable that intelligence would be the single exception to these differences. Some racial differences in intelligence must also have evolved as a matter of general biological principle.

Second, the studies show a consistency of the IQs of the races in a wide range of geographical locations that can only be explained by some genetic determination. For instance, in the 140 studies of general population samples of sub-Saharan Africans, all the IQs lie in the range between 60 and 87 (Table 4.1), while in the 72 studies of indigenous Northeast Asians in six countries, all the IQs fall in the range between 101 and 130 (Table 10.1). Only a genetic factor can explain the consistency of these race differences in so many different environments.

Third, the races differ consistently in IQs when they live in the same environments. Thus, sub-Saharan Africans in the United States, Britain, the Netherlands, and Brazil consistently have lower IQs than Whites. The same is true of South Asians and North Africans in Britain, Continental Europe, Africa, Fiji, Malaysia, and Mauritius; of Native Americans living with Europeans in the United States, Canada, and Mexico; of Arctic Peoples living with Europeans in Canada; of Australian Aborigines living with Europeans in Australia; and of Pacific Islanders living with Europeans in New Zealand and Hawaii. All these differences are consistent and add to the credibility of a genetic explanation.

Fourth, when babies from other races are adopted by Europeans in Europe and the United States, they retain the IQs characteristic of their race. This has been shown for sub-Saharan Africans in the United States, where Black infants adopted by White middle-class parents have the same IQ as Blacks reared in their own communities (Lynn, 1994c); for Australian Aborigines in Australia; and for Northeast Asians in the United States and Europe, where Korean infants adopted by Europeans have IQs in the range between 102 and 110 (Table 10.4) shown in Chapters 4, 8, and 10, respectively.

Fifth, mixed-race individuals have IQs intermediate between those of the two parent races. Thus, in the Weinberg, Scarr, and Waldman (1992) study of children adopted by White middle-class families, at the age of 17, Blacks had an IQ of 89; those of mixed Black-White parentage, an IQ of 98; and Whites, an IQ of 106 (Lynn, 1994c). When the amount of European ancestry in American Blacks is assessed by skin color, dark-skinned Blacks have an IQ of 85 and light-skinned Blacks have an IQ of 92 (Lynn, 2002a), and there is a statistically significant association between light skin and intelligence. Similarly, mixed-race Australian Aborigines have IQs intermediate between full-blooded Aborigines and Europeans (Chapter 8, Section 2); and mixed-race Native Americans have IQs intermediate between full-blooded Native Americans and Europeans (Chapter 12, Table 12.4).

Sixth, the IQs of races explain the extent to which they made the Neolithic transition from hunter-gathering to settled agriculture. This transition was made completely by the more intelligent races: the Europeans, the South Asians, and North Africans, the Northeast Asians, the Southeast Asians, and the Native Americans. The Pacific Islanders advanced beyond hunter-gathering to some extent, but they were handicapped by living in small and dispersed populations on small islands. The Neolithic transition was made only minimally by the sub-Saharan Africans, and not at all by the Bushmen and Australian Aborigines (IQs of 56 and 62). The anomaly is the Arctic Peoples, with their IQ of 91, who remain largely hunter-gatherers; this is due to their very small and dispersed populations and the harsh climate of the Arctic Circle.

Seventh, the IQs of races are consistent with their achievements in the development of early urban civilizations with written languages, systems of arithmetic, and codified laws. This was demonstrated by John Baker (1974), who has documented that only the Northeast Asians, the Europeans, the South Asians, the North

Africans, and the Southeast Asians developed early civilizations. The less intelligent Native Americans developed a half-civilization; and the remaining races failed to develop anything that could be called civilizations. The anomalies here are the Pacific Islanders and Arctic Peoples, with their IQs of 90 and 91, neither of which has ever developed anything resembling a civilization; this can be explained, in the case of the Pacific Islanders, as due to their very small and dispersed populations on isolated islands and, in the case of the Arctic Peoples, due to the severity of their climate, which has made it impossible to sustain urban civilizations. These race differences in the development of early civilizations in the period between approximately BC 4,000 and 500 have persisted from 1 AD to the present. Virtually all the advances that have been made in the last 2,000 years in science, mathematics, technology, and the arts have been made by the Northeast Asians and the Europeans, with some small input from the South Asians and North Africans. This has been documented in detail by Charles Murray (2003). The achievements of the races in making the Neolithic transition, in the development of early civilizations, and in the advances of mature civilizations during the last 2,000 years show that the differences in intelligence go back many thousands of years and are further expressions of genetically based race differences in intelligence.

Eighth, all the twin studies that have been carried out in Europe, India, and Japan, and on Blacks and Whites in the United States, have found a high heritability of intelligence in national populations. It is improbable that these high heritabilities within races could co-exist with the absence of any heritability for the differences between the races.

Ninth, there are race differences in brain size that are associated with differences in intelligence, and brain size has a heritability of 90 percent (Baare, Pol et al., 2001; Rushton and Osborne, 1995). The only reasonable interpretation of this association is that the races with the higher intelligence have evolved larger brains to accommodate higher brain function.

Tenth, the alternative environmentalist theory of race differences in intelligence has difficulty in providing plausible explanations for the reversal of the differences among infants.

The consistency of the racial differences in so many different nations, in the development of early and later civilizations, and the high heritability of intelligence wherever it has been investigated, all need to be considered in terms of Popper's (1959) theory of the logic of scientific explanation. This states that a scientific theory generates predictions that are subjected to empirical testing. A strong theory has few assumptions and generates a large number of predictions that are empirically verified. If the predictions are disconfirmed, the theory is weakened and may even be destroyed, although a single disconfirmation can generally be explained, or the theory can be modified to account for it. For the problem of race differences in intelligence, the theory that these have some genetic basis explains all the numerous phenomena set out in the points listed above, and there are no serious anomalies. The theory that the race differences in intelligence are to a significant extent genetically based fulfills Popper's criteria for a strong theory. Those who assert that there is no evidence for a genetic basis of racial differences in intelligence betray a lack of understanding of the logic of scientific explanation.

8. GENOTYPE-ENVIRONMENT CO-VARIATION

The problem of the relative contributions of environmental and genetic factors to race differences in intelligence is made more difficult by the principle of genotype-environment co-variation, which states that the genes for high intelligence tend to be associated with favorable environments for the optimum development of intelligence (Plomin, 1994). Thus, intelligent women who are pregnant typically refrain from smoking, drinking excessive alcohol, and taking drugs because they are aware that these are likely to impair the growth of the brain and subsequent intelligence of the children they are carrying. Intelligent parents tend to provide their children with nutritious foods because they understand the general principles of what constitutes a healthy diet, and a healthy diet is a determinant of intelligence. Intelligent parents are also more likely to give their children cognitive stimulation, which is widely believed (not necessarily correctly) to promote the development of the intelligence of their children. The same principle operates for races. The races with high intelligence tend to provide their children with the double advantage of transmitting favorable genes to their children and of providing them with favorable environments, for example, nutrition, healthcare, and education that (potentially) enhances the development of their children's intelligence. Conversely, the children of the less intelligent races tend to transmit the double disadvantage of lower quality genes and lower quality environments. Thus, it is questionable whether the standards of nutrition and health that impair the intelligence of many Third World peoples should be regarded as a purely environmental effect or as to some degree a genetic effect, arising from the lower intelligence of the populations. The principle of genotype-environment co-variation implies that differences in intelligence between the races for which the immediate cause is environmental are also attributable to genetic factors that contribute to the environmental differences.

It is difficult to avoid the conclusion that race differences in intelligence have both environmental and genetic factors. The extent of their heritability must be expected to vary according to which pairs of races are compared. The magnitude of the heritability depends on the variability in the environmental determinants of intelligence in the population and, in the case of two populations, the differences in the environmental determinants between the two. In the comparison between sub-Saharan Africans in Africa and Europeans, the environmental differences between the two populations, consisting of the quality of nutrition, health, and education, are quite large. Consequently they will have a significant impact and probably explain about 50 percent of the differences in intelligence between the two populations. In the comparison between sub-Saharan Africans in the United States and Europeans, the environmental differences between the two populations are much smaller, so the environmental effect is much smaller and the heritability correspondingly greater. Similarly, in the comparison between Northeast Asians and Europeans, the environmental conditions in which they live are closely similar in so far as they enjoy approximately the same standards of living, nutrition, healthcare, and education, so the slightly higher IQ of Northeast Asians is probably largely determined genetically.

CHAPTER 15

THE EVOLUTION OF INTELLIGENCE

WE TURN NOW TO THE QUESTION of how intelligence has evolved. Across a species's history, there is a general tendency for it to develop greater intelligence. This chapter gives an account of the principles responsible for this; the next two chapters demonstrate how the evolution of race differences in intelligence has been a continuation of this trend.

1. GENERAL PRINCIPLES OF THE EVOLUTION OF INTELLIGENCE

The general principles underlying the evolution of intelligence in a series of species over the course of approximately 225 million years have been formulated by Henry Jerison (1973, 2000). He focuses on the operation of two of these principles. The first is that from time to time species have occupied new environments or niches that have required greater cognitive ability. When this has occurred, these species have adapted by evolving larger brains to accommodate greater intelligence. The second principle is that carnivores and herbivores have been engaged in an arms race in which carnivores have needed to become more intelligent to catch herbivores, while herbivores have needed to become more intelligent to avoid capture by carnivores. A useful account of this process has been given by Richard Dawkins and John Krebs (1979).

Comparisons between species in terms of brain size and intelligence are problematical because there is a strong association across species between brain size and body size. The reason for this is that much of the brain services the functions of the body, so species with large bodies have large brains. To control for body size in comparing the brain size of different species, Jerison devised the concept of the encephalization quotient (EQ) as a measure of brain size in relation to body size. He sets the EQ of average living mammals at 1.0 and expresses the EQs of other extinct and living species in relation to this standard. Jerison defines the intelligence of species as their EQ, which determines the information-processing capacity of the brain.

The important developments in the evolution of higher EQs as new species have evolved are summarized in Table 15.1. These data have been compiled from Jerison (1973, 2000), Richard Cutler (1976), and Paul Harvey and Timothy Clutton-Brock (1985). Rows 1, 2, and 3 of the table show that 225 million years ago, fish and reptiles had EQs of 0.05 and that their EQs have not increased up to the present day.

2. INTELLIGENCE IN MAMMALS

Row 4 in Table 15.1 shows that the EQ of the first mammals that evolved approximately 225 million years ago was 0.25. This was a five-fold increase from the reptiles from which they evolved and was the first quantum leap in the increase of EQ and intelligence.

Table 15.1. Evolution of encephalization quotients
(MYA =million years ago)

	MYA	SPECIES	EQ
1	225	Fish & reptiles	0.05
2	60	Fish & reptiles	0.05
3	Living	Fish & reptiles	0.05

	MYA	SPECIES	EQ
4	225	First mammals	0.25
5	60	Average mammals	0.75
6	Living	Average mammals	1
7	150	First birds	0.1
8	60	Average birds	0.75
9	Living	Average birds	1
10	60	First primates	0.75
11	Living	Tree shrew	0.85
12	Living	Potto	1.1
13	Living	Senegal galago	1.2
14	Living	Gentle lemur	0.7
15	Living	Black lemur (*Eulemur macaco*)	1.6
16	30	First monkeys	1
17	Living	Marmoset	1.5
18	Living	Squirrel	2.8
19	Living	Brown-capped capuchin (*Cebus apella*)	3.5
20	Living	Gray Langur (*Semnopithecus entellus*)	1.3
21	Living	Rhesus monkey	2.1
22	Living	Hamadryas baboon	2.4
23	16	First apes	2
24	Living	Gorilla	2
25	Living	Siamang	2.1
26	Living	Orangutan	2.4
27	Living	Chimpanzee	2.6
28	Living	Lar gibbon	2.8
29	4	Australopithecus and Paranthropus	3.7
30	1.7	Homo habilis	4.3
31	0.7	Homo erectus	5
32	Living	Homo sapiens	7.5

The explanation of this development is that the reptiles were largely diurnal and relied primarily on vision for information about the world. Like living reptiles, their behavior consisted largely of hardwired responses to visual sign-stimuli. The first mammals were small animals about the size of the rat and occupied a nocturnal niche in which they slept during the day and foraged at night. This niche was advantageous because it afforded protection from predator reptiles, but it had the disadvantage that, for nocturnal animals, vision is seriously inadequate for gathering information about the external world (although it has some value at dusk and dawn and on moonlit nights). To overcome this problem, the early nocturnal mammals developed their senses of hearing, smell, and touch and an integration processor to obtain and analyze information from the three senses, as well as from vision. They were then able to integrate information obtained from the four senses to identify predators, food, and mates. The development of the information-processing capacities of hearing, smell, and touch required the enlargement of the auditory, olfactory, and tactile centers of the brain and the development of an integration capacity to combine the information obtained from the four senses. These new cognitive functions required a five-fold increase of the encephalization quotient over that of the average fish or reptile, from 0.05 to 0.25.

Row 5 shows that 60 million years ago, the EQ of average mammals had increased to 0.75, representing a three-fold increase from 0.25 in the first mammals. Row 6 shows that over the next 60 million years the EQ of average mammals increased further to 1.0. Thus, during the 225 million years following their first appearance, the EQ of average mammals increased approximately four-fold. This increase appears to have taken place largely through the operation of the principle of the "arms race" between carnivores and herbivores, each of which exerted selection pressure on the other for greater intelligence (and higher EQs to accommodate it).

3. INTELLIGENCE IN BIRDS

Row 7 shows the appearance of the first birds approximately 150 million years ago. The first bird, *Archaeopteryx*, had an EQ of 0.10, twice as large as that of the reptiles from which it evolved. This represented the second quantum leap in EQ and intelligence.

Rows 8 and 9 show that by 60 million years ago, the EQs of birds had increased to approximately 0.75, and increased further to 1.0 over the next 60 million years up to the present. Thus, the average living birds have approximately the same EQ of 1.0 as that of average living mammals. The explanation for the increase in the EQs of birds appears to be that they occupied the niche of living largely in the air. This had the advantage of being well away from predators but the disadvantage that newly hatched chicks in nests in the tops of trees had to be fed for several weeks until they had grown sufficiently to be able to fly and fend for themselves. To raise their chicks, the parents had to build nests, learn the location of their nests in spatial maps of their terrain, form pair bonds between mother and father birds, and co-operate in feeding their young and in defending their nests from predators. These tasks evidently required greater intelligence and learning capacities, and a higher EQ than was needed by fish and reptiles, which do not care for their young. The greater intelligence of birds and mammals, such as dogs and rabbits, has been shown in various experimental tasks reviews by Gregory Razrin (1971). The increase in the EQs of birds over time probably occurred largely through the "arms race" between predators and non-predacious birds, each of which exerted selection pressure on the other for greater intelligence.

4. INTELLIGENCE IN PRIMATES

Row 10 shows the EQ of 0.75 of the first primates, who appeared approximately 60 million years ago following the extinction of the dinosaurs. The EQ of the first primates was about the same as that of average mammals and birds at that time. Rows 11 through 15 give the EQs of the living representatives of the first primates and mammals closely related to primates: tree shrews (EQ 0.85), pottos (EQ 1.1), galagos (EQ 1.2), the gentle lemur (0.7), and the black lemur (*Eulemur macaco*) (EQ 1.6). These five living species have an average EQ of 1.1, an increase of about 50 percent over that of the first primates of 60 million years ago. Row 16 shows the EQ of 1.0 of the first monkeys, which appeared about 30 million years ago. Rows

17 through 22 show the EQs of six typical living species of monkey. Their EQs range between 1.3 for the Gray Langur (*Semnopithecus entellus* synonym *Presbytis entellus*) and 3.5 for the Brown-capped capuchin (*Cebus apella*), so all of them have higher EQs than the first monkeys of 30 million years ago with their EQ of 1.0. Row 23 shows an EQ of 2.0 for the first species of apes that appeared around 16 million years ago. (The principal distinctions between monkeys and apes is that apes have no tails and more flexible shoulders that allow them to raise their arms above their heads and swing from branches of trees, whereas monkeys walk on branches.) Rows 24 through 28 give the EQs of the five species of living great apes. The EQs range from 2.0 (for the gorillas of central Africa) to 2.1 (the siamang of Southeast Asia and Indonesia) to 2.4 (the orangutan of Borneo and Sumatra) to 2.6 (the chimpanzee of central Africa) to 2.8 (the lar gibbon of Southeast Asia and Indonesia). Considered as a family, the apes (excluding humans) do not appear to have evolved higher EQs than the monkeys. The average EQ of the five species of great apes is 2.4, while the average of the six species of monkeys is 2.3. (It's important to note that some of these EQs are derived from quite small numbers and may not be strictly accurate because of sampling errors.)

The rapid evolution in EQs of monkeys and apes, from 1.0 to 2.4 over the 30 million years of their existence, was much greater than that of other mammals and of birds during the same period. This was the third great quantum leap in the evolution of brain size and intelligence. Two reasons for this rapid increase in EQ come to the fore. First, while the early primates were nocturnal like the mammals from which they evolved (Byrne, 2002), the monkeys and apes became diurnal, living by day and sleeping at night. Diurnal species rely heavily on vision to obtain information about the external world, and, in accordance with this principle, the visual centers in the brain increased in size in monkeys and apes to give greater visual processing capacity.

Second, while early primates were solitary, later primates began living in social groups. Living in communities has the advantages of securing the exclusive use of a territory and its resources, as well as cooperating in finding food, rearing the young, and defending against predators. The cost is that the individuals have to learn complex social skills for living harmoniously with other group members, who are also competitors for food and mates. The social system of these animals typically consists of groups of around 30 to 80 animals, in which there are dominance hierarchies in which two or three dominant males have more food, sole access to the females when they are in estrus, and the best sleeping berths in trees. To keep their position, dominant males typically form alliances to fight off challenges from beta males. These non-dominant males belong to the group, but have to be careful to respect the position of the superior males, who will drive them out of the group if they are challenged. Nevertheless, the non-dominant males seem to understand that if they exercise adroit social skills, the time will come when the dominant males will grow old and weak and eventually die, and some of them will be able to succeed them. To maintain their position in the group while awaiting this eventuality, non-dominant males have to exercise restraint and judgement in biding their time until they have a good chance of successfully challenging and displacing a dominant male. Meanwhile they form alliances with other non-dominant males to maintain their position in the group and strengthen their chances of becoming dominant. The acquisition of these social skills requires rapid learning and the capacity to inhibit challenges to the dominant males. These social skills have come to be designated "social intelligence," and they appear to need a relatively large EQ for understanding and manipulating the social relationships, observing, learning, and memorizing the characteristics of other group members, and inhibiting impulsive actions. Males with high social intelligence eventually become dominants and are able to reproduce, and this drives up the social intelligence of the species. The theory that becoming highly social animals was the niche that drove up the EQs of monkeys and apes has been developed by Robin Dunbar (1992), who has shown that among primates the size of the social group in primate species is correlated with the EQ, suggesting that primates that live in larger groups need a higher EQ to deal with the more complex social relationships present among their members. Thus, the monkeys and apes occupied a new niche as co-operative social species that required greater intelligence (and higher EQs).

In various ways, monkeys and apes display a high level of intelligence consistent with their high EQs. The most studied species is the chimpanzee. In the 1920s Wolfgang Kohler (1925) demonstrated that when confronted with a difficult problem, such as how to retrieve a banana hanging from the ceiling and out of reach, chimpanzees can figure out how to use boxes to build a platform, onto which they can climb and grab the banana. Later, Jane Goodall (1986) showed that chimpanzees in the wild learn to make and use tools for a variety of purposes. They take sticks from which they pare off the side stems; they then lick them to make tacky, insert them into the holes in termite mounds and ant nests, pull out the tacky sticks, and eat the termites or ants adhering to them. They make pestles to pound the pulp from wood into an edible paste and chisels to open bees' nests; they use stones to break open nuts, use leaves for drinking cups and to clean themselves, and take up pieces of wood to threaten and hit predators and intruders into their territories. They also have a vocabulary of around a dozen cries to convey information, including the presence of predators, intrusion into their territories of neighboring groups, the location of a supply of food, willingness or unwillingness to share food, and so on. More recently, it has been discovered that orangutans also make and use tools (Fox, Sitompul, and Van Schaik 1999). In laboratory studies, only monkeys and apes can master oddity problems, in which three objects are presented, two of which are the same, and the correct choice is the odd one; and one-trial learning sets, where two different objects are presented and the correct choice varies from day to day.

5. INTELLIGENCE IN HOMINIDS

The fourth quantum leap in EQ and intelligence took place with the evolution of the hominids. This is the series of species that led eventually to the appearance of *Homo sapiens*. It began about four million years ago in central East Africa, in what is now Kenya and Tanzania, with the appearance of the australopithecines; this was followed by the three successive species of *Homo habilis*, *Homo erectus*, and finally *Homo sapiens*. The times of these species and their

EQs are given in Rows 29 to 32 of Table 15.1. The first of these, the australopithecines, comprised several species. The first to appear was *Australopithicus afarensis*, which evolved from an ape closely resembling the chimpanzee. Over the next two million years, further species of australopithecines evolved including *Australopithicus africanus*, *Paranthropus robustus*, and *Paranthropus boisei*. The later species were larger and their brain sizes increased, but not in proportion to their body size, so their encephalization quotients remained the same. The reason for the evolution of the australopithecines was that apes are adapted to live in forests, but in central East Africa the climate became dryer; as a result, much of the forest disappeared and was replaced by grasslands with some brushwood and the occasional clump of trees. Hence the apes in central East Asia had to adapt to survive in the new niche of open savanna. Their three most distinctive adaptations were that they stood upright, whereas apes normally move by knuckle walking on all fours; their thumbs evolved in opposition to the fingers; and their EQs increased. The principal adaptive advantages of the upright posture were that, first, it afforded them better vision that enabled them to see predators at a greater distance, second, to walk over long distances to forage for food, and, third, that it freed the hands. The freeing of the hands and the development of the thumb in opposition to the fingers made it possible to use the hands to carry food from a distance back to the camp, to make stone tools, and to grip stones and pieces of wood more effectively and use them to drive off predators.

The EQs of the hominids showed approximately a threefold increase over the course of about four million years, from about 2.6 of the apes from whom they evolved to 7.5 of *Homo sapiens*. This was a very rapid rate of increase as compared with the 56 or so million years for the same rate of increase to evolve in the primates, from 0.75 of the first primates some 60 million years ago to 2.6 of the most encephalized monkeys and apes. The explanation for this increase is that the hominids entered a new niche of the open savanna in which survival was more cognitively demanding than that of the apes from which they evolved. The cognitive demands of the new niche would have consisted principally of finding a variety of different kinds of foods and protecting themselves from predators.

The australopithecines and the succeeding hominids continued to live largely on plant foods, like the apes from whom they evolved, but in open savanna these had to be more varied and dispersed over a larger terrain. To obtain these foods, they would have needed spatial maps of a large area, and this would have required a larger brain. The foods they ate can be determined from the wear of their teeth, which shows that they subsisted largely on a diet of leaves and fruits, and that they also ate tubers, nuts, grass seeds, and insects (Isaac, 1978; Parker and Gibson, 1977; Grine and Kay, 1988; Stahl, 1984).Some of them lived on the shores of lakes Baringo and Turkana in present-day Kenya. Here they could pick up shellfish and crack them open by hitting them with a rock, which they were able to grip between their thumbs and fingers.

The hominids supplemented their plant and insect diet with a certain amount of meat obtained by scavenging and possibly by occasionally killing small animals. Baboons and chimpanzees sometimes kill small animals for food, although meat has never become more than a small part of their diets (Strum, 1981). Possibly the australopithecines and the later hominids, *Homo habilis*, did the same. They were also scavengers of the remains of animals killed by lions, cheetahs, and leopards. The sites of *Homo habilis* contain the bones of large herbivores with carnivore teeth marks on which stone-cut marks made by the hominids have been superimposed. This suggests that the large herbivores had been killed by lions, cheetahs, and leopards; then *Homo habilis* would have scavenged the bones, which they broke up to extract the marrow and brains, which the feline predators were unable to get at (Binford, 1985; Blumenschine, 1989). With their increased EQ of 4.3, *Homo habilis* became the first hominids with the brain power to make stone tools on an extensive scale. By knapping flints to produce sharp cutting implements, they produced spears and knives to dismember the carcasses of large mammals killed by lions, cheetahs, and leopards.

In addition to obtaining food, the other principal problem of the hominids living in open grasslands would have been to protect themselves against these big-cat predators Apes and monkeys escape from danger by climbing into trees and swinging or jumping from one tree to another. For the australopithecines and the later hominids in open grasslands, this was no longer possible. They must have warded off lions, leopards, and cheetahs by throwing stones at them and hitting them with clubs made from pieces of wood collected from the few trees that remained. For this, their newly evolved thumbs, which increased their gripping power, would have been a great advantage. Chimpanzees sometimes use sticks to ward off predators, but they do not collect an arsenal of sticks and stones for this purpose. The australopithecines would have had to do this, and this would have required greater foresight and intelligence.

Three further selection pressures have been proposed for the increase in the EQs of the hominids. First, at some point, inter-group warfare developed, in which victorious groups generally killed the males of the defeated groups and took over their women and territories. The victorious groups would have tended to have higher IQs than the defeated groups, with the result that alleles would have been selected for. Second, it has been proposed by Richard Alexander (1989) that more intelligent individuals were more effective as tool makers and hunters and had greater social intelligence, which enabled them to secure higher rank in dominance hierarchies, through which they increased their fertility. Third, Jessica Ash and Gordon Gallup (2007) have shown that brain size, from *Homo habilis* through archaic *Homo sapiens*, increased in times of cooler and more variable climates and with distance from the equator; they argue that these required greater intelligence to survive in these more novel conditions.

6. IQS OF MONKEYS, APES, AND PRE-HUMAN HOMINIDS

A number of attempts have been made to assess the intelligence of monkeys, apes, and pre-human hominids by using Piaget's theory of the development of intelligence in children. Piaget's theory states that children progress through four stages of cognitive development. The first of these is the sensorimotor stage of infancy in which the child learns about the properties of objects, space, time, and causality. At about the age of two, children make the transition to the "preoperational" stage, in which they acquire language and abstract concepts but are not yet able to understand logical principles. This stage lasts until the age of about six. In Western societies children at around the age of seven make the transition to the "concrete operations" stage when they can grasp logical principles but only in concrete terms. At around the age of twelve years children progress to the fourth and final stage, "formal operations," when they become able to think logically in terms of general principles divorced from concrete examples.

The applications of this theory to the intelligence of monkeys, apes, and pre-human hominids have been summarized by Parker and McKinney (1999). Their conclusion is that most species of monkeys do not progress beyond the first of Piaget's stages, so they remain at the cognitive level of human toddlers at the ages of about two years. On the scale of human intelligence, their IQ would be about twelve (12). Apes are at Piaget's early pre-operations stage and reach the cognitive level of the average European three- to four-year-old. Their IQ would be about 22. Estimates of the Piagetian level of ability achieved by successive species of hominids from tools they made have been attempted by Wynn (1989). His conclusion is that *Homo habilis*, living in East Africa around 2.4 million years ago, was making simple stone tools that required the early stage of pre-operational ability, about the same as that of apes. *Homo erectus*, who appeared about 1.7 million years ago with a somewhat larger brain, made the more sophisticated Acheulian stone tools, including bifaced hand axes, that would have required the concrete operational thinking of the kind achieved by contemporary European seven- to eight-year-olds. From this it can be inferred that their IQ would have been about 50.

CHAPTER 16

CLIMATE, RACE, BRAIN SIZE, AND INTELLIGENCE

THIS CHAPTER GIVES AN ACCOUNT OF THE GENERAL PRINCIPLES of the evolution of race differences in intelligence. The crucial selection pressure responsible for the evolution of race differences in intelligence is identified as the temperate and cold environments of the northern hemisphere, imposing greater cognitive demands for survival and acting as selection pressures for greater intelligence. The South Asians and North Africans, the Europeans, the Northeast Asians, Arctic Peoples, and Native Americans adapted to these cognitive demands by evolving greater brain size and intelligence. The genetical processes consisted of increases in the frequencies of high intelligence alleles and of mutations for higher intelligence.

1. EVOLUTION OF THE RACES

The consensus theory of the evolution of the races is that humans evolved from apes in sub-Saharan Africa during the last four million years or so. During this time a succession of species known collectively as the hominids evolved with increasingly large brains. These were the australopithecines, followed by *Homo habilis* and then by *Homo erectus*, who appeared about 1.5 million years ago, and finally by *Homo sapiens* (modern humans), who appeared around 150,000 years ago (Relethford, 1988). From around 100,000 years ago, groups of *Homo sapiens* began migrating from equatorial Africa into other regions of the world, and by around 30,000 years ago, they had colonized most of the globe. In the early part of this period, they spread through most of sub-Saharan Africa, and by 100,000 years ago, they were established in the south of Africa, where they evolved into the Bushmen. By 88,000 years ago, they were settled in southwest Asia. By 60–40,000 years ago, they were established throughout Asia, and by about 40,000 years ago, they were settled in Europe, the Indonesian archipelago, Australia, and the Americas. During the last 6,000 years or so, they colonized the Pacific islands (Foley, 1997; Mellars and Stringer, 1999; Cavalli-Sforza, 2000). A map showing the approximate times and directions of the migrations of modern humans indicated from the archeological record is given in Figure 1.

It is a general principle of evolutionary biology that when populations are isolated from one another in different locations, they inevitably develop genetic differences and evolve into different breeds or, in the case of humans, races. These differences evolve through the processes of founder effects, genetic drift, mutation, and adaptation to different environments. The founder effect occurs when a small group breaks away from a population, migrates to a new location, and establishes a new population. The migrating group is likely to differ genetically by chance from the group it has left, bringing about two groups with different genetic characteristics. It is not considered likely that this process played any significant part in the development of genetic differences in intelligence between the races. The second process through which races diverge genetically is through genetic drift. This is a process in which the frequencies of some genes increase, while those of others decrease, through chance. It is possible that the racial differences in the frequencies of different blood groups and of genetic diseases may have arisen in this way, but again this process is not likely to have played any significant part in the development of race differences in intelligence. It is believed that it is through the two remaining processes of adaptation to different environments and genetic mutations that race differences in intelligence have come about.

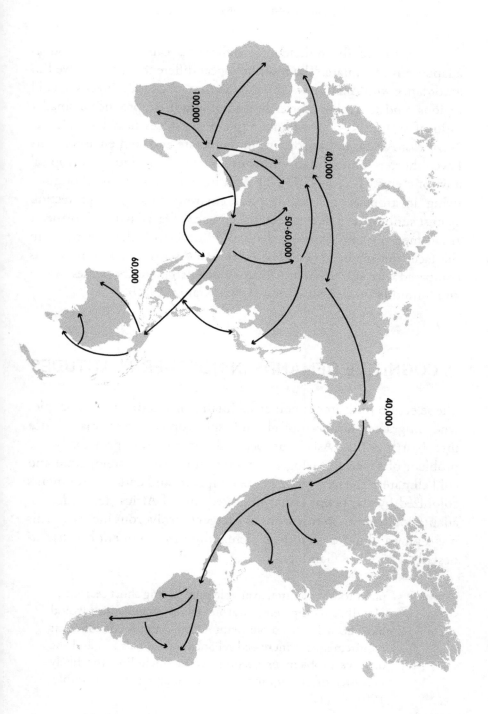

Figure 2. Migrations of modern humans, beginning in Africa about 100,000 years ago

Many of the human race differences can be understood as adaptations to climate. The morphological differences have evolved in accordance with Allen's law, which states that species and breeds in cold regions tend to evolve shorter limbs because these produce a smaller ratio of surface to body volume, and this reduces heat loss. Hence, Northeast Asians and Europeans in temperate and cold environments have shorter limbs than Africans in tropical and sub-tropical environments. The dark skin of Africans and Australian Aborigines living in tropical and sub-tropical environments gives protection against sunburn and skin cancer; the absence of facial hair in Northeast Asian men prevents frostbite that would develop if the hair froze on the face; the smaller nostrils of Northeast Asians and Europeans, as compared with sub-Saharan Africans and Australian Aborigines, warm and humidify inhaled air (Coon, 1962; Krantz, 1980).

2. COGNITIVE DEMANDS IN NORTHERN LATITUDES

The selection pressure for enhanced intelligence acting on the peoples who migrated from tropical and sub-tropical equatorial Africa into North Africa, Asia, Europe, and America was principally the problem of survival during the winter and spring in temperate and cold climates. The new niche of the temperate and cold environments colonized by the peoples that migrated out of Africa demanded an adaptation from an herbivorous to a largely carnivorous life style. This was a new and more cognitively demanding environment because, as described by Clive Gamble,

> plant foods are often available only during short seasons . . . [and] . . . compared to warmer environments there would have been fewer edible plant species, and a concomitant requirement for increased reliance on animals . . . and the obvious problem of keeping warm, including the likely necessity of controlling and even making fire. (Gamble, 1993, p. 117)

A particularly important cognitive advance was the invention, around 17,000 years ago in Europe, of the needle, which enabled people to make clothing for warmth and comfort.

The primates from whom humans evolved had lived for a period of approximately 60 million years as herbivores in the tropical and sub-tropical environment of equatorial Africa, in which plant foods are available throughout the year. The hominids that evolved in equatorial East Africa remained largely herbivorous. In contemporary times, hunter-gatherer peoples in tropical and subtropical latitudes continue to subsist largely on plant foods, of which numerous species are available throughout the year (Lee, 1968; Tooby and de Vore, 1989). It has been shown that in 229 contemporary hunter-gatherer societies, the colder the latitude, the less people are dependent on gathered plant foods. There is a quite strong correlation between latitude and subsistence dependence on gathered plant foods of 0.77 ($p < 0.001$) (Cordain, Miller, Eaton et al., 2000).

Because primates are adapted as herbivores in tropical and sub-tropical environments, they have found it difficult to survive in temperate environments in which plant foods are not available for a number of months in the winter and spring. An early instance of primates encountering the problem of survival during the winter and spring in temperate environments occurred during the mid-Miocene between 16 and 14 million years ago. This was a warm period in which much of Eurasia became subtropical. Two species of apes, Pliopithecus and Dryopithecus, migrated from Africa into Eurasia and flourished there. At the end of this period, about 14 million years ago, Eurasia became colder and the climate became temperate. In Europe and in most of Asia, these apes were unable to survive during the winters and became extinct. The only part of Asia where these early apes were able to survive was in the tropical southeast and the Indonesian archipelago, where they evolved into the orangutans and gibbons (Pickford, 1986).

The new niche of the temperate and cold environments colonized exerted selection pressure for enhanced intelligence in the peoples that migrated out of Africa. This theory that race differences in intelligence evolved because the peoples who migrated out of

Africa into the temperate and cold climates of Asia and Europe entered a more cognitively demanding niche that required greater intelligence is a further instance of the general principle that had operated in the evolution of greater intelligence in mammals when they colonized the nocturnal niche, in birds when they colonized the air, in monkeys and apes when they became co-operating social animals, and in hominids when they adapted to the open savannah.

Four further selection pressures may have operated to drive up the intelligence of the North African and South Asian, European, and East Asian peoples. First, in temperate and cold climates, females became dependent on males for provisioning them with food because they were unable to hunt, whereas in the tropics women were able to gather plant foods for themselves. For this, women would have required higher intelligence to select as mates the men who would provision them. Second, women would have selected as mates men who could provision them and their children, and these would have been men with higher intelligence. This is a case of sexual selection, identified by Darwin as one of the driving forces of evolution. In the tropics, where women could collect plant and insect foods that are available throughout the year, women did not need men to provision them and would have been less prone to select men with high intelligence as mates. Third, during the last ice age, the peoples of northern Europe and Asia would have had to migrate south, as their homelands became covered with ice and uninhabitable. During this migration, they would have encountered other groups who would likely not have welcomed them. Wars would have broken out over disputes for territory and, in these conflicts, the groups with higher intelligence would have tended to win. For all these reasons, temperate and cold climates would have exerted selection pressure for higher intelligence. The colder the winters, the stronger this selection pressure: this was the mechanism through which higher intelligence evolved. This explains the broad association between latitude—or, more precisely, the coldness of winter temperatures—and the intelligence of the races, as shown in Table 16.2 and further documented by Donald Templer and Hiroko Arikawa (2005).

A fourth selection pressure for enhanced intelligence acting on the peoples who migrated into Eurasia has been proposed by Satoshi

Kanazawa (2008). He argues that intelligence evolved in hominids to solve novel problems, and that Eurasia presented migrants with these. He shows that mean annual temperature and the novelty of the environments have independent effects on the average intelligence of populations in different parts of the world. This theory has received some support from Valerie Stone (2002, p.420) who writes, "The major selection pressures acting on *Homo erectus* seem to have been those of foragers moving into new habitats with unfamiliar food resources. Archaic *Homo sapiens*, in contrast, were big game hunters and faced somewhat different selection pressures"—i.e., those of catching and killing large animals.

3. RACE DIFFERENCES IN BRAIN SIZE

The races that migrated into the temperate and cold environments of North Africa, Asia, Europe, and the Americas evolved greater intelligence to survive in these more cognitively demanding climates. To accommodate this enhanced intelligence, they evolved larger brains, just as had occurred in previous adaptations in the evolution of mammals, birds, and primates to more cognitively demanding niches. Studies on race differences in brain size have been given for each race in Chapters 3 through 12. It is not possible to average these to give mean brain sizes, because there are different methods for measuring brain size, and these give different results. The principal methods are by measuring the length, breadth, and height of the head of living individuals and calculating the volumes, and by filling skulls with lead shot or seed and transferring these to a container to measure the volume. What is needed is a large collection of brain sizes (from all races), which would be measured by the same method. Only one such data set is available. This is the mean brain sizes of 87 populations worldwide, based on measurements of approximately 20,000 crania, published by Courtland Smith and Kenneth Beals (1990). These are categorized in Table 16.1 into the 10 races with which we are concerned. The figures in bold are the means of the brain sizes of the samples of each race.

Table 16.1. Brain sizes (cc) for ten races

RACE	BRAIN SIZE	RACE	BRAIN SIZE	RACE	BRAIN SIZE
Native Americans	1366	**Arctic Peoples**	1443	**Africans**	1282
Alacaluf	1397	Aleut	1518	Azande	1345
Araucanians	1386	Buryat	1465	Batetela	1274
Arikara	1399	Inuit	1377	Mangbetu	1247
Blackfoot	1365	Inuit	1474	Masai	1245
Botocudo	1350	Inuit	1411	Nubians	1235
Caddo	1345	Inuit	1429	Xhosa	1344
Carib	1315	Koryak	1419		
Cheyenne	1399	Ostyak	1416	**Pacific Islanders**	1317
Chinook	1321	Yakut	1478	Maori	1393
Chippewa	1418	Yukaghir	1439	Marquesians	1336
Choctaw	1292			New Britain	1232
Cowichan	1288	**Australian Aborigines**	1225	New Caledonia	1311
Delaware	1411	NSW	1228	New Ireland	1250
Goadjiro	1263	NT	1232	Tahitians	1380
Gosiute	1338	QL	1215		
Gros Ventre	1394	Tasmanians	1239	**Bushmen**	1270
Haida	1358	West	1212		
Huron	1424			**South Asians**	1293
Koskimo	1330	**Europeans**	1369	Arabs	1315
Mandan	1382	Basques	1368	Burmese	1227
Maya	1342	Czechs	1341	Egyptians	1379
Nahua	1388	Dutch	1373	Hindus	1362
Nez Perce	1483	French	1361	Sinhalese	1222
Ona	1391	Germans	1391	Tamils	1254
Paiute	1328	Italians	1411		
Pawnee	1334	Poles	1315	**Southeast Asians**	1332
Piegan	1381	Scots	1316	Andamanese	1214
Quechua	1296	Swiss	1408	Javanese	1403
Salish	1284			Lawa	1413

RACE	BRAIN SIZE	RACE	BRAIN SIZE	RACE	BRAIN SIZE
Tarahumara	1404	**East Asians**	1416	Papuans	1304
Teton	1454	Chinese	1418	Papuans	1270
Wichita	1309	Gilyak	1443	Seri	1388
Yahgan	1363	Japanese	1318		
Zuni	1235	Kalmyk	1371		
		Mongols	1489		
		Samoyed	1458		

These results showing larger brain sizes in populations that evolved in colder environments have been confirmed by Jessica Ash and Gordon Gallup (2007) in an analysis of a sample of 109 fossilized hominid skulls, which is discussed further in Section 4. A more recent study providing additional confirmation for these results has been published by Pearce and Dunbar (2011). They measured the brain size of 55 skulls from 12 populations from around the world and found that brain size was correlated with distance from the equator at 0.82.

It has now become widely accepted that this evidence for race differences in intelligence and brain size indicates that these race differences have a genetic basis. As Earl Hunt (2011, p.434) has recently written, "the 100% environmental hypothesis . . . cannot be maintained."

4. RACE DIFFERENCES IN BRAIN SIZE AND IQ AND WINTER TEMPERATURES

The evolution of larger brain size to accommodate greater intelligence in the races that occupied the colder environments is shown in Table 16.2.

Table 16.2. Race differences in winter temperatures (degrees centigrade) and brain size

RACE	WINTER TEMP	WURM TEMP	BRAIN SIZE	IQ
Arctic Peoples	-15	-20	1443	91
Northeast Asians	-7	-12	1416	105
Europeans	0	-5	1369	100
Native Americans	7	5	1366	86
South Asians	12	7	1293	84
North Africans	12	7	1293	83
Bushmen	15	15	1270	55
Sub-Saharan Africans	17	17	1280	71
Australians	17	17	1225	62
Southeast Asians	24	24	1332	87
Pacific Islanders	24	24	1317	85

Column 2 gives the races ranked by the severity of the winter temperatures to which they were exposed. Column 3 gives present-day coldest winter monthly temperatures taken from the Encyclopedia Britannica World Atlas and are averages of the regions inhabited by the races. Column 3 gives the coldest winter monthly temperatures during the main Würm glaciation, which lasted between approximately 28,000 and 10,000 years ago and during which winter temperatures fell by about five degrees centigrade in the northern hemisphere but not in the southern hemisphere (Foley, 1987; Roberts, 1989). Column 4 gives average brain sizes taken from Table 16.1. It is apparent that there is a general correspondence between coldest winter monthly temperatures and brain sizes. For the first six races listed, brain sizes decrease with less severely cold winter monthly temperatures. However, in the remaining four races, this linear trend becomes irregular. The Africans inhabit a warmer zone than the Bushmen, but have larger brain size. The Australian Aborigines continue the trend with a warmer zone and lower brain size. However, the Southeast Asians and the Pacific Islanders in tropical and sub-tropical zones have larger brain sizes than the South Asians and North Africans, the Bushmen, the Africans, and the Australian Aborigines.

Column 5 gives the IQs of the races. Here, too, it is apparent that there is a general correspondence between the IQs and the coldest winter monthly temperatures and brain sizes, but once again there are anomalies. First, the Arctic Peoples inhabit the coldest zone and have the largest brain size, but their average IQ is only 91. Second, the Bushmen have the second smallest brain size (1,270cc) but the lowest IQ (55), while the Australian Aborigines have the smallest brain size (1225cc) but a slightly higher IQ (62) than the Bushmen. Apart from these anomalies, there is a perfect correspondence between race differences in brain size and IQ. To explain these anomalies, we have to consider the genetical principles involved in the evolution of the race differences in intelligence. This question is taken up in Section 8.

A related approach to the issue of the relation between winter temperature and intelligence throughout the world has been taken by Donald Templer and Hiroko Arikawa (2006). They examined the relation between average IQ in 129 nations and lowest winter temperatures. The correlation was -0.66, showing that the lower the winter temperature, the higher the national IQ. They also examined the relation between average national IQ and skin color and found a correlation of 0.92: the lighter the skin color, the higher the IQ.

More recent data on the relation between intelligence, low winter temperatures, and latitude has been presented by Drew Bailey and David Geary (2009). They examined 175 skulls dated between 1.9 million years ago and 10,000 years ago and reported a correlation of -.41 between their size (cubic capacity) and temperature of their locations (greater brain size in lower temperature locations) and a correlation of -.61 between their size (cubic capacity) and latitude (greater size in latitudes more distant from the equator). This study show that larger brain size (conferring greater intelligence) evolved more than 10,000 years ago in the peoples inhabiting colder environments. Similar results have been reported by Jessica Ash and Gordon Gallup (2007) in an alalysis of a sample of 109 fossilized hominid skulls. They found that approximately 22 percent of the variance in cranial capacity (brain size) could be accounted for by variation in equatorial distance, such that cranial capacity was larger with greater distance from the equator. They also found that cranial capacities were highly correlated with paleo-climatic changes in temperature, as indexed by oxygen isotope data and sea-surface temperature, and that 52 percent of the variance in the cranial capacity could be accounted for by temperature variation at 100 ka intervals. Further support for these results has been reported by Drew Bailey and David Geary (2009). They examined 175 skulls dated between 1.9 million years ago and 10,000 years ago and reported a correlation of -0.41 between their size (cubic capacity) and the temperature of their locations, showing greater brain size in lower temperature environments, as well as a correlation of -0.61 between their size and latitude, showing larger brain size in latitudes more distant from the equator.

5. BRAIN SIZE AND INTELLIGENCE IN HUMANS

As discussed above, there is a broad correspondence across races between severity of winter temperatures, brain size, and intelligence. The explanation for this is that the colder the winters in the climatic zones occupied by the races, the greater the selection pressure for the higher intelligence required to survive. This theory presupposes that brain size is positively related with intelligence in humans. There has been a marked reluctance among a number of anthropologists and psychologists to concede the existence of this association. For instance, Agnes Reidel, Joerg Klekamp, Clive Harper, and Hans-Joachim Kretschmann (1994, p. 533) reported a study showing that the average brain weight of Australian Aborigines was substantially lower than that of Europeans, but write,

> It has to be emphasized that this difference in cortical volume cannot be interpreted as evidence of intellectual abilities or intelligence in Aborigines. No study has ever shown a correlation between neuroanatomical data and intelligence in man.

John Bradshaw (1997, p.145) writes of "the vexed issue in our species of a possible relationship between brain size and intellectual capacity. Kenneth Beals, Courtland Smith, and Stephen Dodd

(1984) write "no convincing case for such associations has ever been presented" for the association between brain size and intelligence. Similarly "there is ever more evidence accumulating . . . against a direct relationship between cranial capacity and intellectual capacity" (Henneberg, 1984); "there is really no evidence to show that brain size is positively correlated with intelligence" (Lathan, 1974); and "there is no evidence that larger brains are, in any way, better than smaller brains" (Halpern, 2000, p. 196).

Contrary to these assertions, the positive association between brain size and intelligence in humans has been shown in numerous studies carried out from the first decade of the 20th century. The research has been reviewed by Philip Vernon, John Wickett, Gordon Bazana and Robert Stelmack (2000), who report 54 studies that used an external measure of head size. Every single one of the studies showed a positive relationship. The overall correlation was 0.18. They also report 11 studies of normal populations that measured brain size by CT (computerized axial tomography) and MRI (magnetic resonance imaging), which give a more accurate measure of brain size, and for which there was an overall correlation of 0.40. A further study published subsequent to this review found a correlation for 40 subjects between brain size measured by MRI and intelligence of 0.44 (Thompson, Cannon, Narr, et al., 2001). Vernon et al. conclude that the most reasonable interpretation of the correlation is that brain size is a determinant of intelligence. Larger brains have more neurons, and this gives them greater processing capacity. The association between brain volume and intelligence, it has been shown, is of genetic origin (Posthuma, De Geus, Baaré, et al., 2002). And it is not only among humans that brain size is correlated with intelligence. The same association has been found among rats in a study by Britt Anderson (1993), in which rats' ability to learn their way through mazes was positively correlated with their brain weight.

The correlation of 0.40 obtained by Vernon et al. (2000) between brain size and IQ should be corrected for measurement error ("correction for attenuation") of the intelligence tests. Correction for measurement error is obtained by dividing the correlation by the square root of the product of the reliability coefficients of the two measures from which the correlation coefficient is computed. The reliability of intelligence tests is typically around 0.90 (Bouchard, 1993, p. 49; Mackintosh, 1998). The reliability of the brain size measures is not known, but it is assumed to be perfect. Correction of the correlation of 0.40 between brain size and IQ for the imperfect reliability of the intelligence tests (0.90) gives a true correlation coefficient of 0.44.

6. CONTRIBUTION OF RACE DIFFERENCES IN BRAIN SIZE TO DIFFERENCES IN INTELLIGENCE

We now consider the extent to which race differences in brain size can explain the differences in intelligence. To do this we have to calculate the race differences in brain size in standard deviation units (*d*) and multiply these *d*s by the correlation between brain size and intelligence. This gives the IQ differences of the races attributable to the brain size differences. These calculations require means and standard deviations of brain size for the races. The standard deviations are only available for Europeans, Africans, Native Americans, South Asians, and East Asians, as given by Kenneth Beals, Courtland Smith, and Stephen Dodd (1984), so these are the only races for which the calculations can be made. The results are summarized in Table 16.3.

Table 16.3. Race differences in IQs predicted from differences in brain size

	RACIAL COMPARISONS	BRAIN SIZE DIFFERENCE: D	PREDICTED IQ DIFFERENCE: D (IQ)	ACTUAL IQ DIFFERENCE: D (IQ)
1	European-Sub-Saharan African	1.46	0.64 (9.6)	2.1 (29.0)
2	European-North American	0.43	0.19 (2.8)	0.9 (13.5)
3	European-South Asian	0.48	0.21 (3.2)	0.8 (12.0)
4	European-Northeast Asian	1.23	0.54 (8.1)	0.4 (6.0)

Column 1 gives the two races being compared. Column 2 gives the differences in brain size between the two races expressed as d scores (i.e., in standard deviation units) calculated from the figures given in Table 16.1. Column 3 gives the IQ difference between the two races expressed as d scores predicted from the brain size difference, obtained as the product of the d scores given in column 2 multiplied by 0.44 (the correlation between brain size and intelligence corrected for measurement error). Column 4 gives the racial IQ differences predicted from the brain size differences. Column 5 gives the actual IQ of the race in comparison with 99 for Europeans.

Row 1 gives these figures for the European-African comparison. The difference in brain size predicts that sub-Saharan Africans would have an IQ of 91. Their actual IQ is 71, so the brain size difference predicts approximately one third of the IQ difference. The remaining two thirds must be attributed to differences in neurophysiological processes and adverse environmental conditions. Row 2 gives the figures for the European-Native American comparison. The difference in brain size predicts that Native Americans would have an IQ of 97. Their actual IQ is 86, so the brain size difference predicts about a fifth of the IQ difference. Row 3 gives the figures for the European-South Asian and North African comparison. The difference in brain size predicts that South Asians and North Africans would have an IQ of 96. Their actual IQs are 84 and 83, so the brain size difference predicts about a quarter of the IQ difference. Row 4 gives the figures for the European-Northeast Asian comparison. The difference in brain size predicts that Northeast Asians would have an IQ of 109. Their actual IQ is 105, and is four four IQ points lower than would be predicted from their brain size. There are two likely explanations for this. The first is that Northeast Asians suffer environmental disadvantages, probably consisting of sub-optimal nutrition that prevents their genotypic IQ being realized; if this is so, the Northeast Asian IQ can be expected to rise to around 109 when their environmental conditions improve to the level of Europeans. A second possible explanation is that the large Northeast Asian brain serves cognitive abilities not fully represented in intelligence tests. The most likely of these is visualization abilities.

Although the contribution of race differences in brain size to race differences in IQs can only be calculated for the racial comparisons given in Table 16.3, the results showing that race differences in brain size explain some but not all of the differences in intelligence can probably be reasonably be extended to all race differences. The remainder of the differences are attributable to environmental inequalities and differences in neurophysiological processes.

7. SEX DIFFERENCES IN INTELLIGENCE AND BRAIN SIZE

A problem that has sometimes been raised in connection with the existence of race differences in brain size and intelligence is that women have significantly smaller brains than men, and yet it has been virtually universally asserted that there is no difference in intelligence between men and women. For instance, Brian Butterworth claims, "women's brains are 10% smaller than men's, but their IQ is on average the same" (Butterworth 1999, p. 293). Since women, with their smaller average brain size, are just as intelligent as men, it appears to follow that brain size has no effect on intelligence. This is the conclusion not surprisingly drawn by Stephen Jay Gould (1996, p. 132), who writes that it disproves "the myth that group differences in brain size bear any relationship to intelligence."

That women have, on average, smaller brain size has been demonstrated by Davison Ankney (1992) and J.P. Rushton (1992). Ankney calculated that the average male brain, adjusted for larger body size, is 100 grams heavier than that of women. Rushton calculated, from another data set of 6,325 military personnel, that the average male brain, adjusted for larger body size, is 1,442cc and the average female brain is 1,332cc, a male advantage of 110cc. One cc of brain tissue weighs approximately one gram, so the Ankney and Rushton results are closely similar. These results have been confirmed by Uner Tan et al. (1999), who report that among college students in Turkey, men have a larger average brain of 91cc.

Thus we have the apparent paradox that brain size is positively related to intelligence, that men have larger average brain size than women, and yet (presumably) men and women have the same intelligence. In my own work, I have presented the resolution of this paradox (Lynn, 1994b and 1999; Lynn and Irwing, 2004). Up to the age of 15 years, males and females have approximately the same intelligence, except for a small male advantage on the visualization abilities; however, from the age of 16 years, males begin to show greater intelligence, reaching an advantage of from three to five IQ points in adults. This has been further confirmed by Paul Irwing and myself (Irwing & Lynn, 2005; Irwing, 2012), by Victoria Bourne, Helen Fox, Ian Deary, and Lawrence Whaley (2007).

8. GENETICAL PROCESSES IN THE EVOLUTION OF RACE DIFFERENCES IN IQ

Two genetical processes must be assumed to explain the evolution of race differences in intelligence. The first of these is that differences in the frequencies of the alleles for high and low intelligence have evolved between races such that the alleles for high intelligence are more common in the races with higher IQs and less common in the races with lower IQs. The early humans that migrated out of Africa and spread throughout the world would have carried all the alleles for high and low intelligence with them, but those who colonized Asia and Europe were exposed to the cognitively demanding problems of survival during cold winters. Many of those carrying the alleles for low intelligence would have been unable to survive during the cold winters,, and the less intelligent individuals and tribes would have died out, leaving as survivors the more intelligent. This process would have reduced, and possibly eliminated, the alleles for low intelligence, leaving a higher proportion of the alleles for high intelligence. The more severe the winter temperatures, the greater the selection pressure for the elimination of low IQ individuals carrying low IQ alleles. This process explains the broad association between coldest winter temperatures and IQs and brain size shown in Table 16.2.

A parallel genetical process must have been involved in the evolution of race differences in skin color. The first humans who evolved in tropical equatorial Africa must have had black or very dark skins, as these peoples do today, because of the adaptive advantage of dark skin in strong sunlight. When some of these early peoples migrated into North Africa, Asia, and Europe, alleles for paler skins must have appeared as mutations. Individuals with these mutations would have had a selective advantage because they could synthesize vitamin D from sunlight (while at the same time they did not suffer the disadvantage of contracting skin cancer from the excessively strong sunlight of the tropics). Hence, individuals with paler skins left more surviving offspring, with the result that the alleles for paler skins spread through the population and eventually replaced the alleles for dark skin. This process produced the same broad gradient for skin color as evolved for intelligence: the Arctic peoples, East Asians, and Europeans evolved the palest skins; the South Asians and North Africans, Native Americans, Southeast Asians, and Pacific Islanders evolved somewhat paler skins; while the Africans, Bushmen, and Australian Aborigines, who were exposed to the strongest sunlight, retained the darkest skins.

A second genetical process has been proposed by Edward Miller (1996, 2005), in which several new alleles for high intelligence appeared as mutations in some races but did not appear in others, and these were never transmitted to some other races. This assumption is necessary to explain some of the anomalies in the general relationship between severe winters and the race differences in intelligence. The general principles are that new mutant alleles for high intelligence would be most likely to appear in large populations and in populations that are subjected to stress. New mutant alleles for high intelligence would be most likely to appear in large populations, because a mutation is a chance genetic event and hence is more likely to occur in races with large populations. In addition, populations subjected to stress, including extreme temperatures, also experience more mutations (Plomin, DeFries, and McClearn, 1990, p. 91). The effect of these two principles is that mutations for higher intelligence would have been more likely to occur and can be assumed to have occurred more frequently in the South Asians, who had large populations and were subjected to cold stress, and particularly in the East Asians and Europeans, who had large populations and were subjected to extreme cold stress; such mutations are less likely to have occurred in the Africans, who had large populations but were not subjected to extreme cold stress, and in the Australian Aborigines and Bushmen, who had small populations and were not subjected to extreme cold stress. The Arctic Peoples were subject to extreme cold stress but comprised very small populations, so they would be unlikely to have had mutations for higher intelligence. It may also be that "directed mutation" also operated to produce new mutant alleles for high intelligence in the South Asians, and particularly in the East Asians and Europeans. The concept of "directed mutation" is that a mutation is more likely to occur if it is advantageous to the organism. The theory was first proposed by John Cairn, Julie Overbaugh, and Stephan Miller (1988) and has been supported by a number of biologists (Lenski & Mittler, 1993). Higher intelligence would have been more advantageous for the South Asians, and particularly for the Northeast Asians and Europeans, than for the sub-Saharan Africans.

Once a new mutant allele for higher intelligence had appeared, it would confer a selection advantage and would have spread throughout the group of around 50 to 80 individuals in which people lived during the hunter-gatherer stage of human evolution. It would then have spread fairly rapidly to adjacent groups, because hunter-peoples typically have alliances with neighboring groups with which they exchange mating partners, and it is reasonable to assume that this custom was present for many thousands of years during the evolution of the races. These alliances of groups are known as "demes," and a new mutant allele for higher intelligence and which conferred a selection advantage would have spread fairly rapidly through a deme. From time to time, matings would take place between demes, and by this means, new mutant alleles for higher intelligence would spread from one deme to another and eventually throughout an entire race. It has been estimated by Shahin Rouhani (1989), using reasonable assumptions of a selection coefficient of 0.01 and a five percent migration per generation between hunter-gather demes of around 500 individuals, that advantageous alleles would spread at a rate of 0.8 miles a generation. Thus, in 25,000 years, consisting of approximately 1,000 generations, an advantageous allele would be transmitted about 800 miles. Hence, an advantageous allele occurring as a mutant in the region of, say, Beijing some 25,000 years ago would not yet have spread outside China and would take another 50,000 years or so to reach the Arctic Peoples of far Northeast Asia. This model does not, however, take account of the geographical barriers that have generally been present between the races, such as the Gobi Desert between Northeast Asians and Europeans and the Sahara between sub-Saharan Africans and North Africans, which have largely prevented interbreeding between the demes of different races and hence the transmission of new mutant alleles for higher intelligence from one race to another.

CHAPTER 17

THE EVOLUTION OF RACE DIFFERENCES IN INTELLIGENCE

NOW THAT THE GENERAL PRINCIPLES of the evolution of intelligence and the crucial effects of climate on the evolution of race differences in intelligence and brain size have been set out in Chapters 15 and 16, we are able to reconstruct for each race how and when the differences in intelligence evolved. We begin with the *Homo erectus* peoples, who flourished in equatorial Africa from approximately 1.7 million to 200,000 years ago. During this period, their brain size increased from about 885cc to about 1,186cc (Ruff, Trinkaus, & Holliday, 1997). The reason for this increase in brain size is that, in all mammals, intelligence was under continual directional selection, i.e., the more intelligent individuals left more surviving offspring, and this process was speeded up in the evolving hominids. At the end of this period, *Homo sapiens* appeared (Relethford, 1988), and the quality of their tools suggests that they were capable of Piaget's stage of concrete operational thinking of the kind achieved by contemporary European seven- to eight-year-olds, indicating that their IQ might have been around 50 (Chapter 15, Section 6).

1. THE EVOLUTION OF INTELLIGENCE IN SUB-SAHARAN AFRICANS

During the last 200,000 years, the ancestors of the contemporary sub-Saharan Africans continued to inhabit the tropical and sub-tropical environments of equatorial sub-Saharan Africa. This environment was not strongly cognitively demanding for them, and primates had adapted to it for some 60 million years. The hominids up to and including *Homo erectus* were largely plant eaters, but they supplemented their diets with scavenging the carcasses of animals killed by lions, leopards, and cheetahs (Lee, 1968; Tooby and de Vore, 1989). The evolving Africans lived much as hunter-gatherer peoples in tropical and sub-tropical environments do today, subsisting largely on plant foods, of which numerous species are available throughout the year, and on insects and eggs, with only occasional supplementation from animal meats obtained from hunting.

The ready availability of plant foods, insects, and eggs throughout the year meant that the evolving sub-Saharan African peoples in tropical and sub-tropical Africa did not have to hunt animals to obtain meat. In 1966, a conference of anthropologists was convened to debate the "Man, the Hunter" thesis regarding the importance of hunting for contemporary hunter-gatherers, at which "the consensus of opinion . . . was that meat is of relatively little nutritional importance in the diets of the same modern tropical foragers" (Stanford and Bunn, 2001, p. 4). In 1999, a similar conference took place; the consensus here was that "that hominid diets were primarily plant based, as they are among modern tropical foragers" (Stanford and Bunn, 2001, p. 356). The sub-Saharan Africans, it has been argued, had no need to develop the intelligence, skills, tools, and weapons needed for hunting large mammals. Furthermore, the temperature of equatorial Africa varies annually between approximately 32° C (89.5° F) in the hottest month and 17° C (62.5° F) in the coldest. In such a warm climate, the sub-Saharan African peoples did not encounter the cognitively demanding requirements of having to make needles and thread for clothes and tents, of making fires and keeping them alight, or of preparing and storing food for future consumption. It was relatively easy to keep babies, infants, and young children alive because there was no need to provide them with clothing and from quite a young age, they were capable of going out and foraging for food by themselves.

Nevertheless, the brain size of the sub-Saharan Africans increased during the last 200,000 or so years from approximately 1,186 to 1,276cc, and it can be reasonably assumed that this entailed an increase in their intelligence to its contemporary value of approximately 71. This increase occurred because of continual directional selection for intelligence; simply put, the more intelligent individuals had more surviving offspring. The genetical processes will have consisted of the increase in the frequencies of the alleles for higher IQs and probably of one or more mutations for higher intelligence. The anthropologists Richard Klein and Blake Edgar (2002, p. 270) propose that a mutation for higher intelligence appeared about 50,000 years ago in East Africa and spread throughout the world. If this is so, the new mutated allele for higher intelligence would have spread through the populations, because high intelligence is a fitness characteristic, but it would not have spread as rapidly and extensively in Africa as in temperate and cold climates, because the selection pressures for higher intelligence were not so strong in the benign climate of equatorial Africa.

The level of intelligence that evolved in the sub-Saharan Africans was sufficient for them to make slight progress in the transition from hunter-gathering to settled agriculture. But in the end, they developed no written language, arithmetic, or calendar system, and they built no cities in stone. In other words, sub-Saharan Africans did not develop anything that could be called a "civilization" (Baker, 1974).

2. THE EVOLUTION OF INTELLIGENCE IN BUSHMEN

It appears to have been around 100,000 years ago that some groups of archaic sub-Saharan Africans from equatorial East Africa began to migrate south, where they evolved into the Bushmen; they came to occupy most of southern Africa, but only a few tens of thousands of them survive today in the Kalahari Desert. During the last 100,000 years, the brain size of the Bushmen increased by approximately 10 percent to 1,270cc, at which it stands today, and their IQ increased to 56. The climate in southern Africa is warm and temperate with slightly cooler winters than in equatorial Africa. Nevertheless, the Bushmen were able to survive largely on plant foods, insects, and eggs, as they do today. It has been reported by Ann Brower Stahl (1984) that Bushmen eat around 90 different plant foods and these constitute 70–85 percent of their diet. More recently, William Leonard (2008) has noted that the Bushmen have among the lowest levels of animal food consumption among hunter-gatherers.

Hence, the Bushmen were not exposed to the cognitive demands of survival in a cold temperate environment. Nevertheless, on a solely climatic theory of the evolution of race differences in intelligence, they should have evolved a higher level of intelligence than the sub-Saharan Africans. This failed to occur, and the IQ of the Bushmen today is lower than that of the sub-Saharan Africans, at 56 and 71, respectively. The explanation for this is probably that some mutations for higher intelligence appeared in the sub-Saharan Africans, due to their large population size, and did not appear amongst the Bushmen, because of their smaller numbers. However, the brain size of the Bushmen is only slightly smaller than that of Africans (approximately 1,270cc and 1,276cc, respectively). This indicates that the mutant alleles for higher IQs that probably appeared in sub-Saharan Africans and spread through the population were for neurological processes rather than for increased brain size.

3. THE EVOLUTION OF INTELLIGENCE IN SOUTH ASIANS AND NORTH AFRICANS

The first groups to migrate out of sub-Saharan Africa colonized North Africa and South Asia between about 100,000 to 90,000 years ago (Stringer, 2011, p. 26). Other authorities have suggested that this migration may have taken place as recently as 50,000 years ago, but the precise date of these migrations is not needed for our present purposes. In the period between about 90,000 to 50,000 years ago, these peoples colonized the whole of South Asia. The migrants in North Africa and South Asia were isolated from the sub-Saharan Africans by distance and the Sahara desert and evolved into the South Asians and North Africans. Initially, they encountered a temperate climate similar to that of today, with the coldest winter month averaging about 13°C (55.5°F). Around 70,000 years ago, the first Ice Ages began in the northern hemisphere and lasted until around 50,000 years ago. This was followed by a warmer period between around 50,000 and 28,000 years ago, and then by a second and more severe Ice Age (the main Würm glaciation) that began around 28,000 years ago and lasted until around 10,000 years ago, when temperatures rose quite rapidly to the benign climate of today (Roberts, 1989; Foley, 1987). During the main Würm glaciation, winter temperatures in North Africa, Eurasia, and North America fell by approximately 5° C (9° F) (Roberts, 1989). The coldest winter month in North Africa and South Asia fell to approximately 7° C (44.5° F).[CAPITALIZE ICE AGES?]

Survival during the Ice Ages for the peoples in the cold temperate environments in North Africa and South Asia (and later in the sub-arctic environment of Europe and northern Asia) would have presented a number of cognitively demanding problems that would have acted as selection pressures for greater intelligence than was required in the tropical and sub-tropical climates of sub-Saharan Africa. There would have been five major challenges. First: plant foods were not available during the winter and spring, and were not abundant even in the summer and autumn; insects and reptiles were not available either, because these often hibernate. The major source of food, therefore, became large mammals such as antelope, deer, horses, and boars. It would have been difficult to hunt these large mammals in the grasslands that covered much of the northern hemisphere during the last Ice Age, because there is good visibility for several thousand yards and the herbivores have ample warning of approaching predators. Hunting in open grasslands is more difficult than in the woodlands of the tropics and sub-tropics, where there is plenty of cover for hunters to hide. The humans that evolved in equatorial Africa were largely herbivorous and were not adapted for hunting large mammals, so this would have presented new cognitive problems for them. Large herbivores can run fast and are virtually impossible to catch by men on foot. The only way of killing these animals was to make use of natural traps into which the animals could be driven and then killed. One of the most frequently exploited natural traps was narrow ravines, through which the beasts could be driven and where some of them would stumble and could be speared or clubbed by members of the group waiting in ambush. Another was cliffs towards which a group of men could drive a herd of herbivores, so that some of them would fall over the edge and be killed (or sufficiently injured for other members of the hunting group to kill them). Other natural traps were bogs and the loops of rivers, into which hunting groups could drive herbivores and then kill them. Archaeological excavations have shown that all these traps were used by early humans in Eurasia (Geist, 1978; Mellars, 1999). Working out strategies for cooperative group hunting and trapping large herbivores in these ways would have required an increase in cognitive ability.

It has been shown that among contemporary hunter-gatherers the proportions of foods obtained by hunting and by gathering varies according to latitude. Peoples in tropical and sub-tropical latitudes are largely gatherers, while peoples in temperate environments rely more on hunting; peoples in arctic and sub-arctic environments rely almost exclusively on hunting and fishing, as plant foods are unavailable except for berries and nuts in the summer and autumn (Lee, 1968). When early humans migrated into the temperate regions of North Africa and South Asia, many of those with low IQs could not survive the cold winters. This culling process gradually increased the collective IQ of the survivors to 84.

The effective hunting of large herbivores required the manufacture of a variety of tools from stone, wood, and bone for making spears and for cutting up the carcasses. Some of these animals could be brought down by spears that had to be made by hafting or tying a sharp piece of stone, which had to be manufactured, onto the end of a shaft. When these peoples had brought down and killed a large herbivore, they would have had to skin it and cut it up into pieces of a size that could be carried back to the base camp for the women and children. These animals have thick skins and tough ligaments that are difficult to cut, and people would have needed sharp tools manufactured for these specific purposes. In sub-arctic environments, animals that are killed freeze fairly rapidly and become impossible to cut up, so the hunters had to have good cutting tools that would do the job quickly, before the carcasses froze solid.

Peoples in cold environments need more tools of different kinds and greater complexity than peoples in tropical and subtropical environments. Robin Torrence (1983) has demonstrated an association between latitude and the number and complexity of tools used by contemporary hunter-gatherers. He found that hunter-gatherer peoples in tropical and subtropical latitudes, such as the Amazon basin and New Guinea, typically have between 10 and 20 different tools, whereas those in the colder northern latitudes of Siberia, Alaska, and Greenland have between 25 and 60 different tools. In addition, peoples in cold northern environments make more complex tools involving the assembly of components, such as hafting a sharp piece of stone or bone onto the end of a spear and fixing a stone axe head onto a timber shaft.

Another set of problems encountered by the peoples in the northern hemisphere would have been concerned with keeping warm. People had to solve the problems of making fires and shelters. Archaeological excavations have shown that during the Ice Ages peoples in China and Europe were making fires. To do this, they would have had to learn how to make sparks by striking one stone against another and then get these sparks to ignite dried grass. They would have needed a supply of dry grass and dry wood and animal dung stored in caves to get their fires started and keep them going. This would have needed intelligence and forward planning. Peoples in sub-Saharan Africa and Australia also had fire, but it would have been easier to get fires going in the tropics and sub-tropics, because there would have been spontaneous bush fires from which ignited branches could be taken and carried back to camp to start domestic fires. The problems of starting fires and keeping them burning would have been considerably more difficult in Eurasia and North America than in the tropical and sub-tropical southern hemisphere.

A further problem of keeping warm would have necessitated the making of clothing and tents by sewing together animal skins. This entailed the drying and treatment of the skins of large herbivores and the manufacture of needles from bone and thread to sew skins together to make clothes and footwear. It would have been necessary to make clothes for babies and children as well as adults. Some people kept warm by living in caves, but in places where there were no caves, they used large bones and skins sewn together to make tents, resembling the yurts that are still made in Mongolia (Geist, 1978; Mellars et al., 1999).

The final problem for the peoples in temperate and cold environments concerned food storage. This was necessary because, after they had killed and dismembered several large mammals, they could not eat them all within a few days, and they therefore needed to conserve them for future use.

Some animals that could be killed are migratory and appear in any particular territory for only short periods of time each year. This presents opportunities to kill large numbers of them, too many for immediate consumption, and thus the necessity of storage for future use. One example is reindeer, which migrate regularly over long distances at certain times of the year. In many cases, they follow the same routes at the same time of year, so their appearance could be predicted by early humans who had acquired a knowledge of the seasons and the calendar from astronomical observations. Another migratory species is salmon, which migrate in large numbers at a certain time of the year from the sea up rivers in order to spawn. Many of these rivers are quite shallow, and it is not too difficult to spear large numbers of salmon as they swim upstream. It is also possible to catch them in nets, the construction of which was another cognitively demanding problem for peoples in Eurasia. These peoples would have been able to anticipate the arrival of these migrating herds and fish and kill large numbers of them as they passed through.

In very cold environments, the problem of storing food for future consumption could be solved for part of the year by building icehouses, which served as freezers for preserving the carcasses. Another solution was to cut the flesh into thin slices and dry them. When this is done properly, the pieces will remain edible for a considerable time, but if not, they would become toxic. No doubt, some of the less intelligent and conscientious would have died from food poisoning. This would have been another of the many selection pressures acting to increase the intelligence of the peoples colonizing the niche of the temperate and cold environments. It has been suggested by Edward Miller (1991) that the storage of food would also have required the formulation of rules for rationing its consumption, and that this would have involved the development of arithmetic to allocate it equitably.

Among contemporary hunter-gatherers, it has been shown by Lewis Binford (1980, 1985) that there is a relationship between the extent to which they store food and the temperature of the environments in which they live. The colder the environments, the more they store food for future consumption. He reports that in general it is only in colder climates, where growing seasons are less than about two hundred days, that hunter-gatherer peoples store food.

In addition to these cognitive problems of survival in the northern hemisphere, a further selection pressure for greater intelligence would have been the operation of sexual selection by women. In Eurasia and North America, women would have become entirely dependent on men for much of the year to provide food for themselves and their children. In equatorial Africa and the southern hemisphere, where plant and insect foods are available throughout the year, women are relatively independent of men. Even women with infants and young dependent children can take these with them on foraging trips, or can leave them in the care of other women for a few hours while they go out and gather plant foods. It would have been more difficult and frequently impossible for women with infants and young children in the northern hemisphere to go out on hunting expeditions (possibly lasting several days), kill and dismember large mammals, and carry pieces of them for many miles back to camps. The effect of this would have been that women in the northern hemisphere would have depended on men to bring them food. They would, therefore, have tended to accept as mates intelligent men who were good at hunting and making tools and weapons. The effect of this sexual selection by women would have been that intelligent men would have had more children, and this would have increased the intelligence of the group. Another effect of the greater dependence of women on men in Eurasia would have been that men and women would become psychologically more closely bonded. This potentially explains why the marriages and non-marital relationships of European and East Asian peoples are more stable than those of sub-Saharan Africans (Lynn, 2002).

Survival in the cold environment of the northern hemisphere would have required an increase in general intelligence, defined as general problem solving and learning ability, and in most of the primary cognitive abilities of which general intelligence is composed. Stronger reasoning ability would have been needed to solve all the new problems encountered in the cold northern latitudes, such as building shelters and fires, making clothes, and manufacturing more efficient tools for killing, butchering, and skinning large animals. Improved verbal ability would have been needed for better communication in discussions of how to solve these problems, for planning future activities, and for transmitting acquired cultural knowledge and skills to children. Improved visualization ability would have been needed for planning and executing group hunting strategies, for accurate aiming of spears and missiles, and for the manufacture of more sophisticated tools and weapons from stone, bone, and wood. Fathers would have shown sons how to chip flints to produce good cutting tools and to make spears with sharp points, and these skills would have been conveyed largely by watching and imitation (and not just verbal communication), much as craft skills are learned today by apprentices watching skilled craftsmen. Hunting and tool making would have been undertaken principally by males. the legacy of this is that, in virtually all cases, visualization abilities are stronger in males than in females (Linn and Peterson, 1986). There would have been less selection pressure on the peoples in the northern hemisphere to develop better short-term memory and perceptual speed, which explains why these abilities have not become so strongly enhanced among the Europeans as compared with the Africans.

The selection pressures for enhanced intelligence in the temperate environment of North Africa and South Asia, and later in the sub-Arctic environment of Europe and North Asia, would have acted on both men and women. The selection pressure on men for greater intelligence would have come from the need to go on hunting expeditions to kill large mammals and to make the tools required for this and for skinning and cutting them up. This would have required enhanced spatial intelligence and reasoning ability, which are greater on average in men than in women (Linn and Petersen, 1986; Lynn and Irwing, 2004). Women would have needed enhanced general intelligence for lighting and maintaining fires and preserving food and storing it for future consumption, and they would have had the responsibility of keeping babies and young children alive by keeping them warm. The genetic processes occurring in the North Africans and South Asians would have been an increase in the frequencies of the alleles for higher intelligence and probably the appearance of new mutations for higher intelligence and their diffusion through the population. A new mutation for higher intelligence has been proposed by the "cognitive archaeologist" Thomas Wynn, who places the appearance of this at somewhere between 130,000 and 70,000 years ago (Wynn, 2002, p. 397-ff.; Coolidge & Wynn, 2005). The anthropologists Richard Klein and Blake Edgar (2002) also propose a new mutation for higher intelligence, which they place at about 50,000 years ago. They infer that peoples at this time have evolved higher intelligence from the increased complexity of their stone artifacts, which they "knapped" (i.e. struck to produce sharp cutting tools) in advanced ways requiring visualization of the end product before striking the stone.

The most probable scenario is that the intelligence of North Africans and South Asians increased during both of the two ice ages, the first of which lasted between approximately 70,000 and 50,000 years ago and the second, between 28,000 and 10,000 years ago. The increase in intelligence after the end of the first of these two Ice Ages can be inferred from their more sophisticated tools and other artifacts that appeared about 50,000 years ago (Klein and Edgar, 2002; Stringer and McKie, 1996, p. 185–187). However, their intelligence did not increase to the level at which they were able to make the Neolithic transition from hunter-gathering to settled agriculture. A further increase in intelligence must have taken place during the second major Ice Age (the main Würm glaciation). The severity of the climate during this period would have been the main selection pressure that drove the brain size of the South Asians and North Africans up to 1,342cc and their IQ up to around 84. This was sufficient to allow them to make the Neolithic transition to settled agriculture about 9,500 years ago, and then to build the early civilizations along the valleys of the Nile, Tigris, Euphrates, and Indus rivers, in which they developed cities, written languages, arithmetic, legal systems, and all the fundaments of civilization.

4. THE EVOLUTION OF INTELLIGENCE IN SOUTHEAST ASIANS

Some of the peoples in South Asia migrated into Southeast Asia around 70,000 years ago and evolved into today's Southeast Asian sub-race. This region enjoys a tropical and sub-tropical climate where the coldest monthly winter temperature is about 24°C (75°F). These peoples had reached this Southeast Asia before the onset of the Ice Ages, which had little effect on the region. Hence they were under little selection pressure for an increase of intelligence. However, their IQ of 87 is fractionally higher than that of the North Africans and South Asians (84), from whom they mostly evolved. The most probable explanation is that there is some Northeast Asian admixture in the Southeast Asians from Northeast Asians who migrated south and interbred with indigenous populations. There has been substantial migration of Northeast Asians into Southeast Asia. Thus, today in Singapore, 76 percent of the population is Chinese; in Malaysia 30 percent of the population is Chinese; and there are significant Chinese minorities in Cambodia and Thailand (Philip's, 1996). These Northeast Asians have interbred with the indigenous peoples, and this has produced a racial hybrid population in Southeast Asia. As a result of this migration and inter-mating, the Southeast Asian peoples are closely related genetically to the southern Chinese (Cavalli-Sforza, Menozzi, and Piazza, 1994, p. 78). The Chinese admixture in the Southeast Asians has introduced some of the alleles for high intelligence and raised their IQs to 87.

This IQ enabled the Southeast Asians to make the Neolithic transition from hunter-gathering to settled agriculture and then to build moderately impressive civilizations during the first millennia of the common era. Asians and North Africans, because the river valleys in Southeast Asia were densely forested and do not have the flood plains from which the agricultural surpluses were produced to sustain the first civilizations in Mesopotamia, Egypt, and China. However, from around AD 1,000, their IQs were not sufficient for them to be able to compete economically or in science and technology with the Europeans and the East Asians.

5. THE EVOLUTION OF INTELLIGENCE IN PACIFIC ISLANDERS

It was only around 6,000 years ago that some Southeast Asians began to migrate into the Pacific islands, where they evolved into the Pacific Islanders. Their IQ of 85 is not significantly different from that of 87 of the Southeast Asians from whom they largely evolved, and is likewise higher than would be expected from the benign climates they experience, where the coldest monthly winter temperature is about 24° C (75° F). The explanation for this is the same as for the Southeast Asians, namely an admixture with Northeast Asians who migrated south and interbred with indigenous populations. The presence of significant Northeast Asian ancestry in the Pacific Islanders is shown by their small teeth, which are small in Northeast Asians but large among the Australian Aborigines (Brace and Hinton, 1981). Unlike the Southeast Asians, the Pacific Islanders made only moderate progress in the Neolithic transition to settled agriculture and no progress in developing civilizations. The explanation for this is that their populations have been so small, typically numbering only a few thousands and scattered on remote islands separated over huge distances. It was only the Maoris who had a large territory in New Zealand, but they only colonized the islands about the year AD 800 and have had insufficient time to produce a large population, make the full Neolithic transition, and begin to build a civilization.

6. THE EVOLUTION OF INTELLIGENCE IN AUSTRALIAN AND NEW GUINEAN ABORIGINES

Some of the peoples of South Asia and East Asia migrated into the islands of the Indonesian archipelago and reached New Guinea about 65,000 years ago. About 60,000 years ago, some of these peoples migrated into Australia, where they evolved into the Australian Aborigines (Bradshaw, 1997). At this time, the migration could be made on foot, as there was no sea between New Guinea and Australia. A closely related people survived in the highlands of New Guinea as the New Guinea Aborigines.

The ancestors of the Australian Aborigines and the New Guineans were never exposed to the severe winters that began in South Asia with the onset of the first Ice Age about 70,000 years ago. By this time, they would have been in Southeast Asia, Indonesia, or New Guinea, all of which lie on the equator or very close to it. They were not affected by the second Ice Age in the northern hemisphere. Thus the Australian Aborigines and the New Guineans have the morphological features of a people who have evolved in tropical and subtropical environments and have never been exposed to a temperate climate. They are similar to the Africans in their dark skin, wide noses, long legs, slender trunk, and large teeth.

Like other peoples who have evolved in tropical and subtropical environments, the New Guineans and the Australian Aborigines were able to live on plant foods, insects, and eggs throughout the year. When the Australian Aborigines were studied in the desert of Western Australia in the 20th century, their diet remained largely unchanged: they obtained 70–80 percent of their food from plants and most of the remainder from eggs and insects. They had no well-developed group hunting techniques (Gould, 1969). It has been estimated that the Gadio people, a tribe of New Guineans, obtain 96 percent of their food from plants and only four percent from meat (Dornstreich, 1973). The ready availability of plant foods throughout the year, together with insects and eggs, meant that the Aboriginal peoples in tropical and subtropical New Guinea and Australia never had to rely on meat for their food supply and did not come under strong selection pressure to develop the cognitive abilities required to hunt large animals. Neither did they need to make clothes to keep warm. Even in the island of Tasmania off the south of Australia the temperature in July, the coldest month of the year, averages 7° C (45° F), and "the Tasmanians habitually went naked" (Coon, 1967, p. 114). This explains why their intelligence and brain size are both low: an IQ of 62 and an average brain size of 1,225cc. These are both a little lower than those of the sub-Sarahan Africans. with their IQ of 71 and average brain size of 1,280cc. The most probable explanation for this is that the sub-Sarahan Africans were a much larger population in which mutations for higher intelligence had a greater chance of occurring, while the Australian Aborigines were much fewer. The number of Aboriginal New Guineans in the highlands of New Guinea is around a quarter of a million. The number of Australian Aborigines in the 18th century, when the Europeans first arrived, is estimated at about 300,000. In such a small population, the probability of new mutations for higher intelligence occurring would have been low, and the geographical isolation of the Aborigines of Australia and New Guinea would have prevented the acquisition of these mutations from other races.

When Europeans discovered Australia in the late 18th century, they found the Aborigines at a primitive level of cultural development. "Their Mesolithic (stone age) culture was (and still is in remote areas) without pottery, agriculture, or metals" (Cole, 1965, p. 82). They did not plant seeds to grow food or keep herds of animals (Elkin, 1967). They did not store food for future consumption. As described by John William Bleakley (1961, p. 18), "the aboriginal seems to have had no idea of conserving supplies against a 'hungry time'." Northcote Whitridge Thomas (1925, p. 295) described the Aborigine as "a nomad, who knows neither pottery nor metal work; has no domesticated animals, for the dingo is at most tamed, and he does not till the ground, depending for his sustenance on snakes and lizards, emus, grubs, and simple vegetable foods." FIRST NAME Cole added, "Their main stone implements include the hafted stone axe and knife, and microliths (tiny flakes) mounted as barbs of spear-heads, teeth of saw-knives, and so on. Weapons consist of clubs, spears, spear throwers, and the boomerang. Women use digging sticks to uproot yams and other roots" (Cole, 1965, p. 83). They never invented or acquired the bow and arrow (Coon, 1967). Several of the British explorers and early anthropologists who studied the Aborigines in the 19th century concluded that they had a low level of intelligence: "the Australian aborigines are still but children in their general mental development" (Wake, 1872, p. 80). Their languages lacked numbers, except for one and a pair (Crawfurd, 1863, p. 177), and they were also lacking in abstract concepts and "poor in collective nouns" (Curr, 1886, p. 20), indicative of the inability to formulate general concepts, which is one of the principal characteristics of intelligence. The Aborigines did, however, make primitive drawings of the human form, which survive in the Jinmiun rock shelter in the Northern Territories and which have been dated at about 58,000 years ago (Bradshaw, 1997).

In his popular book *Guns, Germans, and Steel*, Jared Diamond (1997, p. 309) attributes the failure of the Australian Aborigines to domesticate animals or develop agriculture to "the lack of domesticable animals, the poverty of domesticable plants, and the difficult soils and climate"; however, on the same page, Diamond tells us that yams, taro, and arrowroot grow wild in northern Australia and could have been planted and that there are two indigenous wild grasses that could have been bred to produce cereals. The kangaroo and the dingo could have been domesticated by selective breeding for tameness over a number of generations. The climate of Australia is quite varied and, apart from the deserts of the central region, is potentially suitable for the agriculture that was developed during the 19th and 20th centuries by Europeans.

It has sometimes been argued that the deserts of central Australia must have been a harsh and cognitively demanding environment that should have selected for higher intelligence. This suggestion is misconceived, because most of the Aboriginal population lived in the fertile south east (Gamble, 1993, p.217).

The Tasmanians had an even lower level of cultural development than the Aborigines of the Australian mainland. The Russian anthropologist Vladimir Kabo (1985, p. 603) has written that they are "the only society that persisted at the level of the late

Palaeolithic right up to the beginning of European colonization." Captain William Bligh (1754-1817) visited Tasmania in 1788 and described them as nomadic hunter gatherers who had "some miserable wigwams, in which were nothing but a few kangaroo skins spread on the ground"; they "moved from one area to another, foraging as they went, seeking out berries and fruits and the seeds of various trees and bushes." Apart from kelp, they rarely carried food of any kind with them and "they usually went naked, but occasionally draped a kangaroo skin over their bodies" (Bowdler and Ryan, 1997, pp. 318–326). They are the only known people who never discovered how to make fire (Gott, 2002). They were sometimes able to obtain fire from spontaneous bush fires, but if these went out, they had to wait for another natural flare-up or acquire fire from a neighboring band. They never invented the device of hafting a sharp stone into a wooden shaft to make a spear or axe (Ryan, 1992).

When Europeans discovered the New Guineans in the 17th and 18th centuries, they found them at a slightly more advanced stage of cultural development than the Australian Aborigines. The New Guineans were largely hunter-gatherers, but they had some agriculture, consisting of planting yams and bananas, and they had domesticated chickens and pigs. However, "until Europeans began to colonize them, all New Guineans were non-literate, dependent on stone tools, and politically not yet organized into states, or (with few exceptions) chiefdoms" (Diamond, 1997, p. 299). Following European colonization, some of them moved into towns and villages and others remained in rural areas living as subsistence farmers. Europeans built and staffed schools for those in towns and villages and boarding schools were established for those in rural areas, although some rural children did not attend school. Writing in the 1970s, Max Kelly (1977) reported that rural and village tribes in Papua New Guinea lived largely by subsistence slash-and-burn agriculture, carried out mainly by women. The men did some hunting, and some of them worked for wages on coffee plantations run by Europeans. The clothing of the less developed tribes consisted of skirts made from leaves and bark. Some of the tribes had counting systems that enabled them to count to 1,000, while others only had words for "one," "one plus," and "many." The principal reason that the New Guineans were a little more advanced than the Australian Aborigines is that the coastal regions of the island were settled by Southeast Asians and Melanesian Pacific Islanders, who brought with them the taro, an edible root that they cultivated, and also domesticated chickens and pigs. The New Guineans adopted some of these cultural innovations, but never developed anything that could properly be called a civilization: they failed to develop towns, substantial and permanent buildings, metal working, a written language, and arithmetic.

7. THE EVOLUTION OF INTELLIGENCE IN EUROPEANS

Some of the peoples who colonized the Near East between 100,000 and 70,000 years ago migrated northwards; around 60,000 years ago, they reached the Caucasus, from which they spread into the Ukraine and then, around 40,000 years ago, into central and western Europe. Other peoples from Southwest Asia began to colonize Southeast Europe from Anatolia. These peoples evolved into the Europeans, with their paler skins and, in the north of Europe, their fair hair and blue eyes. The Europeans were largely isolated from the South Asians and North Africans on the south by the Mediterranean Sea and on the east by the Black and Caspian Seas, the high mountains of the Caucasus and Himalayas, and the Kara Kum desert in present-day Turkmenistan. In the last ice age, which lasted from around 28,000 to 10,000 years ago, the winters were significantly colder than those in South Asia, with the coldest winter month falling to about -5° C (23° F). The terrain in Europe became similar to that of present-day Alaska and Siberia. The north of England, Germany, Russia, and the whole of Scandinavia were covered with a permanent ice sheet, and the remainder of Europe featured cold grasslands and tundra with a few clumps of trees in sheltered places.

These cold winters must have been the main selection pressure for an increase in the brain size and intelligence of the Europeans, which eventually drove their average brain size up to 1,369cc and their IQ up to 99. Europeans' and Northeast Asians' greater reliance on hunting also exerted selection pressure for high intelligence, and spatial abilities in particular. Hence, Europeans have an advantage of approximately 7.5 IQ points on spatial ability over sub-Saharan Africans (Jensen, 1998, p.379), and North East Asians score even higher on spatial ability than Europeans (see chapter 10).

By about half way through the Würm glaciation, the Europeans had evidently evolved higher intelligence. This was expressed in artifacts made from wood and bone, such as barbs carved from antler for fixing on to the heads of spears, and from the cave paintings made with iron and manganese oxide pigments from about 17,000 years ago at Lascaux and other sites in south west France, and at Altamira in northern Spain at from the same period (Wynn, 2002, p. 397-ff.; Klein & Edgar, 2002).

By about 10,000 years ago, when the ended and the ice sheets and tundra that covered northern Europe receded, the Europeans emerged with higher intelligence shown by an increase in their encephalization quotients (EQ), i.e. brain size in relation to body size. Richard Cutler (1976) estimated that pre-Würm Europeans had an EQ of 7.3, and by the end of the Würm glaciation they had an EQ of 8.1. With this increased intelligence, Europeans were able to make the Neolithic transition from hunter-gathering to settled agriculture. However, despite their high IQ, they were not able to develop early civilizations, such as those built by the South Asians and North Africans, mainly because the continent was still cold, covered with forest, and featured heavy soils that were difficult to plough. This environment was unlike that in which the early civilizations were built, which had light soils and river flood plains, which provided annual alluvial deposits that allowed for agricultural surpluses, which could sustain an urban civilization and intellectual class (Landes, 1998). From around 2500 BC, the Europeans overcame these problems in the relatively benign climate of southern Europe, where they developed the first European civilizations in Crete and Greece. From around 700 BC, the Italians began to build a civilization that eventually became the Roman Empire; by AD 200, they embraced the whole of Europe west of the Rhine, including the Danube basin, the Near East, and North Africa. These first European civilizations in Greece and Rome surpassed those of the South Asians and North

Africans in science, mathematics, technology, literature, philosophy, and the arts. The western Roman Empire had collapsed by the end of the 5th century AD, and European culture suffered a setback in the ensuing period, commonly called the Dark Ages. However, from about the year AD 1,000, it revived, and by the year 1500, Europeans became the foremost people in virtually all areas of civilization (Murray, 2003).

The genetical processes through which the higher IQs of the Europeans have evolved will have consisted of changes in allele frequencies towards a greater proportion of alleles for high intelligence, and probably also through the appearance of one or more new mutations for higher intelligence and the rapid spread of these through the population. The probability of new mutations for higher intelligence in the Europeans may have been increased by the stress of the extreme cold to which the Europeans were exposed.

The lower IQs in the range 90 to 94 in Southeast Europe are attributable to some gene flow between South Asians and Europeans across the Dardanelles and Aegean, producing a cline of South Asian and European hybrids in the Balkans with IQs intermediate between those of central and western Europeans (100) and South Asians (84). The same cline is present in Turkey where the IQ of around 90 is only fractionally lower than in the Balkans. The lower IQs in southern Italy and southern Spain are also attributable to hybridization with North African immigrants.

8. THE EVOLUTION OF INTELLIGENCE IN NORTHEAST ASIANS

Some 60,000 to 50,000 years ago, various peoples from South and Central Asia began to colonize Northeast Asia in the region of present-day China, where they evolved into the Northeast Asians and later into the Arctic Peoples of the far Northeast. The archaic Northeast Asians were largely isolated from the Europeans by the Gobi desert to the west and from the South Asians by the Himalayas to the south.

The winters to which they were exposed were much more severe than in South Asia and somewhat more severe than in Europe, with the coldest winter temperatures falling to about -12°C (10.5°F) during the main Würm glaciation. The reasons for the intense winters is that Northeast Asia is a much larger land mass than Europe and that Europe is warmed by prevailing westerly winds from the Atlantic. It was in response to the cold winters that the Northeast Asians evolved the cold adaptations of the flattened nose to prevent frost bite, the short legs and thick trunk to conserve heat, the subcutaneous layer of fat that gives the skin a yellowish appearance, the sparse facial hair in men (because profuse beards would freeze and produce frost bite), and the epicanthic eye-fold to mitigate the effect of dazzle of reflected light from snow and ice. The severe winters would have acted as a strong selection for increased intelligence and raised the IQ of the Northeast Asian peoples to 105. The genetic processes involved probably consisted of an increase in the frequencies of the alleles for high intelligence and also of new mutations for higher intelligence resulting from chance and from severe cold stress. The appearance of new mutations may explain why Northeast Asians have particularly strong visualization abilities, as compared with Europeans. New mutations for enhanced visualization abilities may have appeared in Northeast Asians and spread through the population because they were useful for hunting, tool making, and navigation over long distances through featureless terrain.

As with the Europeans, it is probable that most of the increase in the intelligence of the Northeast Asians occurred during the main Würm glaciation. This would have acted as the selection pressure for greater brain size and must have driven their IQ up to its present value of 105. It was not until after the end of the Würm glaciation that their intelligence reached the level at which they were able to make the Neolithic transition to settled agriculture. This appeared together with the domestication of rice in the valley of the Yangtze river as early as 7,000 years ago (Fuller, Harvey & Qin, 2007) and provided the groundwork for a civilization to arise in the same river valley, which, in turn, birthed subsequent cultures and civilizations in China, Japan, and Korea. During the period between around AD 0 and 1500, the Chinese built impressive civilizations that were in some respects more advanced than those in Europe. For instance, the Chinese invented printing, paper, paper money, gunpowder, the magnetic compass, and the construction of canals with locks several centuries before the Europeans. During the period from 1500 to the present, however, the intellectual achievements of the Northeast Asians have been less impressive than those of the Europeans, as has been documented quantitatively by Charles Murray (2003). Historians regard this as a major puzzle to which there is no consensus solution. One factor may be that the Northeast Asians have evolved a higher degree of social conformity than the Europeans, as studied by Jüi Allik and anu Realo (2004); this trend is also expressed in Northeast Asians low level of psychopathic personality, which I have documented (Lynn, 2002). A low level of social conformity and an element of psychopathic personality appear to be ingredients in creative achievement because they reduce anxiety about social disapproval and appear to facilitate the generation of the original ideas that are required for the highest levels of scientific discovery, artistic expression, and economic enterprise. There is also evidence for lower levels of creativity in the East Asians (Lynn, 2007). Another factor may be an historical accident, which has been discussed by Erich Weede and Sebastian Kampf (2002): throughout much of its history, China was a single state whose autocratic rulers were able to suppress liberties, including freedom of thought, more effectively than the rulers of the numerous European states, who were forced by competition to concede liberties to their peoples.

9. THE EVOLUTION OF INTELLIGENCE IN ARCTIC PEOPLES

Sometime between 50,000–40,000 years ago, some archaic Northeast Asian peoples migrated into the far northeast of Asia, where they evolved into the Arctic Peoples. These peoples became a separate race because they were geographically isolated from the Northeast Asians on the south by the high Chersky, Khrebet, Khingan, and Sayan Mountains, and about a thousand miles of forest north of the Amur

River. The Arctic Peoples experienced the severest winter conditions of all the races, with winter temperatures of about -15°C (5°F) and falling to about -20°C (-4°F) during the main Würm glaciation. In response to these cold winters, the Arctic Peoples evolved more pronounced forms of the morphological cold adaptations of the Northeast Asians, consisting of the flattened nose, the short legs and thick trunk, the subcutaneous layer of fat that gives the skin a yellowish appearance, and the epicanthic eyefold. These severe winters would be expected to have acted as a strong selection for increased intelligence, but this evidently failed to occur, as their collective IQ is only 91.

The explanation for this must lie in the small numbers of the Arctic Peoples, whose population, at the end of the 20th century, was approximately 56,000, as compared with approximately 1.4 billion Northeast Asians. While it is impossible to make precise estimates of population sizes during the main Würm glaciation, there can be no doubt that the Northeast Asians were many times more numerous than the Arctic Peoples. The effect of the difference in population size would have been that mutations for higher intelligence, which occurred and spread in the Northeast Asians, never appeared in the Arctic Peoples. The Northeast Asians (consisting of the Chinese, Koreans, and Japanese) would have formed a single extended breeding population of demes in which mutant alleles for high intelligence would have spread, and these would not have been transmitted to the Arctic Peoples, isolated as they were by high mountain ranges and long distance. The Arctic Peoples did, however, evolve a larger brain size, approximately the same as that of the Northeast Asians, so it is curious that they do not have the same intelligence. A possible explanation for this is that the Arctic Peoples have evolved a strong visual memory, which would have been necessary when they went out on long hunting expeditions and needed to remember landmarks in order to find their way home in the largely featureless environments of snow and ice. An increase of this ability would have required an increase in brain size; however, the Arctic People's visualization ability has not been properly measured through intelligence tests. A further possibility is that one or more new mutant alleles for more efficient neurophysiological processes underlying intelligence may have appeared in the Northeast Asians but not in the Arctic Peoples.

10. THE EVOLUTION OF INTELLIGENCE IN NATIVE AMERICANS

The Native Americans evolved from peoples who migrated from Northeast Asia across the Bering Straits into Alaska and then made their way southward into the Americas. The dates at which these crossings were made are disputed, and it has frequently been claimed that they occurred about 12,000 to 11,000 years ago. Contrary to these claims, there is some evidence that they made these crossings much earlier, at around 40,000 years ago. This evidence comes both from the archaeological record and from genetic analysis. Archaeological finds of Amerindian artifacts have been dated by radiocarbon analysis at 24,000 years ago in Mexico (Lorenzo and Mirambell, 1996), 30,000 years ago in California (Bada, Schroeder, and Carter, 1974), 32,000 years ago in the northeast of Brazil (Guidon and Delibrias, 1996), 35,000 to 43,000 years ago for a rock wall painting in the Serra da Capivara National Park in northeast Brazil (Watanabe, Ayta, Mamaguchi, et al., 2003), and 33,000 years ago at Monte Verde in Chile (Dillehay and Collins, 1998). It must have taken several thousand years for these peoples to make their way from Alaska to South America, so the archaeological evidence points to the first peoples making the crossing at least 40,000 years ago. This archaeological evidence is corroborated by genetic analysis that also puts the first migration into the Americas at approximately 40,000 years ago (Cavalli-Sforza, 2000).

It seems most probable that there was an archaic Northeast Asian people in Northeast Asia around 50,000 years ago, some of whom migrated northwards into Kamchatka and the Chersky Peninsula and then made the crossing of the Bering straits into Alaska around 40,000 years ago. Some of these peoples migrated southwards until they colonized the whole of the Americas and evolved into the Native American Indians, while the archaic Northeast Asian peoples that remained in Northeast Asia evolved into the present-day East Asians. The relatively recent common origin of these two races is apparent from a number of genetic similarities. For instance, the Rhesus negative blood group allele is rare in both races, the Diego blood group is unique to these two races, and they both have similar coarse, straight black hair, shovel incisor teeth, and the Inca bone in the skull (Krantz, 1990).

The archaic Northeast Asian ancestors of the Native Americans who were present in Northeast Asia around 60,000–50,000 years ago were exposed to cold winters, but these were not so severe as those of the main Würm glaciation of approximately 28,000 to 10,000 years ago (Roberts, 1994), by which time the ancestors of the Native Americans had colonized the Americas. Hence, the Native Americans were never exposed to extreme cold and do not have the morphological adaptations that evolved in the Northeast Asians. The Native American nose is not recessed but is quite prominent, and the full Northeast Asian eyefold, as well as the short legs and thick trunk of the Northeast Asians, are not present. In these respects, Native Americans are similar to the Ainu, the original inhabitants of Japan, a few of whom survive on Hokkaido, and who also do not have the cold-adaption morphology of the Northeast Asians, because the climate of the Japanese islands was more maritime and less severe than that of mainland Northeast Asia.

Thus, the Native Americans were established throughout the Americas by around 33,000 to 30,000 years ago. Those in the southern part of the United States and in Central and South America were not exposed to the severe conditions of the main Würm glaciation, so they did not evolve either the morphological cold adaptations or the high IQ of the Northeast Asians. Furthermore, once the ancestors of the Native Americans had crossed the Bering Straits and made their way down into the Americas, they would have found life a good deal easier than their ancestors had been accustomed to in Northeast Asia. They would have found a number of herbivorous mammals such as mammoth, antelope, sloth, armadillo, and bison, which were unused to being hunted by man. Normally predators and prey evolve together: predators become more intelligent in order to catch prey, and prey become more intelligent in order to evade predators. But the herbivorous animals of the Americas had no experience of predation by man and would have been easy game for the skilled hunters who had evolved for many thousands of years in the more severe environment of Northeast Asia. The Native Americans would have found large numbers of these herbivores that were easy to catch.

As they migrated southward, they would have found plant foods more readily available, and these would come to play a significant part in their diets (MacNeish, 1976; Hayden, 1991).

The evolution of intelligence in the Native Americans can be reconstructed as follows. The archaic Northeast Asians from whom they evolved would have had higher intelligence than the South Asians, because they were exposed to the cold climate of Northeast Asia for around 20,000 years, between around 60,000 and 40,000 years ago. The ancestors of the Native Americans spent another few thousand years in Alaska, during which they experienced a severe climate that will have driven up their collective intelligence further. Once they were in the Americas south of Alaska, the selection pressure for any additional increase in intelligence would have been weak because of the benign climate and the ease of survival in the continent hitherto unexploited by humans. This explains their present IQ of 86, a little higher than the 84 of the South Asians, but much below the 105 of the Northeast Asians. This reconstruction provides further evidence that it was the selection pressure exerted by the main Würm glaciation of approximately 28,000 to 10,000 years ago that must have raised the intelligence of the Northeast Asians by around 19 IQ points above that of the Native Americans.

There is one problem with this reconstruction: Native Americans in the northern part of North America would have been exposed to severely cold winters during the main Würm glaciation, and it would be expected that this experience would have increased their intelligence. The most probable explanation for why this did not occur is that the population of the Native Americans was quite small. The earliest reliable estimate of population sizes is for 400 BC, at which time they numbered approximately one million in North America (Biraben, 1980). Hence, the probability of mutations for higher intelligence appearing in the Native Americans in the north of North America was quite small and possibly did not occur, or else fewer of them appeared than in the much more numerous populations of Northeast Asians and Europeans.

The Native Americans have the same profile of intelligence as the Northeast Asians and the Arctic Peoples: strong visualization abilities and weaker verbal abilities. The probable explanation for this common profile is that one or more mutations for higher visualization abilities appeared in the ancestral archaic Northeast Asians around 50,000 years ago and were transmitted to the subsequent Northeast Asians, Arctic Peoples, and Native Americans, all of whom evolved from this ancestral population. Genetic studies have shown that there are genes determining the strength of visualization ability in addition to those determining the strength of the verbal abilities and of g (Plomin, DeFries, and McClearn, 1990).

With their IQ of 86, the Native Americans were able to make the Neolithic transition from hunter-gathering to settled agriculture; they then built the civilizations of the Maya, Aztecs, and Incas. The reason that these civilizations appeared in Central and South America, and not in North America, is probably that their numbers were much greater in these part, at approximately 11 million as compared with only two million as of AD 500 (Biraben, 1990). However, despite their impressive civilizations, the Native Americans were no match for the Europeans, who from the 16th and 17th centuries onwards, had little difficulty in defeating them in battle, taking most of their lands, and killing large numbers of them.

11. CONCLUSIONS

The IQs of the races set out in Chapters 3 through 12 can be explained as having arisen from the different environments in which they evolved, in particular from the struggle for survival during the Ice Ages and from the appearance of mutations for higher intelligence among the races with larger populations and under the greatest stress from cold winters. The IQ differences between the races explain the differences in achievement in making the Neolithic transition from hunter-gathering to settled agriculture, the building of early civilizations, and the development of mature civilizations during the last 2,000 years.

The position of "environmentalists"—that over the course of some 100,000 years peoples separated by geographical barriers in different parts of the world evolved into 10 distinct races with pronounced genetic differences in morphology, blood groups, and the incidence of genetic diseases, and yet have identical genotypes for intelligence—is so improbable that those who advance it must either be totally ignorant of the basic principles of evolutionary biology or else have a political agenda to deny the importance of race. Or both.

INTELLIGENCE TESTS

Brief descriptions of the tests abbreviated in the tables are given below.

AAB. The American Army Beta constructed for testing the IQs of military personnel in World War 1. A nonverbal test of general intelligence on which the performance subtests of the Wechsler tests were based.

AFQT. Armed Forces Qualification Test. A mainly verbal test of general intelligence.

AH. Alice Heim. Tests of verbal and nonverbal reasoning ability.

AP. Alexander Passalong Test. A nonverbal test of intelligence and visualization consisting of a succession of shallow boxes in which are placed a number of colored square and rectangular blocks. The task is to rearrange the blocks so that the red ones are all at one end and the blue all at the other.

Arthur Point Performance Scale. A nonverbal test of general intelligence. BAS. British Ability Scales. A test of general intelligence, verbal and nonverbal ability.

BG. Bender Gestalt. A drawing test of general intelligence.

BTBC. Boehm Test of Basic Concepts. A test of general intelligence measuring verbal understanding of spatial and quantity concepts.

BTBC-R. Boehm Test of Basic Concepts-Revised. A revised version of the BTBC.

CCAT. Canadian Cognitive Abilities Test. A test of verbal, quantitative and nonverbal reasoning.

CEFT. Children's Embedded Figure Test. A children's version of the EFT. Test of the ability to find a simple figure embedded in a larger figure.

CF. Cattell's Culture Fair Test. A nonverbal test of general intelligence. CITO. A Dutch test measuring numerical reasoning and verbal comprehension.

CMM. Columbia Mental Maturity Scale. A verbal and nonverbal reasoning test of general intelligence.

CPM. Colored Progressive Matrices. A nonverbal reasoning test for ages 5-11. CPMT. A test of visualization.

CTMM. California Test of Mental Maturity. A nonverbal reasoning test of general intelli- gence.

DAM. Goodenough Draw a Man test. A drawing test of general intelligence.

EFT Embedded Figure Test. A test of the ability to find a simple figure embedded in a larger figure. Correlates 0.65 with WISC performance and 0.30 with verbal scale (Witkin et al., 1962).

EPVT. English Picture Vocabulary Test.

FF. Fergusson Form Boards. A test of visualization involving fitting pieces of different shapes into spaces as in a jig-saw puzzle.

GALO. A Dutch test of general intelligence.

GFT. Gottschalt Figures Test. A test of visualization.

GMRT. Group Mental Rotations Test. A test of visualization.

GSAT. General Scholastic Aptitude Test. A South African test of reasoning, verbal, visuali- zation and other abilities.

ITPA. Illinois Test of Psycholinguistic Abilities. Measures 12 auditory (verbal) and visual language abilities.

JAT. Junior Aptitude Test. A South African test with 10 subtests measuring reasoning, ver- bal, spatial, etc abilities.

KABC. Kaufman Assessment Battery for Children. A test of general intelligence resembling the Wechsler tests.

KAIT. Kaufman Adolescent and Adult Intelligence Test. A test of general intelligence re- sembling the Wechsler tests.

LPT. Learning Potential Test. A test of general intelligence.

LT. Lorge-Thorndike. A test of general intelligence. Matrix Analogies Test. A nonverbal reasoning test.

MFFT. Matching Familiar Figures Test.

MH. Moray House. A verbal test of general intelligence.

MHV. Mill Hill Vocabulary. A measure of verbal ability.

MMFT. Matching Familiar Figures Test. A mainly visualization test.

MMSE. Mini-Mental State Examination. A test of general intelligence.

NFER. British National Foundation for Educational Research Test of nonverbal reasoning and verbal ability.

OT. Otis Test. A mainly verbal test of general intelligence.

PAT. Progressive Achievement Test. A verbal test of general intelligence.

PIPS. Pacific Infants' Performance Test. A nonverbal test of general intelligence.

PNL. Pintner Non-Language Test. A nonverbal test of general intelligence.

PPMA. Primary Test of Musical Audation. A test of musical ability.

PPVT. Peabody Picture Vocabulary Test. A set of four pictures of different objects that have to be named.

QT. Queensland Test. A nonverbal test of general intelligence.

RACIT. A Dutch test with a number of subtests measuring reasoning, verbal, spatial, etc. abilities.

SA. Stanford Achievement Test. A verbal test of word meaning, spelling, and arithmetic.

SB. Stanford-Binet. A mainly verbal test of general intelligence. Seashore. A test of musical ability.

SON-R. The Snijders-Ooman nonverbal intelligence test. A nonverbal test of general intel- ligence.

SOT. Spiral Omnibus Test. A reasoning test.

SRAT. Science Research Associates Test. A test of general intelligence.

STAS. Stanford Test of Academic Skills. A test of a range of academic subjects.

TOSCA. Test of Scholastic Abilities. A verbal and numerical test of general intelligence.

WAIS. Wechsler Adult Intelligence Scale. Gives measures of general, verbal and visualiza- tion intelligence

WB. Wechsler Bellevue. Gives measures of general intelligence, verbal and visualization abilities

WCST. Wisconsin Card Sorting Test. A nonverbal test of general intelligence.

WISC. Wechsler Intelligence Scale for Children. Gives measures of general, verbal and visualization intelligence.

WPPSI. Wechsler Preschool and Primary Scale for Intelligence. Gives measures of general, verbal and visualization intelligence for 4-6-year-olds.

WRAT. Wide Range Achievement Test. A test of general intelligence. 3DW. An Austrian test of general intelligence.

REFERENCES

Abbink, J. G. (2002). Ethnic trajectories in Israel. *Anthropos*, 97, 3-19.

Abdel-Khalek, A. M. (1988). Egyptian results on the Standard Progressive Matrices. *Personality and Individual Differences*, 9, 193-195.

Abdel-Khalek, A. M., and Lynn, R. (2006). Sex differences on a standardisation of the Standard Progressive Matrices in Kuwait. *Personality and Individual Differences*, 40(2), 175-182.

Abell, S. C., Wood, W., and Leibman, S. J. (2001). Children's human figure drawings as measures of intelligence: the comparative validity of three scoring systems. *Journal of Psychoeducational Assessment*, 19, 204-215.

Abul-Hubb, D. (1972). Application of Progressive Matrices in Iraq. In L. J. Cronbach and P. J. Drenth (Eds.). *Mental Tests and Cultural Adaptation*. The Hague: Mouton.

Adcock, C. J., McCleary, J. R., Ritchie, J. E., and Somerset, H. C. (1954). An analysis of Maori scores on the Wechsler-Bellvue. *Australian Journal of Psychology*, 6, 16-29.

Afzal, M. (1988). Consequences of consanguinity on cognitive behavior. *Behavior Genetics*, 18, 583-594.

Agrawal, N., Sinha, S. N., and Jensen, A. R. (1984). Effects of inbreeding on Raven matrices. *Behavior Genetics*, 14, 579-585.

Ahmed, R. A. (1989). The development of number, space, quantity and reasoning concepts in Sudanese schoolchildren. In L. L. Adler (Ed.). Cross *Cultural Research in Human Development*. Westport, CT: Praeger.

Albalde Paz, E., and Munoz, C. J. (1993). El test PMS de Raven y los escolares de Galicia. Universidade da Coruna: Servicio de Publicaciones.

Alexander, R. D. (1989). Evolution of the human psyche. In P. Mellors and C. Stringer (Eds.). The Human Revolution. Edinburgh: University of Edinburgh Press.

Al-Heeti K., Ganem, A., Al-Kubaldl, A., and Al-Nood, Y. (1997). Standardization of Raven's Coloured Progressive Matrices Scale on primary school children ages 6-11 in Yemen schools. Indian Psychological Review, 48, 49-56.

Allik, J., and Realo, A. (2004). Individualism collectivism and social capital. Journal of Cross-Cultural Psychology, 35, 29-49.

Alvi, S. A., Khan, S. B., Vegeris, S. L., and Ansari, Z. A. (1986). A cross-cultural study of psychological differentiation. International Journal of Psychology, 21, 659-670.

Alzobaie, A. J. (1964). The Cattell Culture-Free Test as tried on Iraqi students. Journal of Educational Research, 57, 476-479.

Amir, Y. (1975). Perceptive articulation in three Middle Eastern cultures. Journal of Cross-Cultural Psychology, 6, 333-344.

Anderson, B. (1993). Evidence from the rat for a general factor that underlies cognitive per- formance and that relates to brain size: intelligence. Neuroscience Letters, 153, 98-102.

Ankney, C. D. (1992). Sex differences in relative brain size: the mismeasure of intelligence in women, too? Intelligence, 16, 329-336.

Anderson, H.D. & Eells, W. C. (1935). Alaska Natives: A Survey of their Sociological and Educational Status. Stanford: Stanford University Press.

A. P. E. (1960). Australia. Encyclopedia Britannica. Chicago: Benton.

Ardila, A., Pineda, D., and Rosselli, M. (2000). Correlation between intelligence test scores and executive function measures. Archives of Clinical Neuropsychology, 15, 31-36.

Arthur, G. (1941). An experience in testing Indian school children. Mental Hygiene, 25,188-195.

Ausubel, D. P. (1961) Maori Youth. New York: Holt, Rinehart & Winston.

Avenant, T. J. (1988). *The Establishment of an Individual Intelligence Scale for Adult South Africans*. Report No. P-91. Pretoria: Human Sciences Research Council.

Avolio, B. J., and Waldman, D. A. (1994). Variations in cognitive, perceptual and psychomo- tor abilities across the working life span: examining the effects of race, sex, experience, edu- cation and occupational type. *Psychology and Aging*, 9, 430-442.

Baare, W. R C., Pol, H. E. H., Boosma, D. L, Postuma, D., and Geus, E. J. C. (2001). Quanti- tative genetic modelling of variation in human brain morphology. *Cerebral Cortex*, 11, 816- 824.

Backman, M. E. (1972). Patterns of mental abilities: ethnic, socioeconomic and sex differences. *American Educational Research Journal*, 9, 1-12.

Bada, J. L., Schroeder, R. A., and Cater, G. F. (1974). New evidence for the antiquity of man in North America deduced from aspartic and recemization. *Science*, 184, 791-793.

Badri, M. B. (1965a). The use of finger drawing in measuring the Goodenough quotient of culturally deprived Sudanese children. *Journal of Psychology*, 59, 333-334.

Badri, M. B. (1965b). Influence of modernization on Goodenough quotients of Sudenese children. *Perceptual and Motor Skills*, 20, 931-932.

Bagley, C., Iwawaki, S., and Young, L. (1983). Japanese children: group-oriented but not field dependent? In C. Bagley and G. K. Verma (Eds.). *Multicultural Childhood, Education, Ethnicity and Cognitive Styles*. Aldershot, UK: Gower.

Baker, D. B., and Jones, D. P. (1993). Creating gender equality: cross-national gender stratifi- cation and mathematical performance. *Sociology of Education*, 66, 91-103.

Baker, J. R. (1974). *Race*. Oxford, UK: Oxford University Press.

Bakhiet, S.F.A. and Lynn, R. (2014).

Bakhiet, S.F.A. and Lynn, R. (2014a)

Barnabus, I. P., Kapur, M., and Rao, S. (1995). Norm development and reliability of Coloured

Progressive Matrices Test. *Journal of Personality and Clinical Studies*, 11, 17-22.

Bart,W., Kamal, A., and Lane, J. F. (1987). The development of proportional reasoning in *Qatar. Journal of Genetic Psychology*, 148, 95-103.

Beals, K. L., Smith, C. L., and Dodd, S. M. (1984). Brain size, cranial morphology, climate and time machines. Current Anthropology. 25, 301-330.

Bean, Kenneth L. (1936). The Musical Talent of Southern Negroes as Measured with the Seashore Tests. *The Pedagogical Seminary and Journal of Genetic Psychology*, 49, Issue 1.

Beaton, A. E., Mullis, I. V. S., Martin, M. O., Gonzales, E. J., Kelly, D. L., and Smith, T. A. (1996). *Mathematics Achievement in the Middle School Years*. Chestnut Hill, MA: Boston College, TIMSS International Study Center.

Beaton, A. E., Martin, M. O., Mullis, I. V. S., Gonzales, E. J., Smith, T. A., and Kelly, D. L., (1996). *Science Achievement in the Middle School Years*. Chestnut Hill, MA: Boston College, TIMSS International Study Center.

Beaumont, P. B., De Villiers, H., and Vogel, J. C. (1978). Modern man in sub-Saharan Africa prior to 49,000 years B. P. : A review and evaluation with particular reference to border cave. *South African Journal of Science*, 74, 409-419.

Beck, L. R., and St. George, R. (1983). The alleged cultural bias of PAT: reading comprehen- sion and reading vocabulary tests. *New Zealand Journal of Educational Studies*, 18, 32-47.

Beiser, M. and Gotowiec, A. (2000). Accounting for native/non-native differences in IQ scores. *Psychology in the Schools*, 37, 237-252.

Benton, D., and Cook, R. (1991). Vitamin and mineral supplements improve intelligence scores and concentration of six year old children. *Personality and Individual Differences*, 12, 1151-1158.

Benton, D., and Roberts, G. (1988). Effect of vitamin and mineral supplementation on intelligence in a sample of school children. *The Lancet*, 1, 140-143.

Bere, M. (1924). A comparative study of the mental capacity of children of foreign parentage. *Columbia University Contributions to Education*, no. 154.

Berlioz, L. (1955). Etude des progressive matrices faite sur les Africains de Douala. *Bulletin du Centre Etude Recherce Psychotechnique*, 4, 33-44.

Berry, J. W. (1966). Temne and Eskimo perceptual skills. *International Journal of Psychology*, 1, 207-229.

Berry, J. W. (1971). Ecological and cultural factors in spatial perceptual development. *Canadian Journal of Behavioral Science*, 3, 324-336.

Bhatnagar, J. (1970). *Immigrants at School*. London: Cornmarket.

Bhogle, S., and Prakash, I. J. (1992). Performance of Indian children on the Colored Progressive Matrices. *Psychological Studies*, 37,178-181.

Biesheuvel, S. (1949). Psychological tests and their application to non-European peoples. In G. B. Jeffrey (Ed.). *Yearbook of Education*. New York: Evans.

Binford, L. R. (1980). Yellow smoke and dogs' tails: hunter gatherer settlement systems and archeological site formation. *American Antiquity*, 45, 4-20.

Binford, L. R. (1985). Human ancestors: changing views of their behavior. *Journal of Anthropological Archaeology*, 4, 292-327.

Binnie-Dawson, J. L. (1984). Bio-social and endocrine bases of spatial ability. *Psychologia*, 27,129-151.

Biraben, J. N. (1980). An essay concerning mankind's evolution. *Population*, 4,1-13.

Black Peoples. (1978). *Cause for Concern: West Indian Pupils in Redbridge*. Ilford: Black Peoples Progressive Association.

Blatchford, P., Burke, J., Farquhar, C., Plewis, L, and Tizard, B. (1985). Educational achievement in the infant school: the influence of ethnic origin, gender and home on entry skills. *Educational Research*, 27, 52-60.

Bleakley, J. W. (1961). *The Aborigines of Australia*. Brisbane: Jacaranda Press. 165

Bleichrodt, N., and Born, M. P. (1994). A meta-analysis of research on iodine and its relation- ship to cognitive development. In J. B. Stanbury (Ed.). *The Damaged Brain of Iodine Deficiency*. New York: Cognizant Communication Corp.

Bleichrodt, N., Drenth, P. J. D., and Querido, A. (1980). Effects of iron deficiency on motor and psychomotor abilities. *American Journal of Physical Anthropology*, 53, 55-67.

Bleichrodt, N., Garcia, I., Rubio, C., Morreale, D. E., and De Escobar, M. (1987). Develop- mental disorders with severe iodine deficiency. In B. S. Hetzel, J. T. Dunn and J. B. Stanbury (Eds.). *The Prevention and Control of Iodine Deficiency*. Amsterdam: Elsevier.

Blumenbach, J. F. (1776). *De generis humaniuarietate nativa liber*. Goettingen: Vandenhoek.

Blumenschine, R. J. (1989). Man the scavenger. *Archaeology*. July, 26-32.

Bodmer, W. F. and Cavalli-sforza, L. L. (1976). *Genetics, Evolution and Man*. San Francisco: Freeman.

Bohannon, A. D., Fillenbaum, G. G., and Pieper, C. F. (2002). Relationship of race/ethnicity and blood pressure to change in cognitive function. *Journal of the American Geriatrics Society*, 50, 424-429.

Boissiere, M., Knight,]. B. and Sabot, R. H. (1985). Earnings, schooling, ability and cognitive skills. *American Economic Review*, 75,1016-1030.

Boivin, M. J. and Giordani. B. (1993). Improvements in cognitive performance for school children in Zaire following an iron supplement and treatment for intestinal parasites. *Journal of Pediatric Psychology*, 249-264.

Boivin, M. J., Giordani, B., and Bornfeld, B. (1995). Use of the tactual performance test for cognitive ability testing with African children. *Neuropsychology*, 9, 409-417.

Boivin, M. J., Giordani, B., Crist, C. L., and Chounramany, C. (1996). Validating a cognitive ability testing protocol with Lao children for community development applications. *Neuropsychology*, W, 588-599

Borkowski, J. G. and Krause, A. (1983). Racial differences in intelligence: the importance of the executive system. *Intelligence*, 7, 379-395.

Bouchard, T. J. (1993). The genetic architecture of human intelligence. In P. A. Vernon (Ed.). *Biological Approaches to the Study of Human Intelligence*. Norwood, NJ: Ablex.

Bouchard, T. J. (1998). Genetic and environmental influences on adult intelligence and special mental abilities. *Human Biology*, 70, 257-279.

Bourdier, G. (1964). Utilisation et nouvel etalonnage du P. M. 47. *Bulletin de Psychologie*, 235, 39-41.

Bovvd, A. D. (1973). A cross-cultural study of the factorial composition of mechanical aptitude. Canadian Journal of Behavioral Science, 5, 13-23.

Bowdler, S. and Ryan, L. (1987). Southeast Tasmania. In: D. J. Mulvaney and J. P. White (Eds.). *Australians to 1788*. Sydney, Australia: Fairfax, Syme and Weldon.

Boyd, W. (1950). *Genetics and the Races of Man*. Boston: Little, Brown.

Brace, C. L. and Hinton, R. J. (1981). Oceanic tooth size variation as a reflection of biological and cultural mixing. *Current Anthropology*, 22, 549-569.

Brace, C. L. (1999). An anthropological perspective on "race" and intelligence: the non-clinal nature of human cognitive capabilities. *Journal of Anthropological Research*, 55, 245-264. 166

Bradshaw, J. L. (1997). *Human Evolution: A Neuropsychological Perspective*. Hove, UK: Psychology Press.

Brandon, P. R., Newton, B. J., and Hammond, O. W. (1987). Children's mathematics achievement in Hawaii: differences favoring girls. *American Educational Research Journal*, 24, 437-461.

Brandt, T. (1978). Growth dynamics of low birth weight infants with emphasis on the perina- tal period. In: *Human Growth*, vol. 2. F. Falkner and J. M. Tanner (Eds.), pp 557-617. New York: Plenum Press.

Broca, P. (1861). Sur le volume et la forme du cerveau suivant les individus et suivant les races. *Bulletin Societe de Anthropologie Paris*, 2, 139-207, 301-321,441-446.

Brody, N. (1992). *Intelligence*. San Diego, GA: Academic.

Brody, N. (2000). Comment. In: Novaris Foundation Symposium. *The Nature of Intelligence*. New York: Wiley.

Brody, N. (2003). Jensen's genetic interpretation of racial differences in intelligence: critical evaluation. In H. Nyborg (Ed.). *The Scientific Study of General Intelligence*. Amsterdam: El- sevier.

Broer, M. (1996). Rasch-homogene Leistungstests (3DW, WMT). im Kulturvergleich Chile-Osterreich: Erstellung einer spanischen Version ein-er Testbatterie und deren interkulturellen Validierung in Chile [Rasch-homogeneous achievement tests (3DW, WMT) in a cross- cultural comparison of Chile and Austria: development of a Spanish test-battery version and its cross-cultural validation in Chile]. Unpublished M. Sc. thesis, University of Vienna.

Broman, S. H., Nichols, P. L., and Kennedy, W. A. (1975). *Preschool IQ*. New York: J. Wiley.

Broman, S. H., Nichols, P. L., Shaughnessy, P., and Kennedy, W. (1987). *Retardation in Young Children*. Hillsdale, New Jersey: Lawrence Erlbaum.

Brown, R.T., Reynolds, C. R., and Whitaker, J. S. (1999). Bias in mental testing since Bias in Mental Testing. *School Psychology Quarterly*, 14, 208-238

Browne, D. B. (1984). WISC-R scoring patterns among Native Americans of the northern plains. *White Cloud Journal*, 3, 3-16.

Bruce, D. W, Hengeveld, M., and Radford, W. C. (1971). *Some*

Cognitive Skills in Aboriginal Children in Victorian Primary Schools. Victoria: Australian Council for Educational Re- search.

Bruner, F. G. (1908). The hearing of primitive peoples.*Archives of Psychology*, no. 11.

Buj, V. (1981). Average IQ values in various European countries. *Personality and Individual Differences*, 2, 168-169.

Bunn, H. T, and Stanford, C. B. (2001). Conclusions. In C. B. Stanford and H. T. Bunn (Eds.). *Meat Eating and Human Evolution.* Oxford, UK: Oxford University Press.

Burg, B., and Belmont, I. (1990). Mental abilities of children from different cultural backgrounds. *Journal of Cross-Cultural Psychology*, 21, 90-108. Butterworth, B. (1999). The Mathematical Brain. London: Macmillan.

Byrne, R. W. (2002). The primate origins of human intelligence. In R. J. Sternberg and J. K. Kaufman (Eds.) *The Evolution of Intelligence.* Mahway, NJ: Lawrence Erlbaum.

Cairns, J., Overbaugh, J. and Miller, S. (1988). The Origin of Mutants. *Nature*, 335,142-145. 167

Callan, V. J. (1986). *Australian Minority Groups.* Sydney: Harcourt Brace Javanovich.

Carr, A. (1993). Twenty years a growing: a research note on gains in the intelligence test scores of Irish children over two decades. *Irish Journal of Psychology*, 14, 576-582.

Carroll, J. B. (1993). *Human Cognitive Abilities.* Cambridge: Cambridge University Press.

Cashdan, E. (2001). Ethnic diversity and its environmental determinants: effects of climate, pathogens, and habitat diversity. *American Anthropologist*, 103, 968-992.

Cattell, R. B. (1951). The fate of national intelligence—test of a thirteen year prediction. *Eugenics Review*, 17, 136-148.

Cattell, R. B. (1971). *Abilities: Their Structure, Growth and Action.* Boston: Houghton Mifflin.

Cavalli-Sforza, L. L. (2000). *Genes, Peoples and Languages*. New York: North Point.

Cavalli-Sforza, L. L., and Bodmer, W. (1971). *The Genetics of Human Populations*. San Francisco: Freeman.

Cavalli-Sforza, L. L., Menozzi, P., and Piazza, A. (1994). *The History and Geography of Human Genes*. Princeton, NJ: Princeton University Press.

Cazden, C. B., and John, V. P. (1971). Learning in American Indian children. In M. L. Wax, S. Diamond, and F. O. Gearing (Eds.). *Anthropological Perspectives on Education*. New York: Basic Books.

Ceci, S. J. (1991). How much does schooling influence general intelligence and its cognitive components? A reassessment of the evidence. *Developmental Psychology*, 27, 703-722.

Chagnon, N. A. (1983). *Yanomamo: The Fierce People*. New York: Holt, Rinehart & C Winston.

Chaim, H. H. (1994). Is the Raven Progressive Matrices Valid for Malaysians? Unpublished.

Chakraborty, R., Kamboh, M. L, Nwankwo, M., and Ferrell, R. E. (1992). Caucasian genes in American blacks: new data. *American Journal of Human Genetics*, 50, 145-155.

Chambers, C. M. and Grantham-McGregor, S. M. (1986). Research note:patterns of mental development among middle class Jamaican children. *Journal of Child Psychology and Psychiatry*, 27, 117-123.

Chan, J., Eysenck, H. J., and Lynn, R. (1991). Reaction time and intelligence among Hong Kong children. *Perceptual and Motor Skills*, 72, 427-433.

Chan, J. and Lynn, R. (1989). The intelligence of six year olds in Hong Kong. *Journal of Biosocial Science*, 21, 461-464.

Chan, J. and Vernon, P. E. (1988). Individual differences among the peoples of China. In Ir- vine, S. H. and Berry, J. W. *Human Abilities in Cultural Context*. Cambridge, UK: Cambridge University Press.

Chandra, S. (1975). Some patterns of response on the Queensland Test. *Australian Psychologist*, 10,185-191.

Chavaz, A., Matrinez, B., and Soberanes, B. (1995). Effect of malnutrition on infant devel- opment. In N. S. Scrimshaw (Ed.). *Longitudinal Community Based Studies of the Impact of Early Malnutrition on Child Health and Development.* Boston, MA: INFDC.

Chen, C., Lee, S., and Stevenson, H. W. (1996). Long term prediction of academic achievement of American, Chinese and Japanese adolescents. *Journal of Educational Psychology*, 98, 750-759.

Cheung, P. (2003). Congo's Pygmies accuse rebels and army of cannibalism; demand U. N. genocide tribunal. *Associated Press*, May 22, 2003.

Chisholm, J. S. (1989). Biology, culture and the development of temperament-a Navajo ex- ample. In J. K. Nugent, B. L. Lester, and T. B. Brazelton (Eds) *The Cultural Context of Infancy.* Norwood, NJ: Ablex.

Chopra, S. L. (1966). Family size and sibling position as related to measured intelligence and academic achievement. *Journal of Social Psychology*, 70 133-137.

Chorley, M. J., Chorley, K., Seese, N., Owen, M. J., Daniels, J., McGuffin, P., Thompson, L. A., Detterman, D. K., Benbow, C., Lubinski, D., Eley, T., and Plomin, R. (1998). A quantitative trait locus associated with cognitive ability in children. *Psychological Science*, 9, 159- 166.

Chovioto, L., Aghini-Lombardi, R, and Vitti, P. (1994). The impact of iodine deficiency on neurological and cognitive development: the European experience. In J. B. Stanbury (Ed.). *The Damaged Brain of Iodine Deficiency.* New York: Cognizant Communication Corporation.

Claassen, N. C. W. (1990). The comparability of General Scholastic Aptitude Test scores across different populations groups. *South African Journal of Psychology*, 20, 80-92.

Clark, E. A., and Hanisee, J. (1982). Intellectual and adaptive performance of Asian children in adoptive American settings. *Developmental Psychology*, 18,595-599.

Clay, M. M. (1971). The Polynesian language skills of Maori and Samoan school entrants. *International Journal of Psychology*, 6, 135-145.

Codd, J. A. (1972). Cultural factors in the cognitive development of Maori children. *Delta*, 11, 26-36.

Codwell, J. E. (1947). *A Study of the Kind and Amount of Change in Motor Function as the Amount of Negro Blood Increases or Decreases in the Negro-White Hybrid*. Ph. D. thesis, University of Michigan.

Cohen, M. N. (2002). An anthropologist looks at race and IQ testing. In J. M. Fish (Ed.). *Race and Intelligence*. Mahwah, NJ: Lawrence Erlbaum.

Cole, S. (1965). *Races of Man*. London: Her Majesty's Stationery Office.

Coleman, J. S. (1966). *Equality of Educational Opportunity*. Washington, D.C.: U. S. Office of Education.

Colom, R., Garcia, L. R, Juan-Espinoza, M., and Abad, R (2002). Null differences in general intelligence: evidence from the WAIS-R. *Spanish Journal of Psychology*, 5, 29-35.

Colom, R., Juan-Espinosa, M., Abad, R, and Garcia, L. R (2000). Negligible sex differences in general intelligence. *Intelligence*, 28, 57-68.

Colom, R., and Lynn, R. (2004). Testing the developmental theory of sex differences in intelligence on 12-18 year olds. *Personality and Individual Differences*, 2004, 36, 75-82.

Coombs, L. M. (1958). *The Indian Child Goes to School*. Washington, D.C.: U. S. Department of the Interior, Bureau of Indian Affairs.

Coon, C. S., Garn, S. M., and Birdsell, J. B. (1950). *Races*. Springfield, Ill: Thomas.

Coon, C. S. (1962). *The Origin of Races*. New York, Knopf.

Coren, S. (1994). *The Intelligence of Dogs: Canine Consciousness and Capability*. New York: Free Press.

Costenbader, V., and Ngari, S. M. (2000). A Kenya standardisation of the Coloured Progressive Matrices. *School Psychology International*, 22, 258-268.

Cottereau-Reiss, P., and Lehalle, H. (1998). Comparaison des performances d'enfants Kanak et d'enfants francais dans une situation de jugements de morphismes: structuration spatiale et moulin a vent. *Archives de Psychologie*, 66, 3-21.

Counter, S. A., Buchanan, L. H., Rosas, H. D., and Ortega, F. (1998). Neurocognitive effects of chronic lead intoxication in Andean children. *Journal of Neurological Sciences*, 160, 47- 53.

Court, J. H. (1983). Sex differences in performance on Raven's Progressive Matrices: a re- view. *Alberta Journal of Educational Research*, 29, 54-74.

Cox, M. V., Perara, J., and Fan, X. U. (1998). Children's drawing ability in the UK and China. *Psychologia*, 41, 171-182.

Cox, M. V., Koyasu, M., Hranamu, H., and Perara,]. (2001). Children's human figure draw- ings in the UK and Japan: the effects of age, sex and culture. *British Journal of Developmental Psychology*, 19, 275-292.

Craig,]. D. (1974). *A Study of the Education and Abilities of Young Australian Male Adults*. Australian Department of Labor Research Report. Canberra: Government Printing Service.

Cravioto, J. (1966). Malnutrition and behavioural development in the pre-school child. In National Academy of Sciences. *Pre-school Child Malnutrition*. Washington, D.C.

Cravioto, J., Birch, H. G., Licardie, E., Resales, L., and Vega, L. (1969). Ecology of growth and development in a Mexican pre-industrial community. Report 1: Method and findings from birth to one month of age. *Monographs of the Society for Research in Child Development*, vol. 35, no. 129.

Crawfurd, J. (1863). On the antiquity of man, from the evidence of language. *Transactions of the Ethnographic Society of London*, 1, 170-181.

Cropley, A. J., and Cardey, R. M. (1975). Contact with the dominant culture and cognitive competence in Canadian Indians and whites. *Canadian Journal of Behavioral Science*, 7, 328- 238.

Cundick, B.P., Gottfredson, D.K., and Willson, L. (1974) Changes in scholastic achievement and intelligence of Indian children enrolled in a foster placement program. *Developmental Psychology*, 10, 815-820.

Curr, E. M. (1887). *The Australian Race*. Melbourne: Government Printer.

Cutler, R. G. (1976). Evolution of longevity in primates. *Journal of Human Evolution*, 5,169-202.

Dague, P., Garelli, M., and Lebettre, A. (1964). Recherches sur l'echelle de ma-turite mentale de Colombia. *Revue de Psychologie Applique*,14,71-96.

Daley, T. C., Whaley, S. E., Sigman, M. D., Espinosa, M. P., and Neuman, C. (2003). IQ on the rise: the Flynn effect in rural Kenyan children. *Pychological Science*, 14, 215-219.

Dan, L., Yu, J., Vandenberg, S. G., Yuemei, Z., and Caihong, T. (1990). Report on Shanghai norms of the Chinese translation of the Wechsler Intelligence Scale for Children-Revised. *Psychological Reports*, 67, 531-541.

Dasen, P. R., de Lacey, P. R., and Seagrim, G. N. (1973). Reasoning ability in adopted and fostered Aboriginal children. In G. E. Kearney, P. R. de Lacey, and G. R. Davidson (1973). *The Psychology of Aboriginal Australians*. New York: Wiley.

Davidson, G. R. (1974). Linguistic determinants of choice reaction time among Aborigines and white Australians. *Journal of Cross-Cultural Psychology*, 5,199-210.

Davies, M., and Hughes, A. G. (1927). An investigation into the comparative intelligence and attainments of Jewish and non-Jewish school children. *British Journal of Psychology*, 18, 134-146.

Dawkins, A., and Snyder, R. (1977). Disadvantaged junior high school students compared with norms of the Seashore tests. *Journal of Research on Music Education*, 20, 438-444.

Dawkins, R. (1988). *The Blind Watchmaker*. London, UK: Penguin.

Dawkins, R., and Krebs, J. R. (1979). Arms races within and between races. *Proceedings of the Royal Society*, 205B, 489-511.

Darwin, C. (1868). *The Variation of Animals and Plants under Domestication*. London: Murray.

Dawson, I., Colder, R. Y, and Jonas, E. G. (1982). Birthweight by gestational age and its ef- fect on perinatal mortality in white and in Punjabi births. *British Journal of Obstetrics and Gynaecology*, 89, 896-899.

Dayi, E., Okuyan, M., and Tan, U. (2002). Predictability of hand skill and cog nitive abilities from craniofacial width in right and left-handed men and women: relation of skeletal structure to cerebral function. *International journal of Neuroscience*, 112, 383-412.

Deary, I. J. (2000). *Looking Down on Human Intelligence*. Oxford, UK: Oxford University Press.

De Jong, M. J. (1988). Ethnic origin and educational careers in Holland *Netherlands Journal of Sociology*, 24, 65-75.

De Jong, M. J., and van Batenburg, T. A. (1984). Etnische heromst, intelligentic en school-keuzeadvies. *Pedagogische Studien*, 61, 362-371.

De Lacey, P. R. (1971a). Classificatory ability and verbal intelligence among high-contact aboriginal children and low socio-economic status white Australian children. *Journal of Cross-Cultural Psychology*, 3, 393-396.

De Lacey, P. R. (1971b). Verbal intelligence, operational thinking and environment in part- Aboriginal children. *International Journal of Psychology*, 23, 145-149.

De Lacey, P. R. (1972). A relationship between classificatory ability and verbal intelligence. *International Journal of Psychology*, 7, 243-246.

De Lacey, P. R. (1976). Lifeways and cognitive performance in Australia and the United States. In G. E. Kearney and D. W. McElwain (Eds.). *Aboriginal Cognition*. Canberra: Australian Institute of Aboriginal Studies.

De Lemos, M. M. (1969). The development of the concept of conservation in Aboriginal children. *International Journal of Psychology*, 4, 255-269.

De Lemos, M. M. (1979). *Aboriginal Students in Victoria*. ACER Research Monograph No. 3. Melbourne: ACER.

De Lemos, M. M. (1989). *Standard Progressive Matrices: Australian Manual*. Camberwell, Vic.: Australian Council for Educational Research.

De Maeyer, E., and Adiels-Tegman, M. (1985). The prevalence of anaemia in the world. *World Health Statistical Bulletin*, 38, 302-316.

Dennis, W. (1957). Performance of Near Eastern children on the Draw-a-Man test. *Child Development*, 28, 427-430.

Dennis, W., and Najarian, P. (1963). Development under environmental handicap. In W. Dennis (Ed.). *Readings in Child Psychology*. Englewood Cliffs: Prentice-Hall.

Dent, G. R. (1937). An investigation into the applicability of certain performomance and other mental tests to Zulu children. In E. G. Malherbe (Ed.). *Report of New Education Conference*. Cape Town, p. 456.

De Silva, H. A., and Gunatilake, S. B. (2002). Mini Mental State examination in Sinhalese: a sensitive test to screen for dementia in Sri Lanka. *International Journal of Geriatric Psychiatry*, 17, 134-139.

Diamond, J. (1997) *Guns, Germs and Steel: The Fates of Human Societies*. New York; Random House.

Dickenson, L., Hobbs, A., Kleinberg, S. M., and Martin, P. J. (1975). *The Immigrant School Leaver*. Windsor, UK: National Foundation for Educational Research.

Dillehay, T. D., and Collins, M. B. (1988). Early cultural evidence from Monte Verde in Chile. *Nature*, 332, 150-152.

Dixon, E. J. (1999). *Bones, Boats and Bison*. Albuquerque, NM: University of New Mexico Press.

Dobbing, J., and Smart, J. L. (1974). Vulnerability of developing brain and behaviour. *British Medical Bulletin*, 30, 164-168.

Dodge, P. R., Palkes, H., Fierro-Benitez, R., and Ramirez, I. (1969). Effect on intelligence of iodine in oil administration to young adult Andean children. In J. B. Stanbury (Ed.). *Endemic Goitre*. Washington, D.C.: Pan American Health Organization.

Dolan, C. V, and Hamaker, E. (2001). Investigating black-white differences in psychometric IQ: multi-group factor analysis and a critique of the method of correlated vectors. In F. Co-lumbus (Ed). *Advances in Psychological Research*, vol. 6, Huntington: Nova Science.

Dornstreich, M. D. (1973). Food habits of early man and the balance between hunting and gathering. *Science*, 179, 306.

Drennan, M. R. (1937). *A Short Course on Physical Anthropology*. Cape Town: Mercantile- Atlas.

Driessen, G. W. (1997). Islamic primary schools in The Netherlands: the pupil's achievement levels, behavior and attitudes and their parents' cultural backgrounds. *Netherlands' Journal of Social Sciences*, 33, 42-75.

Drinkwater, B. A. (1976). Visual memory skills of medium contact Aboriginal children. *Australian Journal of Psychology*, 28, 37-44.

Du Bois, W. E. B. (1939). *Black Folk: Then and Now*. New York: Henry Holt.

Du Chateau, P. (1967). Ten point gap in Maori aptitudes. *National Education*, 49,157-158.

Dunbar, R. I. (1992). Neocortex size as a constraint on group size in primates. *Journal of Human Evolution*, 20, 469-493.

Dunn, J. T. (1994). Societal implications of iodine deficiency and the value of its prevention. In J. B. Stanbury (Ed.). *The Damaged Brain of Iodine Deficiency*. New York: Cognizant Communication Corporation.

Dunn, L. M. (1988). *Bilingual Hispanic Children on the U. S. Mainland*. Honolulu: Dunn Educational Services.

Dunbrow, E. H., Schaefer, B. A., and Jimerson, S. (2002). Diverging a paths in rural Carib- bean children. *School Psychology International*. 155-168.

Dyck, M. J. (1996). Cognitive assessment in a multicultural society: comment on Davidson. *Australian Psychologist*, 31, 66-69.

Edwards, L. D. (1970). Malnutrition and disease in pre-school Aboriginal children in the Walgett area of N. S. W. *Medical Journal of Australia*, 2, 1007-1010.

Edwards, L. D., and Craddock, L. J. (1973). Malnutrition and intellectual development. *Medical journal of Australia*, 5 May, 880-884.

Eells, W. C. (1933). Mental ability of the native races of Alaska. *Journal of Applied Psychology*, 17, 417-438.

Elkin, A. P. (1964). *The Australian Aborgines*. Sydney: Angus and Robertson.

El-Mneizel, A. F. (1987). Development and psychometric analysis of a Jordanian adaptation of the Kaufman Assessment Battery for Children. Ph.D. dissertation, University of Alabama.

Evans, E. M., Schweingruber, H., and Stevenson, H. W. (2002). Gender differences in interest and knowledge acquisition: the United States, Taiwan, and Japan. *Sex Roles*, 47,153-167.

Eyferth, K. (1961). Leistungen verschiedener Gruppen von Besatzungskindern im Hamburg Wechsler Intelligenz Test fur Kinder. *Archive fur die Gesamte Psychologie*, 113, 222-241.

Eysenck, H. J. (1971). *Race, Intelligence and Education*. London: Temple Smith.

Eysenck, H. J. (1981). *Intelligence: The Battle for the Mind*. London: Pan. Eysenck, H. J. (1995). Genius. Cambridge, UK: Cambridge University Press.

Eysenck, H. J. (1998). *Intelligence: A New Look*. New Brunswick, NJ: Transaction.

Eysenck, H. J., and Schoenthaler, S. J. (1997). Raising IQ with vitamins and minerals. In R. J. Sternberg and E. Grigorenko (Eds.). *Intelligence, Heredity and Environment*. Cambridge, UK: Cambridge University Press.

Fahmy, M. (1964). Initial exploring of the intelligence of Shilluk children. *Vita Humana*, 7,164-177.

Fahrmeier, E. D. (1975). The effect of school attendance on intellectual development in Northern Nigeria. *Child Development*, 46, 281-285.

Falconer, D. S. (1960). *Introduction to Quantitative Genetics*. London: Longman.

Farron, O. (1966). The test performance of coloured children. *Educational Research*, 8, 42-57.

Fatouros, M. (1972). The influence of maturation and education on the development of abilities. In L. J. Cronbach and P. J. Drenth (Eds). *Mental Tests and Cultural Adaptation*. The Hague: Mouton.

Faverge, J. M., and Falmagne, J. C. (1962). On the interpretation of data in intercultural psychology. *Psychologia Africana*, 9, 22-96.

Feldman, D. H. (1971). Map understanding as a possible crystallizer of cogni tive structures. *American Educational Research Journal*, 8, 485-500.

Fergusson, D. M., Lloyd, M., and Horwood, L. J. (1991). Family ethnicity, social background and scholastic achievement - an eleven year longitudinal study. *New Zealand Journal of Educational Studies*, 26, 49-62.

Fergusson, D. M., and Horwood, L. J. (1997). Sex differences in educational achievement in a New Zealand birth cohort. *New Zealand Journal of Educational Studies*, 32, 83-95.

Fernandez, M. (2001). A study of the intelligence of children in Brazil. *Mankind Quarterly*, 42,17-21.

Fernandez-Ballesteros, R., Juan-Espinoza, M., Colom, R., and Calero, M. D. (1997). Contex- tual and personal sources of individual differences in intelligence. In J. S. Carlson (Ed.). *Advances in Cognition and Educational Practice*. Greenwich, CT: JAI Press.

Pick, M. L. (1929). Intelligence test results of poor white, native (Zulu), coloured and Indian school children and the social and educational implications. *South African Journal of Science*, 26, 904-920.

Fierro-Benitez, R. (1994). Impact of iodine deficiency on development in the Andean world. In J. B. Stanbury (Ed.). *The Damaged Brain of Iodine Deficiency*. New York: Cognizant Communication Corporation.

Fierro-Benitez, R., Cazar, R., and Sandoval, H. (1989). Early correction of iodine deficiency and late effects on psychomotor capabilities and migration. In De Long, G. R., Robbins, J., and Condliffe, P. G. (Eds.). *Iodine and the Brain*. New York: Plenum.

Fierro-Benitez, R., Ramirez, L, Estrella, E., and Stanbury, J. B. (1972). Effect of iodine cor- rection in early fetal life on intelligence quotient. In J. B. Stanbury and R. L. Kroc, R. L. (1972). *Human Development and the Thyroid Gland: Relation to Endemic Cretinism.* New York: Plenum.

Fierro-Benitez, R., Ramirez, I., Estrella, E., and Stanbury, J. B. (1974). Effect of iodine in intellectual development in an area of endemic goitre. In J. R. Dunn and G. A. Medeiros-Neto (Eds.). *Endemic Goiter and Cretinism: Continuing Threats to World Health.* Washington, D.C.: Pan American Health Organization.

Fish, J. M. (ed.) (2002). *Race and Intelligence.* Mahvvah, NJ: Lawrence Erlbaum.

Flaherty, M. (1997). The validity of tests of visuo-spatial skills in cross-cultural studies. *Irish Journal of Psychology,* IS, 439-412.

Flaherty, M., and Connolly, M. (1996). Visual memory skills in Japanese and Caucasians. *Perceptual and Motor Skills,* 82, 1319-1329.

Flaughter, R. L. (1971). PROJECT ACCESS RESEARCH REPORT NO. 2. Princeton, NJ: Educational Testing Service.

Flores, M. B., and Evans, G. T. (1972). Some differences in cognitive abilities between selected Canadian and Filipino students. *Multivariate Behavioral Research,* 7, 175-191. Flynn, J. R. (1980). Race, IQ and Jensen. London: Routledge & Kegan Paul.

Flynn, J. R. (1984). The mean IQ of Americans: massive gains 1932 to 1978. *Psychological Bulletin,* 95, 29-51.

Flynn, J. R. (1987). Massive IQ gains in 14 nations: what IQ tests really measure. *Psychological Bulletin,* 101, 171-191.

Flynn, J. R. (1991). *Asian Americans: Achievement Beyond IQ.* Hillsdale, NJ: Lawrence Erl- baum.

Flynn, J. R. (1998). WAIS-111 and WISC-III IQ gains in the United States from 1992 to 1995: how to compensate for obsolete norms. *Perceptual and Motor Skills,* 86, 1231-1239.

Foley, R. (1987). *Another Unique Species.* New York: Wiley.

Fowler, H. L. (1940). Psychological tests on natives in the north west of Western Australia. *Australian Journal of Science,* 2, 124-127.

Fox, E., Sitompul, A., and Van Schaik, C. P. (1999). Intelligent tool use in wild Sumatran orangutans. In S. T. Parker, H. L. Miles, and R. W. Mitchell (Eds.). *The Mentality of Gorillas and Orangutans*. Cambridge:Cambridge University Press.

Fraser, A. (1995). *The Gypsies*. Cambridge, MA: Blackwell.

Freedman, L., Blumer, W. E, and Lofgren, M. (1991). Endocranial capacity of Western Australian Aboriginal crania: comparisons and association with stature and latitude. *American Journal of Physical Anthropology*, 84, 399-405.

Frydman, M., and Lynn, R. (1989). The intelligence of Korean children adopted in Belgium. *Personality and Individual Differences*, 10, 1323-1326.

Gaddes, W. H., McKenzie, A., and Baensley, R. (1968). Psychometric intelligence and spatial imagery in two northwest Indian and two white groups of children. *Journal of Social Psychology*, 75, 35-42.

Gamble, C., Dunbar R., & Gowlett, J. (2010), *Social Brain, Distributed Mind*. Oxford: Oxford University Press.

Caller, J. R., Ramsey, R, and Forde, V. (1986). A follow-up study of the influence of early malnutrition on subsequent development. *Nutrition and Behavior*, 3, 211-222.

Caller, J. R., Ramsey, R, Solimano, G., Lowell, W. E. and Mason, E. (1983). Influence of early malnutrition on subsequent behavioural development. *Journal of the American Academy of Child Psychiatry*, 22, 8-15.

Galton, R (1869). *Hereditary Genius*. London: Macmillan.

Galton, R (1888). Head growth in students at the University of Cambridge. *Nature*, 38, 14-15.

Garrett, H. E. (1945). Facts and interpretations regarding race differences. *Science*, 102,404- 406.

Garrett, H. E. (1961). The equalitarian dogma. *Perspectives in Biology and Medicine*, 4, 480- 484.

Garth, T. R. (1931). *Racial Psychology*. New York: Macmillan.

Garth, T. R., and Smith, O. D. (1937). The performance of full-blood Indians on language and non-language intelligence tests. *Journal of Abnormal and Social Psychology*, 32, 376-381.

Geary, D. C., Hamson, C. O., Chen, G-R, Liu, R, Hoard, M. K., and Salthouse, T. A. (1997). Computational and reasoning abilities in arithmetic: cross-generational change in China and the United States. *Psychonomic Bulletin and Review*, 4, 425-430.

Geary, D. C., Liu, R, Chen, G-R, Salts, S. J., and Hoard, M. K. (1999). Contributions of com- putational fluency to cross-national differences in arithmetical reasoning abilities. *Journal of Educational Psychology*, 91, 716-719.

Geelhoed, G. W., and Downing, D. (1994). Goiter and cretinism in the Uele Zaire endemia. In J. B. Stanbury (Ed.). *The Damaged Brain of Iodine Deficiency*. New York: Cognizant Communication Corporation.

Geist. V. (1978). *Life Strategies, Human Evolution and Environmental Design*. New York: Springer-V erlag.

Georgas, J. G., and Georgas, C. (1972). A children's intelligence test for Greece. In L. J. Cronbach and P. J. D. Drenth (Eds.). *Mental Tests and Cultural Adaptation*. The Hague: Mouton.

Georgas, J., Weiss, L. G., van der Vijver, R J., and Saklofske, D. H. (2003). A cross-cultural analysis of the WISC-III. In J. Georgas, L. G. Weiss, R van der Vijver and D. H. Saklofske (Eds.). *Culture and Children's Intelligence*. Amsterdam: Academic Press.

Gill. P.. and Byrt, E. (1973). *The Standardization of Raven's Progressive A Matrices and the Mill Hill Vocabulary Scale for Irish School Children Aged 6-12 Years*. University College, Cork: MA Thesis.

Ginsburg, H. P., Choi, E., Lopez, L. S., Netley, R., and Chao-Yuan, C. (1997). Happy birthday to you: early mathematical thinking of Asian, South American and U. S. children. In T. Nunes and P. Bryant (Eds.). *Learning and Teaching Mathematics: An International Perspective*. Hove, UK Psychology Press.

Giordani, B., Boivin, M. J., Opel, B., Nseyila, D. N., and Lauer, R. E. (1996). Use of the K- ABC with children in Zaire. *International*

Journal of Disability, Development and Education, 43, 5-24.

Glewwe, P., and Jaccoby, H. (1992). *Estimating the Determinants of Cognitive Achievement in Low Income Countries.* Washington, D.C.: World Bank.

Globerson, T. (1983). Mental capacity and cognitive functioning: developmental and social class differences. *Developmental Psychology*, 19, 225-230.

Goa, Y., Qian, M. and Wang, D. (1998). Changes in intelligence over 10 years (in Chinese). *Chinese Journal of Clinical Psychology*, 6, 185-186.

Gobineau, A. de (1853). *Essai sur l'inegalite des races humaines.* Paris: Didot.

Godman, A. (1964). *The attainments and abilities of Hong Kong primary IV pupils: a first study.* Hong Kong: Hong Kong University Press.

Goodall, J. (1986). *The Chimpanzees of Gombe: Patterns of Behavior.* Cambridge, MA: Cambridge University Press.

Goodenough, F. L. (1926a). *The Measurement of Intelligence by Drawings.* New York: World Books.

Goodenough, F. L. (1926b). Racial differences in the intelligence of school children. *Journal of Experimental Psychology*, 9, 388-397.

Goodenough, F. L., and Harris, D. B. (1950). Studies in the psychology of children's drawings: 11. 1928-49. *Psychological Bulletin*, 27, 396-433.

Goosens, G. (1952a). Etalonnage du Matrix 1947 de J. C. Raven. *Revue Beige de Psychologie et de Pedagogie*, 14,74-80.

Goosens, G. (1952b) Une application du test d'intelligence de R.B

Gordon, E. E. (1980). Developmental music aptitudes among inner city primary children. *Bulletin of the Council for Research in Music Education*, 63, 25-30. 176

Gott, B. (2002). Fire making in Tasmania: absence of evidence is not evidence of absence. *Current Anthropology*, 43, 650-655.

Gottfredson, L. S. (1997). Editorial: Mainstream science on intelligence. *Intelligence*, 24, 13- 24.

Gottfredson, L. S. (2005). What if the hereditarian hypothesis is true? *Psychology, Public Policy, and Law*, 11, 311-319.

Gould, R. A. (1969). Subsistence behaviour among the Western Desert Aborigines of Australia. *Oceania*, 39, 253-274.

Gould, S. J. (1978). Morton's ranking of races by cranial capacity. *Science*, 200, 503-509.

Gould, S. J. (1981; 1996). *The Mismeasure of Man*. New York, Norton.

Grantham-McGregor, S, M., and Hawke, W. A. (1971). Developmental assessment of Jamaican infants. *Developmental Medicine and Child Neurology*, 13,582-589.

Grantham-McGregor, S. M., Powell, C., Walker, S. P., and Himes, J. H. (1991). Nutritional supplementation, psychosocial stimulation and the mental development of stunted children: the Jamaica study. *The Lancet*, 338, 1-5.

Grantham-McGregor, S. M., Powell, C., Walker, S. P., Chang, S., and Fletcher, P. (1994). The long-term follow-up of severely malnourished children who participated in an intervention program. *Child Development*, 65, 428-439.

Grantham-McGregor, S. M., Walker, S. P., and Powell, C. (1994). Methodological approaches used in Kingston, Jamaica, to determine the effect of nutrition and stimulation on child development. In J. B. Stanbury (Ed.). *The Damaged Brain of Iodine Deficiency*. New York: Cognizant Communication.

Graves, J. L. (2002). An anthropologist looks at race and IQ testing. In J. M. Fish (Ed.). *Race and Intelligence*. Mahwah, NJ: Lawrence Erlbaum.

Greenfield, P. M. (1998). The cultural evolution of IQ. In U. Neisser (Ed.). *The Rising Curve: Long Term Gains in IQ and Related Matters*. Washington, D.C.: American Psychological Association.

Grieve, K. W, and Viljoen, S. (2000). An exploratory study of the use of the Austin maze in South Africa. *South African Journal of Psychology*, 30, 14-18.

Grigorenko, E. L., and Sternberg, R. J. (2001). Analytical, creative and practical intelligence as predictors of self-reported adaptive functioning: a case study in Russia. *Intelligence*, 29, 57-73.

Grine, R E., and Kay, R. R (1988). Early hominid diets from quantitative image analysis of dental microwear. *Nature*, 333, 765-768.

Groves, C. P. (1991). Genes, genitals and genius: the evolutionary ecology of race. In P. O'Higgins (Ed.). *Human Biology: An Integrative Science*. Perth, Australia: Center for Human Biology.

Guenole, N., Englert, P., and Taylor, P. J. (2003). Ethnic group differences in cognitive ability test scores within a New Zealand applicant sample. *New Zealand Journal of Psychology*, 32, 49-54.

Guidon, N., and Delibrias, G. (1986). Carbon-14 dates point to man in the Americas 32,000 years ago. *Nature*, 321, 769.

Gupta, G. C., and Gupta, S. (1966). Norms for Raven's Colored Progressive Matrices. *Manns*, 13, 87-89.

Gupta, S. (1991). Effects of time of day and personality on intelligence test scores. *Personality and Individual Differences*, 12, 1227-1231.

Gustafsson, J. E. (1984). A unifying model of the structure of mental abilities *Intelligence*, 8, 179-203.

Guthke, J., and Al-Zoubi, A. (1987). Kulturspezifische Differenzen in den Coloured Progressive Matrices (CPM) und in einer Lerntestvariante der CPM. *Psychologie in Erziehung und Unterricht*, 34, 306-311.

Hadidjaja, P., Bonang, E., Suyardi, A., Abidin, A. N., Ismid, I. S., and Margono, S. S. (1998). The effect of intervention methods on nutritional status and cognitive function of primary school children infected with ascaris lumbricoides. *American Journal of Tropical Medicine*, 59, 791-795.

Halpern, D. (2000). *Sex Differences in Cognitive Abilities*. Mahwah, N. J.: Lawrence Erl- baum.

Halsey, A. H. (1972). *Educational Priority*. Volume 1. London: HMSO.

Hamers, J. H. M., Hessels, M. G. P., and Pennings, A. H. (1996). Learning potential of ethnic minority children. *European Journal of Psychological Assessment*, 12, 183-192.

Hammer, M. E, Redd, A. J., and Wood, E. T. (2000). Jewish and Middle Eastern non-Jewish populations share a common pool of Y-chromosome biallelic haplotypes. *Proceedings of the National Academy of Sciences*, 97, 6769-6774.

Hanushek, E. A., and Kimko, D. D. (2000). Schooling, labor force quality, and the growth of nations. *American Economic Review*, 90, 1184-1208.

Harker, R. K. (1978). Achievement and ethnicity: environmental deprivation or cultural difference. *New Zealand Journal of Educational Studies*, 13,107-124.

Harris, S. A. (1977). Milingimbi Aboriginal Learning Contexts. Ph.D. dissertation, University of New Mexico, Albuquerque, New Mexico.

Hart, J. A. (1965). A study of Cognitive Capacity of a Group of Australian Aboriginal Children. M.A. thesis, University of Queensland.

Harvey, P. H., and Glutton-Brock, T. H. (1985). Life history variation in primates. *Evolution*, 39, 559-581.

Haught, B. F. (1934). Mental growth of the southwest Indians. *Journal of Applied Psychology*, 18, 419-433.

Havighurst, R. J., and Hilkevitch, R. R. (1944). The intelligence of Indian children measured by a performance scale. *Journal of Abnormal and Social Psychology*, 39, 419-433.

Hayden, B. (1981). Subsistence of Modern Hunter Gathers. In R. O. S. Harding and G. Telela (Eds.). *Omnivorous Primates*. New York: Columbia Univ. Press.

Heim, A. W. (1968). *AH4 Group Test of General Intelligence Manual*. Slough,UK: National Foundation for Educational Research.

Helms-Lorenz, M., Van de Vijver, F. J. R., and Poortinger, Y. P. (2003). Cross-cultural differences in cognitive performance and Spearman's hypothesis. *Intelligence*, 31,9-29.

Henneberg, M. (1983). Trends in cranial capacity and cranial index in sub-Saharan Africa during the Holocene. *American Journal of Human Biology*, 5, 473-479.

Henneberg, M. (1984). Comment on Beals Dodd and Smith. *Current Anthropology*, 25, 321- 322.

Henneberg, M., Budnik, A., Pazacka, M., and Puch, A. E. (1985). Head size, body size and intelligence: intra-specific correlations in Homo sapiens. *Homo*, 36, 207-218.

Herrnstein, R. J., and Murray, C. (1994). *The Bell Curve: Intelligence and Class Structure in American Life*. New York: Free Press.

Hertzig, M., Birch, H. G., Richardson, S. A., and Tizard, J. (1972). Intellectual levels of school children malnourished during the first two years of life. *Pediatrics*, 49, 814-824.

Hetzel, B. S. (1994). Historical development of the concepts of brain-thyroid relationships. In J. B. Stanbury (Ed.). *The Damaged Brain of Iodine Deficiency*. New York: Cognizant Communication Corporation.

Heyneman, S. P., and Jamison, D. T. (1980). Student learning in Uganda. *Comparative Education Review*, 24,207-220.

Hirszfeld, L., and Hirszfeld, H. (1919). Essai d'application des methods au probleme des races. *Anthropologie*, 29, 505-537.

Ho, H.-Z., Baker, L. A., and Decker, S. N. 1988. Covariation between intelligence and speed of cognitive processing: genetic and environmental influences. *Behavior Genetics*, 18, 247- 261.

Ho, K.-C, Roessmann, U., Straumfjord, J. V., and Monroe, G. (1980). Analysis of brain weight: 1 & 11. Adult brain weight in relation to sex, race and age. *Archives of Pathology and Laboratory Medicine*, 104, 635-639; 640-645.

Holding, P. A., Taylor, H. G., Kazungu, S. D., and Mkala, T. (2004). Assessing cognitive out- comes in a rural African population:

development of a neuro-psychological battery in Kilifi district, *Kenya. Journal of the International Neuropsychological Society*, 10, 246-260.

Horn, J. L. (1991). Measurement of intellectual capabilities: a review of theory. In K. S. McGrew, J. K. Werder, and R. W. Woodcock (Eds.). *Woodcock-Johnson Technical Manual.* Chicago: Riverside.

Houghton, V. (1966). Intelligence testing of West Indian and English children. *Race*, 8, 147- 156.

Howell, R. J., Evans, L., and Downing, L. N. (1958). A comparison of test scores from the 16-17 year age group of Navajo Indians with standardisation norms from the WAIS. *Journal of Social Psychology*, 47, 355-359.

Hsu, C.-C. (1971). Chinese children's responses to Raven's Colored Progressive Matrices. *Journal of the Formosan Medical Association*, 70, 579-593.

Hsu, C.-C., See, R., and Lin, C-C. (1973). Assessment of learning potential of Chinese children with Raven's Standard Progressive Matrices. *Journal of the Formosan Medical Association*, 72, 658-670.

Hsu, C.-C. (1976). The learning potential of first graders in Taipei city as measured by Raven's Coloured Progressive Matrices. *Acta Pediatrica Sinica*, 17,262-274.

Humphreys, L. G. (1988). Trends in level of academic achievement of blacks and other minorities. *Intelligence*, 12, 231-260.

Hunkin, V. (1950). Validation of the Goodenough Draw-a-Man test for African children. *Journal for Social Research*, 1, 52-63.

Hunter, B., and Schwab, R. G. (1998). *The determinants of indigenous educational outcomes.* Canberra: Australian National University,

Hunter, J. E., and Hunter, R. F. (1984). Validity and utility of alternative predictors of job performance. *Psychological Bulletin*, 96, 72-98.

Hunter, W. S., and Sommermier, E. (1922). The relation of the degree of Indian blood to score on the Otis Intelligence Test. *Journal of Comparative Psychology*, 2, 257-275.

ILEA. (1967). *The Education of Immigrant Pupils in Primary Schools*. London: Inner London Education Authority.

Isaac, G. (1978). The food sharing behavior of protohuman hominoids. *Scientific American*. 238, 90-109.

Ishikuma, T, Moon, S., and Kaufman, A. S. (1988). Sequential-simultaneous analysis of Japanese children's performance on the Japanese McCarthy scales. *Perceptual and Motor Skills*, 66, 355-362.

Jahoda, G. (1970). Supernatural beliefs and changing cognitive structures among Ghanaian university students. *Journal of Cross-Cultural Psychology* 1,115-130.

Jaworowska, A., and Szustrowa, T. (1991). *Podrecznik Do Testu Matryc Ravena*. Warsaw: Pracownia Testow Psychologicznych.

Jencks, C, (1972). *Inequality*. London: Penguin.

Jencks, G., and Phillips, M. (1998). *The Black-White Test Score Gap*. Washington, D.C.: Brookings Institution.

Jensen, A. R. (1969). How much can we boost IQ and scholastic achievement? *Harvard Educational Review*, 39, 1-123.

_____ (1972). *Genetics and Education*. London: Methuen.

Jensen, A. R. (1973). *Educability and Group Differences*. London: Methuen.

_____ (1974). How biased are culture-loaded tests? Genetic Psychology Monographs, 90, 185-244.

_____ (1977). Cumulative deficit in IQ of blacks in the rural south. Developmental Psychology, 13, 184-191.

_____ (1980). Bias in Mental Testing. London: Methuen.

_____ (1981). Obstacles, problems and pitfalls in differential psychology. In: S. Scarr (Ed). Race, Social Class and Individual Differences in IQ. Hillsdale, NJ: Lawrence Erlbaum.

_____ (1982). Reaction time and psychometric g. In H. J. Eysenck (Ed.). A Model for Intelligence. Berlin: Springer-Verlag.

_____ (1993). Spearman's hypothesis tested with chronometric information-processing tasks. *Intelligence*, 17, 47-77.

_____ (1998). *The g Factor*. Westport, CT: Praeger.

Jensen, A. R., and Figueroa, R. A. (1975). Forward and backward digit span interaction with race and IQ: predictions from Jensen's theory. *Journal of Educational Psychology*, 67, 882- 893.

Jensen, A. R., and Inouye, A. R. (1980). Level I and Level II abilities in Asian, white and black children. *Intelligence*. 4, 41-49.

Jensen, A. R., and Reynolds, C. R. (1982). Race, social class and ability patterns on the WISC-R. *Personality and Individual Differences*, 3, 423-438.

Jensen, A. R., and Rohwer, W. D. (1970). An experimental analysis of learning abilities in culturally disadvantaged children. Washington, D.C.: Office of Economic Opportunity.

Jensen, A. R., Saccuzzo, D. P., and Larson, G. E. (1988). Equating the standard and advanced forms of the Progressive Matrices. *Educational and Psychological Measurement*, 48, 1091- 1095.

Jensen, A. R., and Whang, P. A. (1993). Reaction times and intelligence: a comparison of Chinese and Anglo-American children. *Journal of Biosocul Science*, 25, 397-411.

Jensen, A. R., and Whang, P. A. (1994). Speed of accessing arithmetic facts in long term memory: a comparison of Chinese-American and Anglo-American children. *Contemporary Educational Psychology*, 19,1-12.

Jerison, H. (1973). *Evolution of the Brain and Intelligence*. New York, Academic Press.

Jerison, H. (2000). The evolution of intelligence. In R. J. Sternberg (Ed.). *Handbook of Intelligence*. Cambridge: Cambridge University Press.

Jinabhai, C. C., Taylor, M., Rangongo, N. J., Mkhize, S., Anderson, S., Pillay, B. J., and Sullivan, K. R. (2004). Investigating the mental abilities of rural primary school children in South Africa. *Ethnicity and Health*, 9, 17-36.

Johnson, D. L., Johnson, C. A., and Price-Williams, D. (1967). The Draw-a-Man test and Raven Progressive Matrices performance of Guatemalan boys and Ladino children. *Revista Interamericana de Psicologia*,l,143-157.

Johnson, G. B. (1948). Musical talent and the Negro. *Musical Supervisors Journal*, 15, 81-96.

Jordheim, G. D., and Olsen, I. A. (1963). The use of a non-verbal test of intelligence in the trust terriNtory of the Pacific. *American Anthropologist*, 65, 1122-1125.

Joseph, A., and Murray, V. F. (1951) *Chamorros and Carolinians of Saipan*. Westport, CT: Greenwood.

Jurgens, H. W., Aune, I. A., and Pieper, U. (1990). *International Data on Anthropometry*. Geneva, Switzerland: International Labor Office.

Kabo, V. (1985). The origins of the food-producing economy. *Current Anthropology*, 26, 601-616.

Kagitcibasi, C. (1972). Application of the D-48 test in Turkey. In L. J. Cronbach and P. J. D. Drenth (Eds.). *Mental Tests and Cultural Adaptation*. The Hague: Mouton.

Kaniel, S., and Fisherman, S. (1991). Level of performance and distribution of errors in the Progressive Matrices test: a comparison of Ethiopian immigrant and native Israeli adolescents. *International Journal of Psychology*, 26, 25-33.

Kaplan, G. J., Fleshman, J. K., Bender, T. R., and Clark, P. S. (1973). Long term effects of otitis media: a ten-year cohort study of Alaskan Eskimo children. *Pediatrics*, 52, 577-585.

Kaszycka, K. A., and Strkalj, G. (2002). Anthropologist's attitudes towards the concept of race: the Polish sample. *Current Anthropology*, 43, 329-335.

Kaszycka, K. A., and Strzalko, J. (2003). Race - still an issue for physical anthropology? Re- sults of Polish studies seen in the light of the U. S. findings. *American Anthropologist*, 105, 114-122.

Kaufman, A. S., and Doppelt, J. E. (1976). Analysis of WISC-R standardization data in terms of the stratification variables. *Child*

Development, 47 165-171.

Kaufman, A. S., and Kaufman, N. L. (1983). *KABC Interpretive Manual*. Circle-Pines: MN: American Guidance Service.

Kaufman, A. S., and Lichtenberger, E. (2002). *Assessing Adolescent and Adult Intelligence*. Boston: Allyn & Bacon.

Kaufman, A. S., McLean, J. E., Ishikuma, T., and Moon, S. B. (1989). Integration of literature on the intelligence of Japanese children and analysis of the data from a sequential-simultaneous perspective. *School Psychology International*, 10, 173-183.

Kaufman, A.S., and Wang, J. J. (1992). Gender, race and educational differences on the K- BIT at ages 4-90. *Journal of Psychcoeducational Assessment*, 10, 219-229.

Kaufman, J. C, McLean, J. E., Kaufman, A. S., and Kaufman, N. L. (1994). White-black and white-Hispanic differences on fluid and crystallized abilities by age across the 11 to 94 year range. *Psychological Reports*, 75, 1279-1288.

Kearins, J. M. (1981). Visual spatial memory in Australian Aboriginal children of desert regions. *Cognitive Psychology*, 3, 434-460.

Keith, A. (1922). The dawn of national life. In J. A. Hammerton (Ed.). *Peoples of All Nations*. London: Amalgamated Press.

Kelly, M. (1977). Papua New Guinea and Piaget - an eight-year study. In P. R. Dasen (Ed). *Piagetian Psychology*. New York: Gardner Press.

Kendall, I. M. (1976). The predictive validity of a possible alternative to the Classification Test Battery. *Psychologia Africana*, 16, 131-146.

Kendall, I. M. (1977). Some observations concerning reasoning styles of black South African workers: perceptual versus conceptual considerations. *Psychologia Africana*, 17, 1-29.

Kennedy, W. A., and Lindner, R. S. (1964). A normative study of the Goodenough Draw-a- Man Test on Southeastern Negro elementary school children. *Child Development*, 35, 33-62.

Kennedy, W. A., Van der Reit, V, and White, J. C. (1963). A normative study of intelligence and achievement of Negro schoolchildren in the southeastern United States. *Monographs of the Society for Research in Child Development*, 28, no. 6.

Kimura, D. (2002). Sex hormones influence human cognitive pattern *Neuroendocrinology Letters*, Special Issue Supplement 4, vol. 23.

Klaatsch, H. (1908). The skull of the Australian aboriginal. *Reports of the Pathology Laboratory Lunacy Department*, 1, 43-167.

Kleinfeld, J. (1971). Visual memory in village Eskimo and urban Caucasian children. *Arctic*, 24, 132-138.

Klekamp,J.,Reidel, A., Harper, C, and Kretschmann,H.J.(l 987). Morphometric study of the postnatal growth of the visual cortex of Australian aborigines and Caucasians. *Journal of Brain Research*, 35, 541-548.

Kline, C. L., and Lee, N. (1972). A transcultural study of dyslexia: analysis of language disabilities in Chinese children simultaneously learning to read and write in English and in *Chinese. Journal of Social Education*, 6, 9-26.

Klingelhofer, E. L. (1967). Performance of Tanzanian secondary school pupils on the Raven Standard Progressive Matrices test. *Journal of Social Psychology*, 72, 205-215.

Knapp, P. A., and Seagrim, G. N. (1981). Visual memory in Australian Aboriginal children and children of European descent. *International Journal of Psychology*, 16, 213-231.

Kohler, W. (1927). *The Mentality of Apes*. New York: Vintage.

Kozulin, A. (1998). Profiles of immigrant students' cognitive performance on Raven's Progressive Matrices. *Perceptual and Motor Skills*, 87, 1311-1314.

Kramer, R. A., Allen, L., and Gergen, P. J. (1995). Health and social characteristics and children's cognitive functioning: results from a national cohort. *American Journal of Public Health*, 85, 312-318.

Krantz, G. S. (1980). *Climatic Races and Descent Groups*. North Quincy, Mass: Christopher.

Kuhnen, U., Roeder, B. H. U., Ahah, A. A., Upmeyer, B. S. A., and

Zakaria, S. (2001). Cross-cultural variations in identifying embedded figures. *Journal of Cross-Cultural Psychology*, 32, 365-371.

Kunce, J., Rankin, L. S., and Clement, E. (1967). Maze performance and personal, social and economic adjustment of Alaskan natives. *Journal of Social Psychology*, 73, 37-45.

Kurth, von E. (1969). Erhohung der Leistungsnormen bei den farbigen progressiven Matrizen. *Zeitschrift fiir Psychologic*, 177, 85-90.

Kuttner, R. E. (1962). Prehistoric technology and human evolution. *Mankind Quarterly*, 3, 71- 87.

Kyostio, O. K. (1972). Divergence among school beginners caused by different cultural influences. In L. J. Cronbach and P. J. Drenth (Eds.). *Mental Tests and Cultural Adaptation*. The Hague: Mouton.

Lai, T. J., Guo, Y. L., Guo, N. W., and Hsu, C. C. (2001). Effects of prenatal exposure to polychlorinated biphenyls on cognitive development in children: a longitudinal study in Taiwan. *British Journal of Psychiatry*, 178, 49-52.

Lancer, I., and Rim, Y. (1984). Intelligence, family size and sibling age spacing. *Personality and Individual Differences*, 5, 151-157.

Landes, D. S. (1998). *The Wealth and Poverty of Nations: Why Some Are So Rich and Some So Poor*. New York: W. W. Norton &t Company.

Landman, J. (1988). *Appendix to the Manual of the junior South African Individual Scales*. Pretoria: Human Sciences Research Council.

Laosa, L. M., Swartz, J. D., and Diaz-Guerrero, R. (1974). Perceptual-cognitive and personality development of Mexican and Anglo-American children as measured by human figure drawings. *Developmental Psychology*, 10, 131-139.

Laroche, J. L. (1959). Effets de repetition du Matrix 38 sur les resultats d'enfants Katangais. *Bulletin du Centre d'Etudes et Recherches Psychotechniques*, 1, 85-99.

Laros, J. A., and Telegren, P. J. (1991). *Construction and Validation of the Son-R Non-Verbal Test of Intelligence*. Groningen: Wolters-Noordhoff.

Lathan, M. C. (1974). Protein-calorie malnutrition in children and its relation to psychological development and behavior. *Physiological Reviews*, 54, 541-565.

Latouche, G. L., and Dormeau, G. (1956). *La foration professionelle rapide en Afrique Equatoriale Française*. Brazzaville: Centre d'Etudes des Problems du Travail.

Lee, R. B. (1968). What hunters do for a living. In *Man the Hunter*. In R. B. Lee and I. Devore (Eds.), Chicago, Aldine Press.

Lenski, R., and Mittler, J. E. (1993). The directed mutation controversy and neo-Darwinism. *Science*, 259,188-194.

Lesser, G. S., Fifer, G., and Clark, D. H. (1965). Mental abilities of children from different social-class and cultural groups. *Monographs of the Society for Research in Child Development*, 30, no.4.

Levin, M. (1994). Comments on the Minnesota Transracial Adoption study. *Intelligence*, 19, 13-20.

Levin, M. (1997). *Why Race Matters*. Westport, CT: Praeger.

Levinson, B. M. (1957). The intelligence of applicants for admission to Jewish day schools. *Jewish Social Studies*, 19, 129- 140.

Lewis, B. (1990). *Race and Slavery in the Middle East*. New York: Oxford University Press.

Li, D., Jin,Y., Vandenberg, S. G., Zhu,Y., and Tang, C. (1990). Report on Shanghai norms for the Chinese translation of the Wechsler Intelligence Scale for Children - Revised. *Psychological Reports*, 67, 531-541.

Li, X., Sano, H., and Merwin, J. C. (1996). Perception and reasoning abilities among Ameri- can, Japanese and Chinese adolescents. *Journal of Adolescent Research*, 11, 173-193.

Lieberman, L., and Reynolds, L. T. (1996). Race: the deconstruction of a scientific concept. In L. T. Reynolds and L. Lieberman (Eds.). *Race and Other Misadventures: Essays in Honor of Ashley Montagu*. Dix Hills: General Hall.

Lieblich, A., and Kugelmas, S. (1981). Patterns of intellectual ability of Arab school children in Israel. *Intelligence*, 5, 311-320.

Lieblich, A., Ninio, A., and Kugelmas, S. (1972). Effects of ethnic origin and parental SES on WPPSI performance of pre-school children in Israel. *Journal of Cross Cultural Psychology*, 3, 159-168.

Lim, T. K. (1994). Gender-related differences in intelligence: application of confirmatory factor analysis. *Intelligence*, 19, 179-192.

Linn, M. C., and Petersen, A. C. (1986). A meta-analysis of gender differences in spatial ability: implications for mathematics and science achievement. In J. S. Hyde and M. C, Linn (Eds.). *The Psychology of Gender*. Baltimore: Johns Hopkins University Press.

Linnaeus, C. (1758). *Systema naturae sistens animale Sveciae regni*. Holmae: Salvius.

Lipovechaja, N. G., Kantonistowa, N. S., and Chamaganova, T. G. (1978). The role of heredity and of intellectual function. *Medidskie Probleing Formirouaniga Livenosti*, 27, 48-59.

Little, A. (1975). Performance of children from ethnic minority backgrounds in primary schools. *Oxford Review of Education*, 1, 117-135.

Liu, J., Raine, A., Venables, P. H., Dalais, C., and Mednick, S. A. (2003). Malnutrition at age 3 years and lower cognitive ability at age 11 years. *Archives of Pediatric and Adolescent Medicine*, 157, 593-600.

Livingstone, F. B. (1962). On the non-existence of the human races. *Current Anthropology*, 3, 279-281.

Llanos, Z. M. (1974). *El funcionamiento intelectuel de los niños en las zones marginales de Lima*. Montevideo, Uruguay: Institute Americano de Nino.

Lloyd, E, and Pidgeon, D. A. (1961) An investigation into the effects of couching on verbal and non-verbal tests with European, Indian and African children. *British Journal of Educational Psychology*, 31, 145-151.

Loehlin, J. C., Lindzey, G., and Spuhler, J. N. (1975). *Race Differences in Intelligence*. San Francisco, CA: Freeman.

Lombardi, T. P. (1970). Psycholinguistic abilities of Papago Indian school children. *Exceptional Children*, 36, 485-493.

Lorenzo,J. L., and Mirambell, L. (1986). *Tlapacoya: 35,000: Anos de Historic del Lago de Chalco*. Mexico City: Instituto Nacional de Antropologia e Historia.

Lovegrove, M. N. (1966). The scholastic achievement of European and Maori children. *New Zealand Journal of Educational Studies*, 1, 15-39.

Lubinski, D. (2000). Scientific and social significance of assessing individual differences. *Annual Review of Psychology*, 51, 405-444.

Lucas, A., Morley, R., Cole, T. J., Lister, G., and Leeson-Payne, C. (1992). Breast milk and subsequent intelligence quotient in children born pre-term. *The Lancet*, 339, 261-264.

Lucas, A., Morley, R., Cole, T. J. (1998). Randomised trial of early diet in pre-term babies and later intelligence quotient. *British Medical Journal*, 317, 1481-1487.

Lynn, R. (1977a). The intelligence of the Japanese. *Bulletin of the British Psychological Society*, 30, 69-72.

_____ (1977b). The intelligence of the Chinese and Malays in Singapore. *Mankind Quarterly*, 18, 125-128.

_____ (1979). The social ecology of intelligence in the British Isles. *British Journal of Social and Clinical Psychology*, 18, 1-12.

_____ (1980). The social ecology of intelligence in the France. *British Journal of Social and Clinical Psychology*, 19, 325-331.

_____ (1987). The intelligence of the Mongoloids: a psychometric, evolutionary and neurological theory. *Personality and Individual Differences*, 8, 813-844.

_____ (1988). *Educational Achievement in Japan*. London: Macmillan.

_____ (1990a). The role of nutrition in secular increases of intelligence. *Personality and Individual Differences*, 11, 273-285.

_____ (1990b). Differential rates of secular increase of five major primary abilities. *Social Biology*, 38, 137-141.

_____ (1991 a). Race differences in intelligence: a global perspective. *Mankind Quarterly*, 31,254-296.

_____ (1991b). The evolution of race differences in intelligence. *Mankind Quarterly*, 32,99- 173.

_____ (1991c). Intelligence in China. *Social Behavior and Personality*, 19,1-4.

_____ (1992). Sex differences on the Differential Ability Test in British and American adolescents. *Educational Psychology*, 12, 101-106.

_____ (1993). Nutrition and intelligence. In R A. Vernon (Ed.), *Biological Approaches to the Study of Human Intelligence*. Norwood, NJ: Ablex. 185

_____ (1994a). The intelligence of Ethiopian immigrant and Israeli adolescents. *International Journal of Psychology*, 29, 55-56.

_____ (1994b). Sex differences in brain size and intelligence: a paradox resolved. *Personality and Individual Differences*, 17, 257-271.

_____ (1994c). Some reinterpretations of the Minnesota Transracial Adoption Study. *Intelligence*, 19, 21-28.

_____ (1996). Racial and ethnic differences in intelligence in the United States on the Differential Ability Scale. *Personality and Individual Differences*, 20,271-273.

_____ (1997). Intelligence in Taiwan. *Personality and Individual Differences*, 22, 585-586.

_____ (1998a). Sex differences on the Scottish standardisation sample of the WAIS-R. *Personality and Individual Differences*, 24, 289-290.

_____ (1998b). In support of the nutrition theory. In U. Neisser (Ed.). *The Rising Curve: Long Term Gains in IQ and Related Matters*. Washington, D.C.: American Psychological Association.

_____ (1998c). Sex differences in intelligence: a rejoinder to Mackintosh. *Journal of Biosocial Science*, 30, 529-532.

_____ (1998d). New data on black infant precocity. *Personality and Individual Differences*, 25, 801-804.

_____ (1998e). Has the black-white intelligence difference in the United States been narrowing over time? *Personality and Individual Differences*, 25, 999-1002.

_____ (1999). Sex differences in intelligence and brain size: a developmental theory. *Intelligence*, 27, 1-12.

_____ (2001). Intelligence in Russia. *Mankind Quarterly*, 42, 151-154.

_____ (2002). Racial and ethnic differences in psychopathic personality. *Personality and Individual Differences*, 32, 273-316.

_____ (2002a). Skin color and intelligence in African Americans. *Population and Environment*, 23, 365-375.

_____ (2004). The intelligence of American Jews. *Personality and Individual Differences*, 36, 201-207.

Lynn, R., Allik, J., Pullmann, H., and Laidra, J. (2002). A study of the IQ in Estonia. *Psychological Reports*, 95, 611-612.

Lynn, R., Backhoff, E., and Contreras, L. A. (2005). Ethnic and racial differences on the Standard Progressive Matrices in Mexico. *Journal of Biosocial Science*, 37, 107-113.

Lynn, R., Chan, J. W. C., and Eysenck, H. J. (1991). Reaction times and intelligence in Chinese and British children. *Perceptual and Motor Skills*, 72, 443-452.

Lynn, R., and Chan, P. W. (2003). Sex differences on the Progressive Matrices: some data from Hong Kong. *Journal of Biosocial Science*, 35, 145-154.

Lynn, R., and Dziobon, J. (1980). On the intelligence of the Japanese and other Mongoloid peoples. *Personality and Individual Differences*, 1, 95-96.

Lynn, R., and Hampson, S. (1986). The rise of national intelligence: evidence from Britain, Japan and the USA. *Personality and Individual Differences*, 7, 23-332. 186

_____ (1986a). The structure of Japanese abilities: an analysis in terms of the hierarchical model of intelligence. *Current Psychological Research and Reviews*, 4, 309- 322.

_____ (1986b). Intellectual abilities of Japanese children: an assessment of 2-8 year olds derived from the McCarthy Scales of Children's Abilities. *Intelligence*, 10, 41-58.

_____ (1987). Further evidence on the cognitive abilities of the Japanese: data from the WPPSI. *International Journal of Behavioral Development*, 10, 23-36.

Lynn, R., Hampson, S., and Bingham, R. (1987a). Japanese, British and American adolescents compared for Spearman's *g* and for the verbal, numerical and visuo-spatial abilities. *Psychologia*, 30, 137-144.

Lynn, R., Hampson, S., and Iwawaki, S. (1987b). Abstract reasoning and spatial abilities among American, British and Japanese adolescents. *Mankind Quarterly*, 27, 397-434.

Lynn, R., Hampson, S., and Lee, M. (1988). The intelligence of Chinese children in Hong Kong. *School Psychology International*, 9, 29-32.

Lynn, R., Hampson, S., and Magee, M. (1984). Home background, intelligence, personality and education as predictors of unemployment in young people. *Personality and Individual Differences*, 5, 549-558.

Lynn, R., and Harland, E. P. (1998). A positive effect of iron supplementation on the IQs of iron deficient children. *Personality and Individual Differences*, 24, 883-887.

Lynn, R., and Hattori, K. (1990). The heritability of intelligence in Japan. *Behavior Genetics*, 20, 545-546.

Lynn, R., and Holmshaw, M. (1990). Black-white differences in reaction times and intelligence. *Social Behavior and Personality*, 18, 299-308.

Lynn, R., and Irwing, P. (2004). Sex differences on the Progressive Matrices: a meta-analysis. *Intelligence*, 32, 481-98.

Lynn, R., and Kazlauskaite, V. (2002). A Study of the IQ in Lithuania. *Perceptual and Motor Skills*, 95, 611-612.

Lynn, R., and Owen, K. (1994). Spearman's hypothesis and test score differences between whites, Indians and blacks in South Africa. *Journal of General Psychology*, 121, 27-36.

Lynn, R., and Pagliari, C. (1994). The intelligence of American children is still rising. *Journal of Biosocial Science*, 26, 65-68.

Lynn, R., Pagliari, C., and Chan, J. (1988). Intelligence in Hong Kong measured for Spearman's *g* and the visuospatial and verbal primaries. *Intelligence*, 12, 423-433.

Lynn, R., Plaspalanova, E., Stetinsky, D., and Tzenova, B. (1998). Intelligence in Bulgaria. *Psychological Reports*, 82, 912-914.

Lynn, R., Pullmann, H., and Allik, J. (2003). A new estimate of the IQ in Estonia. *Psychological Reports*, 97, 662-664.

Lynn, R., and Shigehisa, T. (1991). Reaction times and intelligence: a comparison of Japanese and British children. *Journal of Biosocial Science*, 23, 409-416.

Lynn, R., and Song, J. M. (1993). Sex differences in reaction times, decision times and movement times in British and Korean children. *Journal of Genetic Psychology*, 154, 209- 313.

_____ (1994). General intelligence, visuospatial and ver bal abilities of Korean children. *Personality and Individual Differences*, l6, 363-364.

Lynn, R., Wilson, R. G., and Gault, A. (1989). Simple musical tests as measures of Spearman's *g*. *Personality and Individual Differences*, 10, 25-28.

Lynn, R., and Vanhanen, T. (2002). *IQ and the Wealth of Nations*. Westport, CT: Praeger.

Lynn, R., and Vanhanen, T. (2006). *IQ and Global Inequality*. Augusta, GA: Washington Summit Publishers.

Mabey, C. (1981). Black British literacy: a study of reading attainment of London black children from 8 to 15 years. *Educational Research*, 23, 83-95.

MacArthur, R. S. (1965). *Mackenzie District Norming Project*. Ottawa:

Department of Northern Affairs.

MacArthur, R. S. (1967). Some cognitive abilities of Eskimo, white and Indian-Metis children aged 9 to 12 years. *Canadian Journal of Behavioral Science*, 1, 50-59.

MacArthur, R. S., Irvine, S. H., and Brimble, A. R. (1964). *The Northern Rhodesia Mental Ability Survey*. Lusaka: Rhodes Livingstone Institute.

MacDonald, K. (1994). *A People That Shall Dwell Alone*. Westport, CT: Praeger.

Mackintosh, N. J. (1977). Stimulus control: attention factors. In W. K. Honig and J. E. R. Staddon (Eds.). *Handbook of Operant Behavior*. Englewood Cliffs: Prentice-Hall.

Mackintosh, N. J. (1996). Sex differences and IQ. *Journal of Biosocial Science*, 28, 559-572.

Mackintosh, N. J. (1998). *IQ and Human Intelligence*. Oxford: University Press.

Mackintosh, N. J., and Mascie-Taylor, C. G. N. (1985). The IQ question. In *Education for All*. Cmnd paper 4453. London: HMSO.

MacLean, A. W., and McGhie, A. (1980). The AH4 group test of intelligence applied in a Canadian high school sample. *Canadian Journal of Behavioral Science*, 12, 217-291.

MacNeish, R. S. (1976). Early man in the New World. *American Scientist*, 64, 316-327.

Maity, H. (1926). A report on the application of the Stanford adult tests to a group of college students. *Indian Journal of Psychology*, 1, 214-222.

Majumdar, P. K., and Nundi, P. C. (1971). Raven's Standard Progressive Matrices in two different populations. *Journal of the Indian Academy of Applied Psychology*, 8, 30-33.

Manley, D. R. (1963). Mental ability in Jamaica. *Social and Economic Studies*, 12, 51-77.

Mann, V. A., Sasanuma, S., Sakuma, N., and Masaki, S. (1990).

Sex differences in cognitive abilities: a cross cultural perspective. *Neuropsychologia*, 28, 1063-1077.

Marinkovich, R. I., Sparosvich, H. E, Santana, M. C. D., Game, J. H., Gomez, C. C., and Marinkovich, D. I. (2000). Estudio de la capacidad intellectuel (test de Matrices Progressivas de Raven) en escolares Chilerios de 5 a 18 años. *Revista de Psicologia General y Aplicada*, 53, 5-30.

Martin, W. A. (1969). Word fluency: a comparative study. *Journal of Genetic Psychology*, 114, 253-262.

Martinelli, V., and Lynn, R. (2005). Sex differences on verbal and non-verbal abilities among primary school children in Malta. Unpublished.

Martorell, R., Malina, R. M., Castillo, R. O., Mendoza, F. S., and Pawson, I. G. (1988). Body proportions in three ethnic groups: children and youths 2-17 years in NHANES 11 and NHANES. *Human Biology*, 60, 205-222.

Martorell, R. (1997). Undernutrition during pregnancy and early childhood: consequences for cognitive and behavioural development. In M. E. Young (Ed.). *Early Child Development: Investing in Our Children's Future*, Amsterdam: Elsevier.

Matarazo, J. D. (1972). *The Measurement and Appraisal of Adult Intelligence*. Baltimore: Williams and Wilkins.

Maugham, B., and Rutter, M. (1986). Black pupils' progress in secondary schools: examination attainments. *British Journal of Developmental Psychology*, 4, 19-29.

McElwain, D. W, and Kearney, G. E. (1970). *Queensland Test Handbook*. Hawthorne, Australia: Australian Council for Educational Research.

McElwain, D. W, and Kearney, G. E. (1973). Intellectual development. In G. E. Kearney, P. R. de Lacey and G. R. Davidson (Eds.). *The Psychology of Aboriginal Australians*. New York: Wiley.

McFie, J., and Thompson, J. A. (1970). Intellectual abilities of immigrant children. *British Journal of Educational Psychology*, 40,

348-351.

McGrew, K. S., and Flanagan, D. P. (1998). *The Intelligence Test Desk Reference*. Oston: Allyn and Bacon.

McGurk, F. C. F. (1953a). On white and Negro test performance and socio-economic factors. *Journal of Abnormal and Social Psychology*, 37, 448-450.

McGurk, F. C. F. (1953b). Socio-economic status and culturally weighted test scores of Negro subjects. *Journal of Abnormal and Social Psychology*, 37, 276-277.

McIntyre, G. A. (1938). *The Standardisation of Intelligence Tests in Australia*. Melbourne: University Press.

McShane, D. A., and Plas, J. M. (1984). The cognitive functioning of American Indian children: moving from the WISC to the WISC-R. *School Psychology Review*, 17, 39-51.

Mehrotra, K. K. (1968). A comparative study of the WISC and Raven's Progressive Matrices. *Psychological Studies*, 13, 47-50.

Mehryar, A. H., Shapurian, R., and Bassiri, T. (1972). A preliminary report on a Persian adaptation of Heirn's AH4 test. *Journal of Psychology*, 80, 167-180.

Mehryar, A. H., Tashakkori, A., Yousefi, R, and Khajavi, F. (1987). The application of the Goodenough-Harris Draw-a-Man test to a group of Iranian children in the city of Shiraz. *British Journal of Educational Psychology*, 57,401-406.

Mellars, P., and Stringer, C. (1989). *The Human Revolution*. Edinburgh: Edinburgh University Press.

Mercer, J. R., and Lewis, J. F. (1984). *System of Multicultural Pluralistic Assessment: Manual*. San Antonio, TX: Psychological Corporation.

Michael, R. T. (2003). Children's cognitive skill development in Britain and the United States. *International Journal of Behavioral Development*, 27, 396-408.

Miller, E. M. (1991). Climate and intelligence. *Mankind Quarterly*, 32, 127-131.

Miller, E. M. (1996). The evolution of Australoid and Amerindian intelligence. *Mankind Quarterly*, 37,149-186.

Miller, E. M. (2005). Geographical Centrality As an Explanation for Racial Differences in Intelligence. *Mankind Quarterly* (forthcoming)

Miron, M. (1977). A validation study of a transferred group intelligence test. *International Journal of Psychology*, 12, 193-205.

Misawa, G., Motegi, M., Fujita, K., and Hattori, K. (1984). A comparative study of intellec- tual abilities of Japanese and American children on the Columbia Mental Maturity Scale. *Personality and Individual Differences*, 5,173-181.

Modiano, N. (1962). Mental testing among Tzeltal and Tzotzil children. *Proceedings of the 35th International Congress of Americanists*. Mexico City.

Mohan, V. (1972). Raven's Standard Progressive Matrices and a verbal test of general mental ability. *Journal of Psychological Researches*, 16, 67-69.

Mohan, V., and Kumar, D. (1979). Performance of neurotics and stables on the Standard Progressive Matrices. *Intelligence*, 3, 355-368.

Mohanty, A. K., and Babu, N. (1983). Bilingualism and metalinguistic ability among Kond tribals in Orissa, India. *Journal of Social Psychology*, 121, 15-22.

Montagu, A. (1945a). *Man's Most Dangerous Myth: The Fallacy of Race*. New York; Columbia University Press.

Montagu, A. (1945b). Intelligence of northern Negroes and southern whites in the First World War. *American Journal of Psychology*, 58, 161-188.

Montagu, A. (1999). (Ed.). *Race and IQ. Expanded Edition*. New York: Oxford University Press.

Montie, J. E., and Pagan, J. F. (1988). Racial differences in IQ: item analysis of the Stanford- Binet at 3 years. *Intelligence*, 12, 315-332.

Moon, S. B. (1988). A Cross Cultural Study of the Kaufman Assessment Battery for Children with Korean Children. Ph.D. thesis,

University of Alabama.

Morant, G. M. (1927). A study of Australian and Tasmanian skulls based on previously studied measurements. *Biometrika*, 19, 417-440.

Morton, S. G. (1849). Observations on the size of the brain and families of man. *Proceedings of the Academy of Natural Sciences Philadelphia*, 4, 221-224.

Movies, E. W, and Wolins, M. (1973). Group care and intellectual development. *Developmental Psychology*, 4, 370-380.

Murray, C. (1998). *Income Inequality and IQ*. Washington, D.C.: AEI Press.

Murray, C. (2003). *Human Accomplishment*. New York: Harper Collins.

Murray, L. S. (1983). Nutritional Status and Development of St. Lucian Preschool Children. M.Sc. Thesis. UWI, Mona.

Nagoshi, C. T., and Johnson, R. C. (1986). The ubiquity of *g*. *Personality and Individual Differences*, 7, 201-208.

Nardi, N. (1948). Studies in intelligence of Jewish children. *Jewish Education*, 19,41-45.

Nathawat, S. S., and Puri, P. (1995). A comparative study of MZ and DZ twins on Level 1 and Level 11 mental abilities and personality. *Journal of the Indian Academy of Applied Psychology*, 21, 545-546.

National Center for Education Statistics. (2003). *National Assessment of Educational Progress*. Washington, D.C.

National Center for Health Statistics. (1979). Caloric and selected nutrient values for persons 1-74 years of age. *Vital Health Statistics*, No. 209. Hyattsville, MD.

Nei, M., and Roychoudhury, A. K. (1993). Evolutionary relationships of human populations on a global scale. *Molecular Biology and Evolution*, 10, 927-943.

Neisser,U. (1998). Intelligence: knowns and unknowns. *American Psychologist*, 51, 77-101.

Nell, V. (2000). *Cross-Cultural Neuropsychological Assessment.*

Mahwah, NJ: Lawrence Erlbaum.

Nelson, W. E. (1933). *Mitchell-Nelson Textbook of Pediatrics.* Philadelphia: Saunders.

Nettle, D. (2003). Intelligence and class mobility in the British population. *British Journal of Psychology,* 94, 551-561.

Nisbett, R. E. (1998). Race, genetics and IQ. In C. Jencks and M. Phillips (Eds.). *The Black-White Test Score Gap.* Washington, D.C.: Brookings Institution Press.

Nissen, S., Machover, S., and Kinder, E. F. (1935). A study of performance tests given to a group of Native African Negro children. *British Journal of Psychology,* 25, 308-355.

Nkaya, H. N., Huteau, M., and Bonnet, J-P. (1994). Retest effect on cognitive performance on the Raven Matrices in France and in the Congo. *Perceptual and Motor Skills,* 78, 503-510.

Norman, R. D., and Midkiff, K. L. (1955). Navaho children on Raven Progressive Matrices and Goodenough Draw-a-Man tests. *Southwestern Journal of Anthropology,* 11,129-136.

Notcutt, B. (1950). The measurement of Zulu intelligence. *Journal of Social Research,* 1, 195- 206.

Nurcombe, B., de Lacey, P., and Walker, S. L. (1999). *Children of the Dispossessed.* Stamford, CT: Ablex.

Nurcombe, B., and Moffitt, P. (1973). Cultural Deprivation and Language Deficit. In G. E. Kearney, P. R. de Lacey, and G. R. Davidson (Eds.). *The Psychology of Aboriginal Australians.* Sydney: John Wiley.

Nyborg, H. (2003). Sex differences in g. In H. Nyborg (Ed.). *The Scientific Study of General Intelligence.* Amsterdam: Elsevier.

Nyborg, H., and Jensen, A. R. (2000). Black-white differences on various psychometric tests: Spearman's hypothesis tested on American armed services veterans. *Personality and Individual Differences,* 28, 593—599.

Office of the Surgeon General. (1968). *Supplement to Health of the*

Army. Washington, D.C.: Dept. of the Army.

Ombredane, A., Robaye, E, and Robaye, E. (1952). Analyse des resultats d'une application experimentale du matrix 38 a 485 noirs Baluba. *Bulletin Centre d'Etudes et Recherches Psychotechniques*, 7, 235-255.

Ortar, G. (1952). Standardization of the Wechsler Test for Intelligence for children in Israel. *Megamot*, 4, 87-100.

Osborne, R. T. (1980). *Twins: Black and White.* Athens, GA: Foundation for Human Under- standing.

Osborne, R. T, and Gregor, A. J. (1966). The heritability of visualization, perceptual speed and spatial orientation. *Perceptual and Motor Skills*, 23, 379-390.

Osborne, R. T., and McGurk, F. C. (1982). *The Testing of Negro Intelligence.* Athens, GA: Foundation for Human Understanding.

Osmon, D.C., and Jackson, R. (2002). Inspection time and IQ: fluid or perceptual aspects of intelligence. *Intelligence*, 30, 119-127.

Owen, K. (1992). The suitability of Raven's Progressive Matrices for various groups in South Africa. *Personality and Individual Differences*, 13, 149-159.

Packenberg, B., and Gundersen, H. J. (1997). Neurocortical nerurone number in humans: effects of age and sex. *Journal of Comparative Neurology*, 384, 312-320.

Paine, P., Dorea, J. G., Pasquali, L., and Monteiro, A. M. (1992). Growth and cognition in Brazilian school children: a spontaneously occurring intervention study. *International Journal of Behavioral Development*, 15, 169-183.

Pakkenberg, H., and Voigt, J. (1964). Brain weight of Danes. *Acta Anatoma* (Basel), 5, 297- 307.

Pal, S., Shyam, R., and Singh, R. (1997). Genetic analysis of general intelligence g: a twin study. *Personality and Individual Differences*, 22, 779-780.

Parker, S. T., and Gibson, K. R. (1977). A development model of the evolution of language and intelligence in early hominids. *The Behavioral Brain Sciences*, 2, 367-408

Parker, S.T., and McKinney, M. L. (1999). *Origins of Intelligence: The Evolution of Cognitive Development in Monkeys, Apes and Humans.* Baltimore, MD: Johns Hopkins University Press.

Parra, E. J., Marcini, A., and Akey, J. (1998). Estimating African American admixture proportions by use of population-specific alleles. *American Journal of Human Genetics*, 63,1839- 1851.

Paul, S. M. (1985). The Advanced Raven's Progressive Matrices: normative data for an American university population and an examination of the relationship with Spearman's *g. Journal of Experimental Education*, 54, 95-100.

Payne. J. (1974). Educational Priority: EPA Surveys and Statistics, vol. 2, London: HMSO.

Pearson, R. (1974). *Introduction to Anthropology.* New York: Holt, Rinehart and Winston.

_____ (1985). *Anthropological Glossary.* Malabar, FL: Kreiger.

Peoples, C. E., Fagan, J. E, and Drotar, D. (1995). The influence of race on 3 year old chil- dren's performance on the Stanford-Binet Fourth Edition. *Intelligence*, 21, 69-82.

Persaud, G. (1972). *The Performance of Two Samples of Primary School Children on Two Culture Free and Two Culture Bound Tests of Intelligence.* University of Stockholm, Sweden: Institute of Applied Psychology.

Peters, L., and Ellis, E. N. (1970). *An Analysis of WISC Profile Scores of Chinese-Canadian Children.* Vancouver, BC: Board of School Trustees.

Peterson, J., and Lanier, L. H. (1929). *Studies in the comparative abilities of whites and Negroes. Mental Measurement Monographs*, No. 5.

Petrogiannis, K. S., Bardos, A. N., and Randou, E. (1999). Performance of Greek and American students on the Matrix Analogies Test. *School Psychology International*, 20, 233-238.

Philip's. (1996). *World Atlas*. London: Chancellor.

Phillips, C. J. (1979). Educational under-achievement in different ethnic groups. *Educational Research* 21, 116-130.

Pickford, M. (1986). Major events in primate paleontology: possible support for climatic forcing models of evolution. *Antropologia Contemporarea*, 9, 89-94.

Piddington, M., and Piddington, R. (1932). Report of field work in Northwestern Australia. *Oceania*, 2, 327-328.

Pieke, F. N. (1988). The social position of the Dutch Chinese: an outline. *China Information*, 3, 12-23.

Pind, J., Gunnarsdottir, E. K., and Johannesson, H. S. (2003). Raven's Standard Progressive Matrices: new school age norms and a study of the test's validity. *Personality and Individual Differences*, 34, 375-386.

Plomin, R. (1994). *Genetics and Experience: The Interplay between Nature and Nurture*. Thousand Oaks, CA: Sage.

Plomin, R., and Buss, D. (1973). Reflection-impulsivity and intelligence. *Psychological Reports*, 33, 726.

Plomin, R., DeFries, J. C., and McClearn, G. E. (1990). *Behavioral Genetics*. New York: Freeman.

Pollitt, E., Gorman, K. S., Engle, P. L., Martorell, R., and Rivera,J. (1993). *Early Supplementary Feeding and Cognition. Monographs Society for Research in Child Development*, 58, No. 235.

Pollitt, E., Hathirat, P., Kotchabhakdi, N., Missell, L., and Valyasevi, A. (1989). Iron defi- ciency and educational achievement in Thailand. *American Journal of Clinical Nutrition*, 50, 687-697.

Pons, A. L. (1974). *Administration of Tests Outside the Cultures of their Origin*. 26th Congress of the South African Psychological Association.

Popper, K. R. (1959). *The Logic of Scientific Discovery*. London: Methuen.

Poortinga, Y. (1971). Cross-cultural comparison of maximum performance tests: some methodological aspects and some experiments with simple auditory and visual stimuli. *Psychologia*

Africana, Monograph Supplement No. 6.

Poortinga, Y. (1972). A comparison of African and European students in simple auditory and visual tasks. In L. J. Cronbach and P. D. Drenth (Eds.). *Mental Tests and Cultural Adaptation*. The Hague: Mouton.

Poortinga, Y, and Foden, I. M. (1975). A comparative study of curiosity in black and white South African students. *Psychologia Africana*, Monograph supplement No. 8.

Portenier, L. G. (1947). Abilities and interests of Japanese-American high school seniors. *Journal of Social Psychology*, 25, 53-61.

Porteus, S. D. (1917). Mental tests with delinquents and Australian Aboriginal children. *Psychological Review*, 24, 32-42.

Porteus, S. D. (1930). Race and social differences in performance tests. *Genetic Psychology Monographs*, 8, no. 2.

Porteus, S. D. (1931). *The Psychology of a Primitive People*. London: Edward Arnold.

Porteus, S. D. (1933a). Mentality of Australian Aborigines. *Oceania*, 4, 30-36.

Porteus, S. D. (1933b). Correspondence—the psychology of a primitive people. *Oceania*, 4, 30-36.

Porteus, S.D. (1937) Ethnic groups and the Maze Test. In R.E.Kuttner (Ed) *Race and Modem Science*. New York: Social Science Press.

Porteus, S. D. (1965). *Porteus Maze Test*. Palo Alto, CA: Pacific Books.

Porteus, S. D., and Babcock, H. (1926). *Temperament and Race*. Boston, MA: Badger.

Porteus, S. D., Brochner, S., Russell, J., and David, K. (1967). Age a factor in Australid mentality. *Perceptual and Motor Skills*, 25, 3-16

Porteus, S. D., and Gregor, A. J. (1963). Studies in intercultural testing. *Perceptual and Motor Skills*, 16, 705-724.

Post, R. H. (1962). Population differences in red and green colour vision deficiency: review and a query on relaxation selection. *Eugenics Review*, 9,131-146.

Pnfitera, A., Lawrence, L. G., and Saklofske, D. H. (1998). The WISC-III in context. In A. Prifitera and D. H. Saklofske (Eds.). (1998). *WISC-III Clinical Use and Interpretation*. San Diego, CA: Academic.

Prince, J. R. (1968). The effect of western education and science conceptualisation in New Guinea. *British Journal of Educational Psychology*, 38, 64-74.

Proctor, B. E., Kranzler, J. H., Rosenbloom, A. L., Martinez, V., and Guevara-Aguire, J. (2000). An initial investigation of validation of the Matrix Analogies Test-Expanded Form in Ecuador. *Psychological Reports*, 86, 445-453.

Pumfrey, P. D. (1983). The reading attainments of British children of parents of West Indian origin. *Reading*, 17, 111-124.

Rabinowitz, M. B., Wang, J-D., and Soong, W-T. (1991). Dentine lead and child intelligence in Taiwan. *Archives of Environmental Health*, 46, 351-360.

Rahman, A., Macbool, E., and Zuberi, H. S. (2002). Lead-associated deficits in stature, mental ability and behavior in children in Karachi. *Annals of Tropical Paediatrics*, 22, 301-311.

Raine, A., Reynolds, C, Venables, P. H., and Mednick, S. A. (2002). Stimulation seeking and intelligence: a prospective longitudinal study. *Journal of Personality and Social Psychology*, 82, 663-674.

Rao, S. N., and Reddy, I. K. (1968). Development of norms for Raven's Coloured Progressive Matrices on elementary school children. *Psychological Studies*, 13, 105-107.

Raudenbush, S. W, and Kasim, R. M. (1998). Cognitive skill and economic inequality: findings from the national adult literacy survey. *Harvard Educational Review*, 68, 33-68.

Raveau, F. H. M., Elster, E., and Lecoutre, J. P. (1976). Migration et acculturation differentiale. *International Review of Applied Psychology*, 25, 145-163.

Raven, J. (1981). *Irish and British Standardisations*. Oxford: Oxford Psychologists Press.

_____ (1986). *Manual for Raven's Progressive Matrices and Vocabulary Scales*. London: Lewis.

_____ (1998). *Manual for Raven's Progressive Matrices*. Oxford: Oxford Psychologists Press.

Raven, J., and Court, J. H. (1989). *Manual for Raven's Progressive Matrices and Vocabulary Scales*. London: Lewis.

Raven, J. C. (1939). The RECI series of perceptual tests: an experimental survey. *British Journal of Medical Psychology*, 18, 16-34.

Raven, J. C., Court, J. H., and Raven, J. (1994). *Advanced Progressive Matrices*. Oxford: Oxford Psychologists Press.

_____ (1995). *Coloured Progressive Matrices*. Oxford: Oxford Psychologists Press.

_____ (1996). *Standard Progressive Matrices*. Oxford: Oxford Psychologists Press.

_____ (1998). *Advanced Progressive Matrices*. Oxford: Oxford Psychologists Press.

_____ (1999). *Manual for Raven's Progressive Matrices and Vocabulary Scales*. London: Lewis.

_____ (2000). *Standard Progressive Matrices*. Oxford: Oxford Psychologists Press.

Razrin, G. (1971). *Mind in Evolution*. New York: Houghton Mifflin.

Redmond, M., and Davies, F. R. (1940). *The Standardisation of Two Intelligence Tests*. Wellington: New Zealand Council for Educational Research.

Reed, T. E. (1969). Caucasian genes in American Negroes. *Science*, 165, 762-768.

Reed, T. E. (1971). The population variance of the proportion of genetic admixture in human intergroup hybrids. *Proceedings of the National Academy of Science*, 68, 3168-3169.

Reid, N., and Gilmore, A. (1983). Pupil performance on TOSCA: Some additional information. *New Zealand Journal of Educational Studies*, 18, 13-81.

Reid, N., and Gilmore, A. (1989). The Raven's Standard Progressive Matrices in New Zealand. *Psychological Test Bulletin*, 2, 25-35.

Reidel, A., Klekamp,]., Harper, C., and Kretschmann, H. J. (1994). Morphometric study on the postnatal growth of the cerebral cortex of Australian aborigines and Caucasians. *Journal of Brain Research*, 35, 531-540.

Relethford, J. H. (1988). Genetics of modern human origins and diversity. *Annual Review of Anthropology*, 27, 1-23.

Resing, W. C. M., Bleichrodt, N., and Drenth, P. J. D. (1986). Het gebruit van de RAKIT bij allochtoon etnische groepen. *Nederlands Tijdschrift voor de Psychologie*, 41, 179-188.

Reuning, H. (1968). Psychological studies of Kalahari Bushmen. In L. J. Cronbach and P. J. Drenth (Eds.). *Mental Tests and Cultural Adaptation*. The Hague: Mouton.

Reuning, H. (1972). Testing Bushmen in the central Kalahari. In S. H. Irvine and J. W. Berry (Eds.). *Human Abilities in Cultural Context*. Cambridge, UK: Cambridge University Press.

Reynolds, C. R., Chastain, R. L., Kaufman, A. S., and McLean, J. E. (1987). Demographic characteristics and IQ among adults: analysis of WAIS-R standardization sample as a function of the stratification variables. *Journal of School Psychology*, 25, 323-342.

Reynolds, C. R., and Jensen, A. R. (1983). WISC-R subscale patterns of abilities of blacks and whites matched on full scale IQ. *Journal of Educational Psychology*, 15, 207-214.

Reynolds, C. R., Willson, V. L., and Ramsey, M. (1999). Intellectual differences among Mexican Americans, Papagos and whites, independent of g. *Personality and Individual Differences*, 27, 1181-1188.

Richardson, K., and Spears, D. (1972). From biology. In K. Richardson and D. Spears (Eds). *Race, Culture and Education*. Harmondsworth, UK: Penguin Books.

Richter, L. M., Griesel, R. D., and Wortley, M. E. (1989). The Draw-a-Man Test: A 50 year perspective on drawings done by black South

African children. *South African Journal of Psychology*, 19, 1-5.

Rimoldi, H. J. (1948). A note on Raven's Progressive Matrices Test. *Educational and Psychological Measurement*, 8, 347-352.

Rindermann, H., Ngoc, Q. H. S. & Baumeister, A. (2013). Cognitive ability, parenting and instruction in Vietnam and Germany. Intelligence, 41, 366-377.

Risso, W. L. (1961). *El test de Matrice Progressivas y el test Domino*. Proceedings of the 1961 Conference of the Psychological Society of Uruguay.

Ritchie, J. E. (1966). Some observations on Maori and Pakeha intelligence test performance. *Journal of the Polynesian Society*, 66, 351-356.

Roberts, N. (1989). Pleistocene environments in time and space. In R. Foley (Ed.). *Hominid Evolution and Community Ecology: Prehistoric Human Adaptation in Biological Perspective*. London: Academic Press.

Robin, R. W, and Shea, J. D.C. (1983). The Bender Gestalt visual motor test in Papua New Guinea. *International Journal of Psychology*, 18, 263-270.

Rodd, W. G. (1959). A cross cultural study of Taiwan's schools. *Journal of Social Psychology*, 50, 30-36.

Rohrer, J. H. (1942). The test intelligence of Osage Indians. *Journal of Social Psychology*, 16, 99-105.

Roth, P. L., Bevier, C. A., Bobko, P., Switzer, E S., and Tyler, P. (2001). Ethnic group differences in cognitive ability in employment and educational settings: a meta-analysis. *Personnel Psychology*, 54, 297-330.

Rouhani, S. (1989). Molecular genetics and the pattern of human evolution: plausible and implausible models. In P. Mellars and C. Stringer (Eds.). *The Human Revolution*. Cambridge, UK: Cambridge University Press.

Rowe, D. C. (2002). IQ, birth weight, and number of sexual partners in white, African American, and mixed race adolescents. *Population and Environment*, 23, 513-524.

Ruff, C. B., Trinkaus, E. and Holliday, T. W. (1997). Body mass and encephalization in Pleistocene Homo. *Nature*, 387, 173-176.

Rushton, J. P. (1988). Race differences in behaviour: a review and evolutionary analysis. *Personality and Individual Differences*, 9, 1009-1024.

Rushton, J. P. (1992a). Cranial capacity related to sex, rank and race differences in a stratified sample of 6,325 U. S. military personnel. *Intelligence*, 16,401-413.

Rushton, J. P. (1992b). Life history comparisons between Orientals and whites at a Canadian university. *Personality and Individual Differences*, 13, 439-442.

Rushton, J. P. (1994). Sex and race differences in cranial capacity from International Labor Office data. *Intelligence*, 19, 281-294.

Rushton, J. P. (1997). Cranial size and IQ in Asian Americans from birth to seven. *Intelligence*, 25, 7-20.

Rushton, J. P. (2000). *Race, Evolution and Behavior*. Port Huron, MI: Charles Darwin Research Institute.

Rushton, J. P. (2003). Race differences in g and the "Jensen Effect." In H. Nyborg (Ed.). *The Scientific Study of General Intelligence*. Amsterdam: Elsevier.

Rushton, J. P., and Jensen, A. R. (2005). Thirty years of research on race differences in cognitive ability. *Psychology, Public Policy, and Law*, 11, 235-294.

Rushton, J. P., and Osborne, R.T. (1995). Genetic and environmental contributions to cranial capacity in black and white adolescents. *Intelligence*, 20, 1-13.

Rushton, J. P., and Skuy, M. (2000). Performance on Raven's Matrices by African and white university students in South Africa. *Intelligence*, 28, 251-266.

Rushton, J. P., Skuy, M., and Fridjhon, P. (2002). Jensen effects among African, Indian and white engineering university students in South Africa on Raven's Standard Progressive Matrices. *Intelligence*, 30, 409-423.

Rushton, J. P., Skuy, M., and Fridjhon, P. (2003). Performance on Raven's Advanced Progressive Matrices by African, Indian and white engineering university students in South Africa. *Intelligence*, 31, 123-138.

Rushton, J. P., Skuy, M., and Bons, T. A. (2004). Construct validity of Raven's Advanced Progressive Matrices by African and Non-African engineering university students in South Africa. *International Journal of Selection and Assessment*, 12, 220-229.

Ryan, L. (1982). *The Aboriginal Australians*. St. Lucia: University of Queensland Press.

Saco-Politt, C. (1989). Ecocultural context of developmental risk: birth in the high altitudes (Peru). In J. K. Nugent, B. L. Lester, and T. B. Brazelton (Eds.). *The Cultural Context of Infancy*. Norwood, NJ: Ablex.

Sadek, A. A. M. (1972). A Factor Analytic Study of Musical Abilities of Egyptian Students Taking Music as a Special Subject. Ph.D. dissertation, University of London.

Sahin, N., and Duzen, E. (1994). Turkish standardisation of Raven's SPM. *Proceedings of the 23rd International Congress of Applied Psychology*, Madrid.

Salkind, N.J.,Kojima,H.,and Zelniker,T. (1978). Cognitive tempo in American, Japanese and Israeli children. *Child Development*, 49, 1024-1027.

Sandiford, P. and Kerr, R. (1926). The intelligence of Chinese and Japanese children. *Journal of Educational Psychology*, 17, 361-367.

Scarr, S. (1981). *Race, Social Class, and Individual Differences in IQ*. Hillsdale, NJ: Lawrence Erlbaum.

_____ (1981). Comments and replies. In S. Scarr. *Race, Social Class, and Individual Differences in IQ*. Hillsdale, NJ: Lawrence Erlbaum.

_____ (1995). Inheritance, intelligence and achievement. *Planning for Higher Education*, 23, 1-9.

Scarr, S., Carparulo, B. K.,Ferdman, B. M., Tower, R. B., and

Caplan, J. (1983). Developmental status and school achievements of minority and non-minority children from birth to 18 years in a British Midlands town. *British Journal of Developmental Psychology*, 1, 31-48.

Scarr, S., and McCartney, K. (1983). How people make their own environments: a theory of genotype-environment effects. *Child Development*, 54, 424-435.

Scarr, S., and Weinberg, R. A. (1976). IQ test performance of black children adopted by white families. *American Psychologist*, 31, 726-739.

Scarr, S., and Weinberg, R. A. (1978). The influence of family background on intellectual attainment. *American Sociological Review*, 43, 674-692.

Scott, L. H. (1981). Measuring intelligence with the Goodenough Draw-a-Man test. *Psychological Bulletin*, 89, 483-505.

Scottish Council for Research in Education. (1933). *The Intelligence of Scottish Children*. London: University of London Press.

Scottish Council for Research in Education. (1949). *The Trend of Scottish Intelligence*. London: University of London Press.

Seagrim, G. N., and Lendon, R. J. (1980). *Furnishing the Mind*. New York: Academic.

Seshadri, S., and Gopaldas, T. (1989). Impact of iron supplementation on cognitive functions in preschool and school-aged children: the Indian experience. *American Journal of Clinical Nutrition*, 50, 675-686.

Seyfort, B., Spreen, O., and Lahmer, V. (1980). A critical look at the WISC-R with native Indian children. *Alberta Journal of Educational Research*, 16, 14-24.

Sheldon, W. H. (1924). The intelligence of Mexican children. *School and Society*, 19, 139-142.

Shigehisa, T., and Lynn, R. (1991). Reaction times and intelligence in Japanese children. *International Journal of Psychology*, 26, 195-202.

Shockley, W. B. (1968). Proposed research to reduce racial aspects of the environment-heredity uncertainty. *Science*, 160, 443.

——————— (1969). Human quality problems and research taboos. *New Concepts and Directions in Education*, 28, 67-99.

——————— (1971). Hardy-Weinberg law generalized to estimate hybrid variance for Negro populations. *Proceedings of the National Academy of Sciences*, 68, 1390.

Shuey, A. M. (1966). *The Testing of Negro Intelligence*. New York: Social Science Press.

Sidles, C., and MacAvoy, J. (1987). Navajo adolescents' scores on a primary language questionnaire and the Raven Progressive Matrices. *Educational and Psychological Measurement*, 47, 703-709.

Sijtsma, K., and Resing, W. C. M. (1991). Scalability of an intelligence test for different ethnic groups. In: N. Bleichrodt and P. J. D. Drenth (Eds.). *Contemporary Issues in Cross-Cultural Psychology*. Amsterdam: Swets and Zeitlinger.

Simeon, D. T., and Gratham-McGregor, S. (1989). Effects of missing breakfast on the cognitive functions of school children of differing nutritional backgrounds. *American Journal of Clinical Nutrition*, 49, 646-653.

Simeon, D. T., and Gratham-McGregor, S. (1990). Effects of nutritional deficiencies on intelligence and behavior. *Nutrition Research Reviews*, 3, 1-24.

Simmons, K. (1942). Cranial capacities by both plastic and water techniques with cranial linear measurements of the Reserve Collection: white and Negro. *Human Biology*, 14, 473-498.

Simoes, M. M. R. (1989). Un estudo exploratorio com o teste das matrizes progressivas de Raven paracriancas. *Proceedings of the Congress of Psychology*, Lisbon.

Simon, J. A., Schreiber, G. B., Crawford, P. B., Frederick, M. M., and Sabry, Z. I. (1993). Income and racial patterns of dietary vitamin C intake among black and white girls. *Public Health Reports*, 108, 760-764.

Sinha, U. (1968). The use of Raven's Progressive Matrices in India. *Indian Educational Review*, 3, 75-88.

Skandinaviska Testforlaget. (1970). *Manual of the Swedish WISC.* Stockholm: Skandinaviska Testforlaget.

Skuy, M., Gewer, A., Osrin, Y., Khunou, D., Fridjhon, P., and Rushton, J. P. (2002). Effects of mediated learning experiences on Raven's matrices scores of African and non-African students in South Africa. *Intelligence*, 30,221-232.

Skuy, M., Schutte, E., Fridjhon, P., and O'Carroll, S. (2001). Suitability of published neuropsychological test norms for urban African secondary school students in South Africa. *Personality and Individual Differences*, 30, 1413-1425.

Smith, C. L., and Beals, K. L. (1990). Cultural correlates with cranial capacity. *American Anthropologist*, 92, 193-200.

Smith, S. (1942). Language and non-verbal test performance of racial groups in Honolulu before and after a fourteen year interval. *Journal of General Psychology*, 26, 51-93.

Soewondo, S., Husaini, M., and Pollitt, E. (1989). Effects of iron deficiency on attention and learning processes in preschool children: Bandung, Indonesia. *American Journal of Clinical Nutrition*, 50, 667-674.

Sonke, C. J. (2000). *Cross-cultural differences on simple cognitive tasks: a psychophysiological investigation.* Tilberg: University Press.

Sorokin, B. (19 54). *Standardisation of the Progressive Matrices Test.* Unpublished report.

Sowell, T. (1978). Three black histories. In T. Sowell and L. D. Collins (Ed.). *Essays and Data on American Ethnic Groups.* Washington, D.C.: The Urban Institute.

Sowell, T. (1986). *Education: Assumptions versus History.* Stanford, CA: Hoover Institution Press.

Spearman, C. (1923). *The Nature of Intelligence and the Principles of Cognition.* London: Macmillan.

Spicher, P. (1993). *Nouvel étalonnage du SPM*. Fribourg, Switzerland: University of Fribourg.

Stahl, A. B. (1984). Hominid dietary selection before fire. *Current Anthropology*, 25,151-68.

Stams, G. J., Juffer, R, Rispens, J., and Hoksergen, R. A. C. (2000). The development and adjustment of 7-year-old children adopted in infancy. *Journal of Child Psychology and Psychiatry*, 41, 1025-1037.

Stanford, C. B., and Bunn, H. T. (2001). Introduction. In C. B. Stanford and H. T. Bunn (Eds.). *Meat Eating and Human Evolution*. Oxford, UK: Oxford University Press.

Stein, Z., Susser, M., Saenger G., and Marolla, F. (1972). Nutrition and mental performance. *Science*, 178, 708-713.

Sternberg, R. J., Grigorenko, E. L., Ngorosho, D., Tantufuye, E., Mbise, A., Nokes, C., Jukes, M., and Bundy, D. A. (2002). Assessing intellectual potential in rural Tanzanian school children. *Intelligence*, 30, 141-162.

Sternberg, R. J., Nokes, C., Geissler, P. W., Prince, R., Okatcha, E, Bundy, D. A., and Grigorenko, E. L. (2001). The relationship between academic and practical intelligence: a case study in Kenya. *Intelligence*, 29, 401-418.

Sternberg, R. J., Powell, C., McGrane, P., and Grantham-McGregor, S. (1997). Effects of a parasitic infection on cognitive functioning. *Journal of Experimental Psychology: Applied*, 3, 67-76.

Stevenson, H. W., and Azuma, H. (1983). IQ in Japan and the United States: methodological problems in Lynn's analysis. *Nature*, 306, 291-292.

Stevenson, H. W., Stigler, J. W., Lee, S., Lucker, G. W. Kitanawa, S. and Hsu, C. (1985). Cognitive performance and academic achievement of Japanese, Chinese and American children. *Child Development*, 56, 718-734.

Stewart, L. H., Dole, A. A., and Harris, Y. Y. (1967). Cultural differences in abilities during high school. *American Educational Research Journal*, 4, 19-30.

Stewart, R., Johnson, J., Richards, M., Brayne, C., and Mann, A. (2002). The distribution of Mini-Mental State Examination scores in an older UK African-Caribbean population compared to MRC CFA study norms. *International Journal of Geriatric Psychiatry*, 17, 745-751.

St. George, A. (1974). Cross-cultural ability testing. Unpublished.

St. George, R. (1970). The psycholinguistic abilities of children from different ethnic backgrounds. *Australian Journal of Psychology*, 22, 85-89.

St. George, R. (1983). Some psychometric properties of the Queensland Test of Cognitive Abilities with New Zealand, European and Maori children. *New Zealand Journal of Psychology*. 12, 57-68.

St. George, R., and Chapman,J. W. (1983).TOSCA results from a New Zealand sample. *New Zealand Journal of Educational Studies*, 18,178-183.

St. George, R., and St. George, S. (1975). The intellectual assessment of Maori and European children. In R D. K. Ramsay (Ed.). *The Family at School in New Zealand*. London: Pitman.

St. John, J.,Krichev, A., and Bauman, E. (1976). North Western Ontario Indian children and the WISC. *Psychology in the Schools*. 13, 407-411.

Storfer, M. D. (1990). *Intelligence and Giftedness*. San Francisco: Jossey-Bass.

Strauss, M. A. (1954). Sub-cultural variation in Ceylonese mental ability: a study in national character. *Journal of Social Psychology*, 39, 129-141.

Stringer, C. B., and Andrews, R (1988). Genetic and fossil evidence for the origin of modern humans. *Science*, 239, 1263-1268.

Stringer, C. B., and McKie, R. (1996). *African Exodus*. London: Pimlico.

Strum, S. C. (1981) Processes and products of change: baboon predatory behavior at Gilgil, Kenya. In R. Harding and G. Telela (Eds.). *Omnivorous Primates*. New York, Columbia University Press.

Sugishita, M., and Omura, K. (2001). Learning Chinese characters may improve visual memory. *Perceptual and Motor Skills*, 93, 579-594.

Sundberg, N., and Ballinger, T. (1968). Nepalese children's cognitive development as revealed by drawings of man, woman and self. *Child Development*, 39, 969-985.

Sung, Y. H., and Dawis, R. V. (1981). Level and factor structure differences in selected abilities across race and sex groups. *Journal of Applied Psychology*, 66, 613-624.

Symonds, P. M. (1924). The intelligence of Chinese in Hawaii. *School and Society*, 19, 442.

Takeuchi, M., and Scott, R. (1992). Cognitive profiles of Japanese and Canadian kindergarten and first grade children. *Journal of Social Psychology*, 132, 505-512.

Tamaoka, K., Saklofske, D. H., and Ide, M. (1993). The non-verbal reasoning ability of Japanese children measured by Naglieri's matrix analogies test—short form. *Psychologia*, 36, 53- 60.

Tan, U., Tan, M., Polat, P., Ceylan, Y, Suma, S., and Okur, A. (1999). Magnetic resonance imaging brain size/IQ relations in Turkish university students. *Intelligence*, 27, 83-92.

Tarnopol, L., and Tarnopol, M. (1980). Arithmetic ability in Chinese and Japanese children. *Focus on Learning Problems in Mathematics*, 2, 29-48.

Taschinski, R. (1985). Eine Untersuchung zur Kulturfairnws der Progressiven Matrizen von Raven gegeniiber tiirkischen Kindern in Deutschland. *Psychologic in Erziehung und Unterricht*, 32, 229-239.

Taylor, J. M., and Radford, E. J. (1986). Psychometric testing as an unfair labour practice. *South African Journal of Psychology*, 16, 79-86.

Taylor, L. J., and Skanes, G. R. (1976a). Level 1 and level 11 abilities in Inuit and white children from similar environments. *Journal of Cross-Cultural Psychology*, 7, 157-167.

_____ (1976b). Cognitive abilities of Inuit and white children from similar environments. *Canadian Journal of*

Behavioral Science, 8, 1-8.

Taylor, L. J., and Skanes, G. R. (1977). A cross-cultural examination of some of Jensen's hypotheses. *Canadian Journal of Behavioral Science*, 9, 315-322.

Teasdale, G. R., and Katz, F. M. (1968). Psycholinguistic abilities of children from different ethnic and socio-economic backgrounds. *Australian Journal of Psychology*, 20, 133-159.

Teasdale, T. W., and Owen, D. R. (1994). Thirty year secular trend in the cognitive abilities of Danish male school leavers at a high educational level. *Scandinavian Journal of Psychology*, 35, 328-335.

Teasdale, T. W., and Owen, D. R. (2000). Forty-year secular trends in cognitive abilities. *Intelligence*, 28, 115-120.

Teeter, A., Moore, C., and Petersen, J. (1982). WISC-R verbal and performance abilities of Native American students referred for school learning problems. *Psychology in the Schools*, 19, 39-44.

Telford, C. W. (1932). Test performance of full and mixed-blood North Dakota Indians. *Journal of Comparative Psychology*, 14, 123-145.

Templer, D. I., and Arikawa, H. (2006). Temperature, skin color, per capita income and IQ: an international perspective. *Intelligence*, 34, 2.

Te Nijenhuis, J. (1997). *Comparability of Test Scores for Immigrants and Majority Group Members in the Netherlands*. Enschede, the Netherlands: Ipskamp.

Te Nijenhuis, J., Tolboom, E. A., Resing, W. C., and Bleichrodt, N. (2004). Does cultural background influence the intellectual performance of children of immigrant groups? *European Journal of Psychological Assessment*, 20, 10-26.

Te Nijenhuis, J., and van der Flier, H. (2001). Group differences in mean intelligence for the Dutch and third world immigrants. *Journal of Biosocial Science*, 33, 469-475.

Terman, L. M. (1916). *The Measurement of Intelligence*. Boston, MA: Houghton Mifflin.

Tesi, G., and Young, B. H. (1962). A standardisation of Raven's Progressive Matrices. *Archive de Psicologia Neurologia e Psichologia*, 5, 455-464.

Tesser, P. T. M., Merens, J. G., and van Prag, C. (1999). *Rapportage minder heden 1999*. Rijswijk: Social en Cultured Planburewau.

Thernstrom, A., and Thernstrom, S. (2003). *No Excuses: Closing the Racial Gap in Learning*. New York: Simon and Schuster.

Thomas, N. W. (1925). Australia: its native races and their customs. In: J. A. Hammerton (Ed.). *Peoples of All Nations*. London: Amalgamated Press.

Thomas, R. M., and Shah, A. (1961). The Draw-a-Man Test in Indonesia. *Journal of Educational Psychology*, 32, 232-235.

Thompson, P. M., Cannon, T. D., Narr, K. L., van Erp, T, and Poutanen, V-P. (2001). Genetic influences on brain structure. *Nature Neuroscience*, 4, 1253-1258.

Thorndike, R. L., Hagen, E. P., and Sattler, J. M. (1986). *Stanford-Binet Intelligence Scale: Fourth Edition Manual*. Chicago: Riverside.

Thurstone, L. L. (1938). *Primary Mental Abilities*. Chicago: University of Chicago Press.

Tizard, B. (1972). IQ and race. *Nature*, 247, 316.

Tobias, P. V. (1970). Brain-size, grey matter and race—fact or fiction? *American Journal of Physical Anthropology*, 32, 3-26.

Tooby, J., and Devore, I. (1989). The reconstruction of hominid behavioral evolution through strategic modeling. In W. G. Kinzey (Ed.). *The Evolution of Human Behavior: Primate Models*. Albany, NY: State University of New York Press.

Torrence, R. (1983). Time budgeting and hunter-gatherer technology. In G. Bailey (Ed.). *Hunter-Gatherer Economy in Prehistory: A European Perspective*. Cambridge: Cambridge University Press.

Turner, G. H., and Penfold, D. J. (1952). The scholastic aptitude the Indian children of the Caradoc reserve. *Canadian Journal of Psychology*, 6, 31-44.

Tzriel, D., and Caspi, N. (1992). Cognitive modifiability and cognitive performance of deaf and hearing preschool children. *Journal of Special Education*, 26, 235-252.

Ucman, P. (1972). A normative study of the Goodenough-Harris test on a Turkish sample. In L. J. Cronbach and P. J. D. Drenth (Eds.). *Mental Tests and Cultural Adaptation*. The Hague: Mouton.

UNICEF. (1996). *The State of the World's Children*. Oxford, U. K.: Oxford University Press.

United States Bureau of the Census. (1989). The Hispanic population of the United States. *Current Population Reports*, series P-20, No. 444.

United States Department of Health, Education and Welfare. (1970). *Intellectual Maturity of Children*. Washington, D.C.

United States Department of Health, Education and Welfare. (1971). *Intellectual Development of Children*. Washington, D.C.

United States National Aeronautics and Space Administration. (1978). *Anthropometric Source Book, vol. 2: Handbook of Anthropometric Data*. Washington, D.C.

Valencia, R. R. (1979). Comparison of performance of Chicano and Anglo-Saxon third-grade boys on Raven's Colored Progressive Matrices. *Psychology in the Schools*, 16, 448-453. 202

Valentine, M. (1959). Psychometric testing in Iran. *Journal of Mental Science*, 105, 93-107.

Van de Vijver, F. J. R., and Willemse, G. R. (1991). Are reaction time tasks better suited for cultural minorities than paper and pencil tests? In N. Bleichrodt and P. J. D. Drenth (Eds.). *Contemporary Issues in Cross-Cultural Psychology*. Amsterdam: Swets and Zeitlinger.

Vandenburg, S.G. (1962).The hereditary abilities study: hereditary components in a psycho- logical test battery. *American Journal of Human Genetics*, 14, 220-237.

Vejleskov, H. (1968). An analysis of Raven Matrix responses in fifth grade children. *Scandinavian Journal of Psychology*, 9, 177-186.

Verhagen, P. (1956). Utilite actuelle des tests pour l'etude psychologique des autochtones Congolais. *Revue de Psychologie Appliquee*, 6,139-151.

Verive, J. M., and McDaniel, M. A. (1996). Short-term memory tests in personnel selection: low adverse impact and high validity. *Intelligence*, 23, 15-32.

Vernon, P. A. (1989). The heritability of measures of speed of information-processing. *Personality and Individual Differences*, 10, 573-576.

Vernon, P. A., Wickett, J. C., Bazana, P. G., and Stelmack, R. M. (2000). The neuropsychology and neurophysiology of human intelligence. In R. J. Sternberg (Ed.). *Handbook of Intelligence.* Cambridge, UK: Cambridge University Press.

Vernon, P. E. (1969). *Intelligence and Cultural Environment.* London: Methuen.

_____ (1979). *Intelligence: Heredity and Environment.* San Francisco: Freeman.

_____ (1982). *The Abilities and Achievements of Orientals in North America.* New York: Academic Press.

Vernon, P. E. (1984). The abilities and achievements of ethnic groups in Canada with special reference to Canadian natives and Orientals. In S. M. Samuda, J. W. Berry, and M. Laferriere (Eds.). *Multiculturalism in Canada.* Toronto: Allyn and Bacon.

Vincent, P. (1966). The measured intelligence of Glasgow Jewish schoolchildren. *Jewish Journal of Sociology*, 8,92-108.

Vitti, P., Aghini-Lombardi, E, and Antonangeli, L. (1992). Mild iodine deficiency in fetal/neonatal life and neuropsychological performances. *Ada Medica Austriaca*, 19, 57-67.

Wagner, K. (1937). The cranial capacity of the Oceanic races. *Norske Videnskaps-akademi I Oslo*. 1 Mat. Naturv. Klasse No 2.

Wake, C. S. (1872). The mental characteristics of primitive man as exemplified by the Australian Aborigines. *Journal of the Anthropological Institute*, 1, 74-84.

Waldman, D., Weinberg, R. A., and Scarr, S. (1994). Racial-group differences in IQ in the Minnesota Transracial adoption study. *Intelligence*, 19, 29-44.

Waldron, L. A., and Gallimore, A. J. (1973). Pictorial depth perception in Papua New Guinea, Torres Straits and Australia. *Australian Journal of Psychology*, 25, 89-92.

Walters, R. H. (1958). The intelligence test performance of Maori children: a cross-cultural study. *Journal of Abnormal and Social Psychology*, 58, 107-114.

Watanabe, S., Ayta, W. E. F, and Hamaguchi, H. (2003). Some evidence of a date of first humans to arrive in *Brazil. Journal of Archeological Science*, 30, 351-254.

Weede, E., and Kampf, S. (2002). The impact of intelligence and institutional improvements on economic growth. *Kyklos*, 55, 361-380.

Wein,N., and Stevenson, B. (1972). *Pre-school education programme—Dominica: Pilot evaluation of 3 and 4 year olds.* Jamaica: Bernard Van Leer Foundation UWI, Mona.

Weinberg, R. A., Scarr, S., and Waldman, I. D. (1992). The Minnesota transracial adoption study: a follow-up of the IQ test performance at adolescence. *Intelligence*, 16, 117-135.

Werner, E. E., Bierman, J., and French, F (1971). *The Children of Kauai: A Longitudinal Study from the Prenatal Period to Age Ten.* Honolulu: University of Hawaii Press.

Werner, E. E., Simonian, K., and Smith R. S. (1968). Ethnic and socio-economic status differences in abilities and achievements among preschool and school-aged children in *Hawaii. Journal of Social Psychology*, 75, 43-59.

West, A. M., Mackintosh, N. J., and Mascie-Taylor, C. G. N. (1992). Cognitive and educational attainment in different ethnic groups. *Journal of Biosocial Science*, 24, 539-554.

West, L. W, and MacArthur, R. S. (1964). An evaluation of selected intelligence tests for two samples of Metis and Indian children.

Alberta Journal of Educational Research, 10, 17-27.

Weyl, N. (1967a). White Rhodesians: an unrecognised intellectual elite. *Mankind Quarterly*, 7, 207-210.

Weyl, N. (1967b). Personal communication.

Wilgosh, L., Mulcahy, R., and Walters, B. (1986). Assessing intellectual performance of cul- turally different Inuit children with the WISC-R. *Canadian Journal of Behavioral Science*, 18, 270-277.

Williams, W. M. (1998). Are we raising smarter children today? School- and home-related influences on IQ. In U. Neisser (Ed.) *The Rising Curve: Long-term changes in IQ and related measures.* Washington, D.C.: American Psychological Association Books.

Winkelmann, W. von (1972). Normen fur den Mann-Zeichen-Test von Ziler und die Coloured Progressive Matrices von Raven fur 5-7 jahrige Kinder. *Psychologische Beiträge*, 17, 80-94.

Winick, M., Meyer, K. K. and Harris, R. C. (1975). Malnutrition and environmental enrichment by early adoption. *Science*, 190, 1173-1175.

Wober, M. (1969). The meaning and stability of Raven's matrices test among Africans. *International Journal of Psychology*, 4, 229-235.

Woodworth, R. S. (1910). Race differences in mental traits. *Science*, 31,171-186.

Workman, P. L. (1968). Gene flow and the search for natural selection in man. *Human Biology*, 40, 260-279.

Wright, S. C.,Taylor, D. M., and Ruggiero, K. M. (1996). Examining the potential for academic achievement among Inuit children. *Journal of Cross-Cultural Psychology*, 27, 733- 753.

Wycherley, R., and Benjamin, L. (1998). *WAIS-111 UK Manual.* London: Psychological Corporation.

Wynn, T. (1989). *The Evolution of Spatial Competence.* Urbana, II: University of Illinois Press.

Yates, A. J., and Forbes, A. R. (1967). *Raven's Advanced Progressive Matrices: Provisional Manual for Australia and New Zealand.*

Hawthorn, Victoria: Australian Council for Educational Research.

Yee, L. Y., and La Forge, R. (1974). Relationship between mental abilities, social class, and exposure to English in Chinese fourth graders. *Journal of Educational Psychology*, 66, 826- 834.

Yeung, K. T. (1922). The intelligence of Chinese children in San Francisco and vicinity. *Journal of Applied Psychology*, 5, 267-274.

Yousefi, E, Shahim, S., Razavieh, A., Mehryar, A. H., Hosseini, A. A., and Alborzi, S. (1992). Some normative data on the Bender Gestalt test performance of Iranian children. *British Journal of Educational Psychology*, 62,410-416.

Yule, W., Berger, M., Rutter, M., and Yule, B. (1975). Children of West Indian immigrants—11. Intellectual performance and reading attainment. *Journal of Child Psychology and Psychiatry*, 16, 1-17.

Zaaiman, H. (1998). *Selecting Students for Mathematics and Science*. Pretoria: Sigma Press.

Zahirnic, C., Girboveanu, M., Onofrei, A., Turcu, A., Voicu, C., Voicu, M., and Visan, O. M. (1974). Etolonarea matricelor progressive colorate Raven. *Revista de Psihologie*, 20, 313-321.

Zeidner, M. (1987a). Test of the cultural bias hypothesis: some Israeli findings. *Journal of Applied Psychology*, 72, 38-48.

Zeidner, M. (1987b). Validity of college admission indices for Jews and Arabs in Israel. *Personality and Individual Differences*, 8, 587-588.

Zhou, Z., and Boehm, A. E. (2001). American and Chinese children's knowledge of basic relational concepts. *School Psychology International*, 22, 5-21.

Zindi, E (1994). Differences in psychometric performance. *The Psychologist*, 7, 549-552.

Zsembik, B. A., and Peek, M. K. (2001). Race differences in cognitive functioning among older adults. *Journal of Gerontology: Social Sciences*, 56B, 266-274.

INDEX

A

abstract reasoning
    See intelligence
Abell, Steven C. 223
Aborigines 240
  Australian Aborigines 163–179,
  255, 258, 314–316
    adopted by Europeans 259
    brain size 288
    civilization 315
    diet 314
    European hybrids 167, 169,
      174–175, 259
    evolution 171, 173
    intelligence and IQ 164–165,
      173–175
    visual and spatial memory 171
  New Guinea Aborigines 163,
  176, 314–316
    civilization 318
    diet 314
Adojaan, Maarja 45
adoption studies. *See* heritability
  studies
affirmative action 25
African-Americans 10, 74, 78–85,
    88–89, 94, 98, 110–111,
    116, 248, 252, 262

Africans 57–121, 240, 251–252,
    258, 262. *See also* North
    Africans
  adopted by Europeans 114, 202,
  259
  Belgium, in 90
  brain size 104–105, 288, 303
  Britain, in 84–88, 137
  Canada, in 90
  Caribbean, in the 76–78
  civilization 303
  European hybrids 58, 67, 78, 83,
    90–91, 107, 116, 131, 259
  France, in 90
  genetic admixtures 117
  intelligence and IQ xv, 52,
    57–121, 302–303. *See also*
  Israel, in 92
  Latin America, in 76–78
  musical and rhythmic abilities
    96–99, 230
  Netherlands, in the 90, 94
  perceptual speed 93–94
  reaction times 99–102
  short-term memory 82–83,
    93–94
  South Africa 12, 142, 251
  sports 101
  Sub-Sahara 57–121
  university students 101, 103, 145

C

D

Darwin, Charles 17, 284
Dasen, Pierre R. 170, 174
Davies, Mary 150
Dawkins, Richard 257, 265
Deary, Ian J. 99, 295
Deary, I.J. 9
De Lemos, Marion M. 169
demes 297, 323
Dent, George Robinson 68
Development Quotient (DQ) 109
Diamond, Jared 179, 316
diet 326
     plant and meat eating 282–283
Digit Span test *See* IQ tests
Dinaric peoples 29
directional selection. *See* evolution
discrimination 25, 90
disease 21
Dodd, Stephen 160, 290, 292
dogs 18
Dolan, Conor V. 73, 95
domestication of animals 18, 316
Dominica and Dominicans 77, 252
Dominican Republic, the 77
Doppelt, Jerome E. 89
Draw-a-man test. *See* IQ tests
Drennan, Matthew R. 124
Drinkwater, Betty A. 171
Dunbar, Robin 271, 287
Dutch famine study 249–251
Dyck, Murray J. 239

E

East Asians. *See* Northeast Asians
East China Normal University 185

Ecuador and Ecuadorians 235
     intelligence and IQ 225
Edgar, Blake 303, 311
Edgar, Heather 25
education 191
     and IQ 89, 93, 114, 166, 175,
     177, 240, 251–252
     Educational Quotient (EQ) 166
Edwards, L.D. 172, 176
Eells, Walter C. 216
Egypt and Egyptians 135
encephalization quotient (EQ)
     266–269, 319
England and the English 39
English as a second langauge 194,
     209, 223, 226-227, 232
Entine, Jon 132
epicanthic eye fold 120, 155, 181,
     213, 323, 325
Eritrea and Eritreans 65
Eskimos. *See* Arctic peoples
Estonia and Estonians 39
Ethnic and Racial Studies (journal)
     25
Ethnicity and Health journal 25
Europeans 30, 251, 258, 262, 284,
     318–320
     achievement in math and science
     47
     brain size 104–105
     Brazil, in 210
     civilization 319
     Eastern Europeans 39
     evolution 218
     genetic admixture 40–43, 320
     hybrids 320
     intelligence and IQ 10, 29–60,
     30–37, 47–53, 318
          heritability of intelligence
          53–54
          regional differences in IQ

F

G

S

VISIT

WASHSUMMIT.COM

CPSIA information can be obtained
at www.ICGtesting.com
Printed in the USA
BVHW042028240920
589466BV00013B/893

9 781593 680190